In Your Eyes I See My Words

IN YOUR EYES I SEE MY WORDS

Homilies and Speeches from Buenos Aires
Volume 1: 1999–2004

Jorge Mario Bergoglio

Pope Francis

Edited and with an Introduction
by Antonio Spadaro, S.J.

Foreword by Patrick J. Ryan, S.J.

Translated by Marina A. Herrera

Introduction translated by Elena Buia Rutt and Andrew Rutt

Fordham University Press

NEW YORK ✝ 2019

This book was originally published in Italian as Jorge Mario Bergoglio, *Papa Francesco, Nei tuoi occhi è la mia parola: Omelie e discorsi di Buenos Aires, 1999–2013, Introduzione e cura di Antonio Spadaro S.I.* © 2016 Rizzoli Libri S.p.A / Rizzoli, Milan.

The translation could not have been possible without the generous donations from Charles F. and Helen A. Dolan and Dr. and Mrs. William Baker.

Visit us online at www.fordhampress.com.

Library of Congress Cataloging-in-Publication Data available online at https://catalog.loc.gov.

Printed in the United States of America

21 20 19   5 4 3 2 1

First edition

The last printed pages of the book are a continuation of this copyright page.

Contents

2003

2004

Foreword

Patrick J. Ryan, S.J.

I preach regularly on Sundays at a parish on the Upper West Side of Manhattan. When I sometimes wax more than ordinarily academic, I tell the congregation that they can apply for credit from Fordham University if they pay the requisite tuition.

The Vatican reporter John Allen reported that Pope Francis, speaking at a Wednesday audience early in 2018, had some words of advice especially made for me: "The homily is not a casual discourse, nor a conference or a lesson." In the course of the same Wednesday audience, Francis told a story that can serve as a warning for all who preach. "A priest said to me once that he had gone to another city, where his parents lived. His dad told him, 'You know, I'm happy, because me and my friends found a church where they do the Mass without a homily.' How many times have we seen people sleeping during a homily, or chatting among themselves, or outside smoking a cigarette?" When people laughed at the image, Francis said, "It's true, you all know it . . . it's true!" Concluding that line of reflection, Francis said, "Please be brief . . . no more than 10 minutes, please!"

As one who has seen his own first cousins in rural Ireland ducking out for a cigarette while he was preaching for much less than ten minutes, I have learned that brevity is the soul of homiletic wit. Even in more patient New York City, I seldom exceed Pope Francis's time limit. The babies in the congregation can serve all of us preachers as timers.

In his 2013 Apostolic Exhortation, *Evangelii gaudium,* a sketch of the themes he hoped to emphasize in his years of papal service, Pope Francis had already suggested, provocatively, that the homily is a maternal form of communication. "The Church is a mother, and . . . she preaches in the same way that a mother speaks to her child, knowing that the child trusts that what she is teaching is for his or her benefit, for children know that they are loved. Moreover, a good mother can recognize everything that God is bringing about in her children, she listens to their concerns and learns from them." Like every good mother, the homilist should never nag, and especially the homilist should never nag at great length.

In this first volume of his pre-papal homilies and discourses, the former Archbishop of Buenos Aires—Papa Bergoglio, as the Italian press calls him today—shares with us some notably succinct homilies. The down-to-earth style of these homilies should not deceive the casual reader. There is depth of insight as well as pastoral wisdom everywhere. In a Chrism Mass at which he presided and preached during Holy Week of 1999 in Buenos Aires, Bergoglio urged the clergy gathered with him for that annual liturgical event to take seriously the symbolism of all anointing in the Church: the anointing of candidates for baptism and confirmation, the anointing of the seriously sick, the anointing of deacons, priests, and bishops as they take up their roles of service:

> By anointing the 'reviled and glorified' body of his beloved Son, God our
> Father has anointed all our sufferings and our joys. Therefore, our hands
> anointed with chrism should be hands close to our faithful people, hands that
> make them feel in their flesh the anointing of the Father, especially where that
> flesh—which is ours!—'is hungry and thirsty, is sick and wounded, is atoning
> for its sins in prison, has nothing to wear, knows the bitter diminishment of
> loneliness born of contempt.'

The longer discourses from Papa Bergoglio's pre-Roman days—not homilies during liturgical celebrations, but addresses at conferences organized for various constituencies—examine with great insight the so-called postmodern situation. Speaking in 1999 to a conference of business executives interested in education, Bergoglio decried certain elements of the modern cultural and intellectual situation: "Postmodern culture presents a model of person that is strongly associated with the image of young people. Those who look young are beautiful, who undergo treatments to have the traces of time disappear. The model of beauty is a youthful model, informal, *casual*. Our model of adulthood is an adolescent." The limitations of such worship of youth, such disregard for the wisdom of the past, are many. A year later, in a message delivered to Argentinian Catholic educators, Bergoglio called for a humanistic education that deepens people in their cultural past: "But will it be that the postmodern disenchantment, present not only in politics but also in culture, art, and everyday life, brings down with it every glimpse of hope based on the expectation of the kingdom?"

Speaking to Argentinian Catholic teachers in 2001, Bergoglio returned to the problematic of postmodernity: "The postmodern primacy of experience brought with it piety of heart, a more personal search for God and a new appreciation of prayer and contemplation. But it also brought a kind of religion à la carte, a unilateral subjectivizing of religion that places it less in the dimension of worship, commitment, and self-giving and more as an element of 'well-being,' similar to a great extent, to the various New Age, magical, or pseudo-psychological religious offerings." The continuity between the thought of Pope Saint John Paul II and Pope Benedict XVI on faith and reason and the thought of then Archbishop Bergoglio is striking. In 2004 Bergoglio told Argentinian Catholic teachers that they should not form conservative ideologues in Catholic schools. "Our schools should never aspire to build a hegemonic army of Christians who will know all the answers; they should instead be places where all questions are welcomed, where, by the light of the Gospels, the search for personal fulfillment is actually encouraged, instead of being blocked with verbal walls, walls that are quite weak and will irreparably collapse soon afterward."

We are reminded periodically in these homilies and addresses that they were first preached in Argentina, a nation tracing its past to the gauchos, heroic cowboys who once ranged its open plains. Today's more urban Argentina has given birth to less heroic types, habitués of the coffee house and practitioners of the tango. At a catechetical conference held during the season of Lent in 2000, Bergoglio evoked scenes that we in North American settings may have only seen on the silver screen: "We have no right to be comfortable loving ourselves. . . . We must go out and tell that, two thousand years ago, there lived a man who wanted to re-create the earthly paradise, and that was his purpose for coming: to reharmonize things. And we must tell 'Doña Rosa,' whom we saw on the balcony. We must tell the children, tell those who lost all their dreams and those who find everything depressing, everything is a tango." Bergoglio could sometimes make his fellow Argentinians squirm, and in English he can now share the same healthy experience with those of us who live far north of Argentina.

Bergoglio quotes at some length the work of the nineteenth-century poet José Hernández, and especially his epic poem *Martín Fierro*. He also cites the example of major figures in Argentina's past, especially Manuel Belgrano (1770–1820), one of the founding figures of the state. For those of us raised on stories of the Boston Tea Party and Molly Pitcher, the Pope introduces us to the historical realities prevailing in the southern half of the Americas.

The Argentinian setting of Bergoglio comes out most vividly in a lengthy discourse delivered in 2002 when he refers to the spontaneous protests of "pot-bangers" (*cacerolazos*) against the government's systematic mismanagement of the nation's economy and the pressure to devalue its currency then being exerted by the International Monetary Fund:

> We need to know where we can rest our hope, the point from which to rebuild the social bonds that have been so bruised by these times. The pot-banging protest was a self-defensive spark, spontaneous and popular (although forcing its repetition over time causes it to lose some of its original expression). We know banging pots was not enough; what we most need today is to find the wherewithal to fill them. We need to reclaim, in an organized and creative way, the leading role we should never have relinquished, which also means we cannot now bury our heads in the sand again, leaving the leaders to do and undo.

It was to such "pot-banging" that Bergoglio referred in his first days as Pope to describe "the racket" he wished to raise in the halls of the Papal Curia, where indolence and resistance to change have long prevailed.

No one comes from nowhere. The homilies and public lectures in this volume introduce us to the serious but also lighthearted intellectual background of the first Jesuit pope and the first Pope to bear the name of Francis of Assisi. This Franciscan-crossed Jesuit has much to teach us.

Introduction

Antonio Spadaro, S.J.

To gather the homilies and speeches of Monsignor Jorge Mario Bergoglio, Archbishop of Buenos Aires from 1999 to 2013, entails immersing oneself into the breadth and depth of a pastoral ministry that has shaped the life, heart, and mind of Pope Francis, the universal pastor of the Catholic Church. Upon approaching these texts, the reader can therefore not only envisage the bishop who walks the streets of his city and diocese or travels by subway but can also see the Holy Father in greater perspective when he appears at the central loggia of Saint Peter's Basilica for the Sunday Angelus. One of the reasons why these books should be read is, in fact, to enter Jorge Mario Bergoglio's world, the local, and now, universal pastor of the Church.

A warning to the reader prior to commencing: It is not in his "mind" but in his gaze, in his way of seeing and processing reality, that we come to know the Pope here. On March 13, 2013, the experience of the Church in Argentina and, more generally, the Latin American one became the experience of a "wellspring" and not just a "reflective" Church.

Could the election of a Pope change the global meaning of a local Church? It is difficult to answer this question in general and absolute terms. In our case we are sure it could, because a Pope who comes from afar has strategic and charismatic value. The Latin American Church is the most mature of the younger Churches, thanks above all to the five General Conferences of the Latin American bishops that have followed one another from 1955 to 2007, held in Rio de Janeiro (Brazil), Medellín (Colombia), Puebla (Mexico), Santo Domingo (Dominican Republic), and Aparecida (Brazil), and that have given the churches of the continent a strong awareness of their identity and their mission. Pope Francis is the son of this often exciting ecclesial experience. In his preaching and in his speeches there is ample evidence of this experience because it is a consequence of it.

A Photographic Laboratory, the Soul's Stomach

This trilogy is not to be counted among the numerous anthologies which have appeared since 2013, nor is it a collection of various and heterogeneous texts; instead, it contains all of Archbishop Bergoglio's homilies and discourses, of which there is an orderly and identifiable trace. The corpus is presented chronologically, not by thematic extracts or extemporaneous and temporary combinations. It therefore should be read progressively, in my opinion, as it was intended. This is in fact the only way to enjoy the pastoral experience that has prepared Pope Francis to be a pastor of the universal Church. Other readings (by subject, by genre, by chance) are extremely useful and interesting, but in their aim to group ideas they are overshadowed by functionalism. Focusing in such a manner would be like picking blackberries or raspberries while wearing blinkers, and hence it would miss the collective beauty of the landscape and the context thereof. This collection intends to push for a freer and more spiritual and profound reading, the one that only the temporal process is able to communicate.

I would like to present this *opera omnia* with two metaphors. The first is that of a photographic laboratory, for those immersed in reading these volumes will be able to see what Bergoglio saw during his long years of Episcopal ministry. Those scenes made a lasting impression and provoked a homily, a speech, or a message. Therefore, reading these pages is like entering the "darkroom" that has developed—in every sense—Pope Francis's pontificate. And this photographic laboratory serves to better understand the ecclesiastical epoch we are experiencing. If we consider that Francis is not only the Catholic Pope but also one of the major moral and spiritual leaders of the world—perhaps the most widely listened to on a global level, as a Gallup International poll found—then we can appreciate the value of this heritage of life and words.

The other metaphor I would like to use for this body of words—spoken, or shared publicly—is that of a processing stomach, which plays a "digestive" role. Here we recall a mystic who is much loved by Bergoglio, the Jesuit Jean-Joseph Surin (1600–65), who described meditation as a gesture of rumination; hence, he spoke of the "stomach of the soul." The words of Bergoglio's pastoral ministry are a language capable of transforming the world and experiences in themselves. They feed on a life lived, on open issues, crossed frontiers, traveled suburbs, challenges that have faces and names. Therefore, they go beyond pastoral exercises, school reflections, or meditations that have emerged from within a chapel without doors and windows, sheltered from the world, from its lights and its shadows. Bergoglio's pastoral words gathered here are like plants extracted from the earth with soil still clinging to the roots. In this sense, of course, we do not hear them pronounced in the context in which they were scribed, which is obviously impossible, but what we do perceive when we read these pages is the scent of the roots and of indeed the earth—the human experience—they refer to.

Here, therefore, the pastor loses all his traits as an "ideologue," that is, a dispenser of ideas, and assumes those of the human being, of his biology (young, old, sick, healthy, and so on) and of his destiny. In short, those who decide to traverse each of these pages, one after the other, will experience an adventure, a journey, a discovery, an attempt to decipher the world, sometimes even a profound existential act of embracement or struggle. This trilogy is a boxing ring. There is no word of Bergoglio's that is not formed by his silence as a Jesuit who contemplates and acts without chronological distinction between the two, according to the Ignatian maxim *contemplativus in actione.*

The Eyes of the People

"With the entire being, hands, heart, word": these are the key words of the first homily in this collection, and no coincidence that they represent the master key to interpreting this trilogy. The gesture of preaching is a gesture of "total self-giving, a gesture that wants to be fruitful and vital." Succinctly put, it is a "father's gesture," and Bergoglio's preaching adds form and intensity to this totality. This is not an elaboration of a concept that is in the mind and that is expressed outside the person, and therefore purely explanatory. Concisely, these are words that embrace the Pope's and the interlocutor's humanity; when uttered, they create a language of interlocution itself.

For Bergoglio, the homily has a dialogic linguistic structure that facilitates dialogue between God and his people. The Pope expresses this dimension in his homilies with the warm language of this encounter, speaking of his mission as preacher to aggregate the hearts that love each other—those of the Lord and of his people—which for the duration of his homily are silent, and so the silence may speak to them.

Therefore, its meaning transcends the "communication of a truth" because dialogue is much more than this: realized for the sake of speaking and for the good that consists in bringing people closer to one another. Thus, God unfolds his power through the human word. The preacher is an aggregator, permitting the encounter between God and his people.

Obviously, the Lord and his people dialogue in a thousand different ways: in a direct way, without intermediaries, beyond the meeting space that is the homily. However, in the homily, a mediator who expresses the feelings of both is engaged, so that each person present chooses how to continue his personal conversation with God. This is why a purely moralistic or exegetical sermon impoverishes the communication between hearts, which, for Bergoglio, has an almost sacramental character, inasmuch "faith comes from hearing, and hearing through the word of Christ" (Rm 10:17). If the homily does not create a language between God and his people, so that each one can develop their personal relationship with God, then it really is a waste of time.

Therefore, the title of these volumes is not a coincidence for it comes from an expression used by the Pontiff in our conversation here. But, it is also something more besides. When I proposed the initial title, *My Word Is in Your Eyes*, to the Holy Father, I saw he was initially perplexed. What made him so was that the phrase "My word" was placed at the beginning. I shared his discomfort, which immediately became mine too, almost by heart. No, the center must not be "my word," but "your eyes." It is the eye of the faithful, of the *santo pueblo fiel de Dios*, the holy and faithful people of God, who must generate the paternal, fruitful, vital word. Beyond being paternal, Bergoglio's word is maternal, a fruitful, unique expression full of the "mother tongue" that generates a personal and communal relationship with God. In this sense, the homily generates faith and community. It is generative.

The Warm Rigor of an Amniotic Environment

The same dialogue between the Lord and his people develops also a "maternal frame." Bergoglio once said: "I think that the image of a Mother with her son best clarifies what it means to have to teach the one who already knows. The Church is mother and preaches to the people as a mother who speaks to her child, with that confidence that the child already knows that everything that is taught to him or her will be for their own good, because they know they are loved." Moreover, "a good mother can recognize everything that God is bringing about in her children; she listens to their concerns and learns from them. The spirit of love that reigns in a family guides both mother and child in their conversations; therein, they teach and learn, experience correction and grow in appreciation of what is good. Something similar happens in a homily" (EG 139).

For Bergoglio, the cordial closeness of the preacher, the warmth of the tone of his voice, his gestures, foster and nurture the "maternal and ecclesial frame" in which the Lord's dialogue with his people develops. Those who preach create a communicative and effective amniotic environment so that the Lord may hold a dialogue with his people. Therefore, it is the living relationship that creates pastoral language. The references of these homilies and of these discourses to human flesh, and therefore to that of Christ, are innumerable.

Bergoglio offers—and still continues today to do so from the Casa Santa Marta—an "oral doctrine," a definition that will appear even more plausible when reading this trilogy. Among these pages there is a "broken" word to be shared when it is uttered. The reader will find a logos that welcomes in itself the force of orality. There is a vital tension that cannot really be "tamed" with a *labor limae*, with a laboring workshop chisel. And this is even evident in those more analytical and structured and wide-ranging speeches in which Bergoglio gives proof of a paradoxical, nonacademic, "warming rigor."

The first fruit of this warm and rigorous orality is its comprehensibility. Abstract speeches can also be simple and clear for academics, journalists, lovers of thought, but they may not really be understood by people in the wider sense. Bergoglio's discourses overcome the surface of awareness and penetrate it. The apparent crystalline clarity of a doctrine enunciated abstractly and without discernment can sometimes be transformed into a polished slab on which one simply slips, without having any chance of finding a foothold. Beyond just relentless "clear" speeches, the man of today needs speeches that are credible, bearers of the complexity of situations, of experiences, of life that sometimes is not and cannot be so "clear." In fact, quite the contrary, for true life is never clear and as distinct as an idea. Bergoglio's clarity is on another level, for it is that of choices, of commitment, of action, of motivation to act, of the prophecy that names something for what it is. In some of his homilies, especially those addressed also to civil society, he carries out memorable feats, as in the case of voicing unequivocal complaints that leave no way out for the interlocutor, and even saw one president of the Republic get up and leave during one of his sermons.

It would be, of course, a tragic mistake to believe that all this is the result of a certain ingenuity or extemporaneousness in expression. Here we must remember that Pope Francis taught literature, not only its history but also creative writing. Bergoglio has loved many poets and writers: from Borges to Hölderlin, from Marechal to Manzoni, from Bloy to Pemán, from

Dante to Dostoyevsky, to name just a few. These and other authors besides are from whom he derives cryptoquotations that appear as spontaneous parts of his speech, metabolized by an inner process, but that are never used as examples of his learnedness. The same must be said for the Magisterium documents of the Mother Church, of the Popes, of the Second Vatican Council and of the General Conferences of Latin American Bishops, especially Medellín, Puebla, and Aparecida. Bergoglio draws from them as milk is drawn from a mother. Therefore, these authors and their texts are found in his homilies for reasons beyond pure respect and formal praxis of supporting details for his own speeches; instead, they show a recognition that he is a pastor, a child of the Mother Church. In addition, there is also a challenge to theological language: Bergoglio is aware that this very language, unsuspectingly uttered, risks in its sum to be influenced by a "technocratic" paradigm. There is nothing worse than a bureaucratic sermon, "theo-technique," one might say. Preaching is a maternal act. And so we understand how Pope Francis's preaching intends both to speak to the hearts of the faithful and to present to them a missionary Church with its doors open.

As a consequence of his experience, and as illustrated in this anthology, Pope Francis has developed a vision of what it means to be a preacher. During an interview with him for La Civiltà Cattolica in 2013, I touched on this point, to which he replied by speaking of the balance between dogmatic and moral teachings and the missionary proclamation of the Church: "A beautiful homily, a true homily, must begin with the first proclamation, with the announcement of salvation. There is nothing more solid, deep and secure than this announcement. Then a catechesis must be done. Finally, a moral implication can also be drawn. But the announcement of the saving love of God is prior to moral and religious obligation. Today, sometimes, the reverse order seems to prevail." And instead "the Gospel message cannot therefore be reduced to some of its aspects which, although important, do not manifest of themselves the heart of Jesus' teaching." With these words, I think it is possible to grasp the meaning that, in general, the homily has for Pope Francis: an announcement that concentrates on the essential, on the necessary, that is also what is most fascinating and attractive and sets the heart on fire, as it did so for the disciples at Emmaus. In these volumes we find the construction site that has led Bergoglio to formulate these indications. In addition, the Pope has specified, as he did so in his apostolic exhortation Evangelii gaudium, that the homily is a litmus test: It is a clear, incontrovertible index. In fact, it is the touchstone with which to calibrate the proximity and the ability of a pastor's encounter with his people. Therefore, the homily cannot break the link between the pastor and his people. Those who preach must recognize the heart of their community to discern where God's desire is alive and ardent, also on the basis of an inspiration and a grace linked to that special celebration (cf. EG 137).

How Does Pope Francis Prepare His Homilies?

In *Evangelii gaudium* the Pontiff offers certain very precise indications on how to prepare a homily, and as such they are the fruit of his experience, and not of reading homiletic manuals. "The first step, after calling upon the Holy Spirit in prayer, is to give our entire attention to the biblical text, which needs to be the basis of our preaching" (EG 146). Priority therefore is not given to study, which remains fundamental, but to the invocation of the Holy Spirit. God comes first, above all else. Without him, even the most appropriate word becomes ineffective. In fact, effectiveness depends on God, and not on the human word.

The disposition that Francis asks of every preacher is therefore of humility and amazed veneration of the Word, even a sort of sacred fear of its manipulation. And further: "To interpret a biblical text, we need to be patient, to put aside all other concerns, and to give it our time, interest and undivided attention. We must leave aside any other pressing concerns and create an environment of serene concentration" (ibid.). It takes love: "We only devote periods of quiet time to the things or the people whom we love; and here we are speaking of the God whom we love, a God who wishes to speak to us. Because of this love, we can take as much time as we need, like every true disciple" (ibid.).

Thus, the homilies are prepared with calm attention and with love for the fact that God speaks to his people. The Word of God is approached with a docile and praying heart, so that it penetrates deeply into thoughts and feelings (see EG 149). He who preaches "must be the first to let the word of God move him deeply and become incarnate in his daily life" (EG 150), the Pope writes. The word must become flesh in the one who preaches, Francis continues: "before preparing what we will actually say when preaching, we need to let ourselves be penetrated by that word which will also penetrate others, for it is a living and active word, like a sword 'which pierces to the division of soul and spirit, of joints and marrow, and discerns the thoughts and intentions of the heart' (Heb 4:12)" (ibid).

Therefore, we know that Bergoglio is well aware that the Word of God has to really pass through his person, not only through his reason but also through the possession of "his entire being" (EG 151). And that is how he finds "words which he could not find by himself" (ibid.). Therefore, preaching is indeed a spiritual experience that is full of surprise and mystery for those who experience it. In *Evangelii gaudium*, there are some useful questions that we can imagine are those that Bergoglio has learned to pose himself over time: "In the presence of God, during a recollected reading of the text, it is good to ask, for example: 'Lord, what does this text say to me? What is it about my life that you want to change by this text? What troubles me about this text? Why am I not interested in this?' Or perhaps: 'What do I find pleasant in this text? What is it about this word that moves me? What attracts me? Why does it attract me?'" (EG 153).

But this is the first step. The second is the extension in concentric circles of this personal relationship to involve the faithful people of God. The preacher, writes the Pope, "also needs to keep his ear to the people and to discover what it is that the faithful need to hear. A preacher has to contemplate the word, but he also has to contemplate his people" (EG 154). In this way the Pope, like any preacher, tunes in with the aspirations and situations of time by reading them in the light of the Word. It is a necessary spiritual sensitivity to know how to read God's message in events, and this signifies much more than just finding something interesting to say. So the question is: What does the Lord have to say on this occasion? Therefore, as is well understood, the personal prayer of a reading becomes a fundamental time for the Pope—to put it in musical terms, almost the *basso continuo* of his action.

Preparation for preaching becomes an exercise of evangelical discernment, in which Francis tries to recognize, in the light of the Spirit, the call that God makes to resonate in the historical context, at that specific moment (cf. EG 154). He therefore—we repeat it once more—has a strong relationship with his action and the development of his ministry. To sum up, it is akin to an explication of a method of action that without a shadow of a doubt must be accompanied with a living, pastoral, natural relationship with the people of God.

A Word Pulsing with the Rhythm of Our Lives, and the Liturgical Calendar

A reader may ask: Are there specific situations when these sermons and speeches were given? Obviously, we find a multiplicity of events and situations that led Bergoglio to speak, and we only have to scroll through the videos of his Masses that are on YouTube, sometimes videoed by nonprofessional and precarious means, to realize the extent of the range of occasions. But a father's gesture cannot be collected because it often leaves no trace. In this trilogy, however, we find the main occasions, the central "beacons" at which the fundamental messages reach every kind of person: from the poor person who goes to the shrine to ask for work and bread to the politician in public office; from the teacher to the consecrated; from the priest to the congregations who crowd the churches for Christmas and Easter celebrations. But we also find funeral masses, ample speeches during ecclesial assemblies, and interventions addressed to non-Catholics. There is a complete spectrum herein, and though the register changes, the voice is the same. Here, I would like to give credit to the translator who has been able to maintain this unity of voice so well in the English translation, despite the plethora of occasions and audiences to whom each sermon or discourse was addressed.

These volumes, therefore, cover that magisterium of which Archbishop Bergoglio has left traces, thanks also to his collaborators who have preserved these records. There are some recurring and particularly significant circumstances, and they are those which have been recorded over time. Here is a list of the main ones:

Te Deum for May 25, Argentina Independence Day
Homilies for the feast of Saint Cajetan, August 7
Pilgrimage to Luján
Chrism Masses
Corpus Christi
Masses with consecrated persons
Messages, meetings, and Masses for catechists
Messages, meetings, and Masses for educators
Christmas Masses
Easter Vigils

Te Deum, May 25

An important date for Argentines is most certainly the May 25 national holiday. This date celebrates the anniversary of the formation of the first autonomous government, when Argentina achieved independence in 1810. In the cathedral of Buenos Aires, a *Te Deum* is solemnly sung each year to mark the anniversary, and the president and the most important political authorities take part in the thanksgiving. When Cardinal Bergoglio spoke, the occasion was transformed into a truly "prophetic" event for the city both because he preached justice and social friendship, and by working for the construction of a democratic culture, especially at times of serious crisis for the nation.

The "power" that emerges from the May 25 homilies is a form of service for the common good and of the social bond: a form of "feet washing" rather than "washing one's own hands," let's say. Argentina's moments of crisis should not lead us to imagine politics simply as a crisis management system; instead, politics has a much higher constructive, positive purpose, for it serves "to create, to nourish" social life.

Bergoglio devoted a lot of energy in this direction, constantly encouraging the different political parties to meet through dialogue, pushing "to revitalize the fabric" of society. But he did not hesitate in certain circumstances to launch clear challenges to the government in the name of the people and to fight against those elites who had become blinded by ideology. The Pope recognizes the complex history of Argentina, its crossroads, the dilemmas between globalization and solidarity; with the acute perspective infused with faith, he sees in the suppression of the crisis the Passion of Christ. He sees a people in front of him "whose history is full of questions and doubts, with its institutions barely standing, its values dangling from question marks, its basic tools only sufficient for short-term survival."

He never avoids addressing complex themes, and never remains silent when confronted with dramatic events. An example of such an occasion was the tragedy of the fire at the Cromagnon Republic disco in the city of Buenos Aires, on the night of December 30, 2004, during a rock concert. The fire caused the death of 194 people, and more than 700 were wounded. Bergoglio comments in his homily marking the fifth anniversary of the tragedy (a transcription of which is included in the third volume): "This vain, frivolous, proud, easily bribed city. This city that disguises the wounds of its children so as not to suffer. It does not cure them, it disguises them. This city, which hides its malnourished elderly, puts them aside because it does not want to see the suffering of those who gave us life. A city that abandons its children, and elegantly calls them 'kids of the street.' It casts them off and abandons them in the street. This city does not cry, and since this city does not know how to weep it is not a mother. We have come here today to cry so that this city may be more of a mother." And what about the definition of the city of Buenos Aires as "a factory of slaves and a meat grinder"? These terrible words were pronounced July 12, 2010, during the Mass for victims of human trafficking at Constitución railway station.

In his speeches, the Archbishop speaks directly to the people to remind them they have a "soul." Indeed, he speaks to this soul, which is "a way of seeing reality, a conscience" consisting also of "memory." From there, only dignity, wisdom, and culture can emerge. It is in this context that Bergoglio speaks openly about "inner revolution," which is not "against a system," but in favor of a new awareness. It serves, in his opinion, "to *rebuild the social bond between Argentines,* a hopeful bond." But this must have nothing to do with either ideologies or "disaffected and destructive" pragmatism, as Bergoglio defined it, or with strictly administrative matters. On the contrary, it must be a "constant conviction *expressed in actions,* in the personal approach, in a distinctive stamp, where this will be expressed to change our way of kneading, in hope, a new culture of *encounter,* of proximity." It is the "inner emptiness" that breaks the bonds between men.

In this line, Bergoglio does not reject "utopia" as a mere abstraction. On the contrary, he recognizes its positive role and its political value. He states: "Utopias are primarily the fruit of the imagination, which projects into the future a constellation of desires and aspirations." A utopia takes strength from the dissatisfaction and malaise generated by current reality, but also from the belief that a different world is possible. It is not pure evasion, but a form that hope assumes in a concrete historical situation and that is accompanied by a concrete search for the mechanisms or strategies to achieve it. A utopia springs from the intelligent rejection of a situation considered bad, unjust, dehumanizing, alienating. So utopia for Bergoglio is critical of reality, but also the search for new ways.

One of the most important factors of Bergoglio's criticism of reality concerns the drama of being deprived of relationships and bonds. This for him is the true drama of a people, today favored by big cities and the spatial eradication thereof. The districts "explode" from within, while being a people also means "inhabiting the space together," opening our eyes together on what surrounds us in the everyday. The sense of belonging to a space and at a time disappears. And for Bergoglio, who has repeated it often and in various contexts, it is what it means to belong. The fracturing of space, combined with those of time in the transition from young to old, destroys coexistence. A road to recovering these bonds is exemplified by the *fiesta,* in free and spontaneous organizations, in the image of the people taking to the streets. But this culture today seems to leave room for the "throwaway" culture, which is the opposite of all rootedness.

Above all else, for Bergoglio, the task of reconstructing the social fabric is entrusted to the young people whom he defines in a strong and evocative way as "embers of memory." In fact, in a close alliance with the old people, those custodians of memory that founded the country, the youth are called upon to keep it alive and alight, passing it from one generation to another. In fact, memory is "the richness of the road walked by our elders" that becomes a seed for the future and an impulse to "keep walking." His speech is never nostalgic for a lost past, but remains focused on a horizon that is always before our eyes as the "vocation of a people, of a nation": the vocation of "a society where there is room for everyone: the trader from Buenos Aires, the coastal *gaucho*, the northern shepherd, the northeastern craftworker, aboriginals and immigrants, insofar as none of them wants to keep everything for himself, ejecting others from the territory." For Bergoglio, the people are "a call, a summons to emerge from the confines of individualism, self-interest and restriction, from our personal pond, and throw ourselves into the broad stream of a river which flows on and on, gathering into itself the life and history of the wide land it crosses and nourishes."

Speaking to the communicators, he affirms that there is a singular beauty "in each man and woman who lovingly live out their personal vocation in selfless service to the community, for the homeland; in the generous work for the happiness of the family . . . engaged in the anonymous and impartial hard work of restoring social friendship. . . . To discover, show, and highlight this beauty is to lay the foundations of a culture of solidarity and social friendship," thanks to which there is room for everyone in society. There must be no opposition between solidarity and excellence in view of an inclusive and fraternal society.

Bergoglio's message is clear and strong for everyone: "Each of us, based on our responsibilities, must *put our country on our shoulders.*" And he continues to sink the blade deeper: "Let us take responsibility for our crimes, dissensions, and lies, because only a reconciliation that makes reparation will raise us up and make us lose our fear of ourselves." In these words there is the key to understanding how Pope Francis stands before the situations of tension within the various countries or the conflicts that seem inextinguishable. And finally the appeal to his country: "Argentina, Arise!"

Saint Cajetan

The feast of Saint Cajetan of Thiene is celebrated on August 7. On this day, hundreds of thousands of the faithful go to the suburbs of the city, in the Liniers area, to the shrine where the statue of the saint is kept. There, kissing the glass fronting a small recess containing the statue, they ask for "bread and work." Bergoglio has also preached there in very difficult times, always in favor of the workers and the unemployed. This preaching has become a sort of examination of the Argentine society's religious and civil conscience, with the aim that it would be achieved thanks to a newfound sense of responsibility, not least among the political classes.

Bergoglio preaches:

> Our people know very well what power is and what service is. Our people know very well that coming to Saint Cajetan, to the feet of the powerful Saint Cajetan, is a religious gesture and—for that reason—is a political gesture—in the highest sense of the word. By touching the feet of the saint, washing them with their tears, whispering their petitions and begging for Jesus' forgiveness that cleanses and dignifies, our people are telling us all that the power that Jesus gave to the saint is service, that all power is service and it cannot be used for anything else. They say it quietly, with gentle and patient gestures of this endless line of tired and perhaps dirty feet which, in the eyes of Jesus, are the most beautiful feet in the world.

People come on foot to ask for bread and work. Bergoglio knows that being without work is dehumanizing, hurts that person in the depths of their dignity as a person. For him, the right to earn bread is fundamental: One of the greatest humiliations for a human being is not being in a position to earn their daily bread. It is the worst form of exclusion and humiliation. Saint Cajetan therefore becomes the protector of hope.

Bergoglio develops this rich symbolism of bread in various contexts well, but above all in one of his homilies on August 7:

> There is a bread for celebration, a bread that is the product and reward of work, the joy of eating together. But bread is also bread that is eaten on the way to work, that gives us the strength to do difficult tasks. That is the bread we're looking for today: the bread that gives us strength. The bread that provides energy. The bread that makes us feel like working and persevering. The bread that is shared along the way with our companions. That bit of bread we eat as we're working, and that helps us make it through the day. This is the bread we want to leave to our young people, because they are our hope; the bread of work that restores dignity and pulls us through.
>
> This bread that gives us a beautiful image of the Eucharist, the one that travels with us, meaning bread for the road. It's like the bread roll carried in our bag as a token of family love, it's the warmth of home that reaches all the way to our workplace, if we have one, or the places where we look for work.

Luján

The Shrine of Luján is central to Marian devotion in Argentina. It is based on a story. Around 1630 a caravel arrived in the port of Buenos Aires, led by a sailor who brought with him two small terracotta statuettes from Brazil: one representing Our Lady of Consolation, the other representing the Immaculate Conception. The statuettes were intended for a Portuguese man who lived in Sumampa. After journeying for three days, the caravan, headed for Tucumán, arrived at the Luján River, where it spent the night. The following morning the oxen refused to pull the carts. The only way to persuade the oxen to resume the journey was to leave the box, which contained a two-foot-tall statue depicting the Immaculate Conception, on the ground. The statue thus remained in that place, in the silence of the pampas. Those present understood that this event was miraculous and decided not to take the statue beyond the river. Traveling with the men of the caravan, there was a servant named Manuel who became the exclusive custodian of the statue until his death.

In 1890, following various other events, the first shrine dedicated to Our Lady of Luján was built in that place, and she subsequently became the patron saint of Argentina. The building is in a Gothic style, with fifteen altars inside, with the front towers measuring more than three hundred feet in the recesses where the statues of sixteen apostles are placed. Every year, four million pilgrims go there from all over Argentina and Latin America. Leo XIII established the feast on the Saturday before the fourth Sunday after Easter. The shrine was recognized as a basilica by Pius IX in 1930. On December 8, the statue of the Virgin leaves the basilica and is carried by hand through the main streets of Luján. Why go on a pilgrimage to Luján?

Bergoglio says: "We need her tender gaze, the Mother's gaze, that unlocks our soul." In his homilies that reference the shrine, Mary is a model of Christian life but above all a welcoming mother: "There is much in life that overwhelms us, but we know that here she waits for us; she does not ask us why we came, and she welcomes us. She knows we walked here because we need this *encounter*. She also knows that we came a long way to gaze at each other and meet, in order to be more neighborly."

Mary is therefore a presence who unites people, who places the desire for mutual help, for solidarity in the heart. Mary's welcome leads Bergoglio to invite people to pray: "Mother, we want to be one people"; and again: "Mother, we need to live as brothers. And for that we ask you, Mother, the grace to know how to take care of one another, because we are of your same flesh, Mother." The shrine therefore becomes "a home for all," "the house of the Argentines," a living symbol of unity. In Luján there is "a sign for our country: Everyone has a place, everyone shares hope, and everyone is recognized as a child."

Thus, Luján becomes the place for the celebration of an inclusive homeland, which assumes from Mary the role of welcoming, of the maternity of the home, of the "homeland for all," without exclusion.

Chrism Masses

There are occasions when Bergoglio's homilies are invitations to prayer, and the first homily in this collection, a Chrism Mass, is an example of this. But first, what is a Chrism Mass? It is the Eucharistic celebration, presided over by the bishop in a cathedral on the morning of Holy Thursday. In this circumstance the majority of the clergy of the diocese are present. In fact, this Mass intends to signify the unity of the local Church gathered around its pastor. After the bishop's homily, the priests renew their promises made on the day of their priestly ordination. The bishop consecrates the holy oils: the chrism, the oil of the catechumens, and the oil for anointing that will be used throughout the course of the liturgical year to celebrate and administer the sacraments: baptism, confirmation, ordination of presbyters and bishops, anointing of the sick.

A central moment, therefore, in the life of the local Church. And with these words Archbishop Bergoglio, in 1999, exhorted: "*We beseech* the Father to anoint us so that we can be fully his children. May his merciful fatherly hands rest on us and heal our wounds, prodigal sons and daughters that we are. May the love that flows gently and patiently from his fatherly heart spill over the totality of his People—the Church—by reconciling us as brothers and sisters and leaving no room for resentment and division." In this petition there is a vision of the Church, the "field hospital" he spoke to me of in our interview in August 2013, and a constant certainty of mercy. And earlier, in 1999, he stated: "By anointing the reviled and glorified body of his beloved Son, God our Father has anointed all our sufferings and our joys. Therefore, our hands anointed with chrism should be hands close to our faithful people, hands that make them feel in their flesh the anointing of the Father, especially where that flesh—which is ours!—'is hungry and thirsty, is sick and wounded, is atoning for its sins in prison, has nothing to wear, knows the bitter diminishment of loneliness born of contempt.'"

In this regard, an image which Bergoglio recalls as Pontiff in his apostolic exhortation *Evangelii gaudium* is that of the "caravan" (cf. EG 87): "God enters this human caravan, undertakes this journey and proceeds with us. God is always present in the events of our existence, he is one of us." In this sense, the consecrated person with the sacred chrism is called to proceed "next to every human limitation, to every human joy, to every human misery." To anoint, therefore, does not separate or remove the anointed in a disdainful and conservative manner; it does not make him fear the loss of his integrity, but on the contrary pushes him toward the mission, toward the dusty roads.

Here is Bergoglio's very evocative synthesis: "Within, the priest must be like oil in the flask, like the fire in the torch, like the wind in the sails, like the crumbs in bread."

Corpus Christi

In his Corpus Christi homilies the sense of God's generosity and his disproportionate abundance prevails. The miracle of the multiplication of the loaves is not a "magical solution" but Jesus himself, who breaks and multiplies without measure. Jesus is "omnipotent with the loaves and the fish": "the Lord is almighty with these humble things." And his disproportionate gestures are not made with a magic wand, but with his hands. It is from those hands we receive warm bread. And so, Bergoglio says, "May the warmth of the consecrated bread burn into our hands the effective desire to share such a great gift with those who hunger for bread, for justice, and for God."

In this way, our hands are able to experience the abundance of God. This disproportion also takes the form of the "loving fragility of the Eucharist," that is, the fact that the Eucharist is broken, or rather, the Lord "becomes little pieces . . . of bread and gives himself." Bergoglio comments: "How curious! We see fragmentation as the greatest danger for our social life and also for our inner life. On the other hand, in Jesus, this fragmentation under the form of tender bread is his most vital, most unifying act: to give himself whole he has to be broken! In the Eucharist, fragility is strength. Strength of love that becomes weak to be received. Strength of love that is broken to feed and give life. Strength of love that is fragmented to be shared in solidarity."

The "hunger" that people have for Jesus is interpreted and accepted as it is; above all, it is recognized without placing legalistic obstacles to hinder this recognition: "People follow Jesus. Although they may not always attend the ceremonies to which the Church invites them, because the invading pagan culture tends to diminish our traditions and tries to replace them, the faithful people of God continue to listen to the voice of the Good Shepherd and follow him. I like to think that the petitions for bread, work, health . . . and the promises that people bring to the Lord, besides constituting true needs are beautiful pretexts for being close to Jesus. The faithful people of God still yearn with true hunger for the One who is their Bread of Life."

The Consecrated, Catechists, and Educators

A key theme of Bergoglio's discourses and homilies is that of education and formation, which he frames within a broad vision of society. "An education that strengthens the fabric of civil society (civilized or for citizens) is necessary. Education must be a place of *encounter* and for the common efforts where we learn to be a society, where society learns to be a society of solidarity. We must learn new ways of building the city of man." This is the core of his teaching: education is oriented toward the growth of a society striving for solidarity, the "city of man." And education is not a technique but a generative fruitfulness.

The consecrated—religious men and women in the Church—are called upon to be fruitful, not to be people "without children." It is interesting to note the direct link between religious consecration and fruitfulness. The drama for Bergoglio is to have religious men and women defined by their civil status of being without a spouse (once he even said "spinster") and without children. And Bergoglio gained this understanding when he became a Jesuit and provincial father, and this is clearly evident by reading his writings from that time.

A section, treating the broadest of all Bergoglio's topics, is dedicated to the speeches delivered to educators. In sum, we realize that his prevailing interest is precisely that of education. His conviction is that "every day, every morning, when a teacher meets with a student, a new story begins" though through speaking with educators and catechists, the archbishop reveals his anxieties. Why? Because Bergoglio senses the urgency to build the world, to make the world a better place. The teacher teaches from the heart, transmits a lived life, and does not "trade" knowledge. This educational pact basically consists of a familial way of seeing; in fact, Bergoglio speaks of the father and a mother, a brother and a sister. This way of seeing conveys "the warmth born of a mature heart as a result of memory, struggle, defects, grace, sin" to a young or adolescent heart. If this way of seeing has strength and endurance, then the young person will be able to suffer in life, and in times of crisis they will not risk losing their mind. Why? Because they have not lost their compass with which to orientate themselves. This way of seeing is also capable of learning to "discover," "contemplate," and "grasp" the questions of the youngest, who are sometimes those who fail to express their needs and their questions in a complete and clear manner. We must never answer questions that no one poses; this is a fundamental criterion for education and pastoral care. In this sense, catechesis must never run the risk of becoming an "insipid teaching of doctrine, a frustrating transmission of moral norms."

This open and far-reaching approach corresponds to an inclusive concept of "truth." He affirms in a truly enlightened passage addressed to educators:

> We must advance toward an idea of truth that is ever more inclusive, less restrictive; at least, if we are thinking about God's truth and not some human truth, however solid it may appear to us. God's truth is unending; it is an ocean of which we can barely see the shore. It is something that we are starting to discover these days: not to enslave ourselves to an almost paranoid defense of 'our truth' (if I 'have it,' he does not 'have it'; if he 'can have it,' then it means that 'I don't have it'). The truth is a gift that is too big for us, and that is precisely why it makes us bigger, amplifies us, raises us up. And it makes us servants of such a gift. There's no relativism to it, just that the truth forces us to follow a continuous path toward a deeper understanding of it.

Bergoglio likewise detests a "theism spray," meaning every form of abstract spiritualism; instead, he wants a spirituality incarnated and down to earth. He even expresses contempt for a sort of "elitism of the spirit" present in some ecclesial contexts "that exhausts all wisdom" and denies the "fundamental truth of our faith: The Word became flesh."

Only a healthy educational process, including the catechetical, can contribute to forming a Christian capable of making a serious contribution to society. He has stated:

> More often than we would like, we Christians have transformed the theological virtues into a pretext to stay comfortably settled in a poor caricature of transcendence, disregarding the hard task of building the world in which we live and where our salvation is at stake. The fact is that faith, hope, and charity constitute, by definition, fundamental attitudes that trigger ecstasy, a leap of man toward God. They transcend us, really. They make us transcend and transcend us. And in their reference to God they present such purity, such

splendor of truth that can dazzle us. That bedazzlement of contemplation can make us forget that these same virtues rest on a whole foundation of human realities, because the subject who finds his way to the divine in this way is human. Dazzled, we can be distracted without plan or guidance until we bang our heads.

It is therefore impossible to confuse, in the preaching of Bergoglio, Christian hope with "spiritual comfort," a "distraction from the serious tasks that require our attention." Christian hope is "a dynamic that frees us from all determinism and from every obstacle to build a world of freedom, to free this history from the chains of selfishness, inertia, and injustice, in which it tends to fall so easily." These are fundamental words to understand the *mens* of Pope Francis. Hence the appeal to educators to be "bold and creative." Not only to "resist an adverse reality," therefore, nor to become fundamentalist officials linked to rigid planning. The call is to "create," to "start laying the bricks for a new building in the midst of history," to express the genius and the soul. In fact creativity is the "characteristic of an active hope" because it takes charge of what is there, of reality, and finds "the path from which something new can appear."

From this vision follows a vision of maturity—an important topic for an educator—that no longer coincides with adaptation. "Jesus, no less," Bergoglio states provocatively, "could have been thought of by many people of his time as poorly adjusted, and, by extension, as immature." Without eulogizing anarchy, Bergoglio argues: "If maturity were purely and simply adjustment, the aim of our educational task would be to 'adjust' children, these 'anarchic creatures,' to the accepted norms of our society, whatever they might be. At what cost? At the cost of being gagged, and the submission of subjectivity. Or worse still, at the cost of losing what is most intrinsic and sacred to the person: his freedom."

Therefore, maturity involves much more than adaptation to a model. In fact, it implies the ability to personally take a position on the specific situation in which one finds oneself. Here, then, is the meaning of the educational task: as an exercise in discernment and freedom. Therefore, any vision of "discipline" as a form of "mutilation of desire" should be avoided. Bergoglio writes: "A 'restless' child . . . is a child sensitive to the stimuli of the world and society, one open to the crises that life throws at them, one who rebels against limits but, on the other hand, demands them and accepts them (not without pain) if they are fair. One who does not conform to the cultural clichés put forward by the worldly society; a child who wants to learn to argue." So we need to "read" this restlessness and enhance it because all the systems that try to "quiet down" mankind are pernicious. They lead, in one way or another, to "existential quietism."

A specific form of anarchism and restlessness is what Bergoglio attributes to children. But it appears educational for the educator! A child's vitality is, in the first instance, a challenge that measures the ability of those around him to go beyond rigid patterns. And this leads Bergoglio to ask the educators a question:

> Do we have a heart that is open enough to let us be surprised every day by the creativity of a child, by the dreams of a child? Do I allow myself to be surprised by the crazy ideas of a child? Do I let myself be surprised by the transparency of a child? Do I also let myself be surprised by the thousand and one pranks of a child, those ineffable 'little Johnnys' that are in our classrooms? Is my heart open, or have I already closed it, sealed in a kind of museum of settled knowledge, of settled methods in which everything is perfect and that I have to impose but do not have to receive anything? As an educator, do I have a receptive and *humble* heart to see the freshness of a child? If I don't have it, something very serious can happen to me: I will start to get stale. And when the heart of a parent, of an educator, becomes stale, the child keeps the five loaves and the two fish without knowing to whom he should give them, he is frustrated in his dreams, he is frustrated in his solidarity.

Christmas

When it comes to celebrating Christmas, it is very interesting to follow Bergoglio's itinerary over the years. In his years as a Cardinal, the Christmas contemplation greatly influenced his sensibility and led him to understand that God, the center of the Universe and the Lord of history, became a child in silence, illuminated by a "hidden light" in a periphery of the Empire. This light is—as John Henry Newman would say—"a kindly light." It is not a blinding, dazzling light, but a light that comes near, like the light of a torch that helps on a journey. For Bergoglio, the light does not evoke static contemplation; instead, the light is used for walking. Here, then, the strength of the manger lies in triggering a process, in starting a journey. For Bergoglio, the Christmas mystery is intimately dynamic, for it awakens the numb conscience, collects the soul, and sees us starting off as pilgrims who believe with the steadfast faith of those who do not sell their consciences. Who can be born from the light? Those who receive this light are the simple ones, the faithful ones: the shepherds, the wise men, Elizabeth, Zechariah,

Simeon, Anna, Joseph, Mary. Everyone is summoned by light, in the apparent darkness, in the ordinariness of a common life. It is as if we were told here: If you believe you are living with spotlights on you, living a life illuminated by success or a truth perceived as a possession, the hidden light of Christmas cannot touch you. Confronted by the manger, so many of our things, which perhaps shone brightly to us, or we believed important and solid, crumble away. But sometimes that glimmering light has only the quagmire of our ambitions for foundation. Only the "middle class of holiness," to quote Joseph Malègue, a writer so dear to Pope Francis, can be reached by this regenerating Christmas light. It is when standing before simplicity, the everyday of the nativity scene, that glory can be experienced.

Consistent and extremely realistic would be how best to describe Jorge Mario Bergoglio's Christmas considerations, which contain nothing "ideal" or fabled about them. The tenderness of the Nativity does not recall anything childish or pertaining to nursery rhymes. For the Pope, Bethlehem is the place of an extremely concrete service, where Mary, Joseph, and each one of us who contemplate are called to serve God and to take care of him in the people around us, in the ordinary and sometimes restricted space of everyday things. This Jesuit maxim is very dear to the Pope: "To suffer no restriction from anything however great, and yet to be contained in the tiniest of things, that is divine." The root of this maxim is precisely the Son of God, of whom nothing greater can be thought of, who became a little child. In the horizon of the Kingdom of God the infinitesimal can be infinitely large, and the immensity can be a cage. It seems a paradox, but not for God who became flesh. The great project is realized in the minimal gesture, in the small step: God is hidden in what is small and in what is growing, even if we are unable to see it.

Easter

"The One who existed before Abraham was born, who wanted to become a close companion on our journey, the Good Samaritan who picks us up when we are defeated by life and by our volatile free will, the One who died and was buried and whose sepulcher was sealed; that One has risen and lives forever." This is the resounding Easter proclamation that the then Archbishop of Buenos Aires, Monsignor Bergoglio, made on April 22, 2000, in his cathedral on Easter night.

His Easter message is radical, for it confronts history with its bearing of sufferance, of death, of sorrow, and offers a reading of that in light of Christ's

Resurrection. This message is not afraid of approaching the many "tombs" of history and of the human soul to make resound within them the announcement that death has been defeated. As we noted previously, the homily—every homily—must always begin, one way or another, with the Christian proclamation, the *kerygma*. Everything else comes later.

In his Easter preaching, he is very attentive to what happened on Easter night. The first of the central elements in the scene of the stories of Christ's death and Resurrection is the stone that covers and closes the tomb of the dead Christ. "It was a very large stone," remembers the Pope. "As I listened to the Gospel, I was thinking of the centuries of history that we have relived here today, with the readings of the history of salvation, the Jewish people, the people of God . . . all those centuries of history crash and collapse before a stone that seemed no one could move. All the promises of the prophets, the expectations, the hopes, end here, crashed on a stone."

The stone creates a sealed environment that deprives of oxygen the desires of salvation that Jesus' life and preaching had aroused and opened, disclosing hearts. So we ask Bergoglio: how many times in our Christian life do we suddenly find ourselves wondering who will roll away this stone that "does not allow us to fly. It does not let us be ourselves." The sepulcher stone in the Pope's consideration assumes all the negative connotations of what weighs on our lives like a boulder, preventing us from living, from opening ourselves to existence; but it is also the symbol of the failures of history, of the path of humanity over time.

The unbearable scene of Christ's death on the cross is accompanied by an earthquake, which, for Bergoglio, is the second great element of the paschal mystery setting, for it embodies the cry of humanity. We can imagine *The Scream* by the Norwegian painter Edvard Munch, but also the cry that comes from the many "peripheries" of humanity that seem to confirm that God is dead, that there is nothing else to do. And yet that universal spasm is "the timid confession of faith from the soldiers, the pain of those who loved Jesus and a lukewarm hope . . . a kind of embers hidden there in the depths of the soul." Even within this infernal cry, timidly and under the ashes, the embers of something else, of a possibility, hides. It is a fundamental intuition: The Lord acts within every existential situation. Even in the most desolate and closed to hope, He acts inadvertently, but He can act and "nurture" red and warm embers under the gray ash.

And here, after the Sabbath, another earthquake arrives, the one that accompanies the manifested Resurrection: An angel of the Lord rolls away the stone and rests upon it, leaving the guards stunned (Mt 28:1–4). Bergoglio comments: "Two earthquakes, two shocks of the earth, the sky and the heart." And "with a 'do not be afraid' Jesus destroys the prop of the first earthquake. It had only been a cry born of the triumphalism of pride. The 'fear not' of Jesus, on the other hand, is the gentler proclamation of the true triumph, which will be passed from mouth to mouth, faith to faith, down through the centuries." The voice of the Lord, therefore, resounds "in the midst of personal, cultural and social earthquakes; in the midst of those earthquakes manufactured by the prop of self-sufficiency and arrogance, pride and petulance; in the midst of the earthquakes of the sin of each one of us." In the midst of all this we must decide to listen to the voice of the Lord. The earthquake becomes the symbol of a profound shaking; first it releases a human cry of anguish, then it allows the voice of the Lord to make his presence resound everywhere.

Afterward, everything in the Easter scene becomes movement. Women run to give the news and to meet with Christ. The scene of the Resurrection does not imply the static contemplation of a mystery that happened once before; instead, it is an impulse that set history in motion that had stopped because of that tombstone. The earthquake, the scream, the stone rolled away, the stunned soldiers, the running women, running Peter, the coming angel. . . . The meeting with God is always a historical mystery, part of the dynamics of events, and transmits energy, at times also acceleration to bodies that rediscover an inner strength and a reaction of intense capacity.

It is from this Easter earthquake that it is possible to deduce an urgency that runs under the surface of Bergoglio's words. He once said at a catechetical meeting: "Time is running out. We do not have the right to be caressing our souls. To close ourselves away in our little . . . little things." The power of Easter must be proclaimed. And to whom? He answers: "We must tell 'Doña Rosa,' whom we saw on the balcony. We must tell the children, tell those who lost all their dreams and those who find everything depressing, everything is a tango, everything is *cambalache*. We must tell it to the hoity-toity fat lady, who believes that stretching her skin will earn her eternal life. We must tell all those young people who, like the one we saw on the balcony, denounce us for wanting to put them in the same mold."

This three-volume series concludes with a homily dated March 28, 2013. Cardinal Jorge Mario Bergoglio was elected Pontiff on March 13, two weeks earlier. Before leaving for Rome, and sure that he would come back, he had written the text of his homily for the Chrism Mass of that year so as to have it ready for his return. It is therefore a precious document that, beyond all expectations, bears witness to an important step. In this homily, Cardinal Bergoglio wrote: "The precious oil that anoints Aaron's beard does not only perfume his person, but spreads and reaches the margins. The Lord will say it clearly: his anointing is for the poor, the prisoners, the sick, those who are sad and alone. The anointing is not for perfuming ourselves, nor for keeping in its bottle, because the oil would become rancid . . . and the heart bitter." Since the early days of his Pontificate, these are the penetrating words that Pope Francis has repeated and implemented with powerful gestures, and also with words that the years spent as a pastor in Buenos Aires have shaped, warmed, and made effective.

Translator's Notes

Marina A. Herrera

Reading the homilies of Archbishop Jorge Mario Bergoglio to the faithful of the Archdiocese of Buenos Aires and to politicians and civic leaders and his letters to catechists and to other groups needing pastoral care is like stepping into a time capsule that provides a vivid, intriguing, and inspiring panoramic view of the theological, social, anthropological, and technological developments that were foremost in the mind of someone who was being formed to be the successor of Peter, the Rock. With this volume, covering his writings and speeches as Archbishop from 1999 to 2004, we are rewarded with a privileged, insightful, and often prophetic analysis of the political, religious, social, and cultural events affecting Argentina, mostly Buenos Aires, where the life of that country is centered. Through these homilies, speeches, and lectures the Archbishop provides a critique of the technological and economic forces at play in the transformation, positive and negative, of the world and the Latin American Church at the turn of the twenty-first century.

Translating the various subjects covered and the need to be faithful to the Archbishop's tone and artful references to the contexts of the audiences he addressed in his many roles and settings—pastor, preacher, educator, communicator, theologian, Jesuit, man of the people and for the people— required me to conduct research into many of the subjects included in this volume. The research deepened the knowledge I had acquired through my strong connections with Argentina, which began in 1968, when I first visited my parents while my father was the Dominican ambassador to that country. More than a dozen extended visits throughout different regions and their impressive natural beauty in the following forty-five years have deepened and strengthened those connections. The providential task of bringing the Archbishop's writings to American audiences has now cemented my appreciation of and admiration for that all-important segment

of our continent and given me a privileged window into the making of the
first Pope from Latin America and the unsettling forces that have been un-
leashed in the Church by someone who sees the world from the bottom up
(from South to North) rather than the opposite.

In 1999 the name Jorge Bergoglio would not have been known outside
his native country and the Latin American communities of Jesuits. Today,
however, the homilies, letters, and papers delivered between 1999 and 2004,
when searched for online, appear countless times and in a variety of lan-
guages. This is a welcome development, but it is also one tainted by the
many translations produced by "machine" translators such as Google Translate and Babelfish, which often distort the words of the Archbishop, rendering them unintelligible to readers without a knowledge of Spanish. The
same is true of some of the "human translations" done with little or no familiarity with Argentine idioms or history, or without understanding the
pastoral language unique to the Church in the United States, the development of which has been spurred on by the dialogue with Latin American
pastoralists referring to the same realities as those of North America. The
use of those pastoral terms would be more in keeping with the context of
readers for whom this work is intended, but they were set aside in favor of
those developed by the Vatican translators. This disconnect between translators without pastoral experience in the American or Argentine context
within which the writings of Bergoglio were born has given rise to some false
cognates that veil the full meaning of some important concepts the Archbishop has brought into the pastoral vocabulary of his papacy. An attempt
has been made in the translation to explain these terms.

The bottomless linguistic creativity of a thinker and writer of Jorge Bergoglio's caliber will change the way we speak about almost every aspect of
the faith and ecclesial ministry for decades to come. In order to fully understand his political, cultural, and religious critique and inspirational and
motivational homilies to all segments of society, one needs to step out of
the Scripture readings and historical events and wander off into many popular cultural icons of the day and also into the rich literary tradition of Argentina, such as the epic poem *Martín Fierro* by José Hernandez. This
volume and two more to come will help readers in the United States understand where Pope Francis's perspective on the mission of the Church was
born and grew and how he gained his understanding, empathy, and sympa-
thy from all segments of society.

The documents speak directly to their intended audiences without an interlocutor. They show the Archbishop's intimacy with the feelings for the

pilgrims to the Shrines of Saint Cajetan or Our Lady of Luján, the priests, and the catechists or the teachers, his pulling them out of their complacency or inaction, but always affirming them in their dignity, deep Christian values, and importance in the eyes of God. He speaks so directly that you feel the listeners' being drawn into a dialogue with the homilist and into the homilist's deep dialogue with God, history, and human achievements and follies. To educators, politicians, and communicators, he presented brilliant analyses of the situation of their country, Argentina, and of the challenges and opportunities their professions or positions of power offered, always finding in their common history as a people the seeds and the resources for the transformation required to make the future different. Who would want to relinquish the call to be a part of the transformation of society as he convinces the listeners that they are indispensable laborers alongside him in the vineyard?

The chronological and nonthematic order of this volume is missing the ambience and rhythms of an Easter Vigil, or Midnight Mass at church, or of the schools and cultural centers where some of the papers were presented to very different audiences. As a result, some readers might skip those homilies intended for the bishops or the politicians. Those documents can feel cold and difficult to understand because they are filled with concepts rooted in the dialectic tradition of Romano Guardini, one of Jorge Bergoglio's great inspirations—a dialectic of antinomies, two equally valid principles that seem to be in opposition (contemplation/action, immanence/transcendence), realities that need to be kept in tension to generate a new reality. Those readers, if they follow along, will be rewarded with the discovery of how a mind destined to lead the Church in this turbulent time was shaped in the laboratory of a life lived among the people he served, traveling in public buses and shunning the trappings of hierarchical privilege. One senses that he gleaned his insights into how the Church should relate to the people it serves from his exchanges and engagement with all he met from the extensive literary and cultural history of Argentina and the Spanish language—the stories and the songs, the poems and the prayers that he knows as well as the Scriptures. These poems and prayers, stories and songs—the new, the old, and the ancient—held the threads of the lives, values, and hopes of all he addressed. The thought of a Pope-in-the making embodied in this volume could have been brewed only in the Latin American context—520 years after the Catholic missionaries accompanying the Spanish conquistadors arrived in this continent, leaving in their wake so much destruction of culture and native peoples, but also the construction of the largest bloc of nations that consider themselves sisters in language, religion, love of family, *fiesta*, music, and poetry. Nowhere in the remnants of Catholic Europe or the English- or French-speaking Catholic portions of North America could a thinker, pastor, teacher, and preacher like Bergoglio be nurtured or flourish. The production of Bergoglio's mind in these pages is the clearest example of the new and the good that could be born from the antinomy of Europe and America, with its accompanying polarities of destruction and construction, greed and grace, misery and mercy, cruelty and compassion.

Some Conventions Used

These are some conventions that will help readers follow the documents with greater understanding:

1. The titles of each document do not appear in the original. They are phrases from within the documents that contain the kernel of the message. This allows readers to anticipate each document's flavor, which the actual audiences would have sensed by the particular occasions when the homilies were given.
2. Where the Pope used double quotes in the original texts, we have used single quotes. Double quotes are used for all other quoted material.
3. All the footnotes in this volume contextualize and enhance the meaning for readers not familiar with Argentine history, culture, or folklore and appear at the foot of each page.
4. Spanish uses the plural form of personal nouns and adjectives when it wishes to be inclusive of both genders (e.g., *hermanos*), albeit in most cases the nouns have a masculine form (an exception, *personas*). When the Archbishop used both masculine and feminine forms of a noun, this translation does the same. When he used the plural and the context indicated that his noun was inclusive, we used the plural or both genders if it was important to highlight the inclusivity and it was not grammatically awkward. When speaking to priests and religious men and women he uses "*consagrados y consagradas*" but in the next paragraph asks God to anoint them all to make them his *hijos*, which is nicely rendered as *children*, the inclusive plural. If the wording in a biblical passage is noninclusive, it was left as such.
5. Readers will notice a frequent use of ellipses. Besides the normal use to mark text omitted from a quote, they appear in the homilies or extemporaneous talks that were transcribed from recordings. We can

assume that the Archbishop may have been speaking from notes. The transcribers, trying to be faithful to the style of the Archbishop, inserted them in the written texts found in the archdiocesan archives in Buenos Aires, and they are freely accessible through their website, http://www.arzbaires .org.ar/inicio/homilias. Ellipses appear at points in the presentation where as speaker or homilist he was pausing to allow his listeners to reflect on or ponder what he had just said. They were also inserted where you can almost sense the Archbishop was making a nonverbal point with his vivid expressions, eye contact with the audiences, or one of the many other facial expressions he uses to communicate.

6. References to actual Argentine historical and social events were not omitted, as in some translations. To do so would disembody the documents and place in a vacuum the observations and promptings made to the faithful by the Archbishop. These disembodied translations negate one of the most important concepts of Bergoglio's pastoral aim: never to stay in abstract thought that is not born from human experience (idealism) or to detach doctrine from human reality or actual situations (legalism).

And then there are the many newly coined phrases or traditional ones used in a new way, for which Pope Francis has become known, even prompting a book, *A Pope Francis Lexicon* (Liturgical Press, 2017). Many of these phrases and terms, now on the radar of Catholics from all countries, were present in the writings covered here and in subsequent volumes. These are among the most striking ones:

- **Our Father God** = *nuestro Padre Dios.* This phrase is the first indication that Bergoglio is someone with an experience of spiritual realities different from that of most Catholics. *Nuestro Padre Dios* = "our Father God" is not a Spanish idiom because *Dios nuestro Padre* is the commonly used equivalent to "God our Father." Calling God "Father" first immediately gives the listener a new reference point for understanding the paternal dimension of our relationship with the divine. And that is key to following the Archbishop's arguments for becoming involved and responsible for God's creation, made concrete in *Laudato si',* Pope Francis's encyclical on our responsibility for the Earth.

- **Culture of encounter** = *la cultura del encuentro. Encuentro* has come to signify in U.S. pastoral Spanish (and not translated) as a meeting of persons that leads to engagement, new relations, assessments, planning, and commitment to work for the well-being of all. To most American English speakers, an *encounter* is a brief, passing exchange, and in some senses it has come to be a euphemism for a negative, often violent, interaction. To alert the readers who may see *encounter* in that light, when it appears in this work it has been placed in italics to indicate that it is used in its Spanish meaning, not its more conventional English meaning. When *encounter* refers to an exchange with God or Jesus, it is left in roman type, as in those instances it has the same equivalency. The encounters with the divine are not of the same nature as those that Bergoglio would like all believers to have with one another.

- **Gaze** = *mirar.* If there is an activity that for the Archbishop summarizes the attitude of God, Mary, and the saints toward us humans, it is the way in which they gaze at us. It is worth noting that Pope Francis's gaze when he is engaged with someone is transparent and profound. He asks us to gaze at God, Mary, the saints, one another. It is only when we not merely see but *gaze* that we can come closer to the other person. And only then can we feel our common humanity and express our solidarity and compassion.

- **Orphanhood** = *orfandad.* This is the description of the human person who is isolated, depersonalized, estranged from community. It is the person with "a deficit of memory" that results in a fragmented personality that feels no link to the past, to our elders, our traditions.

- *Parrhesia.* A word from the Greek that entered Latin in the Middle Ages and was brought into modern usage by the French philosopher Michel Foucault (1926–84). The Archbishop brought it into pastoral Spanish to convey the same meaning as Saint Paul gave it: the freedom and courage to speak frankly, with audacity, to tell the truth in a way that confronts prejudices and power. The Archbishop mentions that Pope Paul VI points out that the lack of *parrhesia* (fervor, zeal) is a serious shortcoming because it comes from within, and it manifests itself in fatigue, disenchantment, compromise, and "burnout."

- **Solidarity** = *solidaridad* and *solidario.* While *solidaridad* is an easy equivalent for *solidarity*, not so *solidario.* The best word in English to contain all that it means for Bergoglio is to translate *solidario* as supportive or mutually supportive.

- **Spirituality** = *religiosidad.* While English has the word *religiosity*, it has a negative connotation, implying the religious practices of fanatics or fundamentalists. *Religiosidad* does not have such connotations. We don't hear about the religiosity of the Irish or the Italians but of their spirituality, a positive way of naming their relationship to matters of spirit. In that sense, when Bergoglio speaks about *religiosidad*, he means the positive ways in which Hispanics relate to the profound Christian values that are their inheritance. The word *religiosity* was used for *religiosidad* in some of the translations of the documents from the meetings of the Consejo Episcopal Latinoamericano (Episcopal Conference of Latin America, CELAM) in Puebla, Santo Domingo, and Aparecida. It was left there as *religiosity*.

- **The margins = *periferias*.** *Periferias* yields one of the false cognates used by some translators not familiar with pastoral use of the word *margins*. Pastorally speaking, in American English we have always spoken about the people on the margins of society. *Periphery* refers to the outer limit or edge of a geometric figure or geographical boundary. *Margins* is commonly used with reference to the empty edges of paper, in terms of "profit margin," "margin of victory." When Bergoglio uses *periferias*, it refers to people living in the "empty spaces" who do not benefit from the goods that those in the center enjoy.

- **To be the first = *primerear*.** This term, one of Bergoglio's favorites, is a reference to God's being first in loving us, and as a result we should be first in loving others rather than wait for others to love us first. I suppose that a neologist could use *first* as verb and say *first, firsting, firsted*, which is what Bergoglio has done. He finds the image in the prophets who refer to the Lord's love as the almond tree, the first to flower in Israel.

Abbreviations

Old Testament Books

Dt	Deuteronomy
Ex	Exodus
Ez	Ezekiel
Gn	Genesis
Is	Isaiah
Jer	Jeremiah
Jgs	Judges
1 Kgs	1 Kings
Lev	Leviticus
Mi	Micah
Neh	Nehemiah
Num	Numbers
Ps	Psalms
1 Sm	1 Samuel
2 Sm	2 Samuel
Wis	Wisdom

New Testament Books

Acts	Acts of the Apostles
Col	Colossians
1 Cor	1 Corinthians
2 Cor	2 Corinthians
Gal	Galatians
Heb	Hebrews
Jn	John
1 Jn	1 John
Lk	Luke
Mk	Mark

Mt	Matthew
1 Pt	1 Peter
Phil	Philippians
Rm	Romans
2 Tm	2 Timothy
Ti	Titus
Rev	Revelation

Documents from the Magisterium

AG   *Ad gentes divinitus*: The Decree on the Mission Activity of the Church (Vatican II, December 7, 1965)

APR   *Aperite portas Redemptori*: Bull: Open the Doors to the Redeemer for the Jubilee Year Commemorating the 1950th Year of Redemption (John Paul II, January 6, 1983)

CA   *Centesimus annus*: Encyclical Letter on the 100th Anniversary of *Rerum novarum* (John Paul II, May 1, 1991)

CCC   *Catechism of the Catholic Church*, Librería Editrice Vaticana (John Paul II, October 11, 1992)

CL   *Christifideles laici*: Post-synodal Apostolic Exhortation on the Vocation and the Mission of the Lay Faithful (John Paul II, December 30, 1988)

DP   *Puebla Document*: Conclusions of the Third General Conference of the Latin American Episcopate (March 23, 1979)

EDE   *Ecclesia de Eucharistia*: Encyclical Letter on the Eucharist and Its Relationship to the Church (John Paul II, April 17, 2003)

EIA   *Ecclesia in America*: Post-synodal Apostolic Exhortation on the Church in America (John Paul II, January 22, 1999)

EG   *Evangelii gaudium*: Apostolic Exhortation on the Joy of the Gospel (Francis, November 24, 2013)

EN   *Evangelii nuntiandi*: Apostolic Exhortation on Evangelization in the Modern World (Paul VI, December 8, 1975)

FR   *Fides et ratio*: Encyclical Letter on Faith and Reason (John Paul II, September 14, 1998)

GS   *Gaudium et spes*: Pastoral Constitution on the Church in the Modern World (Second Vatican Council, December 7, 1965)

LE   *Laborem exercens*: Encyclical Letter on Human Work on the Ninetieth Anniversary of *Rerum novarum* (John Paul II, September 14, 1981)

NMA   *Navega mar adentro* [Go Into Deeper Waters], Pastoral Guidelines for the New Evangelization, Update (Argentine Episcopal Conference, May 31, 2003).

NMI   *Novo millennio ineunte*: Apostolic Letter at the Close of the Great Jubilee of the Year 2000 (John Paul II, January 6, 2001)

RM   *Redemptoris missio*: Encyclical Letter on the Permanent Validity of the Church's Missionary Mandate (John Paul II, December 7, 1990)

RMA   *Redemptoris mater*: Encyclical Letter on the Blessed Virgin Mary in the Life of the Pilgrim Church (John Paul II, March 25, 1987)

SRS   *Sollicitudo rei socialis*: Encyclical Letter on the Social Concern of the Church on the Twentieth Anniversary of *Populorum progresio* (December 30, 1987).

TMA   *Tertio millennio adveniente*: Apostolic Letter on Preparation for the Jubilee of the Year 2000 (John Paul II, November 10, 1994)

VS   *Veritatis splendor*: Encyclical Letter on the Splendor of Truth (John Paul II, August 6, 1993)

In Your Eyes I See My Words

1999

Anointing Is an Act of the Whole Being

Homily, Chrism Mass—April 1, 1999, Year A

The Gospel according to Luke resonates in our hearts in a special way during this last year of preparation for the Jubilee dedicated to God the Father—Jesus testifies that he has been anointed by the Father "to proclaim a year acceptable to the Lord" (Lk 4:19).

Anointing, especially with perfumed oil, is a symbol of gladness and joy. Anointing is done for different purposes: to heal, consecrate, commission . . . but the quality of all these actions is joy, enveloping like perfume, penetrating like oil, expanding throughout the body and not leaving any unanointed gaps.

Today, in the Chrism Mass, the Mass of anointing, all—bishops, priests, consecrated men and women, the faithful—*ask* the Father to renew in our hearts the anointing of the Spirit, received by all in our baptism, the same anointing received by his beloved Son—the favored one—and bestowed on us abundantly by his holy hands.

We beseech the Father to anoint us so that we can be fully his children. May his merciful fatherly hands rest on us and heal our wounds, prodigal sons and daughters that we are. May the love that flows gently and patiently from his fatherly heart spill over the totality of his People—the Church— by reconciling us as brothers and sisters and leaving no room for resentment and division. May the joy that this glorious and wounded truth gives us— the Father loves us!—fill us with courage to announce this good news to a world thirsting for the gospel, thirsting for Jesus Christ.

Anointing is an act done with the entire being, hands, heart, word. It implies total self-giving, a gesture that wants to be fruitful and vital—a father's gesture.

Therefore, those of us who have been anointed, in a special way those of us who have been anointed as priests, *implore* the Father to please teach us to anoint our brothers with fatherly hearts. A father is one who offers himself totally to his family, in everything and always:

> When he embraces, he embraces all, the just and the sinners.
> When he gives, he does not hold anything back: "Son . . . all that is mine is yours" (Lk 15:31). Therefore, when he forgives, he spares no expense but celebrates with a big feast.
> When he waits he does not tire, he always waits, waits each day, waits for all that is missing, and for all his children.

Dear priests, my desire and prayer in this Eucharist is, that by renewing the promises we made on the day of our ordination, our Father in Heaven will renew in us the grace of fulfilling these anointings, these priestly and fatherly gestures.

We want to treat each other as anointed at all times: at work, united side by side in the service of our faithful people; in prayer, breathing the same perfume of the Gospel's sound doctrine that makes us one with Jesus and the Father; in our self-giving, in total donation to others; and also in the difficulties and conflicts that often arise among us priests . . . especially in those conflicts, we want the anointing that made David say, in the midst of his struggles with Saul, "The LORD forbid I lay a hand on the LORD's anointed" (1 Sm 26:11), so that we may abound in fraternal respect and concord.

We want to anoint our people in the baptismal faith, the faith that makes them a royal, priestly people, the people of God. That faith of our parents marks the true dignity of our people, makes them live joyfully amidst the current tribulations.

We want to anoint our people in hope. A hope placed only in Jesus, to feel that his hands liberate and heal, his lips speak the only truth that consoles, his heart enjoys dwelling in the midst of his people and feeling it as flesh of his flesh.

We want to anoint our people in charity, so that they do not tire of being mutually supportive as they have always been; that each father has his vigor renewed and the strength for the arduous task of advancing his family; that all mothers continue to pour the balm of sweetness and warmth of home in the hearts of their husbands and children; that young people feel the joy of spending their lives in the service of others, especially children and the poor; that grandparents may dare to look hopefully at the future and prophesy like those elders of the Gospel—Simeon and Anna—and transmit the message that life is worthwhile because the Lord keeps his promises; that the sick, the prisoners, those who are lonely or homeless, the poorest can feel close to Jesus, who came especially for them to heal, to give them freedom, to announce to them the good news.

By anointing the 'reviled and glorified' body of his beloved Son, God our Father has anointed all our sufferings and our joys. Therefore, our hands anointed with chrism should be hands close to our faithful people, hands that make them feel in their flesh the anointing of the Father, especially where that flesh—which is ours!—'is hungry and thirsty, is sick and wounded, is atoning for its sins in prison, has nothing to wear, knows the bitter diminishment of loneliness born of contempt.'

To heal that flesh, the Father sent his Son. In his wounds we have been healed! To heal that flesh today we are asked to provide a fatherhood of the anointed, a priestly fatherhood. May Our Lady, who gave flesh to the Word of God, accompany us and take care of us on this road.

→► ◄←

Leave Behind Nostalgia and Pessimism and Open the Way to Our Thirst for *Encounter*

Homily, Solemn Te Deum *on Independence Day—May 25, 1999*

That very day, the first day of the week, two of Jesus' disciples were going to a village seven miles from Jerusalem called Emmaus, and they were conversing about all the things that had occurred. And it happened that while they were conversing and debating, Jesus himself drew near and walked with them, but their eyes were prevented from recognizing him.

He asked them, "What are you discussing as you walk along?" They stopped, looking downcast. One of them, named Cleopas, said to him in reply, "Are you the only visitor to Jerusalem who does not know of the things that have taken place there in these days?" And he replied to them, "What sort of things?" They said to him, "The things that happened to Jesus the Nazarene, who was a prophet mighty in deed and word before God and all the people, how our chief priests and rulers both handed him over to a sentence of death and crucified him. But we were hoping that he would be the one to redeem Israel; and besides all this, it is now the third day since this took place. Some women from our group, however, have astounded us: they were at the tomb early in the morning and did not find his Body; they came back and reported that they had indeed seen a vision of angels who announced that he was alive. Then some of those with us went to the tomb and found things just as the women had described, but him they did not see."

And he said to them, "Oh, how foolish you are! How slow of heart to believe all that the prophets spoke! Was it not necessary that the Christ should suffer these things and enter into his glory?" Then beginning with Moses and all the prophets, he interpreted to them what referred to him in all the Scriptures. As they approached the village to which they were going, he gave the impression that he was going on farther. But they urged him, "Stay with us, for it is nearly evening and the day is almost over." So he went in to stay with them. And it happened that, while he was with them at table, he took bread, said the blessing, broke it, and gave it to them. With that their eyes were opened and they recognized him, but he vanished from their sight. Then they said to each other, "Were not our hearts burning within us while he spoke to us on the way and opened the Scriptures to us?"

So they set out at once and returned to Jerusalem where they found gathered together the eleven and those with them who were saying, "The Lord has truly been raised and has appeared to Simon!" Then the two recounted what had taken place on the way and how he was made known to them in the breaking of the bread.
(Lk 24:13–35)

1. A new celebration of the incipient beginning of patriotic consciousness, the May of the Argentines,[1] brings us together to give thanks for the gifts of *God the Father*, gifts for which *our parents knew how to live*, struggle, and die in pain and toil. To give thanks devoid of a sterile nostalgia or dishonest formal remembrance and let this same God the Father stir us at the close of this millennium and invite us to look onto a new horizon. To give thanks because the invitation "Argentina, Arise!" made by the Holy Father during his visit to our homeland still resonates in this Cathedral (also 'Plaza de Mayo'), an invitation for all inhabitants of this land, no matter their origin, and with one condition—goodwill to search for the well-being of the people.[2] We want to hear that invitation, "Argentina, Arise!" again today, because it is a diagnosis and a hope. To rise up is a sign of resurrection; it is a *call to revitalize the fabric of our society*. The Church in Argentina knows that this

---

1. May 25 is Argentina's Independence Day. In many Latin American countries a *Te Deum* is offered by the head of the church to mark the anniversary of independence.

2. Pope John Paul II used this line from Is 60:1 with the second part "and shine" in his pastoral visit to Argentina on April 10, 1987. The Cathedral stands alongside the Plaza, but the challenge was issued at the Vélez Sarsfield Stadium in Buenos Aires at a Mass for consecrated men and women and pastoral ministers.

is an order for a new evangelization of its own internal life, extending, at
the same time, to the entire society.

The Gospel passage we have just heard uses the Lord's pedagogy; and it
can enlighten us, so we can be faithful to our mission as parents, governors,
pastors . . . and thus, be faithful to our 'being a people' (*ser pueblo*). It is a
pedagogy of closeness and accompaniment. The story about the two disciples
of Emmaus shows them on their walk, and more than a walk, a flight. Indeed, they were escaping from the joy of the Resurrection, mumbling their
bitterness and disappointments, and cannot see the new Life that the Lord
has come to offer them. Recalling the papal injunction, we could say that
they had not risen from their inner stupor and therefore were unable to see
the Gift of Life marching beside them hoping to be found.

We Argentines march through our history accompanied by the gift created from the riches of our lands and by the Spirit of Christ reflected in the
mystique and effort of so many who lived and worked in this home, in the
silent witness of those who give their talent, ethics, creativity, their life.
The people deeply understand what it is to love their land, and the memory
of their deepest convictions! In its most intimate religious feelings, in the
always spontaneous solidarity, in its struggles and social initiatives, in its
creativity and capacity for festive and artistic enjoyment, the Gift of Life of
the Risen One is reflected. Because we are a people capable of feeling our
identity beyond circumstances and adversities, we are a people capable of
recognizing ourselves in our diverse faces. So much talent has not always
been accompanied by projects with continuity over time, nor has it always
managed to bring together the collective conscience. And, therefore, like the
fleeing disciples, we can find ourselves overcome by a certain bitterness in
our march, weary of problems that do not allow us to glimpse the urgency
of a future that never seems to arrive.

2. Fatigue and disappointment do not allow us to see the *main danger.*
The current process of globalization seems to unveil aggressively our antinomies: The advance of economic power and the language that aids it, which
with its excessive interest and use, has captured large areas of national life,
while—as a counterpart—the majority of our men and women see the danger of losing, in practice, their self-esteem, their deepest sense of being,
their humanity, and the possibilities of having access to a more dignified life.
In his Apostolic Exhortation *Ecclesia in America,* John Paul II refers to the
negative aspect of this globalization: "If globalization is ruled merely by
the laws of the market applied to suit the powerful, the consequences cannot but be negative. The absolutizing of the economy, unemployment, the

reduction and deterioration of public services, the destruction of the environment and natural resources, the growing distance between rich and poor, unfair competition which puts the poor nations in a situation of ever increasing inferiority" (EIA 20).

Together with these problems already raised at the international level, we also find ourselves with a certain inability to face real problems. It would seem that fatigue and disappointment can be counteracted only by lukewarm proposals or ethicism that only enunciate principles and emphasize the primacy of the formal over the real. Or, even worse, a growing distrust and loss of interest for all commitment to the common good that ends in 'just wanting to live the moment,' in the immediacy of consumerism. We cannot afford to be naive: The shadow of a cloud of social dismemberment looms on the horizon while diverse interests play their game, oblivious to the needs of all. Emptiness and anomie can emerge as dark consequences of self-neglect and threaten our continuity. Will the Argentines remain, like the disciples of Emmaus, imprisoned in their bitter amazement or plaintive murmuring? Or will we be able to let ourselves be shaken by the call of the Risen One to the disconsolate disciples, and to react, *to remember* the prophetic word, to remember those salvific, constructive moments of our history?

3. As in the Passion of Christ, our history is full of crossroads, tensions, and conflicts. However, this people of faith knew how to shoulder their destiny whenever *solidarity and work* forged a political friendship of racial and social coexistence that marks our way of life. The Argentines learned 'to be' part of, to 'feel' part of, learned *to reach out and be companions to each other*. Because of their *capacity for individual and collective creativity* and from their impetus for spontaneous popular organization, our people have known foundational moments of civil, political, and social changes, cultural and scientific achievements that took us out of isolation and demonstrated our values. Moments that, in short, gave us a sense of identity beyond our complex ethnic and historical makeup. Moments in which an awareness of fraternal work prevailed, sometimes with little elaboration, but always felt and lived to the point of heroism. That is why the call is to leave the sterile historicism manipulated by interests or ideologies or by mere destructive criticisms. History bets on the higher truth, on remembering what unites and builds us up, on our achievements rather than our failures. And when looking at pain and failure, let our remembrance be a wager on peace and rights . . . and if we look at hatred and fratricidal violence, let our memories guide us so that our common interests prevail. The last years have shaken

us, belatedly and cruelly, and the silent voices of so many dead cry out from heaven asking not to repeat the mistakes. Only then will their tragic destinies have meaning.[3] Like the walking and fearful disciples, today we are asked to realize that such a heavy cross cannot have been carried in vain.

The call to *a historical memory* also asks us to delve into our deepest achievements, those that do not appear before a quick and superficial glance. The effort of recent times was none other than the effort to affirm the democratic system to overcome political divisions, which seemed an almost insurmountable social chasm: Today we seek to respect the rules and accept dialogue as a way of civic coexistence. Let go of nostalgia and pessimism and, like the disciples of Emmaus, *give way to our thirst for* encounter: "Stay with us, because it is almost evening and the day is now nearly over." The Gospel sets the course for us: to sit at the table and let ourselves be summoned by the profound action of Christ. The blessed bread should be shared. The same bread that is the fruit of sacrifice and work, that is an image of eternal life, but that must be made real now.

4. In effect, brothers, it is not a mere invitation to share, it is not only to reconcile opposites and adversities: To sit down to break the bread of the Risen One is *to be inspired to live in a different way.* We are challenged by that bread made with the best we can provide, with the leaven that was already put in so many moments of pain, work, and achievements. The evangelical call of today asks us to *rebuild the social and political bond between Argentines.* Political society lasts only if it is framed as a vocation to meet human needs in common. It is the place of the citizen. *To be a citizen is to feel called, summoned for something good, for a purpose with meaning . . .* and to go to the appointment. If we bet on an Argentina where not all will be seated at the table, where only a few benefit, and the social fabric is destroyed, where the gaps are enlarged since the sacrifice belongs to everyone, then we will end up being a society on the road to confrontation.

From the depths of our *conscience as a supportive people,* this call to share bread has deep resonance. Far from superficiality and immediatist conjuncturalism (flowers that do not bear fruit), there is a people with a collective memory that does not renounce walking with the nobility that characterizes them: Community efforts and undertakings, the growth of neighborhood initiatives, the boom of so many mutual aid movements, are signs of God's presence in a whirlwind of participation without tribalism, rarely seen

---

3. This refers to the thousands of Argentines who were killed during the years of military dictatorship dubbed the Dirty War (1976–83).

in our country. In the background there is a supportive people, a people willing to rise again and again. A people that not only seeks survival, not only ignores inefficient bureaucracies, but wants to *rebuild the social bond*; a people that is practicing, almost without knowing it, the virtue of being partners in the search for the common good. A people that wants to conjure the poverty of emptiness and despair. A people with memory, a memory that cannot be reduced to a mere record. Here is the greatness of our people. I see in our Argentine people a strong awareness of their dignity. It is an awareness that has been molded by significant milestones. Our people have a soul, and because we can speak of the soul of a people, we can speak of a hermeneutics, of a way of seeing reality, of a conscience. Today, in the midst of conflicts, these people teach us that we should not pay attention to those who try to distill reality into ideas, that we are not served by intellectuals without talent, nor by ethicists without kindness, but by *appealing to the depth of our dignity as a people, to our wisdom, to our cultural resources*. It is a true revolution, not against a system, but in the interior; a revolution of memory and tenderness: memory of the great founding, heroic deeds . . . and memory of the simple gestures that we have been breast-fed as a family. To be faithful to our mission is to take care of the 'embers' in the heart, protect them from the cheating ashes of forgetfulness or the presumption of believing that our homeland and our family have no history or that it has begun with us. The embers of memory that condense, like the embers in the fire, the values that make us great: the way of celebrating and defending life, of accepting death, of caring for the frailty of our poorest brothers, of opening hands in solidarity before pain and poverty, to celebrate and pray; the hope of working together and—from our common poverty—to amass solidarity.

So that this force that we all carry within and that is bond and life can be made manifest, it is necessary that all, and especially those of us with a high quota of political or economic power or any type of influence, renounce those interests or abuses of those that pretend to go beyond the common good that brings us together; it is imperative that we assume, with austere attitude and greatness, the mission imposed on us.

Our people, who know how to spontaneously and naturally organize themselves as a national community, protagonists of this new social bond, demand to be consulted and have a place for control and creative participation in all areas of social life that concern them. We, the leaders, must accompany the vitality of this new bond. Empowering and protecting it can become our main mission. We do not resign from our ideas, utopias, properties, or rights, but renounce only the claim that they are unique or absolute. We are all invited to this *encounter*,[4] to accept and share this new ferment that—at the same time—is a life-giving memory of our best history of supportive sacrifice, struggle for freedom, and social integration.

5. That historic May, full of ups and downs and interests at stake, united all viceroyalty in a common decision that initiated a different history. Perhaps we ought to feel that our homeland of all is a new town hall, a great table of communion where no longer a desolate nostalgia, but the hopeful recognition, impels us to proclaim like the disciples of Emmaus: "Were not our hearts burning within us while he spoke to us on the way and opened the Scriptures to us?" Let our hearts burn with the desire to live and grow in this our home, be the petition that accompanies this thanksgiving to the Father, and the commitment to fulfill his Word. And let us be convinced once again that *the whole is superior to the parts, time superior to space, reality superior to ideas, and unity superior to conflict.*

→ ←

Remembering the Father Is Not Just Another Memory

Homily, Solemnity of Corpus Christi—June 5, 1999, Year A

"Do not forget the LORD, your God!" These words, which are a command and a plea, resonate here in a special way today. Remember Israel . . . remember who you are and from where you were delivered. Moses speaks to his people in this manner. We just heard it: "Do not forget the LORD, your God,

---

4. The word *encuentro* in Spanish pastoral usage has come to mean an exchange of ideas, hopes, and dreams, evaluation of the present, to discern and make a commitment to collaborate in bringing about the Reign that Jesus preached. These events in pastoral settings always take long planning and follow-up. The word "encounter" in English as defined by Merriam-Webster means to meet as an adversary or enemy, to engage in conflict with, to come upon or experience especially unexpectedly; to meet by chance. The English translators of Pope Francis have chosen *encounter* to translate *encuentro* and have assigned the same meaning as the term in Spanish pastoral usage. In order not to mislead English readers who are not familiar with the word "encounter" in a positive light, when used in the Spanish sense, *encounter* will appear in italics.

who . . . fed you in the desert with manna, a food unknown to your fathers" (Dt 8:11, 16). Manna, that little bit of 'bread' kept in the Ark of the Covenant next to the tablets of the Law, summarized for the people of God *the memory of God's goodness*: a fatherly God, a companion God on the journey, a caring God who lets his people walk in his presence and encourages them with his promises. . . . And the promises were fulfilled in Jesus. In Jesus, all the promises of the Father became reality, a reality as alive, close, and tangible as bread.

Today, on the feast of Corpus Christi, we hear again that old plea: "Remember!"—this time on the lips of Jesus: Remember that my flesh is the food of eternal life that my Father gives you! I live by the Father, and whoever eats me will live by me.

Remembering the Father is not just another memory. One does not remember his father without celebrating and giving thanks. And immediately, the memory makes us look for some concrete action to transmit our affection: a visit, a call, a hug, a letter. For our Father in heaven, that gesture of affection, which makes our memory a living memory, is to go to communion. That was Jesus' teaching at the Last Supper: "Do this in memory of me" (1 Cor 11:24); "Whoever receives me receives He who sent me" (Mt 10:40). And, since that night, the Eucharist is *the memorial of our faith*.

The Eucharist is a *gift from the Father*. Jesus wants us to understand it this way: "My Father . . . gives you the true bread from heaven" (Jn 6:32). This bread is no longer a provisional bread like manna; the Body of Christ is the definitive food, capable of giving life and eternal life. In the Eucharist we have the testimony of what the Father's love is: a close, unconditional love; a love available at all times, 'edible,' pure gift; suitable for every humble and hungry person who needs to renew his strength.

On the feast of Corpus Christi, we celebrate this great gift, and, following Jesus' teachings, all our thanksgiving goes to his Father, who is also ours. Jesus wants us to thank the Father for this food: to him be glory and praise. We give thanks to the Father, and by doing so we do not take anything away from Jesus because he is but a Son; he feels like pure gift from the Father. And he includes us in his thanksgiving and in his offering: "Just as the living Father sent me and I have life because of the Father, so also the one who feeds on me will have life because of me" (v. 57).

Jesus, the son of Mary, is in the Eucharist the living memory of the Father.
Remember your Father, faithful People of God!
Remember your Father to recover your dignity daily, that dignity often not valued today and the reason why you're often exiled in the middle of

your own land. *Remember your Father* to live gratefully; the one who feeds the sparrows also feeds you with the flesh of his beloved Son. *Remember your Father* to feel cared for, certain that no one will be able to snatch you from his hands, as Jesus promised. *Remember your Father* to feel as a brother, support, companion, good friend of your brothers. *Remember your Father* and the best values of your heart will flourish: He has taught you to work for your children and to know how to celebrate as a family. He helps you judge with justice and worry about the weakest; enables you to assume your commitments responsibly. *Remember your Father* who has given you Jesus and gives him to you every day in the Eucharist. People of God, people of Buenos Aires, *the memory of your Father* has made you a humble and hopeful people. People of God, people of Buenos Aires, together with Mary our Mother of Luján who kept all things in her heart, Mother of memory, *remember your Father* all the days of your life.

➤ ◄

God, Our Father, Please Heal Her

*Homily, Meeting of Politicians and
Legislators from Latin America—August 3, 1999*

The living Jesus Christ is here, in our midst, as we celebrate the Eucharist. It is the same Lord of life who multiplied the loaves (Mt 14:17–21), who compelled his disciples to get into the boat (v. 22), who went up the mountain to pray alone (v. 23). The same Lord who, in the early morning, walked on the water to meet the disciples (v. 25), as we heard recently in the Gospel. Before his Lordship we bow our faith-filled hearts and worship him. We join him in this thanksgiving as we begin the work of this meeting focused on the theme: "Family and Life in the 50th Anniversary of the Universal Declaration of Human Rights." He is the Lord of all Life; he is the faithful Witness (Rev 1:5) who remains in his faithfulness because he cannot deny himself (2 Tm 2:13). He came to give life and to give it in abundance; it is God with us, a companion on the journey who, at the crossroads of history—the small and the great history—is present. That is why the Spirit moves us to confess him just as the disciples did in the boat when the storm subsided: "Truly, you are the Son of God" (Mt 14:33).

The small and great storms! The theme of our meeting points to one of the largest in history. The Holy Father warns us that "a model of society appears to be emerging in which the powerful predominate, setting aside and even eliminating the powerless: I am thinking here of unborn children, helpless victims of abortion; the elderly and incurably ill, subjected at times to euthanasia; and the many other people relegated to the margins of society by consumerism and materialism. . . . This model of society bears the stamp of *the culture of death and* is therefore in opposition to the Gospel message. Faced with this distressing reality, the Church community intends to commit itself even more to the defense of *the culture of life*" (EIA 63). The defense of this culture of life must occur in all areas, but we cannot help but notice that its strongest foundations are rooted in the family, the foundation of human life. And today "many insidious forces are endangering the solidity of the institution of the family . . . and these represent so many challenges for Christians" (46).

We are like Peter that night on the lake: On the one hand, the presence of the Lord encourages us to face the waves of these challenges; on the other hand, the atmosphere of self-sufficiency and petulance, pure arrogance, that is creating this culture of death threatens us, and we are afraid of sinking in the middle of the storm. The Lord is there. We believe this with the certainty given to us by the strength of the Holy Spirit. And, defying this Lord, there is the snuffed-out cry of so many unborn children—a daily genocide, silent and shielded. There is also the outcry of the abandoned dying man who asks for a tender caress that this culture of death does not know how to give; and the throng of families torn apart by the promises of consumerism and materialism. In the midst of this antinomy and in the presence of the glorious Jesus Christ, today, united as a faithful People of God, we cry out as Peter when he began to sink "Lord, save me" (Mt 14:30), and we extend our hand to cling to the One who can give true meaning to our walk in the midst of the stormy surge.

We ask our Mother, the Mother of all life and of all tenderness, to teach us the path for building the culture of life, just as she taught it to the first disciples when the persecutions began. And to God, our Father, we humbly ask to look at this society so pregnant with death and, making our own the phrase of Moses, we say: "Please, heal her!" (Num 12:13).

→> <←

Standing in Line and Walking

Homily, Shrine of Saint Cajetan—August 7, 1999

Dear brothers,

I want to greet you all with great joy in the Lord and pray, with each of you, in this shrine that brings us together and shelters us. Here, with Saint Cajetan, we feel that our Father God gives us a place in his heart. We have a place in the heart of the Father! How beautiful is the grace of our faith! We have a safe and tender place. Tender as the little ear of wheat that the Saint has in his hand. That ear of wheat with its grains in a row reminds us that "standing in line and walking" to receive grace from the Saint is a gesture of hope. A safe and strong place like this shrine where the Spirit brings us all together, without excluding anyone, and makes us feel like the People of God, with one soul and one heart.

In the heart of our Father God there is a place for us, as persons and as a people! How many persons do not find a place in our city! Either because they are excluded—they have no home, no steady place of work— or because they are disoriented. They have abandoned their struggle in favor of life, for the good of all, to settle into places of privilege that only provide passing joys.

One knows it when one does not have a place, when one is not accepted or welcomed. . . . For example, it is the feeling felt by the person looking for work who's told, after giving all his personal information, "We'll call you."

With God our Father, the experience is totally different. Here we all feel called, always, again and again we have been, and continue to be, invited. The Father is like the landowner of the parable who goes out at dawn, at midmorning, and in the afternoon to look for workers for his vineyard. The Father is the one who, when we are lost, disoriented like the little lamb, sends Jesus to look for us to return us to our place, so we feel that we have a place in life, to heal us from our wounds, and put us back where we belong.

Our place is the house of the Father, of a Father who not only waits for us but who goes out to look for us with Jesus, a Father who knows our wounds, knows what it is to have a son lost and alone in that desert which our city has become for many: a desert where sometimes it is hard to find friendly faces and a helping hand.

To enter here we also must line up, because we are many, but our waiting in line is full of hope. The one ahead of us is not a competitor but a brother. Just like the one behind. And when we see someone who is poorer, less warmly dressed, needier, we remember that for our Father that person is the most important, the one he has sought the most, who receives the warmest greeting. And just as the Good Shepherd carries the lost sheep on his shoulders, we also want to offer our shoulder and make God feel that his people are with him. We want God and Jesus to know that they are not the only ones carrying out this task of healing wounds, of bringing back home those who are scattered. Offering the shoulder is our Father God's gesture, and we must imitate him. Like when we carry the statue of our saints on the processional platform, everyone wants to offer their shoulder, even for a short distance. When you offer your shoulder—the one close to your heart, so close that you feel the weight directly—you find your place in life. When we offer our shoulder to the needs of our brothers, then we experience, with amazement and gratitude, that Another carries us on his shoulders. Since childhood he has taken us, again and again he has carried us back, with joy, with love, like a father carries his small son. In the end, if we want to define who our saints are, we can say clearly: They are the ones who offered their shoulders. That's who Saint Cajetan is; that's how our people feel; that's how we all feel. That is Jesus, the one who carried us all on his shoulders and takes us to the heart of our Father God.

Our Lord has already said, "You who wish to be my followers must deny your very self, take up your cross every day, and follow in my steps" (Lk 9:23). And under the Cross there is only place for the one who wants to offer his shoulder. Offering the shoulder is a grace of our Argentine people, a grace left to us by our elders and that we must teach our children, a grace that allows us to differentiate clearly between who is a father and who is not, who is a friend and who is a traitor, who wants to help and who is a freeloader.

On the shoulders of Jesus, on the shoulders of our saints, of Saint Cajetan, we sense that we are within the heart of our Father God. And today we ask the Virgin for the grace to be strong, to offer our shoulders to the needs of our brothers, to continue being a People who follow Christ and carry his Cross—without losing hope—suffering and praying, praying to God and giving thanks, a happy people amid life's difficulties. When we do this, we are a people who are protected by the peace of Christ that overcomes everything, a people who know with certainty and feel that under the Cross of Christ they have the best place in the heart of their Father God.

→→ ←←

Educating in the Culture of *Encounter*

Position Paper on Education at the Headquarters of the Christian Business Association—September 1, 1999

Over the entrance of one of Harvard's building it reads, "What is man that thou art mindful of him?" A great question to be addressed by those who want to venture into the field of education—like us today.

What is expressed there, charged with admiration, is taken from Psalm 8. It does not emphasize that it is God, the psalmist's interlocutor, who is interested in his creature: "That you are mindful of him." The emphasis is on the "mindful" *aspect* of the question. It is the quality of care God dispenses to man, that surprises the psalmist. The Scriptures sum up this mindfulness in one word: love.

And after the surprise and the impact that the actions of the Creator have on his favorite work, comes the next question. The ontological question is posed, asking about the being who is the beneficiary of so much mindfulness.

What is man? What is humankind?

The biblical verse taken in context allows a glimpse at two access routes, not antithetical, to the mystery of man. One, the *'via teologica'*; the other, the route that goes from the works, to the nucleus from which they flow, the way of philosophy, culture, science.

The first path leads us, with the same wonder of the psalmist, to the divine pedagogy for humanity, where his Word directs us, and acquires such closeness and presence in the middle of history, that it becomes one of us—Jesus Christ. Christ fully reveals man to himself and shows him his dignity.

The question is appropriate, because man needs *to know what he is*—in any way—*to learn to be what he is*. He is given as essence, as nature, but he must be polished, must become. And it is this process of humanization, that we call education.

Man, together with other persons, puts into practice his potential, and as he reaches self-realization he generates culture. The subject of culture is a community, a people, that assumes a specific lifestyle. Education implies a process for transmitting culture.

Man and nations express who they are with their works, but we must add that we are also who we aspire to be. Therefore, we can be defined by our aspirations as well as our achievements.

At the end of the millennium we speak of a cultural crisis, a crisis of values. And this touches the core of what is human, as persons, as society.

We are concerned about what is happening. We must not forget that evil emerges and takes root only in the absence of that which should be present. Therefore, it is necessary to engage in discernment.

Cultural Discernment

In this globalized culture, remnants of what has been called the 'shipwreck culture' are reaching our shores; elements of modernity are departing, and its successor is gaining ground.

Let us identify and describe some characteristics of this nascent culture:

Profane messianism. It appears under various forms symptomatic of social or political approaches. Sometimes it is a displacement of the ethos from individual acts toward the structures, in such a way that the ethos doesn't give form to the structures but rather the structures produce the ethos. Hence, the path of sociopolitical salvation prefers to follow an 'analysis of structures' and the political and economic actions resulting from them. Underlying this is the conviction that the ethos is a fragile element whereas structures have solid and secure value. This fact flows from the tension between action and structure. The ethos does not maintain the correct tension between action and structure (action is what comes from within the person). Consequently, the ethos moves toward structures because they are naturally more stable and weighty. When the personal sense of the objective is lost (human well-being, God), the strength of 'quantity' possessed by the structure remains.

Relativism. The fruit of uncertainty infected by mediocrity, this is the current tendency to discredit values, or at minimum, proposes an immanent moralism that relegates the transcendent, replacing it with false promises or short-term goals. The disconnect from Christian roots converts values into monads, commonplaces, or simply names.

Relativism is the possibility of fantasizing about reality, positing it as if it could be controlled by commands issued in a game. It leads to valuations and judgments based only on subjective impressions without practical, concrete, objective norms.

Ethics and politics are reduced to physics. There is no inherent good and evil, only a calculation of advantages and disadvantages. A consequence of the displacement of moral reasoning, the law is unable to refer to a fundamental image of justice, becoming instead a mirror of the dominant ideas.

This subjectivist withdrawal of values leads us to 'advance through circumstantial consensus building.' We also enter a process of degradation: go 'leveling downwards' through the negotiatory consensus. Progress becomes a series of pacts, and therefore the logic of strength triumphs.

On the other hand, it establishes the reign of opinion. There are no certainties or convictions. Everything is acceptable, which is only steps away from nothing being acceptable.

The human being today experiences *rootlessness and helplessness*. He was brought there by his excessive desire for autonomy, a legacy of modernity. He has lost the support from something that transcends him.

A new *nihilism* that 'universalizes' everything by erasing and devaluing particularities, or affirming them with such violence that their destruction is achieved; fratricidal struggles; total internationalization of capital and the media; lack of interest in concrete sociopolitical commitments and real participation in the culture and its values.

We want to give ourselves the illusion of an autonomous, undiscriminated individuality . . . and we end up being a number in marketing statistics, an incentive for advertising.

The one-sidedness of the modern concept of reason: only *quantitative reason* (geometries as perfect sciences), reasoning for calculation and experimentation, has the right to be called "reason."

The *technological mentality* together with the search for a profane messianism are two expressive features of the man of today, whom we may well describe as "gnostic man"—knowledgeable, but lacking unity, and, on the other hand, in need of the esoteric, in this case, the secularized type, that is to say, profane. In this sense it could be said that education is tempted to be gnostic and esoteric, because it is unable to handle the power of technology from the inner unity that springs from the real ends and the means used on a human scale. And this crisis cannot be overcome by any type of 'return' (which dying modernity has attempted in every way), but instead is surmounted through an *internal overflow*, that is, in the very core of the crisis, totally assuming it, without staying in the crisis, but transcending it by going inward.

A *false hermeneutics that establishes suspicion*. Fallacy is used, a lie that allures with its apparently innocuous structure. Its pernicious effects manifest themselves slowly.

Either truth or nobility is caricatured, aggressively or cruelly enlarging one perspective and leaving many others in the shadow. It is a way of debasing what is good. It is always easy, in public or in private, to laugh mercilessly at a given value: honesty, nonviolence, modesty; but that leads only to losing the taste for that value and to elevating its antivalue and the debasement of life.

Or slogans are used that, with rich verbal or visual language, and using the richest and most valuable concepts, make one aspect absolute and disfigure the whole.

Postmodernity is no longer averse to religion, nor forces it to the private domain. There is a *diluted deism* that tends to reduce faith and religion to the 'spiritualistic' sphere and to the subjective (from which results a faith without mercy). *Fundamentalist positions* arising in other corners lay bare their impotence and superficiality.

That sad transcendence does not even manage to take charge of the limits of immanence, because it simply fails to face any human limits or reach into any wound.

Closely linked to this paradigm of deism, there is a process of emptying out words (words without their own weight, words that do not become flesh). They are emptied of their contents; then Christ does not enter in as a Person, but as an idea. Words are inflated. It is a *nominalist culture*. The word has lost its weight; it is hollow. It lacks support, a 'spark' that makes it come alive and that consists precisely of silence.

A Culture of *Encounter*

I would like to make a proposal: *We need to generate a culture of encounter.*

Facing the *culture of fragmentation*, as some have wanted to call it, or *of nonintegration*, more is demanded of us in difficult times, not favoring those who pretend to capitalize resentment, forget our shared history, or revel in weakening our ties.

With incarnated realism. Let us never stop from finding inspiration in the suffering, unprotected, and anguished faces to stimulate and commit ourselves to research, study, and work and to create more. Man and woman must be the center of our commitments.

The person of flesh and blood, with a concrete culture and history, and the human complexity with tensions and limitations, is not being respected nor considered. But it is the human person who must be at the center of our concerns and reflections. The human reality of limits, of concrete and objective laws and norms, the always necessary and imperfect authority, the commitment to reality, are insurmountable difficulties for the mentality described previously.

Let us escape from virtual realities. And from the cult of appearances.

You cannot educate disconnected from *memory*. Memory is a uniting and integrating power. In the same way that understanding left to its own powers leads to the precipice, memory comes to be the vital core of a family or a people. A family without memory does not deserve the name. A family that does not respect and care for the grandparents, its living memory, is a disintegrated family; but a family and people that remember are a family and people with a future.

The key is not to inhibit the creative force of our own history, of our remembered history. The educational domain, as a permanent search for wisdom, is a space best suited for this exercise: to reencounter the principles that allowed us to realize a desire, to rediscover the mission hidden there that struggles to continue unfolding.

We see so much sick memory, blurred, torn into remembrances incapable of going beyond their first appearance, entertained by flashes and fashion trends, feelings of the moment, opinions full of self-sufficiency that conceal bewilderment. All these fragments want to obscure and deny history.

The change of juridical status of our city cannot mean 'wipe the slate clean.' For one without a past, nothing has been accomplished. All is in the future, but starting from zero.

From cultural refuges to a foundation's transcendence. An anthropology is needed that discards any path of 'return' conceived—more or less consciously—as a cultural refuge. Humans tend by inertia, to rebuild what was yesterday. This feature is a consequence of the previous point. Modernity—when it loses objective support—resorts to 'the classic' (but in the sense of the classical world, the ancient world; not in the sense we give to it) as an expression of the duty to be cultural. Being divided, divorced from itself, confuses the nostalgia proper of the call to transcendence, with the longing for immanent mediations that have also been uprooted. A culture without roots and without unity does not last.

An integrative universalism through respect for differences. We must enter this culture of globalization from the horizon of universality. Instead of being atoms that only acquire meaning in the whole, we must integrate ourselves in a new 'organicity' of a higher order that subsumes us without nullifying us. We incorporate ourselves in harmony, without giving up what is ours, to something that transcends us.

And this cannot be done through consensus, which negotiates downward, but through the path of dialogue, the confrontation of ideas and the exercise of authority.

Exercising *dialogue*, the most human channel of communication. The need to establish in all areas, a space for serious dialogue, effective, not merely formal or distracting. An exchange that destroys prejudices and builds, based on a common search and sharing, and strives for the interaction of wills in favor of a common task or a shared project.

Even more so in times where it is said that we are "children of information and orphans of communication." It requires patience, clarity, good disposition toward the other. It does not exclude confrontation between different points of view, without the use of ideas as weapons, but instead as light. We do not give up our ideas, utopias, properties, or rights, but only the claim that they are unique or absolute.

The exercise of authority. A leader is always necessary, but this means a formality that gives cohesion to the body, and functions not to take sides, but to be totally of service. How impoverishing it is for the dignity of coexistence in society, the policy of fait accompli that prevents legitimate participation, that promotes formality over reality!

Those who govern must respect the various worldviews that inform from within the contents of the most varied areas of knowledge, from the beginning level to the preparation of teachers. It goes with respect for legitimate pluralism and freedom to teach and learn.

So that this force that we all carry within, and is link and life, can manifest itself, it is necessary that all, and especially those of us with a high quota of political or economic power or any type of influence, renounce those interests or abuses of our influence that pretend to go beyond the common good that brings us together. It is necessary that we assume, with seriousness and greatness, the mission imposed on us at these times.

The practice of opening spaces for encounter.[1] At the rearguard of superficiality and immediatist conjuncturalism (flowers that do not bear fruit) there is a people with a collective memory that moves on with their characteristic nobility: Community efforts and undertakings, the growth of neighborhood initiatives, the boom of so many mutual aid movements, which mark the presence of God's sign in a whirlwind, of participation without tribalism, rarely seen in our country. Our people, who know how to spontaneously and naturally organize themselves in the national community, protagonists of this new social bond, demand a space for consultation, control, and creative participation in all areas of social life that concern them. We the leaders

---

1. Encounter that leads to engagement, relationships, commitments to work for the well-being of all.

must be companions to the vitality of this new bond. Empowering and protecting it can become our main mission.

It's hard not to think of schools as a privileged space for exchange!

Openness to a religious experience that is committed, personal, and social. The religious dimension is a creative force within the life of humanity, its history, and invigorates every being that opens to that experience.

How is it possible that in some educational environments all issues and questions are allowed, but there is one outlaw, a great outcast: God?

In the name of a neutrality acknowledged as impossible, a dimension is silenced and excised that, far from being pernicious, can greatly contribute to the formation of hearts and coexistence in society.

It is not through suppressing the differences of valid options of conscience, nor the open treatment of what is related to one's worldview that we will achieve a formation respectful of each person and that recognizes diversity as a path to unity.

It would seem that the public arena has to be 'lite,' watered down, lacking any conviction; the only acceptable stances will be vagueness, frivolity, or in favor of the interests of the powerful.

Educate, and Then? Educate

Faced with this landscape where there is no shortage of internal and external family difficulties, economic problems, violence, and disaffection, it seems necessary to ask ourselves: How to educate? without at the same time needing to ask, how not to educate? How can we not continue to place our trust in education? How can we not continue to trust education?

The educational institution is not understood, without the teacher, the instructor. But neither is it understood without putting the human being in the center. And this comes to mind when structures, curricula, programs, content, assessment, management methods, fight to be the focus of attention.

Postmodern culture presents a model of person that is strongly associated with the image of young people. Those who look young are beautiful, who undergo treatments to have the traces of time disappear. The model of beauty is a youthful model, informal, *casual*. Our model of adulthood is an adolescent.

Adolescents are presented with new ways of feeling, thinking, and acting. But at the same time, they are considered to lack the critical tools for interpreting the world they live in, and hope for the future. To these young people, school knowledge is presented as outdated, meaningless. They devalue what schools present as necessary to live in this society.

The most experienced teachers, confident in their successful ways of teaching, sometimes find the adolescent's world dark and distant. That is, we find an adolescent who devalues school knowledge and a teacher who does not know the adolescent's questions. This is a 'disencounter.'

Young people, too, are being invited insistently to pursue pleasure, the source of satisfaction of desires instantaneously and painlessly; submerged in the culture of the image as their most natural habitat. The knowledge presented by the school appears as unappetizing and is considered unimportant. It does not emphasize sensory satisfaction, nor provide the tools that ensure social climbing or simply access to a job.

Young people do not find at school what they look for. The modern school receives a postmodern student, we could say with a certain ease, but it is not only this.

There is an essential need for coherence. Exchanges of accusations do not work. As a society we must shed light to overcome the disengagement, to not waste energy building on one side what we destroy on the other.

What to teach? The same variety and multitude of what is knowable is immeasurable. How to organize yourself in this multiplicity of what to teach, what to learn? Starting simply from the material to be known, there is not a truly organizing point of view. The object of knowledge does not necessarily indicate a goal and a perspective. The organizing perspective must be found in the human person and in the *encounter* with others, because education must serve formation, that is, the way life is constituted. That point of view, even with all the necessary connection with the thing itself, must be at the same time a path, a way of meeting where those who teach and those who learn can understand themselves better in relation to their time, their history, society, culture, and the world.

Education must overcome the risk of shrinking in the mere distribution of knowledge. It is not only about the selection of concrete offers of contents or methods but also about interpretation and evaluation.

Teacher and student must reach an understanding that cements the common desire for truth. Not only to feel connected to things, but to show integrity in understanding existence.

The education needed must keep what is fundamental and keep the foundation.

What is true, beautiful, and good exists. What is absolute exists. It can, moreover, it must, be known and perceived.

An education that strengthens the fabric of civil society (civilized or for citizens) is necessary. Education must be a place of *encounter* and for the common efforts where we learn to be a society, where society learns to be a society of solidarity. We must learn new ways to build the city of man.

Not Only Words: Life

You all know of growing needs of education in your capacity as students, alumni, or parents. Also, as business leaders surely, you are linked to the world of the school by committing yourselves to internships and education projects for community action. Today I ask you to concern yourself with education, manifest in your invitation to me, and which encourages me to ask you as a friend for continued efforts to support the development of a project sponsored by the Archdiocesan Department for Parochial Schools that cares for and supports structurally weak or weakened areas through the building of community centers that can respond to diversity, poverty, families, and education.

The Church's presence in education, here in Río de la Plata, dates back almost four hundred years. Specifically, a school of the Society of Jesus was the first in this area. And we want to be always present. The Church longs to offer completely free education in areas where school failure and problems are most acute in our city, such as Lugano, Soldati, La Boca, Barracas. We already have works in those sectors, but we aspire to increase our presence and accompaniment, offering the discipline, formation, and follow-up that those children and their families need.

Dear friends, education and the smallest of our society expect much from you, and from us. I know the effort and the work you have been doing. I also know the enthusiasm and ability you can show at this crucial hour in favor of the future of education in our city.

A people that wants to conjure the poverty of emptiness and despair. A people with memory, a memory that cannot be reduced to a mere record. Here is the greatness of our people. I see in our Argentine people a strong awareness of their dignity. It is an awareness that has been molded by significant milestones. Our people have a soul, and because we can speak of the soul of a people, we can speak of a hermeneutics, a way of seeing reality, a conscience. Today, amid conflicts, these people teach us that we should not pay attention to those who try to distill reality into ideas, that we are not served by intellectuals without talent, nor by ethicists without kindness, but by appealing to the depth of our dignity as a people, appealing to our wisdom, appealing to our cultural resources. It is a true revolution, not against a system but internal; a revolution of memory and tenderness: memory of the great heroic founding deeds. . . . And memory of the simple gestures that we sucked at the breast in the family. To be faithful to our mission is to take care of the 'embers' in the heart, protect them from the cheating ashes of forgetfulness or the presumption of believing that our homeland, our city, and our family have no history or that it has begun with us. The embers of memory that condenses, like the embers of fire, the values that make us great; the way of celebrating and defending life, of accepting death, of caring for the fragility of our poorest neighbors, of opening hands in solidarity in the face of pain and poverty, to celebrate and to pray; the illusion of working together and—from our common poverty—to amass solidarity.

We are all invited to build this culture of *encounter*, to realize and share this new ferment that—at the same time—is a revivifying memory of our best history of sacrifice in solidarity, of the struggle against various enslavements and social integration.

We should be convinced once again that the whole is superior to the parts, time is superior to space, reality is superior to the idea, and unity is superior to conflict.

Last, we often ask ourselves with some concern: What kind of world are we leaving to our children? It might be better to pose a different one: What children are we giving to this world?

→ ←

Consecrated Life Makes Sense Only in Light of Fruitfulness

Homily, Mass with Consecrated Men and Women—September 8, 1999

"God with us" is the name of our Redeemer, God with us. Today I want to underscore the *us*. This singular way that we have tonight of being us: the consecrated women, the consecrated men of the diocese together with their bishop.

Us/We. A Church woven by the charity of the Holy Spirit and today *we* come to meet this God, who is always close to us, but we come to greet him, to worship him, to tell him one more time, "yes," with the renewal of our vows, and "yes" in this diocesan church. And "yes" inserted in this holy, faithful people of God who walk in Buenos Aires. We are here today.

And the Church, to us here present today, presents us with the image of the Mother, the one who will give birth. The one who will bring him to be with us.

"Therefore, the Lord will give them up, until the time when she who is to give birth has borne" (Mi 5:2). And in the Gospel, we are also told about motherhood. How Jesus was conceived. The Church poses a question to us consecrated women and men that is also an invitation of the fruitfulness of the Church.

"She who is to give birth" is Mary, and the one who should be a mother is the Church. Mary as a figure of the Church, the Church as a figure of Mary.

And the one who should be mother, doing some exegesis following one of the Church fathers, is also our soul, our most intimate self: Mary, the Church, and the soul.

We hear of ecclesial fruitfulness, and in this assembly looking at Mary, the Church, and our soul, we question ourselves about our own fruitfulness as consecrated women and men. Our fruitfulness is here in Buenos Aires where obedience sent us to work, if we accept head-on the challenge of being mothers and fathers, not merely qualified single men and women. Consecrated life only makes sense in the light of fatherhood and motherhood; that is, in the light of fruitfulness, according to the style of the consecrated family to which one belongs. Without fruitfulness we are just a group of pensioners with religious culture, more or less pious, workers perhaps, but not consecrated.

Consecration anoints us in fruitfulness, as the Mother of the Lord was fruitful in her salvation and as the Church is fruitful.

And fruitfulness implies a deeper generosity of continually denying oneself to give life to others. The same life of self-denial is what gives life; not the selfish Pelagian emptying of self, which ultimately worships one's own personality, but the self-denial of a father and a mother who walk with the sole purpose of relinquishing themselves so that another may have life and that their own lives may have meaning inasmuch as they can give life and make it grow in others. In the light of this Word that the Church puts before us today looking at the Virgin, in light of what our mother Church is, we look at what our soul is as consecrated persons: It is fruitful. Consecrated life will always be tempted by cosmetics, being self-absorbed in its own project, in its own sphere, its own work, in the *little thing*. And that is when consecrated life loses meaning. Good people, very good, but without children. And when I say without children, I mean without hope, because what a father and mother have when they bring a child into the world, when they play the most intimate part of themselves for another life, is the hope that this life that brings the world, that life that it raises in the Lord, in our case, it will grow, it will be adult, it will overshadow me, it will surpass me, and it will close my eyes.

A fruitful consecrated life is a hopeful consecrated life that believes that through its spiritual depth passes the power of the Spirit that gives life to others.

A fruitful consecrated life is a consecrated life that looks beyond the doors of its convent, has broader horizons, and continually poses the questions that the Lord asks through the things that are happening each day, what kind of life the Lord asks through the thousand and one daily occurrences, in the intimacy of prayer and in the sharing of community life. What does Jesus ask me today in order to give life? Broad horizons, horizons past our noses. And this is the mission that we consecrated men and women have in the Church—to reflect the fruitfulness of Mother Church, the fruitfulness of Mother Mary in our own fruitfulness. To reflect the hope of the Church, to reflect the apostolic courage of the Church, which does not remain locked up worshipping itself, its little thing, its little work, its own organizational chart.

The worst enemy of religious fruitfulness is functionalism, that artificial fruitfulness of the test tube. If there is no previous fruitfulness, any functionalism does not serve, it adulterates. We must be intelligent in the means we choose. We must look for them and plan for them, but in the light of our hope, of our apostolic daring that entails that fruitfulness. Let us not believe that we are serving the Church if we have beautiful apostolic plans made only by single men and women.

Today we contemplate "she who is to give birth" and congratulate her on her birthday. I thought that one of the good sisters would think of bringing a cake. No one felt the impulse to do that. The birthday of the Virgin. We congratulate her, but the great glory of Mary is that her virginity was fruitful. It brought us the meaning of our existence; it brought us "God with us."

And today, fruitful in our mother Church, we come to tell Mary that we want to belong to her, that we want to belong to the Church, that we want to be fathers and mothers. That we want to lavish hope, lavish fruitfulness, lavish apostolic courage. We ask her for the grace of a fruitful insertion in the Church to which we belong, generous, bountiful; and the grace that, when our moment comes, there will be many children to close our eyes. May it be so.

→> <+-

Open the Doors to Christ

Letter to Priests of the Archdiocese—October 1, 1999

Dear brothers,

The Advent season will begin in a few weeks, and this year will be the liturgical start of the Jubilee. The desire to let the Lord visit us at his coming acquires a singular force in light of this event. At Christmas the Holy Door will open and, foreseeing this moment, the oft-repeated invitation of the Pope resonates in my heart: "Open the doors to the Redeemer" (APR 1), "Open the door to Christ" (RM 3). The Nativity of the Lord must find us thus, "like servants who await their master's return . . . ready to open immediately" (Lk 12:36). This letter to you arises from the desire to exhort you, as pastor and brother, to open the doors to the Lord: the doors of the heart, the doors of the mind, the doors of our churches . . . all doors. Opening doors is a Christian and a priestly task.

Jesus did it too, as we read in the Gospel. At the beginning of his mission, he appears opening the book of the prophet Isaiah (cf. Lk 4:17); and the book of Revelation ends in a similar manner, with Jesus as the slain Lamb, the Lion of Judah, the only one "worthy to open the scroll and break its seals" (Rev 5:2). The risen Jesus 'opened the minds' of the disciples of Emmaus "to understand the scriptures" (Lk 24:45) and made them recall: "Were not our hearts burning [within us] while he spoke to us on the way and opened the scriptures to us?" (v. 32). Many miracles happened because of this openness to the Word: Jesus touched the eyes of two blind men "and their eyes were opened" (Mt 9:30); "He said to him, '*Ephphatha!*' (that is, 'Be opened!'). And [immediately] the man's ears were opened" (Mk 7:34). When Jesus "opens his mouth" the Kingdom of Heaven opens in parables: "He began to teach them" (Mt 5:2); "I will open my mouth in parables" (Mt 13:35). When Jesus humbles himself and is baptized; when he prays (cf. Lk 3:21) the heavens open and the loving voice of the Father is heard: "This is my beloved Son" (Mt 3:17). And it is the Lord who exhorts us: "Knock and the door will be opened to you" (Lk 11:9), and the Church prays "that God may open a door to us for the word" (Col 4:3), because if he "opens . . . no one shall close" (Rev 3:7). All the opening actions of the Lord can be seen clearly and definitively in a personal invitation that we read in the letter to Laodicea: "If anyone hears my voice and opens the door, [then] I will enter his house and dine with him, and he with me" (v. 20).

Today, openness is considered a value, although it is not always well understood. "He's an open priest," people say, contrasting it to "a closed priest." Like any assessment, it depends on who makes it. Sometimes, on a superficial assessment, openness can mean "one who allows anything" or "who is a show-off," who isn't "starched" or "rigid." But some positions that are more superficial always hide something profound that people perceive. Being an open priest means one "who is able to listen but stands firm in his convictions." Once, a man from a small town defined a priest with a simple declaration: "He is a priest who talks to everyone." He meant he doesn't exclude any persons. He was struck by the fact that the priest could easily speak with each person; and he clearly distinguished it both from those who could easily speak with only some, and from those who speak with everyone and say yes to everything.

This is because openness goes hand in hand with fidelity. And true fidelity moves, on the one hand, to open the door of the heart entirely to the beloved and, on the other, to close that door to anyone who threatens that love. Hence, opening the door to the Lord implies opening it to those he loves: the poor, the young, the wayward, the sinners . . . everyone, really. And closing it to "idols": easy flattery, worldly glory, lust, power, wealth, slander, and—insofar as they embody these antivalues—people who want to enter our hearts or our communities to impose these.

Besides being faithful, the attitude of opening or closing the door must give witness. Give witness that, on the last day, there will be a door that opens for some: the blessed of the Father, those who gave food and drink to the little ones, who maintained their lamps with oil, who put the Word into practice. . . . And it will be closed to others: those who did not open their hearts to the needy, who ran out of oil, who only said "Lord, Lord" in word, and didn't love with their actions.

Thus, openness is not a matter of talk but of actions. People express this when talking about the priest who "is always present" and the one "who is never there" (charitably opening their requests saying, "I know you're busy, Father, because you have so many things to do . . ."). Evangelical openness is played out at the entrances: at the door of churches that, in a world where shopping centers never close, cannot remain closed for so many hours, even if you need to pay security guards and come down to the confessional more often; in that door that is the telephone, tiring and inopportune in our hypercommunicated world, but cannot remain long hours at the mercy of an answering machine. But these doors are external and "media technologies." They are an expression of that other door, our face, with our eyes, our smile, slowing down a bit and having the courage to look at the one we know is waiting. . . . In the confessional one knows that half of the battle is won or lost in the greeting, in the way of receiving the penitent, especially the one who peeks and with a gesture seems to say, "May I?" A frank, cordial, warm welcome completes the opening of a soul that the Lord has already made come to the peephole. On the other hand, a cold, hurried, or bureaucratic reception causes the closing of what is ajar. We know that we confess in different ways according to the priest we get . . . and the people too.

A good image for examining our openness is that of our home. There are houses that are open because they are 'at peace'; that are hospitable because they have the warmth of a home; not so neat that one is afraid to sit (not to mention smoke or eat something), nor so disorderly that they make you feel ashamed. It's the same with the heart: The heart that has room for the Lord also has room for others. If there is not time and place for the Lord then the place for the others is reduced according to one's moods, enthusiasm, or weariness. And the Lord is like the poor: he approaches without being called and insists a bit but doesn't stay if we do not ask him. It is easy to get rid of him. Just rush a little, as when passing by beggars or look the other way as when the kids in the subway leave us a holy card in exchange for a coin.[1]

---

1. In Buenos Aires, children beg by giving away holy cards or other trinkets. They place them on your lap and continue down along the rows of cars before returning to yours after giving you time to decide if you want to make an offering.

Yes, openness to others goes hand in hand with our openness to the Lord. He, the openhearted one, is the only one who can open a peaceful space in our hearts, the peace that makes us hospitable to others. That is the job of the risen Jesus: to enter the closed Upper Room that, as a home, is an image of the heart, and open it by removing all fear and filling the disciples with peace. At Pentecost, the Spirit seals with this peace the home and hearts of the Apostles and transforms them into an Open House for all, into the Church. The Church is like the open house of the merciful Father. Therefore, our attitude should be that of the Father and not that of the sons in the parable: neither of the younger one who takes advantage of an opening to make his getaway nor of the older one who thought that with his stubbornness he would be a better caretaker of his father's inheritance.

Open the doors to the Lord! It is the request that I want to make to all the priests of the Archdiocese. Open your doors! Those of your hearts and those of your churches. Do not be afraid! Open them in the morning, in your prayer, to receive the Spirit who will fill you with peace and joy and then go out to shepherd the faithful People of God. Open them during the day so that the prodigal sons feel they are expected. Open them in the evening so that the Lord will not pass you by and leave you alone but will enter and eat with you and accompany you.

And always remember her, the Gate of Heaven, whose open heart was pierced by the sword, who understands all sorrows; the little servant of the Father who knows how to open up completely to give praise; the one who goes out "in haste" (Lk 1:39) to visit and comfort; the one who knows how to transform any hut into a house for "God with us" with some simple diapers and a mountain of tenderness; the one who is always attentive so that wine won't be lacking in our lives; the one who knows how to wait outside so the Lord may instruct his people; the one always in the open wherever men raise a cross and crucify her children. Our Lady is Mother, and—as a mother—knows how to open the hearts of her children: God forgives every hidden sin through her tender eyes; every whim and obstinacy dissolves with a word from her; all fear for our mission dissipates if she joins us on the way.

I ask her to bless all of us, priests of this archdiocese, and with her motherly tenderness teach us each day to open the doors to the Redeemer. With fraternal affection.

The Virgin's Gaze Is a Gift

Homily, Twenty-Fifth Youth Pilgrimage to Luján—October 3, 1999

We heard how Jesus looked at his Mother. From the cross, he looked at her and pointed to all of us saying: "*This is your Son, these are your children.*" And Mary, feeling Jesus' gaze, must have remembered when she was young, thirty or so years earlier, when she felt another gaze that made her sing with joy: the gaze of the Father. And she felt that the Father had looked at her small- ness. Little Mary, our Mother whom we came to see, and engage her gaze today and be engaged by her gaze. Because her look is like the continuation of the gaze of the Father who saw her smallness and made her the Mother of God; like the gaze of the Son on the cross that made her into our Mother; and with that gaze she looks at us today. And today we, after a long jour- ney, come to this place of rest, because the Virgin's gaze is a place of rest, and we come to tell her our concerns.

We need her tender gaze, the Mother's gaze, that unlocks our soul, a gaze full of compassion and care. And that's why today we say to her: *Mother, grant us your gaze.* Because the Virgin's gaze is a gift, it cannot be bought. It is a gift from her. It is a gift from the Father and a gift from Jesus on the cross. *Mother, grant us your gaze.*

We come to give thanks that her gaze is in our stories. In that story each one of us knows, the hidden history of our lives. That story with problems and joys. And after this long road, tired, we meet her comforting gaze and we say: *Mother, grant us your gaze.*

In the Virgin's gaze, we have a permanent gift. It is the gift of God's mercy, who looked at her smallness and made her his Mother. Of the mercy of God, who looked at her from the cross, and made her our Mother. That mercy of the good Father, who waits for us at every turn of the road. And to meet that Father, today we say to our Mother: *Mother, grant us your gaze.*

But we are not alone, we are many, we are a people, and the Virgin's gaze helps us to look at each other in a different way. We learn to be more like brothers, because our Mother gazes at us. To have that gaze that seeks to rescue, accompany, protect. We learn to look at ourselves in her Mother's gaze.

The Virgin's gaze teaches us to look at those whom we naturally notice less, yet need it most: the most vulnerable, those who are alone, the sick, those who have nothing, street children, those who do not know Jesus, those who do not know the tenderness of the Virgin, the young people who lost their way.

Let us not be afraid to go out and look at our brothers with that gaze of the Virgin, that makes us brothers and sisters and thus we will weave with our hearts and our gaze the *culture of encounter* that we need so much, that our homeland so badly needs.

Finally, let us not allow anything to get in the way of the Virgin's gaze. *Mother, grant us your gaze.* Let no one hide it from me. May my filial heart know how to defend itself from so many peddlers who promise illusions; from those who have the avid gaze of the easy life, of promises that cannot be fulfilled. Do not let anyone steal from us the gaze of the Virgin, a gaze of tenderness that strengthens us from within. A gaze that makes us strong in character, that makes us brothers, that makes us supportive of one another. Mother, do not let me wander away from your gaze; we ask her: grant it to me, Mother. Don't let me doubt that you are looking at me with your abiding tenderness, and that your gaze will help me to gaze better at others, to meet Jesus Christ, to work to be more brotherly, more supportive, more open to engaging with others. And so together we can come to this house of rest under the tenderness of your gaze. *Mother, grant us your gaze.*

-»- -«-

To Govern Is to Serve Each One of These Brothers

Homily, Solemn Te Deum *for New National Authorities—
December 11, 1999 (Transcript)*

Ask me anything you would like, God said to Solomon. And Solomon asked him for wisdom to govern. And God praised him. The Lord was pleased that Solomon made that request and said: "Because you have asked for this and you have not asked for a long life, nor wealth, nor the life of your enemies, but you have asked for a wise heart . . ." (1 Kgs 3:11). That gesture of Solomon looking at the sky, because he knows he is small. Your servant, he says to God, is in the middle of your people, I am a boy. We would say in

Buenos Aires: "I am a nobody."[1] The humble heart of a ruler who looks up and asks for wisdom.

Jesus also upends the values and says: "Whoever wants to be great among you must become a servant, whosoever wants to be the first must become his slave, as the Son of man who did not come to be served but to serve" (Mk 10:43). The gaze of Solomon was upward, the gaze that Jesus teaches us, to whom we have some responsibility for government, is also to the sides. Look to the sides! And to govern is to serve each one of these brothers who make up our people.

The word of God is very simple; when one forgets to look up and ask for wisdom, he falls into that nefarious defect—self-sufficiency. And from self-sufficiency to vanity, to pride . . . there is no wisdom. When you forget to look at the sides, you look at yourself, or look at your surroundings, forget your people or fall into the temptation to see your people through their various needs and groups, which perhaps serve as functional, but they do not touch the heart. And to those who are given the mission of serving in government, we are asked never to stop looking up, to avoid falling into self-sufficiency and never stop looking to the sides, so as not to forget our people.

I pray to the Lord today, for all of us who have governing responsibility, but in a special way, for you all: for you, Mr. President, for you Mr. Vice President. For all who will help these two citizens, may the Lord grant them the grace to always look up to ask for wisdom and always look to the sides to perceive, in our flesh and in our hearts, the feelings of our people.

May it be so.

→- -←

"God with Us"

Homily, Christmas of the Millennium—December 18, 1999, Year B

How beautiful to hear all together, here, in silence, the Gospel that reminds us of how God came to be "God with us" (Mt 1:23); how he was received by Mary and by Joseph. We exalt with joy the Holy Trinity that shines

---

1. In Spanish, "*Soy poca cosa.*"

humbly and hidden in this Holy Family. While the Holy Spirit works the
Incarnation in Mary (who is pure availability, totally allowing God to do as
he wishes), the Father—represented in that "angel of God"—makes all the
external arrangements with Saint Joseph (who is pure obedience, just getting up in the morning and doing what he's commanded). And they all
revolve around the Child Jesus, the favorite Son of the Father, the One
anointed by the Holy Spirit, the one anticipated by the nations. The one
who came to save his people from their sins. He who comes every day to be
with us in each Eucharist. Jesus, in whom we believe and whom we wait
until he returns.

The jubilee is Jesus' birthday. The first Christmases were simple family
parties. Joseph and Mary must have celebrated alone, in exile, the first birth-
days of Jesus. The "God with us" seemed to have been only for the two of
them. But—if we listen to the *Magnificat*—we realize that Mary always
loved Jesus with the heart of the people, with the heart of the Church. And
so it was that, after the Resurrection of the Lord, little by little, Christmas
began to be a celebration for all the faithful people of God.

Two thousand Christmases have passed. Seven hundred years before, Isaiah had prophesied that a Child would be born and be called Emmanuel,
"God with us." A God with us who has always wanted to be a God with
everyone.

Two thousand Christmases, and the Child is not disillusioned with his
faithful People, with us. He continues to be confident in our hands, in this
gesture of surrender that is the Eucharist. As if repeating, "I am the God
with you," in his silence that tastes like bread.

"God with us" is a beautiful name for God. *It's like his surname.* His first
name is Jesus, or Father or Spirit . . . but his surname is "God with us."

To speak about him we have to say 'us.' Only if we let him be with us, as
Mary and Joseph did, does *a culture of encounter become possible*, in which
no one is excluded, in which we all see each other as brothers. Because it is
precisely in closeness and in engagement that Jesus, love, is born. That love
that takes root in the memory of a shared grace: "A savior has been born for
you . . . you will find an infant wrapped in swaddling clothes" (Lk 2:11–12).
Love feeds on the common hope, that of the Holy City that will shelter us
all, whose best image is that of shared bread.

That is why today, upon receiving the Eucharist, let us also feel the one
next door, let us feel the presence of all and say: *God with us*. Let us remember Saint Joseph and the Virgin and say: *God with us*. Let us think of the
hope of Isaiah and the Prophets, of our father Abraham and of the Patri-

archs, and let us say: God *with us*. Let us taste the affection of the Saints, that crowd of men and women who "lived in his friendship through the centuries" and pray with them: God *with us*. Let us look for the poorest to say with them: God *with us*. Let us take our children's hands and say: God *with us*. Let us caress our elders and, with them, confess: God *with us*.

United by the memory and hope of Bethlehem, the House of Bread, of the Bread of Life that two thousand years ago the Father gave us, of our Bread each day that he gives us today, and of the Bread that Jesus himself will break for us at the banquet of heaven, now all together, as brothers, we profess our faith in God with us: I believe in one God, the Father . . .

2000

"Repent and Believe in the Gospel"

Archdiocesan Catechetical Encounter (EAC)—March 11, 2000,
Year B (Transcript)

"Repent and believe in the Gospel," the priest told us this past Wednesday, when giving us the ashes.

We begin this Lent with this command. To rend our hearts, to open them, and to believe in the Gospel of truth, not in a caricature of the Gospel, not in the 'lite' Gospel, not in the distilled Gospel, but in the Gospel of truth. And you are asked today, in a special way, as catechists: Repent and believe in the Gospel.

But you also have a mission in the Church: to inspire others to believe in the Gospel. Seeing you, seeing what you do, how you conduct yourselves, what you say, how you feel, how you love, they will believe in the Gospel.

The Gospel says that the Spirit drove Jesus to the desert, and there "he was among wild beasts" (Mk 1:12) without anything bad happening. This reminds us of what occurred at the beginning: The first man and the first woman lived among the beasts, and nothing bad happened. In that paradise everything was peace, everything was joy. And they were tempted, and Jesus, too, was tempted.

Jesus wants, at the beginning of his life, after his baptism, to reprise something like what happened at the beginning of time. And this gesture of Jesus' living in peace with all nature, in fruitful solitude of the heart and in temptation, indicates to us what he came to do. He came to restore, to re-create. In one of the Mass prayers during the year, we say a very nice thing: "O God, who wonderfully created [all things], and still more wonderfully restored [them]."[1]

Jesus came with this marvel of a vocation to obedience to re-create, re-harmonize, and bring harmony even amid temptation. Is this clear? And Lent is this path. In Lent, we all need to make room in our hearts so that Jesus, with the strength of his Spirit, the same Spirit who led him to the desert, will reharmonize our hearts. But this reharmonization won't be with esoteric prayers and cheap intimacies as some pretend. Rather, it will be reharmonized with the mission, the apostolic work, our daily prayer, work, strength, witness. Make room for Jesus because time is running out, the Gospel tells us. We are already in the last times—have been for two thousand years—the times that Jesus established, the times for reharmonizing.

The times push us on. We have no right to keep coddling the soul, to stay locked in our thing . . . little things . . . wee things. We have no right to be comfortable loving ourselves. How much I love myself! No, we have no right. We must go out and tell that, two thousand years ago, there lived a man who wanted to re-create the earthly paradise, and that was his purpose for coming: to reharmonize things. We must tell 'Doña Rosa,' whom we saw on the balcony. We must tell the children, tell those who lost all their dreams and those who find everything depressing, everything is a tango,[2] everything is cambalache.[3] We must tell it to the hoity-toity fat lady, who believes that stretching her skin will earn her eternal life. We must tell all those young people who, like the one we saw on the balcony, denounce us for wanting to put them in the same mold. He did not use the lyrics of the tango, but he could have: "Anything goes, everything is the same . . ."[4]

We must go out and talk to the city people whom we saw on the balconies. We must get out of our shell and tell them that Jesus lives, and that Jesus lives for him, for her, and say it with joy . . . although at times we may seem a bit crazy. The message of the Gospel is madness, says Saint Paul (cf. 1 Cor 1:17–18). Our lifetimes will not be enough to dedicate ourselves to announcing the message that Jesus is restoring life. We must go out to sow hope, we must go out on the street. We must go out and search.

How many old ladies like that 'Doña Rosa' are bored and can't even manage, sometimes, the money even to buy medicines. How many kids are be-

---

1. From the collect for the Christmas Mass during the day.
2. Tango music is typically sad.
3. In Argentine Spanish slang, something cambalache is interchangeable and cheap.
4. In Spanish, "Dale que va, que todo es igual."

ing brainwashed with ideas we think are a great novelty, when ten years ago they were discarded in Europe and in the United States, and we disseminate them as great educational progress.

How many young people spend their lives stunned by drugs and noise, lacking meaning, because no one told them there was something big. How many nostalgics there are also in our city, who need a tin [barroom] counter to imbibe drink after drink to forget.

How many good but vain people are living by appearances and are in danger of falling into arrogance and pride.

And as for us, are we going to stay home? Are we going to stay in the parish, locked in? Are we going to stay in the parish gossip mill, or the school's, or the church's, when all these people are waiting for us? The people of our city! A city that has religious and cultural reserves, a beautiful, great city but that is very tempted by Satan. We cannot stay alone, we cannot stay in the parish and at school. Catechist, go out to the street! To catechize, to seek, to knock on doors. To knock on hearts.

The first thing that she (the Virgin Mary) did, when she received the Good News in her womb was to run to offer her service. Let's run to give the service of our belief in the Good News, and we want to give it to others. May this be our conversion: the Good News of Christ yesterday, today, and forever. May it be so.

-+>- -<+-

Keeping Our Feet on Earth to Avoid Losing the Way to Heaven

Message to the Educational Community—March 29, 2000

He waited against all hope. (Rm 4:18)

Pilgrims or Wanderers

This change of century and millennium raises the question of time. Also the question of direction. We glanced back at the path traveled, and at the same time the question arose about the way and direction of the path that opens ahead. Today is sustained by yesterday and anticipates tomorrow. The image of the future can mobilize the energies of the present. However, for many, the horizon and the vision of the future have shrunk and anguish has arisen.

Why do I invite you to reflect on hope? Are there no other issues more current, more immediate, more relevant to the educational task that we must face? Are we not at a crucial moment for our city, our country, and our Church, a moment of projects and definitions in the *kairos*[1] of the beginning of the new century, which demands that we think about concrete and very urgent issues? Or even if we avoid the temptation of 'immediatism,' should we not focus our attention on the essential problems that give us a substantive, not merely formal, definition of the person we want to form through our educational mission? Many thinkers consider the time that we live in as a real moment of radical change. In some ways, it is also the climate that underlies the Christian celebration of the Jubilee. Is not such an inquiry at this moment a spiritualist escape, an empty discourse, a religious version of the ostrich's behavior?

These precautions are partly reasonable. More often than we would like, we Christians have transformed the theological virtues into a pretext to stay comfortably settled in a poor caricature of transcendence, disregarding the hard task of building the world in which we live and where our salvation is at stake. In truth, faith, hope, and charity constitute, by definition, fundamental attitudes that trigger ecstasy, a leap of man toward God. They transcend us, really. They make us transcend and transcend us. And in their reference to God, they present such purity, such splendor of truth that can dazzle us. That bedazzlement of contemplation can make us forget that these same virtues rest on a whole foundation of human realities, because the subject who finds his way to the divine in this way is human. Dazzled, we can be distracted without plan or guidance until we bang our heads, needing to recognize our reality as an "earth that walks," as the poet said.[2]

And there, while trying to restart the journey keeping our feet on earth to avoid losing the way to heaven, is where the true meaning of hope is revealed. Although its object is God, it is in relation to the itinerary of man toward him. And, therefore, this virtue travels with us all the way, from the cradle to the tomb and heaven, from the well of meaninglessness and sin,

---

1. The Greek word means "the right moment."
2. The reference is to Atahualpa Yupanki (1908–82), an Argentine writer, folk singer, and poet.

through the joyful encounter in prayer that makes everything shine, until the definitive tender embrace of the One who is our foundation.

Therefore, we want to reflect on hope. But not on a 'lite' hope, lifeless, separated from the drama of human existence. We will examine hope, considering the deepest problems that afflict us and constitute our daily struggle in our educational task, our coexistence, and our very interiority. We will ask hope to help us recognize clearly the challenges that we confront when facing responsibility for the education of the younger generations, to live all the dimensions of our existence with greater intensity. We want to ask hope to contribute meaning and substance to our commitments and undertakings, even those we carry with great difficulty, almost like a cross.

Because, on the other hand, what else besides hope is the very substance of every educator's commitment? What sense would it make to consecrate one's own strength to something whose results are not immediately apparent, if all those efforts were not threaded by the invisible, but most solid, thread of hope? To offer some knowledge, propose values, awaken possibilities, and share one's faith are tasks that can only have one motive: the trust that these seeds will develop and produce fruit in their own time and way. To educate is to bet on and to support the present and the future. And the future is governed by hope.

A reflection on hope with such pretensions leads us, no doubt, to travel on difficult routes. It entails crossroads in which it is necessary to draw on the accumulated wisdom represented by the human sciences and theology. And it could acquire an uncomfortable harshness when it forces us to face the limits of the world's concrete reality, and our own. Therefore, what is offered here is, above all, an invitation to look at that reality in a Christian way—that is, in a hopeful way. If in the educational communities it awakens a desire to revise the style of our march or to deepen our way of looking at the landscape in which we move, it will have fulfilled part of its objective.

The Crisis as a Challenge to Hope

There is no doubt that, for some time, we have been living a time of profound changes. It is often said, a time of crisis. This is almost a commonplace. Crisis in education, economic crisis, ecological crisis, moral crisis. At times, the latest news highlights some successful initiative or novel diagnoses of the situation, but soon our attention returns to that kind of general malaise that assumes different faces or pretexts. Some point to a more philosophical level and speak of the 'crisis of man' or the 'crisis of civilization.'

What is this crisis? Let's try to describe it, step by step. In the first place, it is a global, complex crisis. We are not talking about issues that fall within defined and partial realms of reality. If this were the case, the simplistic prescriptions that circulate habitually among us would suffice: "Here the problem is education," "The impunity of crime is to blame for everything," "If corruption ends, everything is fixed." It is evident that education, security, and public ethics are urgent and legitimate demands of society. But it's not just about that. If education cannot be articulated with the social and economic reality of the country in mind; if corruption seems to be a cancer that invades everything, it is because the root of the crisis is broader, deeper. The economy is not alien to politics, nor the latter to social ethics. The school is part of a much larger whole, and drugs and violence are intertwined with complicated economic, social, and cultural processes. All aspects of reality and the relationship between them shape the crisis.

To say that the crisis is global, then, is to look toward the great cultural convictions, the most deeply rooted beliefs, the criteria through which people think that something is good or bad, desirable or disposable. What is in crisis is a whole way of understanding reality and of understanding ourselves.

Second, the crisis is historical. It is not the 'crisis of man' as an abstract or universal being: It is a mode of the evolution of Western civilization, which drags with it the entire planet. It is true that in every era there are things that work badly, changes and decisions to make. But here there is something more. Never as in this time, in the last four hundred years, have the fundamental certainties of human life been shaken so profoundly. Negative tendencies appear with great destructive power. Think only about the deterioration of the environment, social imbalances, the terrible power of weapons. The media, the means of communication and of transportation have never been so powerful either, with their negative factors—the at times compulsive cultural uniformity, together with the expansion of consumerism—but also all the positive ones: powerful means for debate, encounter, and dialogue, and the search for solutions.

What changes, then, is not only the economy, communications, or the relation of forces between the powerful world factors but also the way in which humanity carries out its existence in the world. And this affects politics as well as everyday life, eating habits as well as religion, collective expectations such as family and sex, the relationship between different generations as well as the experience of space and time.

To help visualize the true dimensions of the challenge before us, we will briefly review some issues that are usually presented as marking the turn of the century, pointing out their impact on our educational task, and without forgetting the characterizations provided in the previous messages to the schools:

1. *Technological advances (computer science, robotics, new materials . . .) have profoundly modified the forms of production.* Today manual labor is not considered as important as investment in technology, communications, and knowledge development (of new techniques, new forms of work, the relationship between production and consumption). This obviously brings about important social and cultural changes. And it implies an important challenge for educators.

2. *The globalization of the economy.* Capital does not recognize borders: It is produced by segments, in different parts of the world, and it is sold in a market that has been globalized. All this has serious consequences for the labor market and the social imagination.

3. *International and social imbalances tend to deepen.* The rich are getting richer and the poor, poorer, and in an increasingly accelerated way. Whole continents are excluded from the market, and large sectors of the population (even from developed countries) remain outside the circulation of society's material and symbolic goods.

4. *Unemployment* is growing all over the world, not as a circumstantial problem but as a structural one. The current economy does not consider the possibility of everyone having a decent job. In the same dynamic, entire sectors of workers are turned into the proletariat—among others, educators.

5. *The ecological problem is aggravated.* The environment deteriorates rapidly, traditional energy resources are depleted, the current developmental model is incompatible with ecosystem preservation.

6. *Totalitarianism falls*, and there is a wave of *democratization* throughout the world that does not seem to be circumstantial. Along with this, we are witnessing a strong process of *demilitarization*, with the end of the Cold War and nuclear disarmament and with the fall of military regimes in different parts of the world. But at the same time, *nationalisms* and *xenophobia* reappear, leading to serious acts of social and racial violence and even bloody civil and interethnic wars. And we know from experience that problems in schools due to ethnic, national, or social discrimination are not just the heritage of other latitudes.

7. Large political parties lose validity and representation or feel weaker. In many societies there is a strong *crisis of participation* (people are

disinterested in politics) *and representation* (many do not feel represented by traditional structures). As a result, *new actors and forms of social participation* emerge, linked to more partial demands: the environment, neighborhood problems, ethnic or cultural issues, human rights, minority rights . . .

8. Technological advances produce a true *information and multimedia revolution*. This brings not only important economic and commercial consequences but also cultural ones. Now there is no need to leave home to be in contact with everyone, in 'real time.' 'Virtual reality' opens new doors for creativity and education and questions the traditional forms of communication with serious anthropological implications. Educators are faced with the challenge of trying to stay current despite the poor resources at their disposal or accept with resignation that progress is not for everyone. Many children will be able to take advantage of the Internet, but many others will not have access to knowledge (and even recognition as equal citizens, beyond the formality of the national identity card and the vote).

9. The *process of transforming the social, family, and work role for women* continues and deepens. These new modes of insertion bring with them great changes in the *structure of society* and *family life*.

10. Science and technology open the doors of the *bio-technological revolution and genetic manipulation*: In a short time, one will be able to modify human reproduction, almost at the request of individuals or the needs of societies, deepening current practices of shaping the body and personality by technical means.

11. Far from disappearing, *religion* acquires new strength in today's world. Although additionally, magical practices that seemed to have been overcome are again gaining validity, and mystical conceptions are popularized that before were circumscribed by traditional cultures. At the same time, some fundamentalist positions are radicalized, both in Islam as in Christianity and Judaism.

Each of these points could be extensively treated, and surely more challenges would appear for which we have no definite answers and not even a shallow opinion. There is no need to insist on the consequences that these profound mutations have on individuals, communities, and organizations. How do we stand, as a Christian educational community, in the face of such enormous and thorny conflicts as those we have pointed out? Our reflection on hope will now lead us to try to make our way through the middle of equivocal paths: a discernment of the diverse attitudes that can arise among us in the face of these challenges.

Opening Our Way to Hope

In the first place, there are some who develop a naively optimistic attitude toward changes. They assume that humanity always advances forward (everything new is always better), and rely on various 'data' to certify their optimism: the possibilities offered by the computer revolution, the predictions of the 'gurus' of the first world, the new forms of business organization, the end of ideological conflicts ...

They consider that the great social and international imbalances will be overcome successfully, by strengthening the current path. Technology will undoubtedly solve the problems of hunger and disease. The ecological crisis will be controlled by applying new technical prescriptions. School, thus, is the place where all these advances are offered to the new generations, who will undoubtedly know how to take advantage of them for the good of all. We are almost listening to the enlightened people of past centuries.

What can be said when faced with this stance? On the one hand, this basic belief lacks any serious foundation; nothing guarantees an upward progress in human history. Yes, there may be diverse improvements in different fields. But, in fact, much data, such as the ecological crisis and the recently attenuated (forever?) possibility of a nuclear holocaust, fill us with alarm, rather than confidence. The terrible experiences of this century also teach us about the enormous capacity for irrationality and self-destruction that the human species possesses. Civilization has turned out to be quite barbaric.

This stance has a surprisingly considerable capacity to close our eyes to the negative aspects (quite a few, as we have seen) of scientific-technological progress or to the serious limits shown by different forms of political and social organization; while at the same time exhibiting full confidence in impersonal and indeterminate forces, such as the market, and attributing to it the capacity to obtain the good of all.

It is combined with a self-sufficient pose, whether of an individual, a group, or a state. It does not expect anything outside itself. It imposes the rules of the game. Unable to perceive one's own wound and sin, it does not know how to help others' indigence. It is a defacement of the calm attitude of the one who knows his talents and limits, adequately estimating his possibilities and those of the whole of which he is a part. Because man, with his works, can forget his constitutive finitude and mortality.

On the opposite side, there are those who take a very critical and closed position, pessimistic in the face of all process of change. Being located 'outside' of it, they denounce its most destructive aspects, generalizing its perverse effects and condemning wholesale the movement. They are experts in discovering conspiracies, in deducing disastrous consequences for humanity, in detecting catastrophes. By analogy with a spiritual and theological movement of the second century BC, this mentality is often called 'apocalyptic.' It rests on a basic belief as flimsy as that of the opposite position: the negative aspects of historical realities are imaginatively projected to their most terrible possibility, and that image is taken as the proper expression of the historical process.

The phobia of change makes those who lean toward this attitude unable to tolerate uncertainty, and they retreat before the dangers, real or imagined, that come with every change. The school as a 'bunker' that protects from 'outside' errors is the expressed caricature of this tendency. But that image shockingly reflects what many young people experience when they graduate from educational establishments—an insurmountable inadequacy between what they were taught and the world in which they live.

Of course, this mentality underlies a pessimistic conception of human freedom and, consequently, of historical processes, which are almost left in the hands of evil. And there is a paralysis of intelligence and will. A depressive and sectarian paralysis: Not only is there nothing to be done, but nothing can be done to avoid catastrophe except to protect oneself in the increasingly small nucleus of the 'pure ones.'

They also feel disillusioned with God, whom they blame for things going wrong. They are impatient with the supposed slowness of God's actions. Some choose to take refuge behind a defensive wall, licking their grief, and others choose to escape into inane gratifications. The same happens when it comes to personal failures; they are skirted without taking them on or transcending them, but they leave their entanglements.

We can still find another equally sterile attitude: that of those who realize the difficulty of any concrete action and then wash their hands of it. Interestingly, they share the diagnosis of the pessimists in interpreting the social and historical reality, but remove the burden of ethical resentment: If you cannot improve the situation of humanity as a whole, do what you can. The posture of "what can be done," in general, means acting along the lines of dominant events and trends without analyzing them critically or trying to reorient them ethically. This attitude is usually characterized as pragmatic, because it separates individual or historical praxis from all ethical and spiritual considerations. It necessarily ignores the bare claims of justice, humanity, or historical social responsibility. Its pessimism is as strong as that of the position described before, but it does not lead to paralysis, rather to hypocrisy or cynicism. It happens, too, in our educational reality, in situations more attuned to 'cash' issues or to the appearance of 'excellence' than to trying to contribute something to the construction of a more humane society.

On the Path of Discernment

Faced with these positions, hope, which never rules anything outright, chooses to elaborate a careful discernment that may rescue the kernel of truth contained in each of these attitudes, but finds the way to a more integral and constructive path. And it does it for its own reasons that we will elaborate later.

In today's reality, there are many elements that, well oriented, can greatly improve the lives of human beings on earth. There is no doubt that technology has put in our hands powerful instruments that can be put at the service of man. We cannot deny the advances made with the emancipation of women, communications, the contributions of science to the health and well-being of people, the broadening of horizons brought on by social media to millions who previously subsisted by moving in the reduced world of their local community and their work.

In the same way, we cannot naively ignore the dangers that the current process involves: dehumanization, serious social and international conflicts, exclusion and the death of millions. . . . The pessimism of the apocalyptic minds is not gratuitous: In many aspects, and for many people, the future reveals a threatening face. It is also true that it is difficult for an attitude of genuine hope to emerge in someone who has not suffered the disappointment of what he wanted.

And even then, at some point it is necessary to bite the bullet and continue living, although there is not much room for ideals. "The best is the enemy of the good," and that's also how pragmatism acquires its share of truth.

What do we conclude from all this? That hope is presented, at first, as the ability to weigh everything and stay with the best of everything. To discern. But this discernment is not blind or improvised; it is carried out on the basis of a series of presuppositions and following certain norms of an ethical and spiritual nature. It involves asking what is good, what we want, where we want to go. It includes a recourse to *values*, supported by a given *worldview*. In short, hope is strongly intertwined with faith. Thus, hope looks farther, opens to new horizons, invites other depths.

Hope sustains unseen many of the human expectations, which come at fixed intervals. Hope needs to be legitimized with effective interventions that give it credit; they are incarnations that already introduce and specify—although they do not exhaust—the highest values. Although there are also vain expectations, which are not conducive to a full humanization, because they ignore or atrophy their condition of a thinking being (and reduce it to the order of sensation or matter), they deny their personal condition that is realized in loving and being loved, and they cut off their openness to the Absolute (disdaining their capacity for worship and the practice of prayer).

Therefore, we could enunciate those criteria that allow us to discern better, overcoming the divorce between doing and believing. And at the same time, it will prevent us from being seduced by the always revived idols. Let's give priority to love over reason, but never with your back to truth; to being above having; to integral human action above the transforming praxis that rewards only efficiency; to serving above doing for self-satisfaction; to the ultimate vocation above the penultimate motivations.

The Roots of Hope

If history is not a progressive and linear advance toward a hypothetical kingdom of freedom, a triumphal march of reason—as was believed when the ideals of modernity reigned supreme—but rather presents to us living in these difficult times of disenchantment, postmodernity, and a new century, the stage where the ambiguous human drama takes place, drama without a libretto and without guaranteed success, what can be the foundation of hope? And not just a 'strong' hope, but one inclusive of the motivation to sustain an immediate commitment, face to face, with fruits deferred over time.

It is a concept already thematized by philosophers and theologians: the consistency of the future as an anthropological dimension and, in the perspective of the Christian faith, the relationship between eschatology and history, between the expectation of the Kingdom and the construction of the temporal city. Of course, we will not analyze these questions here, arguing and exposing the biblical, historical, and theoretical foundations that lead to certain affirmations that are, at this point, the patrimony of the whole Church. We will present in a simple way only some themes of our faith that justify and vivify our hope.

For Christians, the belief that bases their position on reality is based on the testimony of the New Testament, which speaks of Jesus Christ, God made man, who with his resurrection inaugurates the kingdom of God among us. A kingdom not purely spiritual or interior, but integral and eschatological, able to make sense of all human history and all commitment in that history. And not "from the outside," from a mere ethical or religious imperative, but "from within," because this kingdom is already present, transforming and orienting the same history until its full realization in justice, peace, and communion between men and God, in a future, transfigured, world.

In recent times, many Christians have felt that this presence of the Kingdom could generate a real, concrete anticipation of that new world and mediate the historical commitment. A better, more just, and humane society, a kind of first draft or prelude to what we expect for the end of time. Moreover, it was believed that the action of Christians could truly "advance" the coming of the Kingdom, since the Lord had left in our hands the possibility of completing his task.

But things did not turn out as expected. Clearly in our country, and not only here, the attempts to humanize the economy, to build a more just and fraternal community, to expand the spaces for freedom, well-being, and creativity, were depleted and bowed to the overwhelming dynamics of concentration of capital that characterizes these last decades. The attempt to concretize utopia was followed by the resignation of accepting internal and external conditions. The affirmation of the desirable was supplanted by the reduction to the possible. The promises were not fulfilled. I dare say: They revealed to have been only an illusion. . . . We should ask ourselves if the current disinterest of younger generations in politics, or in other collective projects, has to do with this experience of frustration.

But will it be that the postmodern disenchantment, present not only in politics but also in culture, art, and everyday life, brings down with it every glimpse of hope based on the expectation of the kingdom? Or, on the contrary, the idea of the kingdom that begins among us—the nucleus of the preaching and action of Jesus—and intimate but not intimist experience among believers after his resurrection, still has something to tell us in these times? Is there, beyond those identifications that are perhaps too linear, some relationship between the theological message of the kingdom and the concrete history in which we are immersed and for which men are responsible?

The parable of the seed that grows by itself has always been extremely inspiring to me (Mk 4:26–29). But each time it becomes more difficult (through experience and intellectual honesty) to understand it from the perspective of development. Jesus would not be talking here about history's 'maturing' in time, through the hidden action of the kingdom, until it reaches its fullness. The idea of 'organic growth' was foreign to ancient man. They were not able to see the continuity between the seed and the fruit, only contrast: an almost miraculous occurrence. Jesus' parable tried to show the Kingdom as a reality hidden from human eyes, but that will produce its fruit by the action of God, regardless of what the sower does.

Does this mean accepting a dissociation between human effort and divine action? Does it justify a position of skepticism or pragmatism? In a way, this is what happens to so many people today. Postmodern individualism and aestheticism, if not contemporary pragmatism and certain cynicism, are the result of the fall of historical certainties, of the loss of the meaning of human action as a builder of something objectively and concretely better. Also, in the case of some Christians, it can be expressed in a mere 'living in the moment' (even if it is the 'moment' of the spiritual experience) passively waiting for the Kingdom to 'fall' from heaven.

But Christian hope has nothing to do with that. In any case, we must recognize that there is no linear continuity between history and the consummation of the Kingdom, in the sense of an uninterrupted advance or ascent. Just as the individual consummation (the encounter with God and the definitive personal transfiguration in the resurrection) happens in most cases by a terrible moment of discontinuity, failure, and destruction (death), there is no reason to reject that the same thing can happen with history as a whole. Here is the truth of the apocalyptic mentality: This world passes. There is no fullness without some form of destruction or loss that we cannot predict. But also, without any continuity: I will be the one who rises! It will be the same humanity, the same creation, the same history that will be transfigured in the fullness of time! Continuity and discontinuity. A mysterious reality of presence-absence, of the promises 'already' fulfilled but 'not yet' fully. A kingdom that essentially is near, in all moments, everywhere, including in the worst of human situations, and that one day will stop being hidden to manifest itself completely and clearly.

Hope and History

What certainties are left to us, then? What elements does faith offer us to ground our hope?

In the first place, that *this history*, and not a pretended 'spiritual dimension,' is the place of Christian existence. The place of the response to Christ, the place of the realization of our vocation. It is here that the risen Lord meets us through signs that we must recognize in faith and respond to in love. The Lord comes, is coming, in many perceptible ways through the eyes of faith: in the sacramental signs and in the life of the Christian community, but also in every human manifestation where communion happens, freedom is promoted, God's creation is perfected. But he also comes in the underside of history: in the poor, the sick, the marginalized (cf. Mt 25:31–45; and DP 31–39). He is coming in all those modes, and the meaning of the final consummation cannot be dissociated from all those comings.

And here, another dimension of hope acquires meaning: the *vitality of memory*. The Church lives from the memory of the Risen One. And more, memory supports the Church's historical path in the certainty that the Risen One is the Crucified One. The Lord who comes is the same one who preached the Beatitudes, who broke bread with the crowds, cured the sick, forgave sinners, who sat at the table with the publicans. Remembering Jesus of Nazareth with faith in the Lord Jesus Christ enables us to "do what he did," in his memory. And here the whole dimension of memory is incorporated, because the history of Jesus is linked with the history of men and peoples in their imperfect searches for a fraternal banquet, a lasting love. Christian hope, in this way, awakens and empowers the perhaps buried energies of our past, personal or collective, the grateful memory of moments of joy and happiness, the passion perhaps forgotten by truth and justice, the sparkles of plenitude that Love has produced on our journey. And, why not, the memory of the Cross, of failure, of pain, this time to be transfigured by exorcising the demons of bitterness and resentment and opening the possibility of a deeper meaning.

But also, the tension toward that consummation tells us that this history *has meaning and a terminus*. The action of God that began with a Creation on whose summit stands the creature who could respond to God as his image and likeness, with whom he could enter into a relationship of love, and matured with the Incarnation of the Son, must culminate in the fullness of that communion in a universal way. Everything created must enter into that definitive communion with God, initiated in the risen Christ. That is to say, there must be a perfect terminus as a positive conclusion of the loving work of God, a terminus that is not an immediate or direct result of human action but is a saving action of God, the final touch of the work of art that God himself initiated and for which he wants us to be associates and free collaborators.

And if this is the case, faith in the *parousia* or eschatological consummation becomes the foundation of the hope and the foundation of *Christian commitment in the world.* History, our history, is not lost time. Everything that follows the line of the Kingdom of truth, freedom, justice, and fraternity will be recovered and fulfilled. And this counts not only for things made with love, but also for those made as if the work did not matter. As Christians, we have often placed too much emphasis on "good intentions" or right intention. The work of our hands—and not only that of our hearts—has value in itself; and insofar as it is oriented in the line of the Kingdom, of God's plan, it will be lasting in a way that we cannot imagine. On the other hand, what is opposed to that kingdom, not only has its days numbered but also will be definitively discarded. It will not be part of the New Creation.

Christian hope is not, then, a "spiritual comfort," a distraction from the serious tasks that require our attention. It is a dynamic that frees us from all determinism and from every obstacle to build a world of freedom, to free this history from the chains of selfishness, inertia, and injustice in which it tends to fall so easily.

Invitations

There are still some final words left. This journey we have made from the disillusionment of the turn of the century to the faith in the coming of the Kingdom, and from there to the recovery of hope and concrete commitment, opens new possibilities for the educational task entrusted to us, which we have embraced with love. I would like to point out these specific invitations to us made by hope:

The invitation to *cultivate personal and social ties*, revaluing friendship and solidarity. The school is still the place where people can be recognized as such, welcomed and promoted. While we should not neglect a valid dimension of efficiency and effectiveness in the transmission of knowledge that allows our young people to take their place in society, it is essential that we be "teachers of humanness." And this can be a very important contribution that Catholic education offers to a society that at times seems to have renounced the elements that constituted it as a community: solidarity, a sense of justice, respect for the other, in particular, for the weakest and smallest. Ruthless competition has a prominent place in our society. Let us contribute to it a sense of justice and mercy.

The invitation to *be bold and creative.* The new realities demand new answers. But first, they demand an open spirit that constructively discerns, that does not cling to stale certainties, and that encourages the envisioning of other ways of expressing values, that does not turn its back on the challenges of the present time. Here is a genuine test for our hope. If it is placed in God and the Kingdom, it will know how to free itself from burdens, fears, and hardened reflexes in order to dare to build the new, starting with dialogue and collaboration.

The invitation *to joy, to gratuity, to celebration*. Perhaps the worst injustice of the present time is the tyranny of utilitarianism, the dictatorship of frugality, the triumph of bitterness. The authenticity of our hope would be demonstrated if we knew how to discover, in everyday reality, the reasons, big or small, to recognize the gifts of God, to celebrate life, to get out of the chains of debt and credit and display the joy of being the seeds of a new creation. To make our schools a place of work and study, yes, but also—and, I would dare to say, above all—a place of celebration, *encounter*, and gratuity.

And finally, the invitation *to worship and to be grateful*. In the dizzying existence of each day, we may forget to address the thirst for communication that lives deep within us. The school can introduce, guide, and help sustain the encounter with the Living One, teaching us to enjoy his presence, to trace his footprints, to accept his 'hiddenness.' Learning to cultivate a relationship with him is something not to be missed.

I encourage you to take these words of sixteenth-century men, to speak to God in this new century, in the continuity of the same love:

> *Thy love so moves me naught to prize above Thee*
> *that were there not a Hell I yet would fear Thee*
> *and were there not a Heaven I would love Thee.*
> *Thou needst not give me more to have me love Thee,*
> *for, had I not such hope of being near Thee,*
> *I yet would love Thee just as now I love Thee.*
> (Anonymous, Spanish)[3]

⤜ ⤛

---

3. Considered a jewel of Spanish mystical poetry, this poem is variously attributed to Saint Juan of Ávila, doctor of the Church, to Miguel de Guevara, Augustine monk, and to Antonio de Rojas, who published it in one of his writings (1628), although it had appeared in manuscript form before that time. It has also been attributed to Saint Teresa of Ávila, Saint Ignatius of Loyola, and even Lope de Vega.

Educating in Peace and Hope

Homily, Mass for the Education Vicariate—March 29, 2000 (Transcript)

How beautiful the expression of the first reading: "What great nation is there that has gods so close to it as the LORD, our God, is to us whenever we call upon him?" (Dt 4:7).

That was how the People of Israel reflected during their journey through the desert. Throughout their history, they felt that their God was near. That our God was near, because our God is close, is the God of all closeness, is more intimate than our own intimacy.

And that intimacy that God has with his people, that he has with each one of us, that makes us a people, he imprints in our hearts. He imprints it in those mandates mentioned here: "Now therefore, Israel, hear the statutes and ordinances I am teaching you to observe" (v. 1). They are not external laws; they are laws of the heart. Laws transferred from the heart of God to the hearts of his people, to the hearts of every woman and man of his people. Laws placed there with tenderness. And there comes the transformation of the heart, when he says, "I will remove the hearts of stone, and give them hearts of flesh" (Ez 11:19). A heart of tenderness, the heart that receives these ten well-known mandates not as an external precept, but as a kiss of love and as the assurance that along that path one becomes more and more woman or man, more mature, more for others, more sowers of peace and hope. These commandments are seeds of peace and hope.

Jesus takes up this idea and says: "Whoever obeys and teaches these commandments will be called greatest in the kingdom of heaven" (Mt 5:19). In other words, those who fulfill and teach this path of love engraved in the heart and summarized by Jesus himself in two great commandments: "You shall love the Lord, your God . . . and . . . You shall love your neighbor as yourself" (cf. Mt 22:37–39).

With that, hatred, contention, bad competition, evil, and lies are displaced. The commandments are a source of peace and hope, and that is why today we are together as educators to decide that in this year we will educate for peace and hope. And to educate together because this is everyone's job. It is the work of a people who have their God very close to them, who have their God in their hearts, to educate in peace and hope.

We do not want a stagnant peace, a peace that does not move. Ultimately, remember that stagnant water is the first to spoil. That is not the peace of our nearby God.

The peace of our nearby God is the peace of the spring that continues to flow, and that continues to create things and give life with its same water and give life with its same peace. It keeps on creating hope. Our peace is the foundation, origin, spring of a hope that will transcend even ourselves, but that we must sow now, today.

To the educators who are here, those who consecrate their lives to make the hearts of so many girls and boys of our country grow, I say to them: Look at that spring, that spring that is the peace that God placed in our hearts with his commandments. And let it run, push it, channel it to give life to others. Make it grow.

And to the students who are here, those being educated, I say: Do not waste the wealth of that spring. Be creative. Know that your life makes sense, to the extent that you take charge of that kiss of love and tenderness that God put in your heart and transformed into peace, so that peace will bring life and make others firm.

That is what I ask today of our God, the nearby God, the God of our hearts. The God who recorded his commands in our hearts. The God of love, the God who brings peace as a spring, so that we can bring it to others. And just as he became our neighbor and close to us, we become neighbors and close to others, bringing this life and message of peace and hope. May it be so.

→→ ←←

God, Your God, Has Anointed You with the Oil of Gladness

Homily, Chrism Mass—April 20, 2000, Year B

God, your God, has anointed you with the oil of gladness. (Heb 1:9)

The framework and center of this Chrism liturgy is jubilation. The Lord comes to announce a Year of Grace, a Holy Year, a Jubilee Year. Although in its roots it refers to a musical instrument, *jubilatio* is the Latin word that is used to describe the peasants' cries of joy, the joy of the humble workers, of the little ones. *Jubilare* is to celebrate and shout for joy like simple people and the poor when they sing. Throw shouts of praise to God. This is what Isaiah describes to us in the first reading: the promised Lord who will come to heal the brokenhearted, to comfort those who mourn and to bring "glad tidings" to the lowly (cf. Is 61:1–3a).

Jubilation is the joy of the little ones: of the farmers who "will return with cries of joy," who "go forth weeping" (cf. Ps 126:6); of the shepherds, the joy that the angels announced on Christmas night; of Our Lady, the joy of Mary and Elizabeth, that joy that fills their souls and makes them brim with a contagious rejoicing; Saint Luke tells us that Jesus "rejoiced [in] the holy Spirit" and praised the Father because he had revealed his things to the childlike (Lk 10:21). And if we look closely, the joy of the poor is *a joy that is given around work*: during harvest, at the beginning of the mission and upon returning. It is the joy that comes after suffering something for Christ, as happened to the Apostles who "rejoiced that they were considered worthy to suffer dishonor for the sake of the name [of Jesus]" (Acts 5:41). It is the song that springs from the heart after being bottled up amid the anguish of labor. It is a song that unites and strengthens: "Do not be saddened this day, for rejoicing in the LORD is your strength!" (Neh 8:10).

Today it would be good to ask ourselves, as a presbytery and as a priestly people: What gives joy to our hearts? It is not a marginal question, a minor question. To ask ourselves if there is joy in our hearts—in order to be grateful and pray for it—is to ask what unites us in holiness and what makes our pastoral task effective; it is to ask for humility and strength.

The Chrism Mass is a Mass of joy for the priests: the joy of unity. It is the same Lord who has sent each one of us on mission and has dispersed us throughout the archdiocese and beyond. (I think of Xai-Xai[1] and those who are helping in other dioceses). It is the same Lord who brings us together on Holy Thursday and places the Eucharist in a ciborium and makes us feel that we are in his hands, united, to break us and distribute us among

---

1. Xai-Xai is a city in southern Mozambique to which the Archdiocese of Buenos Aires has sent missionaries.

the faithful people of God. All joy proceeds from this presbyterial communion that Jesus our Lord gives us: union in the Spirit and union in the
Bride, the Church, one and holy. From this attitude springs all the jubilant
attitudes of a priestly heart.

Pope John Paul II points us to the framework of the great jubilations that
will fill our hearts during this year: the joy of pilgrimage, shepherding the
faithful people of God to the Father's house; the joy of crossing thresholds
and passing through the Door—that is Christ; the joy of having a clear conscience because we were able to ask for forgiveness; the deep joy that is the
fruit of heroic charity and the dramatic joy that overwhelms our memory
as we recall our martyrs. And, along with these great joys—if you can call
them that—the little joys that form part of the daily life of each priestly
heart.

Using the categories of the gospel, we can fearlessly affirm that *a strong
priestly heart* is the one capable of jumping for joy when contemplating, for
example, how his catechists teach the smallest, or how his young people go
out at night to attend to those who are homeless. A priestly heart is strong
if it retains the ability to jump for joy when facing the prodigal son who returns, and for whom he had been waiting patiently in the confessional. *A
priestly heart is strong* if it can allow happiness to light up with the word of
the hidden Jesus who becomes our companion on the road, as happened to
the Emmaus disciples. Let us not forget: *Rejoicing in the Lord is your strength!*
(cf. Neh 8:10), and it protects us against every spirit of complaint that sig-
nals a lack of hope, and against all impatience, more typical of civil authorities than of priestly hearts.

Joy, smallness, and strength are very close together and are the graces we
priests ask the Lord to give us along with all our faithful people on this Holy
Thursday of the Jubilee Year. *To receive the joy* that comes from the Spirit,
we ask Our Lady to teach us how it is that the greatest is the smallest. *To
receive the grace of humility* we ask the Handmaid to teach us what it is like
to sing the *Magnificat* while in humble service and in the daily fraternal encounters. *To receive the grace of strength*, we ask the Virgin to teach us how
to never separate joy and humility. And we ask her, as the friends of her
Son Jesus, to please never allow our hearts be scattered by pride, but that
we humbly love and accept ourselves as brothers so that "Rejoicing in the
Lord [be our] strength!"

⤜ ⤛

The Angel Reassures the Women:
"Do Not Be Afraid"

Homily, Easter Vigil—April 22, 2000, Year B

A short while ago, in the atrium of the Cathedral, we proclaimed that Jesus Christ was yesterday, is today, and will always be while we scribed this year's date into the Paschal Candle, figure of the Risen Christ. This gesture that the Church has been repeating for centuries is the resounding announcement, throughout history, of what happened that Sunday morning in the cemetery of Jerusalem: the One who existed before Abraham was born, who wanted to become a close companion on our journey, the Good Samaritan who picks us up when we are defeated by life and by our volatile free will, the One who died and was buried and whose sepulcher was sealed; that One has risen and lives forever.

It is about the announcement to those women who were surprised by the stone that had been moved and the angel sitting where the dead man had been. An announcement that, from that moment on, was handed down from person to person throughout the history of humanity. An announcement that boldly proclaims that, from now on, in the midst of all death, there is a seed of resurrection. The beginning of this liturgy, in the dark, is nothing but a symbol of darkness and death. In contrast, the light is Christ, a spark of hope in the midst of all the situations and the hearts, even those submerged in the greatest darkness.

The Angel reassures the women: "Do not be afraid" (Mt 28:5). It deals with that instinctive fear of having any hope of happiness and life, that fear that what I am seeing or what they tell me is not true, the fear of joy that is given to us by an outpouring of something totally free. And, after the reassuring advice "Do not fear," they were sent: "Go now to tell your disciples and Peter that he will go before you to Galilee; there you will see it, as he had told you" (v. 7).

It is the Lord that *always precedes us*, the Lord who awaits us. When the Apostle John wanted to explain what love was, he resorted to that *experience of feeling preceded, feeling expected*: "Love is not that we have loved God, but in that he loved us first" (1 Jn 4:10). While in our lives, in one way or another, we seek God, the deepest truth is that we are sought and awaited by him. Like the almond tree flower mentioned by the prophets because it is the first to bloom, that is how the Lord is: He waits first, he is first to love us.

For centuries, our God has been ahead of us in love. It has been two thousand years since Jesus has been "preceding us" and awaits us in Galilee, that Galilee of the first *encounter*, that Galilee that each one of us has somewhere in the heart. Feeling preceded and awaited speeds up the pace of our steps to make the meeting happen sooner. The same God, who "loved us first," is also the Good Samaritan who becomes our neighbor and says—as at the end of that parable—"Go and do likewise" (Lk 10:37). As simple as that, do what he did: Be "first" to love your brothers; do not expect to be loved but instead love first. Take the first step, steps that will make us escape our sleepiness (not having been able to watch with him) or any sophisticated quietism. Steps of reconciliation, steps of love. Take the first step in your family, take the first step in this city; become a neighbor to those who live without what is necessary to subsist—every day there are more. We imitate our God who precedes us and loves first, making gestures of neighborliness toward our brothers who suffer loneliness, indigence, loss of work, exploitation, lack of shelter, contempt for being migrants, illness, isolation in the retirement homes for the elderly. Take the first step and bring, with your own life, the announcement: He has risen. Then, amid so much death, you will light a spark of resurrection, which he wants you to carry. Then your profession of faith will be credible.

On this Easter night, I ask our Mother to help us understand how to be "first" in love. May she, who stayed awake sustained by hope, help us to be unafraid to announce, with the word and the attitudes of neighborliness toward the neediest, that he is alive in our midst. And as a good mother, to lead us by the hand to the silent adoration of that God who precedes us in love.

➤➤ ◄◄

Hope Does Not Disappoint

Homily, Solemn Te Deum *on Independence Day—May 25, 2000*

Jesus journeyed to a city called Nain, and his disciples and a large crowd accompanied him. As he drew near to the gate of the city, a man who had died was being carried out, the only son of his mother, and she was a widow. A large crowd from the city was with her. When the Lord saw her, he was moved with pity for her and said to her, "Do not weep." He stepped forward and touched the coffin; at this the bearers

halted, and he said, "Young man, I tell you, arise!" The dead man sat up and began
to speak, and Jesus gave him to his mother. Fear seized them all, and they glorified
God, exclaiming, "A great prophet has arisen in our midst," and "God has visited
his people." This report about him spread through the whole of Judea and in all the
surrounding region. (Lk 7:11–17)

1. From the call of the Holy Father to the celebration of the Great Jubilee, this year has been *filled with hope* for every Christian. In 2000 we did not have a conventional anniversary, but we celebrated the permanence of Christ himself among us. We remember the grace that transforms humanity, and we also remember the resistance of our nature. The first, to thank and praise; the second, to recognize and ask for forgiveness. We call all this, conversion.

As the Gospel says, "A great prophet has appeared in our midst and God has visited his people" (v. 16b). There is joy because God is with us and among us, and despite the resistance to love that is sin, he offers us the joy of feeling redeemed, of feeling called to love again, as he taught us. We are invited to begin a new time: It is the beginning of Christ, who despite "knowing what is inside man," continues to trust in the *gift of freedom*, in the spark of love that the Spirit infuses in our hearts.

2. I am sure that the desire of all Argentines is to be able to reach this new May anniversary *with the same jubilee hope* that today encourages millions in the world. The Jubilee of Christ incarnate in the faith and in the pain of our people, *hope* to relive those heroic deeds that, beyond the contradictory mistakes and interests, knew how to collaborate to begin the adventure of a new Nation. *Hope deepens the soul and brings it peace*, then, by opening—magnanimously—the heart, trusting in the promise made, in the given word, men are freed from the suspicions and pessimisms brought about by their hasty reasoning and even the weight of certain evidence. He who lives from his expectations shows the dignity of being the image and likeness of the Father. His joy is free; it does not depend on success or the most immediate results.

The deep joy that lasts as peace is cemented and ultimately builds links beyond differences and conditions. We Argentines want to be reborn in the promise of the elders who started the country, and for this we urgently need *the hope* that makes joy sprout; because from it will emerge the bonds that will bring down fears and insecurities, distances that today seem insurmountable. *Hope for joy, joy for bonding.*

3. A year ago, on this same occasion, I highlighted the need to *rebuild the social bond between Argentines, a hopeful bond*: a bond that bridges the pain-

ful gap between those who have more and those who have less; that brings young people closer who do not find their own social task; that rekindles in us the love of a childhood often despised and impoverished; that concerns us for each person who loses his job; that makes us supportive and inclusive of the dispossessed and with goodwill to immigrants, who arrive and must continue to arrive; that makes us especially considerate toward the elderly who have spent their lives for us and now deserve to celebrate and recover their places as wise persons and teachers transmitting hope.

Rebuild with hope our social ties! This is not a cold ethical and rationalistic proposition. It is not a new unrealizable utopia, much less a disaffected and destructive pragmatism. It is the imperative need to live together to build the desired common good, that of a community that surrenders interests to be able to share justly their assets, their interests, and their social life in peace. Nor is it just an administrative or technical management plan. Instead, it is *the constant conviction expressed in actions*, in the personal approach, in a distinctive stamp, where this will be expressed to change our way of kneading, in hope, a new culture of *encounter*, of proximity; where privilege is no longer an impregnable and irreducible power, and exploitation and abuse are no longer a habitual way of surviving. Following this line of promoting an approach, a culture of hope that creates new bonds, I invite you to win over wills, to pacify, and to convince.

4. We have seen in the Gospel our Lord Jesus Christ initiating *the hopeful bond* of a new people. The image of Jesus raising the son of the widow is a strong image—with the force of drama, not of tragedy—depicting death and resurrected life. Pain is not disguised nor hope diminished. The key is that Jesus is moved, draws closer and touches pain and death, and turns them into new life. He did not let that mourning of the dead youth crush hope: "Do not cry," he said to the mother and touched the pain. Sometimes I wonder if we are marching, in certain circumstances of the life of our society, as in a sad funeral cortege, and if we are insisting on putting a tombstone on our search as if we were walking to an inexorable destiny, threaded with impossibilities, and we are settling for small illusions devoid of hope.

5. We must recognize, with humility, that the system has fallen into a broad conical umbra,[1] *the shadow of mistrust*, with some promises and statements sounding like a funeral cortege: Everyone is consoling the mourners

---

1. The umbra is the conical shadow projected from a planet or satellite on the side opposite the sun.

but nobody is raising the dead. Arise! is the call of Christ in his Jubilee. "Arise Argentina!" as the Holy Father told us in his last visit, as our founding fathers dreamed and did. But until we recognize our duplicitous intentions, there will be no trust or peace. Until our conversion is made effective, we will not have joy and gladness. Excessive ambition, whether of power, of money, or of popularity, only expresses a great interior emptiness. Those who are empty do not transmit peace, joy, and hope but suspicion. They do not create links.

6. Touch, Lord, our still young Argentina, not turned inward but open to its neighbors. Show us your gestures of love that make us lose our fear! And, we, let's dare to touch the marginalized of the system, seeing in them men and women who are much more than potential voters. Within the framework of the republican institutions, let us give power and support to those community organizations that lend a hand and make them participate, that give preference to intimacy, fraternity, loyalty to principles and objectives as a new 'productivity.' Thus, young people will recover concrete horizons, discover possible futures leaving aside empty statements, which deepen their own emptiness.

For this you must touch the one who is mourned, whom everyone believes dead. You must value him: "Young man, I tell you, arise." For this, like Christ, we must dare to renounce monopolizing and blinding power and exercise an authority that serves and accompanies. A few have the power of finance and technology; others exercise the power of the State, but only an active community that works jointly and in solidarity can, in its creative diversity, promote the common good, be the custodian of the law and of coexistence.

In the same manner as Christ the Redeemer, who did not take for himself the glory of the young man revived but returned him to his environment, to his mother, let us, who hold some authority, serve the community. Let us give the spotlight to the community, supporting and sustaining those who organize themselves in pursuit of their goals. This will overcome the lack of communication that, paradoxically, exists in this hypercommunicated world. This is how the public realm approaches its true protagonists, who no longer want to mortgage their fate to the voting appeal of unknown representatives.

7. We believe that these community initiatives are the *hopeful signs* of a participatory joy. Here is the beginning of a true internal revolution and—at the same time—social transformation that escapes the 'macro-manipulations' of the systems and structures, foreign to the genuine being of the people.

These initiatives provide an unbeatable solution to the social suicide caused by all philosophies and techniques that expel manual labor, marginalize the tenderness of family affection, and negotiate the values of the dignity of man. It only takes *a bold and hopeful initiative* to give ground, to relinquish futile prominence; an initiative to leave the exhausting infighting, the excess of insatiable power.

We can, yes, we can, we do not have to doubt. We can return a young Argentina to our adults, to our elders: those men and women who today, so often, reach the twilight of their lives and cannot have "jubilation"[2] because they have been defrauded and are on the verge of skepticism. With them we have a debt, not only of justice but also of survival for our young people, because they are the embers of memory. Hopefully we dare to give them back a hopeful Argentina, like the young man returned to his mother, so that they can, *with their smile of hope, encourage* the lives of today's sad young people. And then we will see that the one we thought dead will rise, as we read in the Gospel, and begin to speak. Then we will understand that *"hope does not disappoint"* (Rm 5:5).

→➤ ◄←

Where Do You Want Us to Prepare the Eucharist?

Homily, Solemnity of Corpus Christi—June 24, 2000, Year B

"Where do you want us to go and prepare for you to eat the Passover?" (Mk 14:12), the disciples asked Jesus. And the Gospel tells us that the Lord had everything ready: He knew the man's path with the pitcher of water, he knew the owner of the house with a large room arranged with cushions on the second floor. . . . And he knew, above all, the love with which his friends were going to receive his Body and Blood, that Body and Blood that he so ardently desired to give us as a new Covenant.

Gathered on this feast of the Body and Blood of Christ, we ask Jesus again, as did those disciples: Lord, where do you want us to prepare the

---

2. In Spanish, *jubilarse* means "to retire."

Eucharist? Where do you want us to receive it with love by worshiping you as the living God? And he tells us again: "Go into the city. . . ." Go out to meet *those carrying pitchers of water to give others to drink.* Those who are like the Samaritan woman who, leaving the pitcher of water—she herself pours a pitcher, filled with the water of the Spirit—ran into the city, to announce to the people, to her brothers: "Come and see a man who told me everything I have done! Could he possibly be the Messiah?" (Jn 4:29). The Lord prepares the Eucharist with those who dare to be *human-pitchers,* those who allow themselves to be filled with the living water of the Spirit and let themselves be led by him.

Go out to meet *with those who prepare large rooms for others.* Rooms like the one the King prepares for his son in the parable of the wedding feast (cf. Mt 22:1–14). That room was filled with people because the first guests had excused themselves and did not want to attend the party. The Lord prepares the Eucharist for his people with *those who dare to open their hearts to others,* who have a father's heart, a heart like a large room in which all are invited to share bread.

If we read with simplicity we can discover, in these two men unknown to the Gospel, a sign of the mysterious presence of the Spirit and of the Father collaborating with Jesus for making the Eucharist. At every Mass, when we ask the Father for the power of the Spirit, he will gather his people without ceasing, and sanctify, by the same Spirit, our offerings, and accept them as a holy and living sacrifice converted into the Body and Blood of his Son.

Today we are asked to become like those men: *human-pitchers,* who open paths, who create bonds, because they have a heart full of the living water of the Spirit and show the meaning of life with gestures rather than words. We are asked to *make men and women prepare the table for the Lord and for his brothers,* men and women who create, with their actions, a coming together of neighborliness and welcome. We are all asked to open pathways of hope, but in a special way, for those who are going through moments of darkness. To those who suffer the most, those who walk without seeing, I say to you: You for whom that pitcher may have become a heavy cross, you also have something to give. Remember that it was on the Cross that the Lord, having been pierced, was given to us as a source of living water.

And, if we are all asked, young and old, children and parents, to become men and women mediators of *encounter,* it is asked especially of those who are suffering from this enormous inequality rooted among us (as expressed in our Document *Jesus, Lord of History*). To those who suffer most, to those who feel excluded from the banquet of this world, I say: Look up, keep your heart open to solidarity, that solidarity that no one should steal from the hearts of our faithful people, because it is their reserve, their treasure, the wisdom that our people learn as children in the school of love that is the Eucharist, a school of love of God and love of neighbor.

When we kneel at the moment of consecration, while we worship Jesus saying, "My Lord and my God," let us ask Our Lady, who knows about empty pitchers, to say to Jesus as she did in Cana: "They have no wine" (Jn 2:3). Let us ask her to pray for us, now, so that we can do whatever Jesus tells us. Pray for us, Mother, so that we may be faithful servants, and that by filling our pitchers to the brim, the Lord will turn the water into the wine of his Blood that purifies and gladdens our hearts with hope.

While we are praying to Jesus, let us ask Mary—who put the great hall of her heart at the disposal of the Spirit so that the Word would become flesh and dwell among us—that she pray for us, now, so that our hearts may expand and become a little more like hers: a meeting place for brothers and for neighborliness between us and God our Lord.

→➤ ◄←

For a Millennium of Justice, Solidarity, and Hope

Homily, Shrine of Saint Cajetan—August 7, 2000

Dear brothers, we have just heard in the reading how Saint Paul urges us, "Have in you *the same attitude* that is also in Christ Jesus" (Phil 2:5). The *same attitude* brings us all here to Saint Cajetan, and it is a very profound attitude. That attitude is expressed in many ways: in *the hope* of those in the queue for several days, even weeks; in *the solidarity* of the one who brings a bag of mate[3] or sugar to those who are needier than he is; in the one who wants *to be just*, gives thanks for his bread, and asks for work, touching with great faith the image of the Saint while remembering the faces of the loved ones. . . . *All these attitudes spring from one even deeper*, the attitude described by Jesus in the parable of the Good Samaritan. Jesus says that the Samaritan

---

3. Mate is a tea that is ubiquitous in Argentina.

had pity and *"was moved with compassion"* (Lk 10:33) when he saw the man injured beside the road. And this is what happens to us making the queue to ask for favors and to thank Saint Cajetan—our hearts are moved with compassion.

But let's look closely. The tenderness of the Good Samaritan was not fleeting sentimentality. On the contrary, the feeling of compassion made the Samaritan have the courage and strength to help the wounded man. The others were lazy; they passed by with hardened hearts and did nothing for their neighbor.

Tenderness and compassion made the Samaritan feel that it would be unjust to leave a brother dumped like that. Tenderness made him feel solidarity with the fate of that poor traveler who could have been himself, gave him hope that there was still life in that bloody, exhausted body, and gave him courage to help him. A feeling of justice, solidarity, and hope. These are the attitudes of the Good Samaritan. These are the attitudes Jesus has for all of us who, many times, are like that man, assaulted by thieves, stripped, beaten, and wounded . . . and yet are alive and full of hope, desiring to be healed and hoping that our ailing society will be cured, wanting to improve together with our compatriots, wanting to be helped.

That is why we are here, with hearts that need help like that of the wounded man and—at the same time—willing to help like the Good Samaritan. These are the attitudes that, through the intercession of Saint Cajetan, we want to ask God our Father, so that our hearts become more like that of Jesus, and as a faithful people we will have the same attitudes as Jesus Christ.

Justice, solidarity, and hope . . . are different ways of not passing by, as did the other two characters in the parable. Seeing someone lying on the ground, they went around and passed by. Coming here, to Saint Cajetan, is a way of not passing by. Being grateful for our daily bread is a way of not passing by, *of being just* like our Father in Heaven, who takes care of us in the midst of man's injustices. Asking *in solidarity* for work in this queue where we do not feel like competitors but like brothers, is a way of not passing by. Keeping hope kindled while fighting for justice and living *in solidarity* is a way of not passing by.

Draw closer. Do not take a detour or pass by. Draw closer today, now— that is the key, that is what Jesus teaches us. We must become close to all our brothers and sisters, especially those in need. When one draws closer, one "is moved with compassion." And in a heart not afraid to feel tenderness (the tenderness of a father and mother with their children), the needy one becomes like our son, someone small who needs care and help. Then, *the desire for justice, solidarity, and hope* are expressed with concrete gestures—gestures like those of the Good Samaritan who anoints with wine and oil and bandages wounds, who takes the wounded man to the inn on his donkey, who spends his money so that he is cared for and promises to visit him again.

On the other hand, when we do not draw closer, when we look from afar, things neither hurt us nor move us. There is a saying that goes, "What the eyes don't see, the heart does not mourn." But the reverse is also true, especially today when we see everything, but on television: "Hearts that do not come nearer, that don't touch pain, are hearts that don't mourn . . . and therefore, are eyes that look but do not see."

That is why here, in this moment when we are together, piled up like the grains in the never-ending ear of wheat at Saint Cajetan that is the queue, close to the Child Jesus like Saint Cajetan is, our hearts feel like a single heart. Here, together as a faithful People of God, we have the same attitudes that Jesus had, and we thank the Father because he is the one who softens our hearts. We thank the Virgin Mary, because she—as Mother of all of us—treats us with tenderness and obtains for us from the Father the attitudes Jesus had, the fruitful desires to be *more just, more in solidarity and full of hope.*

→> <←

In Every *Encounter* There Is a New Story at Play

Jubilee Celebration for Educators—September 13, 2000

At the time of Jesus' farewell, some of his disciples still doubted. They had doubts about what would happen to them. They had doubts about themselves. They had doubts about the strength of their hearts.

But all, at that farewell, all of them, surely everyone, remembered the first time he spoke to them.

That first encounter with Jesus Christ was in their hearts, and from the echo of that first encounter they receive the mission: go and teach.

It could be interpreted, go and meet every day with each one of those who are close to you, with each one of those I have entrusted to you.

Father Juan[1] likes to say that every day, every morning, when a teacher meets with a student, a new story begins.

Today I ask you, while giving you, in the name of Jesus, the mission of finding each day in your students a person who awaits, a heart that wants to be loved and to learn to love, a life that wants to hope. Today, as I give you this mission, I ask you not to forget the first meeting, the first meeting with your teacher. Today I continue to visit my first-grade teacher, who is now ninety-one years old.

In every encounter with a boy and a girl there is a new story at play.

You who were found by Jesus Christ and received his outpouring of grace, when approaching each of your boys or girls, you will not sell them anything, because you are not "peddlers of education," you are transmitters of life, of a lived life. Therefore, the teacher teaches from the heart, the teacher is not a merchant.

The whole educational community must put on the 'grill' of life the 'meat' of its memory, the 'meat' of its own life, with successes and failures, with graces and sins; but there is always that first encounter with Jesus Christ. That gaze that created and formed us. That gaze that is conveyed every morning so that I can look at every approaching boy and girl with his eyes.

Teaching, educating, making people grow, although it is work, transcends the model of pure work-for-hire. It exceeds that. To take life and guide it by the hand is to listen to the concerns of that life and not to impose, but to propose the way. And that is only done from the heart.

If an educational community—teachers, administrators, all the staff of the school—does not place the heart there from the beginning, it will fail in the goal of transmitting a memory, a gaze of hope, of transmitting a future.

Boys and girls will remember you when life shakes them. In times of crisis in which everything seems to be in turmoil, we lose orientation, the compass goes awry. If you approached them with the eyes of fathers and mothers, with the eyes of brothers and sisters, you would have put in that little heart, in that adolescent heart or in that young heart, the warmth born of a mature heart as a result of memory, struggle, defects, grace, sin. That boy or girl who is at your side today, when shaken by crisis, will not lose his or her compass. They will suffer, because none of us is exempt from that, but the compass is not going to go awry, and they will know where north is.

---

1. Fr. Juan Isasmendi is a priest in Equipo de Curas Villeros, a group of priests assigned by Archbishop Bergoglio to bring the message of faith to the marginalized in the suburbs of Buenos Aires.

You are women and men of *encounter*; encourage self-*encounters* within each one of your boys and girls.

You are men and women of memory and remembrance; teach them to remember the gazes of tenderness that have been molding them. Teach them to discover the gaze of Jesus Christ.

You are men and women of hope, because you are betting on something that will transcend you.

I ask the Virgin that you may win that bet, because we all win. May it be so.

⤜⤛

Help Us Find Jesus in Each Other

Homily, Twenty-Sixth Youth Pilgrimage to Luján——October 1, 2000

Our visit to the house of the Virgin this year has a special meaning: We have asked her that we may find her Son in each brother and sister.

We have walked for many miles because this love costs us dearly, but we ask for it; we need her help to find Jesus in each neighbor. We do not want to pass by a brother with indifference; we do not want, as brothers, to destroy each other. We want to *encounter* each other as brothers and sisters, to work so that this fraternal culture of *encounter* becomes a reality. And on this path, we make the effort to change in our hearts whatever prevents us from being more neighborly.

We want to be generous, and sometimes we feel pain that we are not, so we ask our Mother: "Help us to find Jesus in each other."

Like other years, we came to gaze at her and to rest with her. There is much in our life that overwhelms us, but we know that here she waits for us; she does not ask us why we came, and she welcomes us. She knows that we walked here because we need this *encounter*. She also knows that we came a long way to gaze at each other and meet, in order to be more neighborly.

She also made a long journey and brought us Jesus. In this current Holy Year, we celebrate in a special way the birth of Jesus. She, with her life, shows us the way to find him, and it is the path of brotherly love.

You young people are always ready to give of yourselves, to go hiking, as we see today in coming to Luján.

You who want to be faithful and who live with passion, aren't you willing to live this path of love with Jesus, a path of brotherly love? This way of *encounter* that we Argentines need so much.

Jesus and his Mother here in Luján welcome you. They want to accompany you and invite you to persevere on this path, to not falter in the fellowship of *encounter*. We came here to meet the sincere and generous love of Jesus that always leaves a footprint in our hearts, a footprint of hope to keep on walking. We need this hope.

We say to ourselves and to her: "Mother, let us see Jesus in each other."

We need it; it is good for us.

2001

To Educate: Blending a 'Warm' and an 'Intellectual' Task

Message to the Educational Community—March 28, 2001

Whoever loves me will keep my word, and my Father will love him, and we will come to him and make our dwelling with him. (Jn 14:23)

I would like to ask you to join me for a moment in a little imagination exercise. It will not be difficult. I will evoke experiences and feelings that we have all had at some time.

We will imagine that we were born and lived in one of the small towns in the north of our country. But not one of those towns visited by tourists and buses and that have television; rather, from a hamlet that does not appear on any map, no route passes through, and vehicles rarely arrive there . . . a place that we cannot call "forgotten" because it was never in the conscience or memory of anyone, except for its few inhabitants. No doubt there are places like this in our country, more than we realize.

We are someone from that place. And one day, now it does not matter how or why, we came to the big city, Buenos Aires, without anyone's address or a specific purpose. Let us use our imagination but also involve the heart. Beyond the details that a cartoon might record (the difficulties in crossing one of the avenues, the astonishment before the big buildings and luminous posters in Avenida 9 de Julio, the fear of the subway), we first focus on the immense isolation in the midst of the crowd, lack of communication, not knowing what to ask, where to look for help or what kind of help one needs. The isolation. Imagine and physically feel your aching feet after hours of walking through the big city. We do not know where to rest. The night falls.

On a bench in a central square, some boys fooling around frighten us, and we know that at the slightest distraction they will take our bag, the only thing we have. Isolation becomes anguish, insecurity, and real fear. It's cold, a while ago it drizzled, and our feet are wet. And ahead of us, the long night.

Our throats, gagged by the knot of loneliness and fear, feel only one question pushing through: Will there be a hospitable soul to open a door for me, offer me something warm and allow me to rest, give me support and encourage me to decide the way ahead?

An open heart? A warm welcome? So the document *Pastoral Lines for the New Evangelization* called it. Because, no doubt, you quickly understood where the proposed exercise was going to focus our attention: on the need for us Christians, educators, members of educational communities, to become welcoming hearts that open doors, that nurture a garden of humanity and affection in the middle of the big city with its machines, its lights, and its widespread orphanhood.

We could have started this reflection in another way: citing authors, documents, theories about the situation of contemporary man, his estrangement, his depersonalization. But I preferred to invite you to see it from the perspective of feeling, from the heart. Because this ministry of warm welcome, of healing the human person through hospitable love, is first a response to an experience, not an idea. It is the human, ethical experience of perceiving the pain and the need of the brother. And in it, the theological experience of recognizing in the pilgrim that is homeless when the night falls and the day is over (Lk 24:29) the Lord who is passing through (Mt 25:35c). And to know that by opening our heart, we will be allowing him "to make his dwelling among us" (Jn 1:14). To discover, full of joy, that at that moment the roles are reversed and that Dwelling, a Heart of brother, father, and mother, opens and receives us, and we have finally arrived home.

I would like then, brothers and sisters, to invite you to reflect together on the school as a place of warm welcome, as a home offering an open hand to the men, women, young people, boys, and girls of this city. And may we do it with all the seriousness and depth that these brief pages allow, and from the perspective of the experience that we have imagined.

But before entering fully into the subject, I want to anticipate a concern that should be considered now. To address the dimensions of hospitality, tenderness, and affection at the school does not mean, in any way, that we leave aside its other dimension: that of a place with an objective, a specific function that must be carried out seriously, effectively, and I would dare to say, professionally. Are these two aspects in opposition? They can be opposites, no doubt. In fact, our society tends to oppose gratuity and efficiency, freedom and duty, the heart and reason—they can be opposites, but they do not have to be. It is our challenge to find the solution in a higher plane: the wisdom perspective that allows us to create a space that is welcoming and nurtures growth. I hope these reflections encourage you to look for that solution.

Growing in the Ashes: Orphanhood in Contemporary Culture

As we clarified earlier, the vocation of our schools to be areas for welcoming and affirming all persons in their fullest dimension springs from the very core of the Gospel message. This is because the school, as an ecclesial community, is called to embody the love of Christ, which dignifies man from the center of his being.

But in addition, this mission has another important motivation in the concrete situation of women and men in our society. Allow me now to introduce some ideas that, at first glance, may seem extremely harsh and even pessimistic. However, they offer the basic recognition of that which cries out for a word of hope.

A while ago, when I spoke about the city, I used the word orphanhood. I would like to take it up again and make it the center of this segment of our reflection. Let's explore the following line of thought: We must develop and strengthen our capacity for offering a warm welcome because many of those coming to our schools do so in a deep state of orphanhood. And I do not mean certain family conflicts, but an experience that equally concerns children, youth and adults, mothers, fathers, and children. For so many orphans—our contemporaries, perhaps, ourselves?—the community that is the school should become family: a space for love freely given and promotion, for affirmation and growth.

Let's try to clarify this idea a bit more. In what sense do we say that we live in a situation of orphanhood?

Recently, in conversation with some young people, I heard these shocking affirmations: "We are children of failure. Our parents' dreams of a new world, the hopes of the '60s, were burned in the bonfire of violence, enmity and everyone for himself. The business culture finished undoing what was left of those embers. We grew up in a world of ashes. How do they want us to have ideals or projects, to believe in the future, in commitment? We don't believe or disbelieve. It is just that we are oblivious to all that. We were born in the desert, among the ashes, and in the desert, nothing is sown nor grows."

Of course, not all young people will identify with this. At least, it seems to me that this painful testimony serves, in my opinion, as an introduction to the three points that characterize the current situation of man and woman's orphanhood in our city—the experience of discontinuity, uprootedness, and the decline of basic certainties.

The Experience of Discontinuity

The first dimension of contemporary orphanhood has to do with the experience of time, or rather, history and stories. Something is broken, fragmented. Something that should be united, precisely the connecting bridge, is broken or absent. How is this? In the first place, it is a deficit of memory and tradition. Memory as the integrating power of history and tradition conceived as the richness of the road walked by our elders. Both do not cancel each other out (in that case they would lack meaning) but open new spaces of hope to keep on walking. The painful experiences lived in our country, coupled with a certain purely economic success that had its peak a few years ago, resulted in a generational break that no longer occurs as part of the normal growth and affirmation cycles of young people, but is due to an inability of the adult generation to transmit the principles or ideals that animated it. Perhaps due to the terrible crises suffered by that generation, to the death experiences that they brought (and I do not mean only the political conflicts that we already know, but also death from AIDS—as a closure or at least a serious limit to the horizon of the sexual revolution—and even the death of love, in so many couples that did not manage to carry out their family projects). How many parents, let's be truthful, have been able to even try an enriching dialogue with their children, that would review and "retell frankly" their diverse experiences, so that the next generation would learn of their successes and mistakes and continue the same road, with all the rectifications of the case? How many things that you do not talk about, how many things you have not talked about, how many things you cannot talk about! How many times have you preferred "to start over, from scratch," both in families and in Argentine society, instead of undertaking the hard task of promoting a reexamination of the questions and concerns that motivated a whole generation, starting with a dialogue, although difficult, in order to overcome bitterness and isolation.

And that discontinuity of generational experience does not come alone: It generates a whole range of discontinuities. The discontinuity—rather, abyss—between society and ruling class (I think of the political class, but not only), a discontinuity that has a dose of indifference and voluntary blindness on both sides, and the discontinuity—or dissociation—between institutions and personal expectations (applicable to the school and the university as well as to marriage and church organizations, among others).

Forms of Uprootedness

Discontinuity: loss or absence of bonds, in time and in the socio-political interweaving that constitutes a people. The first face of orphanhood. But there is more. Along with discontinuity, uprootedness has also grown. We can locate it in three areas.

First, the uprooting of a spatial type, in a broad sense. It is no longer so easy to build your own identity on the basis of 'place.' The city invades the 'neighborhood' and makes it explode from within. I dare to add: the global city, which is identified in the big chains, in eating habits, in the omnipresence of the social media, in the logic, the jargon and the cruel business folklore, supplants the 'local' city. And without exaggerating too much, they are leaving just a laughable remnant "for export"[1] and the tragic reality— also globalized!—of people who spend the night in the street, children exploited and drowned by drugs and the violence of crime and marginality. Both personal and collective identities suffer from this dissolution of the living spaces. The concept of 'a people' has less and less content in the current dynamics of fragmentation and segmentation of human groups. The city is losing its capacity to identify human groups, being populated, as a French anthropologist[2] pointed out a few years ago, by 'non-places,' empty spaces subject exclusively to instrumental logic (functionality, marketing) and deprived of symbols and references that contribute to the constitution of communal identities.

And so, 'spatial' uprooting goes hand in hand with the other two forms of uprooting: the existential and the spiritual. The first is linked to the absence of projects, perhaps to the experience of 'growing up in the ashes,' as the young man I quoted before said. In the absence of continuity or places with history and meaning (breakup of time and space as a possibility for

---

1. The phrase "for export" appears in English in the original, suggesting the invasion of foreign companies in Argentina's economy.
2. Marc Augé (b. 1935), a French anthropologist who, in his book *Non-Places: Introduction to an Anthropology of Supermodernity* (1995), refers to places where relationships, history, and identity are erased.

constituting an identity and forming a personal project), the feeling of belonging to a history and the link with a possible future are weakened, a
future that challenges me and energizes the present. This radically affects
identity, because fundamentally, 'to identify with is to belong to.' Economic
insecurity also plays a part. How can one be rooted in the existential
ground of a personal project if a guarantee of minimum job security is not
assured?

And still this has one more face. Both the blurring of spatial references
and the rupturing of continuity between the past, the present, and the future
emptied the life of city dwellers from certain symbolic references, from those
'windows'—true horizons of meaning—toward the transcendent that
opened here and there, in the city and in human interaction. This openness
to the transcendent, in traditional cultures, was mediated by a rather static
and hierarchical representation of reality, and this was expressed in a multitude of images and symbols present in the city (from the layout itself to
the places impregnated with history or even sacredness). Contrasting with
the modern sense, transcendence had to do with 'going forward,' constituting the backbone of history as a process of emancipation mediated in human
action—a transforming action, in the modern sense—which found its symbolic expression in art, in the strengthening of some festive dimensions, in
free and spontaneous organizations, and in the image of the people in the
street. But now, when spaces that until recently worked as triggers and as
symbols of transcendence are increasingly delimited or emptied of meaning, uprooting also reaches a spiritual dimension.

This last statement could meet two objections. The first has to do with
the role of the media that fills the world with images, that communicates,
generates milestones—and myths—that replace old geographical landmarks
or utopian references. Could it not be that the media culture of the image
is the new system of symbols, the new 'window' to the Other, just as cathedrals and monuments once were? However, there is a fundamental difference here. While an image of the Virgin in a neighborhood club, yes, refers
to the basilica where the original image is, and for some, to the totality of
the conceptual, moral, and disciplinary system of the Catholic faith, beyond
all this, this image also points to a transcendent pole, to something that has
to do with the 'sky,' with the 'miracle.' In short, it is a religious[3] symbol. It
reconnects, relinks earth and heaven, the transitory with the absolute. Man

---

3. Traditionally, the word "religion" comes from the Latin re-ligare, meaning "to bind" or,
more specifically, "to reconnect yourself with God."

and God. As a symbol that reconnects, it does not exhaust itself, but it has its own coherence. The image culture, on the contrary, and in particular the image of the media, of advertising, and, now, the image of the Internet screen, is not a symbol of something else; it does not 'refer to' something, it has no external reference to the media circle itself. We cannot deepen these ideas here, but it is a fact that the multimedia system is increasingly self-referential, it is becoming, more than a medium, a stage, and that stage takes, at times, more importance than the drama that can be represented on it. A series of signs all pointing to themselves and almost nothing else, without a true, objective, and fair reference to the reality outside the media, or, moreover, pretending to build reality through their discourse. What rootedness could they generate, what kind of bonds, what openness to 'the Other' that cements one in being? What will they contribute to the project of humanization other than an endless 'navigating,' 'zapping,' 'surfing' on the bright faces of the screens?

The second objection puts on the table the fact that, against all the secularizing prognoses, religion did not disappear from the cities, and I add, it developed new expressions and references, to the point that again and again marketing tries to ride on this phenomenon to generate profits. This is true without a doubt, but it is also true that all these religious manifestations are generated in good part from uprooting and orphanhood and seek, in faith, prayer, and religious gesture, to remedy in some way those situations. Now, in a society losing its communitarian dimension—its cohesion as a people—such massive religious expressions increasingly need a communitarian correlative, so as not to remain mere individual gestures. While recognizing the dimension of the People of God, present and operating in the popular religious expression, we need to restore that authentic faith and provide elements that allow it to unfold its full humanizing potential. That is, to recognize in it a cry for true liberation (DP 452) that will enable our people to overcome their orphanhood, through the very resources they carry within and that are rooted in the grace of their baptism, and in their memory of belonging to Holy Mother Church.

So, then, discontinuity (generational and political) and uprooting (spatial, existential, spiritual) characterize that situation that we have called, more generically, orphanhood. We could already ask ourselves: What can the school do, degraded from 'temple of knowledge' to 'social expenditure,' to remedy this situation? What can teachers do, who yesterday were living symbols of a free society in search of a future, but today are reduced in social status and unable to live with dignity from their work? What can the entire educational community do, itself crossed by so many situations of discontinuity and uprooting? But first, we want to briefly specify something else.

The Decline of Certainty

A third aspect of contemporary orphanhood, closely related to those we have already seen, is the decline of certainty. In general, civilizations grow in the shadow of some basic beliefs about the world, man, coexistence, the why and wherefore of founding human events, and so forth. These beliefs, often dependent on religions, but not exclusively, constitute a sort of certainty on which the construction of a historical figure rests, and which gives meaning to the existence of communities and people.

So, many of the certainties that have animated our modern society have been diluted, have declined or worn out. A patriotic discourse, in the style of those that moved my generation, tends to be seen with mockery or skepticism. The revolutionary language of thirty years ago can be, at best, cause for curiosity and surprise. The very idea of solidarity has difficulty making itself heard in the middle of the ideology of the 'individual drive.' And this loss of certainties, once unshakable, also reaches the foundations of the person, family, and faith. The principles guiding the generations that preceded us seem outdated: how to continue to maintain that saving is the basis of fortune, for example, when there is no work and the only fortunes that can grow today come from corruption, speculation, and shady deals? How to continue considering that human life is untouchable, when so many humble people, whose only good is their life, ask for the death penalty to protect themselves from urban violence, although we all know that the causes of this violence are not in the extreme perversity of some?

But this decline of certainties is not merely a circumstantial event of a society in the periphery. No. In addition to a widespread mood in the West, it constitutes almost a 'new certainty' that finds its place in the most prestigious discourses of contemporary thought. A brief reference to this will not hurt, since it constitutes the substrata of a whole spiritual state at the beginning of this century.

Reason: Idolized, Reviled, and Reconsidered

From different ideological positions, there was a debate some years ago about the opposition between modernity and postmodernity. Among the many—

very many—dimensions and perspectives that included (and still include, in some vulgar way) that discussion, we want to highlight one: the idea that 'the end of modernity' supposes the loss of the main certainties, an idea that refers, in the last analysis, to a deep discredit of reason. This is how John Paul II describes this position:

> The currents of thought which claim to be postmodern merit appropriate attention. According to some of them, the time of certainties is irrevocably past, and the human being must now learn to live in a horizon of total absence of meaning, where everything is provisional and ephemeral. In their destructive critique of every certitude, several authors have failed to make crucial distinctions and have called into question the certitudes of faith.
>
> This nihilism has been justified in a sense by the terrible experience of evil which has marked our age. Such a dramatic experience has ensured the collapse of rationalist optimism, which viewed history as the triumphant progress of reason, the source of all happiness and freedom; and now, at the end of this century, one of our greatest threats is the temptation to despair. (FR 91)

A deep disenchantment spreads everywhere about the great promises of reason: freedom, equality, fraternity. . . . What remained of all this? At the outset of the twenty-first century, there is no longer a rationality, a meaning, but multiple fragmented, partial meanings. The same search for truth—and the very idea of "truth"—are overshadowed. In any case, there will be "truths" without pretensions of universal validity, perspectives, interchangeable discourses. A thought that travels in the relative and the ambiguous, the fragmentary and the multiple, constitutes the mood that colors not only philosophy and academic knowledge, but the same culture "of the street," as has been confirmed by all those who have dealt with youth. Relativism will therefore be the result of the so-called "consensus policy" whose action always involves a leveling down. It is the era of "weak thinking."

Rescuing Rationality

Hence, disengaged from the certainties of reason (and, as John Paul II pointed out, also from those of faith understood as "knowledge" of salvation), today's culture relies on feeling, impressions, and images. This also creates orphanhood, which requires us to make our schools welcoming places, spaces where people can find themselves and others to re-create their being in the world. But also, and here we will take another step in our reflection, this situation forces us to face in some way the need to rescue a valid rationality, a vigorous way of thinking that allows us to overcome contemporary irrationality. You may ask: And why? Since we are revaluing and in fact recovering and deepening the affective aspects, like tenderness, and the human bonds that have been left aside in our society, why do we have to tilt the balance again to the other side?

It is not about falling into new imbalances, but precisely about finding the right place that makes this warm welcome an authentically human and liberating gesture. Three ideas will help us understand this.

First, things are not all white or black. Denouncing the 'abuses of reason' (totalitarianism of all kinds, historical and political projects that brought more suffering than happiness, devaluation of the affective, personal, and routine aspects of life, reduction of everything to calculation, number, and concept . . .) does not mean throwing away all the benefits that "rational" development has brought. The school itself, without going too far, is the child of this idea. Although we cannot share the line from the old school hymn, "By giving them knowledge, you gave them a soul," we must recognize that 'knowing' is a very important resource for the development of the 'soul,' that is, of the human person. I refer to 'knowledge' that cannot be reduced to mere information or to certain cybernetic 'encyclopedism,' a knowledge with capacity to relate, to advance the posing of questions and elaboration of an-swers. It is a resource that we have no right to be stingy about. On the contrary, we must improve our capacity (even 'technical') to carry out this transmission.

Second, although the "postmodern" discourse that values the emotional, the relative, and even the irrational aspects of life seems to free us from the tyranny of the uniform, the bureaucratic or the disciplinary, on the other hand, it becomes the justification of other tyrannies, not to mention a very important one, that of the economy with its power and technocratic factors. Because if today is governed by feelings, the image, and the immediate, that holds true only for the consumers of goods and services . . . and media ad-vertising. The ability to choose, freedom, not needing to be ascribed to a uni-form norm, diversity and plurality—all of this so dear to the postmodern mentality—are now translated simply as a diversity of goods. It is true that the State and the school, to name institutions that generated strong nor-mative responsibilities, no longer govern the lives of individuals. The Church has a growing appreciation within itself of personal freedom and 'electivity.' But it is also true that this freedom, away from those institutional frame-works that gave it harmony, has been captured by the market. In short, if we do not recover the notion of truth, without a shared, dialogical rational-ity, a search for the best means to achieve the most desirable ends (for each and every one), there remains only the law of the strongest, the law of the jungle. Then, the more we worry about developing critical thinking, refining our ethical sense, improving our skills, our creativity, and our resources, the more we can avoid being slaves to advertising—the planned (by others) exacerbation of the immediate, of the manipulation of information, of the discouragement that holds each one in their individual interest.

And third, arriving at what defines our identity as Christian educators—faith, knowledge, the grasp of the real—has not only an affective component but also an important dimension of wisdom that must be rescued, and that begins with the capacity for admiration. Next, we will focus our attention on this point. The wisdom dimension globally encompasses knowledge, feeling, and doing. It harmoniously conveys the ability to understand, the tension of owning what is good, the contemplation of the beautiful, all synchronized by the unity of a human being that understands, loves, and admires. The wisdom dimension remembers, integrates, and creates hope. It is what opens the disciple's existence and anoints the teacher. Wisdom is only understood in light of the Word of God.

The Word: Revealing and Creative

The 'postmodern' primacy of experience brought with it piety of heart, a more personal search for God, and a new appreciation of prayer and contemplation. But it also brought a kind of religion à la carte, a unilateral subjectivizing of religion that places it less in the dimension of worship, commitment, and self-giving and more as an element of well-being, similar to a great extent to various New Age, magical, or pseudo-psychological religious offerings.

That true reductionism (as much as its opposite, the unilateral affirmation of religion as 'content' and 'discourse') leaves aside the infinite richness of the Word of God. Throughout the Bible (both in the Old and New Testaments), the Word of God presents two dimensions, both equally important: that of 'revelation,' 'discourse,' 'logos,' and as 'action,' 'presence,' 'power,' '*dynamis*.'[4] The Word of God speaks and does. If we consider it only as a salvific presence (because when God acts, God saves, and God saves by creating communion, by bonding with his creatures, making us children), we set aside the aspect of revelation. If, on the contrary, we consider it only under its aspect of truth, of 'content,' we lose its dimension of communion, of

---

4. The Greek means "potential, unrealized power."

loving presence, its salvific dynamics. The Word of God bonds us to him with ties of both knowledge and love. It speaks and does.

In its aspect of 'revelation,' the Word in the Old Testament is presented as Law, as a rule of life through which God offers a path to happiness. "Your Word is a lamp to my feet and a light for my path," says Psalm 119 (v. 105), all of it an impressive hymn to the Word of God expressed as Law. But in addition to this 'practical knowledge,' the Word offers a 'knowledge' about God and man in the world. God reveals his Name and his saving will, and thus shows man the greatness of his filiation and his destiny.

But the Word of God is also the force of God, which does what it announces: "It shall not return to me empty, / but shall do what pleases me, / achieving the end for which I sent it" (Is 55:11b). It is a creative Word, from the beginning of time: "God said . . ." and "saw it happened" (cf. Gn 1). It is a liberating Word that saves the Hebrew slaves and leads them through the desert, the Word that calls them together and constitutes them as a People, the Word that is promised as New Creation at the end of time.

And the New Testament presents Jesus Christ in the same way: as a prophet who teaches and offers a New Law, as a teacher of wisdom that makes us taste the beauty and goodness of God's love, and as God's force who effects salvation, heals the sick, expels demons, and inaugurates, with his Death and Resurrection, the New Creation in the paschal banquet of the Kingdom.

Where does all of this take us? As witnesses of the Word, our presence in society must correspond to this wealth that cannot be enclosed in a single dimension. The creative, dynamic, salvific dimension of the Word will be enacted in the world in the creation of community, of bonding with, recognizing, welcoming, and empowering others. This dimension has an important affective component, not in a superficial sense, but in the deepest and most demanding sense of the commandment of love. The Gospel according to Matthew (25:31 ff.) presents the 'test' that the Lord will administer to his people at the end of time: if they fed the hungry, gave drink to the thirsty, received the stranger. . . . The miracle of the dynamic presence of God is made real, and communion takes place in the disciples who acted accordingly: Christ identifies himself with the one to whom love was given, symbolically inverting the roles, since it is he who offers, gives, transforms, and creates a new reality with your love.

But also, because the Word is revelation, law, teaching, our mission will aim to seriously seek the truth and invite and incorporate others in this search. A whole dimension that, precisely because it includes the whole person, will not ignore the importance of human intelligence, its formation and promotion. This dimension is equally defining, as the Gospel according to John teaches us (12:44–50).

This same dynamic occurs in the liturgical celebration, the sacramental encounter with the Lord: Word and Eucharist, teaching and communion, contemplation and adoration. It is precisely in this delicate balance that the richness of an integral, nonreductive understanding of the Christian mystery is found; an understanding that comes through wisdom.

The concept of wisdom, precisely, is one that harmoniously brings together various aspects: knowledge, love, contemplation of the beautiful, at the same time as a 'communion in truth' and a 'truth that creates communion,' 'a beauty that attracts and enchants.' It is intelligence, heart, eyes of the soul, not dissociated but integrated into the human person at its fullest.

Hence, it is impossible to dissociate the various aspects in our pastoral or educational activity. The authenticity of the Word that we transmit must rely on the integrity with which we assume its dimensions. And this translates precisely into caring for both aspects of doing, linked to the warm welcome, the concrete practice of charity, here and now, the creation of human bonds (which include, of course, any assistance and promotional action that helps a person get on his feet and take his place in the human and Christian community), as well as those dimensions more related to speaking: the careful preparation, remote and near, of the educational activity, the planning for a more effective use of resources, the seriousness with which we undertake our own training, and so on. Both dimensions are constitutive of our mission as Christian educators, and if it is true that we are called to put a bit of humanity and tenderness into an individualistic and exclusive society, it is also true that, faced with the discrediting of the word, we have the obligation to help our brothers to develop the ability to understand and to speak. Not only to create rootedness, but also to re-create the most important certainties, in the form of wisdom of life, the world, and God. A fruitful wisdom begets children and dissipates orphanhood. A wisdom that is a source of beauty that moves the soul toward admiration, contemplation.

Invitation

We are coming to the end of this long reflection. Contemporary orphanhood—in terms of discontinuity, uprooting, and the disappearance of the main certainties that shape life—challenges us to make our schools a 'family,' a 'home' where women and men, boys and girls, can develop their capacity to link their experiences, and to take root in their soil and in their personal and collective history. In doing so, they can find the tools and resources that allow them to develop their intelligence, their will, and all their abilities to be able to reach the human potential that they are called to live.

This dual challenge demands many tasks from us. In this initial segment of the educational year, I would like to draw your attention to three aspects that derive from the reflections I have developed.

First, the development of human bonds of affection and tenderness as a remedy to uprootedness. The school can be a "place" (geographical, in the middle of the neighborhood, but also existential, human, interpersonal) in which roots are enmeshed to allow personal development. It can be shelter and home, firm ground, window and horizon to the transcendent. However, we know that the school is not the walls, the boards, and the record books. It is the people, especially the teachers—that is, teachers and educators who will have to develop their capacity for affection and dedication to create these human spaces. How to develop forms of affective discipline in times of mistrust? How to re-create human relationships when everyone expects the worst from the other? We must find, all of us and each one, the ways, gestures, and actions that allow us to include everyone and to help the most vulnerable generate a climate of serene joy and confidence and to take care of both the progress of the whole and the specifics of each person under our care.

Second, coherence between what is said and what is done to reduce the abyss of discontinuity. We know that in every act of communication there is an explicit message, something that is stated, but that message can be blocked, nuanced, disfigured, and even denied by the attitude with which it is transmitted. There is a whole aspect of communication, 'nonexplicit' and 'nonverbal,' that has to do with gestures, the relationship that is established, and the deployment of the various human dimensions in general. Everything we do is an act of communication. To the extent that we avoid double messages, insofar as we create and try to live with our whole being what we are transmitting, to that extent we will have contributed to restore credibility in human communication.

Of course, this communicational ideal will be hampered time and again by the mystery of sin and human weakness. Who can boast of having absolute coherence, absolute control of their miseries, their dualities, their self-deception, their repressed selfishness, and their unspeakable interests? We know that not everything is achieved with good intentions, "moralizing" purposes, or normative rigidities. But in the same way, we are aware that not everything is excusable and acceptable just like that, since we have a responsibility to other people and to those who entrusted lives to our care. And then? The key to achieving coherence without pretending an impossible perfection will be to walk humbly and willingly, to discern personally and communally, avoiding the condemnatory judgment of the other; to be open to fraternal correction, forgiveness, and reconciliation; to recognize together that we are pilgrims, weak and sinful women and men but with a memory and in search of a fuller love that will heal and help us rise. That can be a way to exchange discontinuity for nearness, to make ourselves close to each other amid the differences.

Third, the effort to generate some basic certainties in the sea of the relative and the fragmentary. Maybe this is extremely difficult. We know that truth by force is contrary to the force of truth. We also know that we cannot adopt the compulsive methods of advertising, which displace real needs for illusory satisfactions. And then? There is a "narrow path" that goes through the search for wisdom, always convinced of the ability to move and fall in love. It consists of learning to discover the other's questions, to contemplate them, and to intuit them (because it is difficult for children and young people to express their needs and questions clearly). Although tiredness and routine sometimes make us a kind of 'speaker' that emits sounds that nobody cares about, we know well that only 'teachings' that respond to a question, to admiration, will have an 'impact' and 'remain.' Sharing the questions (even if we do not have the answers!) is already putting us all, educators and learners, on a searching path of contemplation, of hope.

For all this, it will be necessary to set in motion two dimensions, integrating them always: to amplify the capacity of our heart as servants of the brothers and sisters, and always to further develop our capacity as professional educators. A 'warm' task and an 'intellectual' task well blended. Getting in tune with the Word of God, which speaks, today as always, both to our intelligence and to our hearts. As a Spanish theologian reflects, "individuals are led to a personal life when they are offered science and conscience, knowledge and responsibilities, ends and means, trust and demands." And this is wisdom. May the Lord grant it to all of us. Let us ask for it humbly through the prayer of King Solomon.

> Now, LORD, my God,
> you have made me, your servant,
> king to succeed David my father;
> but I am a mere youth,
> not knowing at all how to act—

I, your servant, among the people
you have chosen,
a people so vast
that it cannot be numbered or counted.
Give your servant,
therefore, a listening heart
to judge your people
and to distinguish between good and evil.

(1 Kgs 3:7–9)

⤜ ⤛

Caring for Another Is Power

Homily, Mass for Educators—March 28, 2001

We just heard about a scene from a representative day (cf. Mt 8:5–13) in the life of Jesus, pressed upon by the people, in the midst of the crowd and taking care of their problems. In this case, the problems of a foreigner, a member of the occupation forces—Jesus took care of everyone. It was enough that someone was in need for him to take responsibility.

And together with the Lord's attitude of taking responsibility, is another, so beautiful, that of the father who was told that there was a man who could heal. In his desperation the father goes to ask Jesus to cure his boy. The attitude of the caregiver, in this case, taking care of his son.

Two attitudes directed to life, to give life, a good life, intended for the maturing of individuals. Because when someone feels that his problem is being taken care of, then he can rest, trust, walk with more strength, mature. When someone feels that he is cared for—with good care, not a suffocating care—he feels like a person and can grow in freedom.

Obviously, the nucleus, the most humane place to take responsibility and care is the family, and together with the family, the school. That is where we men and women learn to take responsibility and to care, because it is there that we allow them to take responsibility and take care of us.

And today, to you who work in education—I do not mean that you are employees of education—but that you work and are "molders" of education—I ask you to be artisans of taking responsibility for the children and of caring for them. To create a culture of caring for each other, of not allowing that the indifference to the problem that I have at my side or of those that I have in my care should overwhelm me, paralyze me, or make me sterile.

Caring for another is a great power too. It is not only an obligation; it is not only the act of taking someone in, but it is power. And it is power that cannot be delegated to the best person available. It is a power that each person, responsible for caring for another, carries in the heart.

My wish is for us to grow in this attitude of mutual care. That we grow in this awareness that we must bear responsibility, and here I would say, beyond the children that we have in our care, also, as men and women of our community, we must bear responsibility and take care of one another without contracting this job out to someone else.

This is a social responsibility that strengthens hearts, that makes our children and our young people, and even our own community mutually supportive. It is to care and to take charge, to encourage each other to have tenderness. Today I ask God to grant to all of you, and to me too, the grace to learn how to be tender every day, because in that way we will take better care of one another and will foster that care warmly, as brothers and sisters.

May God grant this grace to all of us.

→→ ←←

May Our Priesthood Make the Faithful People of God Feel That the Church Loves Them

Homily, Chrism Mass—April 12, 2001, Year C

During this Mass for Holy Thursday, when the Church gathers us year after year with this opening passage of the Gospel according to Saint Luke: "Jesus came to Nazareth, where he had grown up, and went according to his custom into the synagogue on the sabbath day. He stood up to read and was handed a scroll of the prophet Isaiah . . ." (Lk 4:16–17). I want to pause a moment to contemplate, together with you, dear brothers in the priesthood, *the same scene*: a scene so well described, it paints for us *Jesus in the synagogue of his town*, as if we were saying Jesus in the neighborhood church, in our parish. It will do us good to get into the scene imagining that little chapel of Nazareth and, why not, each one imagining Jesus in his parish, in his church.

If we look at what the Lord does, this reading ritual is still current, as when one rises at the Mass and goes up to the altar, the book is brought to you or the acolyte points to the page. The Lord gets up to read, reads from Isaiah, returns it to the minister, and sits down. Simple rituals that speak of family tradition, of Saturdays in the synagogue held by the hand of Saint Joseph and of the Virgin, determined gestures of Jesus that refer us to the life of a parish. The scene of the adult Jesus in the synagogue parallels in Luke that of the lost and found Child in the Temple, to which they also ascend "according to festival custom" (Lk 2:42). Luke, as we know, makes the life of the Lord revolve around the Temple of Jerusalem, from the annunciation to Zechariah, to the final image of those who form the new community, after the Ascension: "They were continually in the temple praising God" (Lk 24:53).

This wide panorama of the relationship of the Lord with the Temple has its correlative in everyday life, those other images of *the small-town synagogues*: in the synagogue of Capernaum a typical day begins when he cures the man possessed by a demon and then goes to the house of Peter—the Church's rock—and when they open the door at dusk, they meet the crowd that had gathered to be attended by Jesus . . . (Lk 4:40). Also, then the emergencies, as we say in our jargon, sometimes took over the day. In the synagogue Jesus heals the man with the paralyzed hand, stalked by the Pharisees (Lk 6:6), where he receives the friends of the centurion who had built the synagogue for the people (Lk 7:1ff.). Leaving the synagogue, Jesus heals the hemorrhaging woman and the daughter of Jairus, the head of the synagogue (Lk 8:49ff.). In the synagogue, he straightens the bent-over woman, so she can give glory to God with dignity again (Lk 13:10ff.).

This is the image that I want to highlight today: *that of Jesus in the midst of the faithful people of God*, of Jesus, priest and good shepherd in the midst of the universal and local Church. Because *in this image is the strength of our priestly identity*. The Lord wants to continue being, through us his priests, in the midst of his faithful people (of which we are a part). He wants to need us to celebrate the Eucharist, to walk as Church. That Church is a shrine that summons all the faithful people of God and—at the same time—a small chapel in which the life of each community is conceived; that Church is a holy place in the midst of the cities where the Father continues to call those who want to worship him in Spirit and in truth.

It is good for us to contemplate Jesus surrounded by all the characters that we see daily in our temples: They never fail, in the midst of the community that gathers to worship God, nor the one who is not completely healthy in body and soul, neither the beggar of the paralyzed hand, nor the bent-over woman, nor the silent hemorrhaging woman who knows how to touch the mantle of the Lord. There is no shortage of those who may not practice, like the centurion, but who help with their alms and good will. There is no shortage of people who come to hear the Word and who pray, admire, and praise God, nor those who are scandalized, those who come to cheat, the Pharisees who are always stalking others with their regulations without charity. . . . Not missing either are the elder saints like Simeon and Anna, the youth of the catechism classes who stay after. . . . And very often the Pharisee and the publican enter to pray. And every day, although only Jesus sees it, some widow throws her last two coins into the alms box for the poor.

How does this Jesus, who enters the synagogue and reads "*according to his custom,*" challenge us? This Jesus, who walks in processions with his people and queues among sinners to be baptized by John, this Jesus, who celebrates Easter and who is immersed in the traditions of his people, renewing everything from within? People realize that everything is renewed around him. Therefore, this impressive contradiction between exultant praises and blasphemies poisoned with hatred before someone who merely says, this scripture is fulfilled today. What does he tell us, priests, and what does he invite us to?

He invites us to be *men of the Church*, which is the most current translation—and the most controversial—of "imitating and following Christ." Today, as then, the Lord *invites us to be amid our faithful people*, steeped in their traditions and customs, without pretensions or exterior elitism and enlightenment of any kind, and with a heart that burns inside us so that the Spirit can renew the face of the earth and light the fire that the Lord himself brought.

He invites us to be *priests who feel the Church is their Mother*, priests who remain in love with the Holy and Immaculate Church, true Spouse of Christ, and who do not lose the hopeful gaze of first love. Priests capable of seeing and feeling the Catholic Church as one and the same, both in the great celebrations and in the hidden confessional. Priests with an open heart like that of the Church to receive everyone, especially and with all possible tenderness, those whom our society excludes and forgets, confirming them in their dignity as beloved sons of the Father. Priests who first rebuke the

Church in themselves, asking for forgiveness of their sins and feeding on the Eucharist and the Word, and then, fraternally as the Gospel says, they encourage themselves to rebuke something in others, without ever throwing away "pearls to the swine" who take advantage of our indiscreet handling of wounds or disagreements to hurt and make fun of our Mother the Church. Priests who summon creatively and tirelessly those whom the Father attracts and brings closer to his Son. Priests who go out to look for those whom Jesus loves to bring them to the flock. Priests who take to the world the Spirit that sanctifies and that creates Church and do not allow the spiritual worldliness to settle in their lives.

I conclude with a fact that appears a little later in this biblical passage. It is striking that those who go from praise to hatred to the point of wanting to throw the Lord over the cliff (cf. Lk 4:29) begin by asking: "Is not this the son of Joseph?" (v. 22). Knowing Jesus and his family was part of ordinary life, and it distanced them from God made flesh. And, on the other hand, to Jesus, the customs of his people do not take him away from the Father or his brothers . . . just the opposite.

I want to ask the Virgin and Saint Joseph today, who knew how to instill in Jesus this love for the ancient Assembly of Israel and its customs, that our love for the Church in all her children and in all her affairs, will have this familiarity. To Our Lady, especially, we priests ask that we may see her face and think in her motherly heart when we speak of the Church and when we attend to the smallest of her children; that we may feel that what we say about the Church we say about her; that what the Lord wants to do in us, as Church, be the same great things that he did in her. We ask her for the grace that our priesthood may make the faithful people of God feel that the Church loves them just as much as they feel loved by Mary.

→� ←

He Is Not Here. He Has Been Raised

Homily, Easter Vigil—April 15, 2001, Year C

The road traveled tonight, through centuries of promises born of the saving heart of God, culminates in a rebuke and an announcement: "Why do you seek the living one among the dead? He is not here, but he has been raised"

(Lk 24:5–6). This rebuke awakens the women from error and deception, and the announcement redirects their lives. As the Gospel indicates, it is a moment of bewilderment and fear for these women who, with much love for Jesus, go early to anoint his dead body. Confusion and fear had already taken hold of them when "they found the stone rolled away from the tomb; but when they entered, they did not find the body of the Lord Jesus" (v. 2–3).

Amid confusion and fear, angels with dazzling garments deliver the announcement that history has reached its fullness, that Jesus has risen. The angels make them come back to themselves, to enter their hearts: "Remember what he said to you . . ."; that it was necessary for the Son of Man to be delivered, crucified, and rise on the third day. "And [the women] remembered his words" (v. 6–8). The memory of the words of Jesus illuminates the event, and their hearts expand: joy, admiration, and the desire to run and announce it. And these feelings are so strong that the disciples think they are delirious.

Tonight, we received the announcement: Christ is risen! The Lord lives! And, for us too, the rebuke is valid: "Why do you look for the living among the dead?" There may be, within us, a kind of impulse that leads us to close the story feeling sadness and failure, to close the door of hope, to prefer to believe that the stone is fixed, and no one can move it. It is true that there are existential moments in which it seems that the dawn comes only to illuminate tombs, and our life is imprisoned there, our search is "among the dead," among the dead things, incapable of giving life hope. Here we are struck by that rebuke: "Why do they look for the living among the dead?" Both in our personal lives and in the society in which we live, sometimes the failures are added to each other and—in a sick way—we get used to living among the graves like the man possessed from among the Gerasenes (cf. Lk 8:26–39). Even more, we can come to believe that this is the law of life, leaving only the fate of yearning for what could have been and was not, and entertaining us by alienating ourselves in an outburst that takes away the memory of God's promise. When this happens to us, then we are sick. When this happens to our society, then it is a sick society.

Today, this Easter in Buenos Aires, the rebuke is directed also to us: "Do not look for the dead among those who are alive." Remember! The rebuke awakens our memory, brings us closer to the power of the promise. We are living in a situation where *we need a lot of memory*. To remember, to bring to our hearts[1] *the great spiritual resource of our people*: the Truth that Jesus is

---

1. *Recordar*, a Spanish word for remembering, comes from the Latin meaning "to bring to the heart."

alive, announced to them in the moments of evangelization and sealed in their simple hearts. To bring to the 'heart' the filial relationship that he won for us with his blood, the validity of the Ten Commandments, the courage to know that sin is a bad business because the devil is a bad payer, that the pacts of impunity are always provisional, and that nobody laughs at God.

We are reminded that it was not a solution of the high priests and elders of that time, who bribed the soldiers to adulterate the truth and "gave a large sum of money" (Mt 28:12) with instructions to say that the disciples had stolen the body. We are reminded that we do not walk alone in history, that we are God's family, and we are asked to look around us and, with the same restlessness of spirit with which the women sought Jesus, look for him in the face of so many of our brothers who live in the margin of indigence, of loneliness, of despair; and we will be judged by the way we treat them.

On this holy night I ask the angels to make us hear those rebukes that will awaken our memory as a faithful people. And, that in the midst of bewilderment and fear, we are given the joy of hope, the one that breaks tombs open and launches the announcement, the one that spends itself conceiving life for others, the one that does not disappoint, which sometimes seems delirious but which every day makes us return to ourselves as did Peter "who went home amazed at what had happened" (Lk 24:12). On this holy night I ask the Virgin Mother to take us out of the quietist resignation of the cemeteries and to whisper in our ears, slowly, as only mothers know how: Jesus rose, he is alive, be encouraged, worship him, and do for your brothers what he did for you. May it be so.

→→ ←←

Whoever Wishes to Be Great Among You Shall Be Your Servant

Homily, Solemn Te Deum *on Independence Day—May 25, 2001*

Then the mother of the sons of Zebedee approached him with her sons and did him homage, wishing to ask him for something. He said to her, "What do you wish?" She answered him, "Command that these two sons of mine sit, one at your right and the other at your left, in your kingdom." Jesus said in reply, "You do not know what you are asking. Can you drink the cup that I am going to drink?" They said to him, "We can." He replied, "My cup you will indeed drink, but to sit at my right and at my left[, this] is not mine to give but is for those for whom it has been prepared by my Father."

When the ten heard this, they became indignant at the two brothers. But Jesus summoned them and said, "You know that the rulers of the Gentiles lord it over them, and the great ones make their authority over them felt. But it shall not be so among you. Rather, whoever wishes to be great among you shall be your servant; whoever wishes to be first among you shall be your slave. Just so, the Son of Man did not come to be served but to serve and to give his life as a ransom for many. (Mt 20:20–28)

1. Clearly, it is not a novelty or something that started in our time—to follow that first impulse when facing someone powerful and wish to obtain some favor. We just heard in the Gospel how the mother of John and James asked Jesus to take her children into account. What is new is the response of the Lord: "You do not know what you are asking. Can you drink the cup that I am going to drink?" What is this cup? The Lord speaks of the cup of *service* and of giving one's life to the point of pouring out one's blood for the loved ones. And even more novel is the change of attitude in his apostles that the Lord achieved. They truly changed, not their lust for greatness but their way of finding it. They went from the whims of small accommodations to the big desire for true power: serving for love. On this Independence Day, I want to dwell on the teaching of the Lord: "Whoever wishes to be great among you shall be your servant; whoever wishes to be first among you must be your slave. *Just so, the Son of Man did not come to be served but to serve* (Mt 20:26–28).

Service is a venerated and manipulated word at the same time. It expresses one of the most original riches of the path traveled by humanity in Jesus Christ, who did not come to be served but to serve, who bent down to wash our feet. . . . Service is bending before the need of the other, to whom, when I bow down, I discover in his need that he is my brother. It is the rejection of indifference and utilitarian selfishness. It is to do on behalf of others and for others. *Service*, a word that gives rise to the desire for a new social bond by letting ourselves be served by the Lord, so that later through our hands, his divine love can descend and build a new humanity, a new way of life. *Service*, a word etched by fire into the heart of our people. From *that spiritual resource* inherited from our grandparents spring our dignity, our ability to work hard and in solidarity, our *tolerant and hopeful serenity*. From service as a central value arise those great attitudes that keep our society integrated, if one knows how to stir the embers of our common heart (nations do have a common heart). I wonder if today we understand, better than those learning disciples, that we have been given a wonderful opportunity, a gift that only God can give: giving ourselves and giving ourselves in full.

2. *Service* is not a mere ethical commitment, nor volunteering from our time of leisure, nor a utopian postulate. . . . Since our life is a gift, to serve is to be faithful to what we are. It is about that intimate capacity to give what one is, to love to the extreme of one's own limits, or, as Mother Teresa taught us, to serve is to "love until it hurts." The words of the Gospel are not directed only to the believer and the practitioner. They address all authority both ecclesiastical and political, since they bring to light the true meaning of power. It is a revolution based on *the new social bond of* service. Power is service. Power only makes sense if it is at the service of the common good. Not much power is needed for the selfish enjoyment of life. In this light we understand that an authentically human society, and therefore also a political one, will not be so, based on the minimalism that merely affirms 'coexistence for survival' or 'the consensus of diverse interests' with economistic aims. Although everything may be thought out and have a place in the always ambiguous reality of men, a society will be authentic only from above, from the best of itself, from the disinterested dedication of ones for the others. When we embark on the path of service, trust is born in us, the desire for heroism is ignited, and our own greatness is discovered.

3. Bearing in mind this reality, it is obvious that cohabiting with power, being determined to deny needs, failing to face contradictions, and accentuating internal hatreds do nothing but prolong the agony of mediocrities. And although we admit the difficulties imposed on us from the outside, ultimately we will always be the ones responsible for our own subjugation and deferral. While some seek to benefit by accentuating the divisions and diverting the focus from the great challenges, the intuitive valuing of the evangelical call that we have heard today arises once again *from the deepest resources of our people*: Drink the cup of service! Our people drink it daily in the service of millions of people who silently give their bodies to work or to search for one, and who do not give it to speculation; in the service of those who support coexistence and silent solidarity and not to the absurd fantasies of the xenophobic ideological minorities, agitators of conflicts; in the service of those who—suffering from the globalization of poverty—have not stopped finding equality in the solidarity of community organizations and in cultural, spontaneous, and creative manifestations. All these women and men of our town, who reject despair and rebel against those mediocrities,

want to say no to anomie, no to nonsense and to the fraudulent superficiality (or even trickery) that encourages consumerism. And finally, no to those who use people who are pessimistic and burdened with bad news to obtain benefits from their pain.

4. From the willingness to serve, shaken by misery and vulnerability, torn by violence and drugs, bombarded by the pressure of escapism of all kinds and forms, we want to be reborn from our own contradictions. We accept the painful cup and we *bring out our best resources as a people* with little press and even less propaganda: with each individual and communitarian effort of solidarity in an extensive network of social organizations; with each researcher and scholar who bets on the search for truth (even if others relativize it or remain silent); with each instructor and teacher who survives adversity; with each producer who continues to bet on the validity of work; with each young person who studies, works, and commits to forming a new family. With the poorest and in all those who work or laboriously seek work, who do not allow themselves to be swept away by destructive marginalization or by the temptation of organized violence, but silently and with the dedication that only faith confers, continue to love their land. They have tasted a cup that, in self-giving and service, has become a *balm and a hope*. In them, *the great cultural and moral resources of our people are manifested*. They are the ones who listen to the word, who avoid ritual applause, who really become an echo and understand that the word is spoken for them, not for others.

5. On this national day I would like us to ask ourselves the question: Are we willing to drink the 'cup' of the 'silent Christs' among our people? To drink from the cup of sorrow and pain of our limits and miseries as a nation but—at the same time—recognizing there the happy wine of conforming to the way of being of the people to whom we belong? To encourage ourselves to serve without pretenses or mediocrities in order to feel worthy and satisfied to be what we are?

We are invited to drink from the cup of *hard and solidary work* that was known from the beginning by the men of our land: work that mixed the indigenous peoples and the Spaniards, despite the many confrontations; work that cost blood for independence and forged the admiration of the world in the dedication of educators, researchers, and scientists; work that awoke the social conscience of millions of underprivileged, as progress for the continent, and who also tasted and taste our arts and letters when they sing with joyful timidity about being Argentines. The cup of *solidary work in service* is the most genuine response to the uncertainty of a country full of unrealized potential or postponed again and again, indefinitely, stopping its course of greatness. It is the answer to the uncertainty of a country damaged by privileges, by those who use power to their advantage on account of representative legitimacy, by those who demand incalculable sacrifices, hidden in their bubbles of abundance, while evading their social responsibility and washing the riches that the effort of all produces; by those who say they listen but do not, who applaud ritualistically without becoming an echo; for those who believe that the words are spoken for others. The rules of the game of today's global reality are a bitter cup, but this must redouble the delivery and ethical effort of a leadership that has no right to demand more from those below if the sacrifice does not come down from above: "Whoever wishes to be great among you will be your servant." "To serve others" before "being served."

6. Today, it is also essential to rescue the *work of solidarity* as a service, the warm embers of *hopeful serenity*, from the embers of bitterness. Indeed, *from the depths of our resources*, in the experiences of the communitarian faith of our history and without being affected by our miseries, so many cultural forms of religiosity and art, of community organizations and of individual or group achievements, must *return to our memory*. Because rescuing *our resources*, the good we have inherited, is the cornerstone to the future.

Just as we cannot promise love going forward without having received it, we cannot feel confident in being Argentine if we do not rescue the goods of the past. And this without sterile resentments, without simplistic revisionisms, without scrutinizing petty things or losing sight of the greatness that helps to build the referential values that every society needs. Let us not forget that when a society takes pleasure in making fun of its intimacy and allows its creative capacity to be trivialized, it becomes dull, and the possibility of being free is eroded by suffocating superficiality. And when these attitudes are proposed to a community whose basic needs are seriously attacked, then violence, addictions, and cultural and social marginality arise as the logical reactions.

Rescuing our memory means, on the contrary, to contemplate the shoots of a soul that resists its oppression. In our people there are popular artistic manifestations where feeling and humaneness come together and there is a return to faith and to the spiritual search before the failure of materialism, scientism, and ideologies. The spontaneous organizations of the community are current forms of socialization and search for the common good. These popular proposals, *emerging from our cultural resources*, transcend sectarianism, partisanship, and petty interests. Now also, as in Argentina yesterday and always, we are seeing a glimpse of indigenes and Spaniards, Creoles and immigrants, and all creeds coming together in pursuit of the common good.

This is what we call *serenity* because it builds solidary goodness, and creative and hopeful joy, because it points beyond self-interests and achievements. It is the outbreak of love as a privileged social bond enjoyed for its own sake, a *serenity* that takes us away from institutionalized violence and is the antidote to disorganized or sponsored violence. And it will be that same serenity that will encourage us to unanimously defend our rights, especially the most urgent: the right to life, the right to receive education and health care (which no policy can postpone), and the irrevocable responsibility to support the elderly, to promote the family (without which there is no humanization or law) and the children, who today are being neglected and despised with impunity.

7. On this Independence Day, the Lord *summons us* to leave all servility and enter the territory of service, that space that extends to where our concern for the common good begins and is the true homeland. Outside the space of service there is no homeland, but a land devastated by struggles of faceless interests.

On this day of the Homeland, the Lord *encourages us* to not be afraid to drink the cup of service. If service makes us equal, displacing false superiorities, if service narrows selfish distances and brings us closer—it makes us neighbors—let us not be afraid: service dignifies us, restoring that dignity that cries out for its place, its height, and its needs.

On this day of the homeland, our people claim us and ask us not to tire of serving, that only then this new social bond that we long for, will be a reality. We have already tasted ad nauseam how our coexistence is eroded by the oppressive abuse of one sector over another, with the inside factions that turn their backs on the big problems, with misguided loyalties, with sectarian or ideological confrontations more or less violent. These dialectics of confrontation lead to national dissolution, annul *encounters* and neighborliness. Service invites us to converge, to mature, to create—in short—a new social dynamic: that of *communion in differences* whose fruit is serenity in justice and peace. A pluralistic communion of all talents and all efforts regardless of their origin. A communion of all those who dare to see others in their deepest dignity.

This is the evangelical proposal that we pose today during the commemoration of the date that is a *living memory of our deepest moral resources as a people*, a proposal that will be, if we take it on, the best tribute to our heroes and to ourselves.

→→ ←←

Everyone Ate Until Satisfied

Homily, Solemnity of Corpus Christi—June 16, 2001, Year C

The Good News of the multiplication of the loaves is one of those events that have been etched forever in the memory of the Church. We will never tire of hearing in amazement what happened that afternoon, the retelling of that 'unprecedented gesture' of Jesus. It was a party, a humble party, a feast of faith. Humble because there were only loaves and fishes, but so superabundant that they gave rise to wonder, faith, the pleasure of sharing the same table and the feeling of fellowship in that bread. . . . We can only imagine the people breaking the bread in surprise and sharing it full of joy with their neighbors.

The memory of the multiplication of the loaves (together with that of the Wedding at Cana) has remained in our hearts as *the gospel of disproportion*. What came out of the Lord's hands giving the blessing was an outpouring of bread: the five loaves became five thousand. The disproportion was beyond all human calculation, that 'realistic' calculation, almost mathematical, that led the disciples to say with skepticism: 'Unless we go to buy bread to feed all this crowd.' There was overabundance, and everyone ate until they were satisfied. And there was even waste: they collected the leftovers, twelve baskets. A waste in which nothing was lost, so different from the scandalous waste that we are used to by some rich and famous people.

The message of the Gospel is clear, transparent, warm, and strong: *Where Jesus is, human measures disappear*. And, paradoxically, the disproportion of God is more human (more realistic, simpler, truer, more realizable) than our calculations. The disproportion of God is realistic and achievable because it looks at the warmth of the bread that invites distribution and not the coldness of the money that seeks the isolation of bank deposits.

The miracle of the loaves is not a magical solution. In the middle of it is the same Jesus with his hands in the dough. It is a Jesus who distributes himself and gives himself in each piece of bread; a Jesus who expands his table, the one he shared with his friends, and makes room for all the people; a Jesus who can do all things with bread and fish. How beautiful it is to look at the simple signs, the small things that Jesus works with: water, wine, bread, and fish! With these simple things the Lord is omnipotent. *His hands* are at ease blessing and breaking the bread. I would be encouraged to say that the Lord overflows only in those actions that he can accomplish with *his hands*: blessing, healing, caressing, distributing, shaking hands, and lifting up, washing feet, showing scars, allowing himself to be scarred. . . . The Lord does not have verbal excesses or pompous actions. Jesus wants to be almighty by breaking the bread with *his hands*.

The action of the Lord is an 'unprecedented gesture' because his best miracle is spent on something as fleeting as a lunch of bread and fish. Jesus bets on the strength of the elementary and the everyday. The action of Jesus is an 'unprecedented gesture' because it is an all-powerful one that uses the mediation of the humble use of *his own hands* together *with everyone's hands*. The miracle of the loaves was a miracle performed ecclesially by all those who shared their bread.

From this miracle of disproportion, we can carry a beautiful image in our hearts today: that of *the hands*. The feast of Corpus Christi is *the feast of the hands*, of *the hands of the Lord* and of *our hands*, of those "holy and venerable hands" of Jesus, wounded hands, that continue to bless and distribute the bread of the Eucharist. And those hands of ours, needy and sinful, extended humbly and opened to receive with faith the body of Christ.

May the divine bread transform our empty hands into full hands, with that measure that the Lord promises to those who are generous with their talents: "packed together, shaken down, and overflowing" (Lk 6:38). May the sweet weight of the Eucharist leave its mark of love in our hands so that, anointed by Christ, they become hands that welcome and support the weakest ones. May the warmth of the consecrated bread burn into our hands the effective desire to share such a great gift with those who hunger for bread, for justice, and for God. May the tenderness of communion with that Jesus who is unreservedly placed in our hands in a true 'unprecedented gesture,' open the eyes of our hearts to *hope* in order to feel present to the God who is "every day with us" and accompanies us along the way.

I ask Mary, who prophesied the multiplication of the loaves in the *Magnificat* when she announced the God who "has shown might with his arm . . . The hungry he has filled with good things; the rich he has sent away empty" (Lk 1:51a, 53), to intercede before her Son so that once again he will look with love on our people who need to make an unprecedented gesture. May she ask Jesus, found in our midst, to once again give us the bread of the Eucharist with his hands so that we may enter into communion with him and learn to share as brothers. Then *our hands* will feel the *disproportion* of God and will be encouraged to amass that 'unprecedented gesture' that inspires us with generosity and brings us out of despair.

➤➤ ◀◀

Be Engaged So You Can Help Engage Others

Letter to Catechists—August 2001

Dear brother and sister catechist,

Every second Saturday of March we have the opportunity to meet at the EAC (Archdiocesan Catechetical *Encounter*). There together we continue the annual time for catechists, focusing on a theme idea that will accompany us throughout the year. It is an intense moment for meeting, celebration, and communion, which I value very much, and I am sure that you do, too.

As we approach the feast of Saint Pius X, patron saint of catechists, I would like to address each one of you through this letter. In the midst of the activities, when fatigue begins to be felt, I wish to encourage you, as a father and brother, and invite you to stop and reflect together on some aspect of catechetical ministry.

I am aware that, as a bishop, I am called to be the first catechist of the diocese. . . . But above all, I would like, by these means, to overcome the anonymity of the great city, which often prevents the personal *encounters* we all seek. In addition, this can be another means to draw common lines within the archdiocesan catechetical ministry, that might allow a deeper unity within the normal and healthy plurality of a city as big and complex as Buenos Aires.

In this letter, I prefer not to dwell on some aspect of catechetical praxis, but rather *on the person of the catechist.*

Numerous documents remind us that the entire Christian community is responsible for catechesis. And that's logical, since catechesis is an aspect

of evangelization. And evangelization is done by the whole Church. Therefore, this teaching and deepening in the mystery of the person of Christ
"should be taken care of not only by catechists or priests, but by the entire
community of the faithful..." (AG 16). Catechesis would be seriously com-
promised if it were relegated to the isolated and solitary action of catechists.
That is why all efforts made in this awareness will never be enough. The path
undertaken years ago, in search of an organic pastoral, has contributed signifi-
cantly to a greater commitment of the entire Christian community in this responsibility of Christian initiation and educating in the maturity of the faith.
In the context of the Christian community's shared responsibility to transmit
the faith, I cannot help but rescue *the reality of the person of the catechist.*

The Church recognizes in the catechist a ministry that, throughout history, has allowed Jesus to be known from one generation to the next. The
Church recognizes in this portion of the People of God, not in an exclusive
way, but in a privileged way, the chain of witnesses about which the *Catechism of the Catholic Church* tells us:

> *The believer [who] has received faith from others ... is thus a link in the great chain
> of believers. I cannot believe without being carried by the faith of others, and by my
> faith I help support others in the faith.* (CCC 166)

All of us, remembering our own personal process of growth in the faith,
discovered the faces of simple catechists who, with their witness of life and
their generous giving, helped us to know and fall in love with Christ. I remember with affection and gratitude Sister Dolores, of the School of Mercy
in Flores. She prepared me for First Communion and Confirmation. Another of my catechists was still living until a few months ago. It was good
for me to visit her, to receive her or call her on the phone. Today there are
many young people and adults who silently, humbly, and *in the field* continue to be the Lord's instruments for building community and making the
Kingdom present.

That is why today I think of each catechist, highlighting an aspect that
has greater urgency given the current circumstances we live in: *The personal
relationship of the catechist with the Lord.*

John Paul II warns us clearly in the apostolic letter *Novo millennio ineunte:*

> *Ours is a time of continual movement which often leads to restlessness, with the risk
> of "doing for the sake of doing." We must resist this temptation by trying "to be"
> before trying "to do." In this regard we should recall how Jesus reproved Martha:
> "You are anxious and troubled about many things; one thing is needful" (Lk
> 10:41–42).* (NMI 15)

The personal encounter with the Lord is in the *very essence and vocation* of every Christian. To seek God is to seek his Face, is to enter into intimacy with him. Every vocation, and much more that of the catechist, presupposes the question: "'Rabbi' . . . , 'where are you staying?' He said to them, 'Come and you will see'" (Jn 1:38–39). *The quality of our catechetical ministry will emerge from the quality of the response, from the depth of the encounter.* The Church is founded on this "come and see." A personal encounter and intimacy with the Master are the foundations of true discipleship and give catechesis its genuine flavor. It also removes the ever-present stalking by any rationalisms and ideologies that take away vitality and sterilize the Good News.

Catechesis needs *holy catechists*, who inspire with their mere presence, who help with their living testimony to overcome an individualistic civilization dominated by "a minimalist ethic and a shallow religiosity" (NMI 31). Today, more than ever, there is an urgent need *to allow ourselves to be found by Love, which always has the initiative, to help men to experience the Good News of the encounter.*

Today more than ever, behind so many demands made by our people, one can discover a search for the Absolute that, at times, takes the shape of a painful cry from an outraged humanity: "We would like to see Jesus" (Jn 12:21). There are many faces making this request of us, through a silence more telling than a thousand words. We know them well. They are in our midst; they are part of that faithful people that God entrusts to us. Faces of children, of young people, of adults. . . . Some of them have the pure look of the "beloved disciple," others the downward gaze of the prodigal son. There is no shortage of faces marked by pain and despair. But all of them hope, seek, want to see Jesus. And that is why they

> "ask believers, not only to 'speak' of Christ, but in a certain sense to 'show' him to them. . . . Our witness, however, would be hopelessly inadequate if we ourselves had not first contemplated his face." (NMI 16)

Today, more than ever, the present difficulties oblige those whom God calls to console their people, to take root in prayer, so that we may "confront the most paradoxical aspect of his mystery, as it emerges in his last hour, on the Cross" (25). Only from a personal encounter with the Lord can we perform a *diaconia* of tenderness, without breaking or letting ourselves be overwhelmed by the presence of pain and suffering.

Today, more than ever, it is necessary that every movement toward the brother, every ecclesial ministry, have the resources and be founded on closeness and familiarity with the Lord, just as Mary's visit to Elizabeth, rich in gestures of service and joy, is understood and becomes a reality only from the profound experience of encounter and listening that took place in the silence of Nazareth.

Our people are tired of words: They do not need so many teachers, but witnesses:

> And the witness is strengthened in interiority, in the encounter with Jesus Christ. Every Christian, but much more the catechist, must be permanently a disciple of the Master in the art of praying. "We have to learn to pray: as it were learning this art ever anew from the lips of the Divine Master himself, like the first disciples: 'Lord, teach us to pray!' (Lk 11:1). Prayer develops that conversation with Christ which makes us his intimate friends: 'Abide in me and I in you'" (Jn 15:4). (NMI 32)

That is why Jesus' invitation to "put out into deep water" must be understood as a call to encourage us to abandon ourselves in the depth of prayer that allows us to avoid being thorns that suffocate the seed. Sometimes our fishing is unsuccessful because we do not do it in his name, or because we are too worried about our nets . . . and we forget to do it with and for him.

These times are not easy; they are not for passing enthusiasms, for spasmodic, sentimental, or gnostic spiritualities. The Catholic Church has a rich spiritual tradition, with numerous and varied teachers who can guide and nurture a true spirituality that today makes possible the *diaconia* of listening and the ministry of *encounter*. In the careful and receptive reading of chapter III of the letter of John Paul II, *Novo millenio ineunte*, you will find the inspiring source of much of what I wanted to share with you. Simply, to finish, I dare to ask you to reinforce three fundamental aspects in the spiritual life of every Christian and much more in that of a catechist.

The Personal and Living Encounter through a Prayerful Reading of the Word of God

I thank the Lord because his Word is more and more present in the meetings of catechists. I also know that there are many advances in the biblical formation of catechists. But it would be risky to remain with a cold exegesis or to use the text of the Sacred Scripture if the personal encounter were missing, the irreplaceable rumination that each believer and each community must make of the Word so that the "life-giving encounter, in the ancient and ever valid tradition of *lectio divina*, which draws from the biblical text the living word which questions, directs and shapes our lives" (NMI 39).

The catechist will thus find the inspiring source of all his pedagogy, which will necessarily be marked by the love that becomes a reaching out, an offering and communion.

The Personal and Living Encounter through the Eucharist

This close and daily presence of the Risen Lord until the end of time is experienced joyfully by all, as Church. It is the central mystery of our faith, which makes communion real and strengthens us in the mission. The *Catechism of the Catholic Church* reminds us that in the Eucharist we find all the goodness of the Church. In it we have the certainty that God is faithful to his promise and has remained until the end of time (cf. Mt 28:20).

During the visit and adoration of the Blessed Sacrament, we experience the closeness of the Good Shepherd, the tenderness of his love, the presence of a faithful friend. We have all experienced the great help that faith offers, the intimate and personal dialogue with the Sacramental Lord. And the catechist cannot give up this beautiful vocation of telling what he has contemplated (cf. 1 Jn 1ff.).

As we break bread we are once again challenged to imitate his dedication and to renew the unprecedented gesture of multiplying the actions of solidarity. From the Eucharistic banquet the Church experiences Communion and is invited to make real the miracle of *closeness* by which it is possible in this globalized world to give a space to the brother and make the poor feel at home in each community (cf. NMI 50). The catechist is called to make the doctrine become message and the message become life. Only in this way can the proclaimed Word be celebrated and be truly constituted as a sacrament of Communion.

The Communal and Festive Meeting of the Sunday Celebration

In the Sunday Eucharist, the Passover is relived, the Passing of the Lord who wanted to enter history to make us sharers in his divine life. It gathers us every Sunday as the family of God gathered around the altar, who feeds on the Living Bread, and who brings and celebrates what happened on the way, to renew its strength and keep on shouting that he lives among us. In each Sunday Mass we experience the warmth of belonging to the People of God to which we were incorporated by Baptism and we "remember" the "first day of the week" (Mk 16:2,9). In today's world, often sick of secularism and consumerism, it seems we are losing the ability to celebrate, to live as a family.

For this reason, the catechist is called to commit his or her life so that Sunday will not be taken from us, helping to ensure that the party continues in the heart of man and that his weekly pilgrimage takes on meaning and fullness.

Saint Therese of Lisieux, with that power of synthesis proper to great and simple souls, writes to one of her sisters, summarizing what the Christian life consists of: "To love him and make him be loved. . . ." This is also the reason for being of every catechist. *Only if there is a personal encounter can one be an instrument for others to find him.*

In greeting you for Catechist Day, I would like to thank you from the bottom of my heart for all your dedication to the service of the faithful People. And to ask Mary, Most Holy, to keep that thirst for God alive in your heart so that you never tire of looking for his face.

Do not stop praying for me to be a good catechist. May Jesus bless you and the Blessed Virgin take care of you.

→→ ←←

The Word Seemed Already to Wipe Away Our Tears

Homily, Shrine of Saint Cajetan—August 7, 2001

Blessed are they who mourn, for they will be comforted! (Mt 5:4)

Dear brothers, dear friends and faithful of Saint Cajetan,

Last year we read here the parable of the Good Samaritan through whom Jesus always opens our eyes to that great truth: He is mysteriously present within the poorest; he is present in the suffering and needs of every person in the flesh. When we approach the one who has needs and we draw closer, our hearts soften, our eyes open, and we see Jesus. When we pass by or look at those in need from afar, our hearts harden, and we do not see Jesus. Do you remember? And I recalled that the way to not pass by such a need as there is in our people today is to keep our hope burning. While we fight for justice and live in solidarity, we must keep our hope alive.

On this day, with the Gospel of the Beatitudes, the Lord goes a step further in his teaching: pain is not only something that calls for help and

demands solutions. Pain, if it is lived as Christ teaches us, also hides a blessing and even a certain joy; a painful joy, certainly, but genuine. How comforting it is to listen all together, as a people gathered by faith, to this
Gospel about the Beatitudes of Jesus! Jesus approaches the things that hurt
us, that give us fear, that worry us, that give us anguish . . . and transforms
them with his Word, with that Word so nearby and such a companion, word
of a friend and word of God.

We can say that when *Jesus approaches our pain, things look differently*:
Jesus speaks to us about the poor, those who are hungry, those who mourn,
those who are unjustly persecuted . . . but there is hope in his tone of voice,
it even comforts us to hear it. Blessed are you who now mourn because you
will be consoled, he says. And that word seems as if it were already wiping
away our tears.

And something else happens. When Jesus says: Poor you, the rich, those
who are now satisfied, those who now laugh, those who only receive praises . . .
rather than making us angry, we feel sorry for these people that Jesus talks
about. It is as if we see their folly, and know that they will end up badly.

The contrasting images that Jesus uses in the beatitudes remind me of
those we see in the news: poor people in the street and rich people celebrating lavishly; the poor persecuted for demanding jobs and the rich who elude
justice and, on top of that, are applauded; people who cry because of violence and people having fun as if they lived in the best of all possible worlds;
people who are hungry and people who throw food away. . . . It seems like a
newscast. And yet, Jesus values things differently from how the news does.
He looks deeply into the reality of life and tells us: Alas! to the heart that
does not know how to mourn. Alas! to the heart that does not hunger and
thirst for justice; alas! to the heart that does not feel poor in love. Alas! to
the heart that is swollen by vanity . . . it is a poor heart, a heart that will end
up hardened, despised, alone.

Jesus looks deep into the hearts of each one of us, who is saddened and
burdened by problems of getting a job, and he says: Blessed are you here,
waiting in line to ask for bread and work. Blessed are you who have a humble
heart and do not feel either better or worse than your brother at your side.
Blessed are you who have no privilege to take pride in, except for being my
beloved child. Blessed are you who have that pain that is hunger and thirst
for justice and who know how to denounce and protest, but without harming anyone, and before doing anything you come to ask your God and Lord.
Blessed are you who do good and many times are misunderstood and criticized, but do not lower your embrace of hope. Blessed are you who know

how to cry meekly and wait only for God. . . . Blessed, not for what you lack
or because all your sufferings will be resolved (there is always some suffering), but blessed because the gift of God is so great that you can receive it
only if your heart is wide open. That is why *Jesus calls blessed those who allow
their hearts to be opened and enlarged by the things that happen to them.*

From among all the beatitudes I want to stop for a moment on the bless-
edness of tears, because it makes us taste the blessings of Jesus and *opens
our hearts* to God while we pray waiting in line and ask our beloved Saint
Cajetan for all our needs.

The blessing of those who mourn invites us to mourn for our country,
with that prayer as old as the prayer of lamentation, in which a people, leaving behind vain illusions and false gods, know to repent of their sins and
turn their eyes to the only true God, the only one capable of saving. It is as
if Jesus told us: Blessed are you who mourn for our country with those tears
that are not only from one but from everybody, with the tears of the one
who prays the Lord's Prayer and when he says bread, he says *our* daily bread,
and when he says forgiveness, he says "forgive us *our* trespasses."

The blessing to those who mourn also reminds us of the weeping of our
family. It is as if Jesus were telling us: Blessed are you who mourn when the
family sleeps and no one sees you, and squeeze my cross hard between your
hands until you are strengthened. Because within the tears of a mother or
a father who cries for their children hides the best prayer that can be made
on this earth: that prayer of silent and meek tears that is like the prayer of
Our Lady at the foot of the Cross, who knows how to be at her Son's side,
accompanying and interceding without making outbursts or scandals.

Blessed are those who weep when approaching Saint Cajetan, asking for
bread and work, and in that tear that barely appears, they confide their request and their prayer with few words, assured that they have been heard
and taken care of. Saint Cajetan intercedes for your faithful people, for all
the Argentine people. And in these hard times, we redouble our faith and
our trust in Jesus our Lord. He has promised us that he himself, in person,
will take care of wiping away our tears. Blessed are we if we put all our hope
in him.

The blessing to those who mourn reminds us, finally, of our crying as
children. It is as if Jesus told us: Blessed are you who cry as you did when
you were children and your mother consoled you. It is true what they say
that only God our Lord and our mothers can truly comfort us. For that reason, we placed our tears before the eyes of the Virgin, and while "we send
up our sighs, mourning and weeping in this vale of tears" we say to her: "Turn

then, most gracious Advocate, thine eyes of mercy toward us, and after this our exile, show unto us the blessed fruit of thy womb, Jesus. . . ."

→» ‹←

The Human Dimension Is Key
to the Sociopolitical Task

*Spontaneous Remarks at Archdiocesan Days for Social Ministry—
December 13, 2001 (Transcript)*

This is a place for *encounter*, dialogue. A place without exclusions. A place where all present are responsible, in one way or another, for helping our people through social and political activity.

Some things you said impressed me, and I want to revisit them very briefly, by way of conclusion.

The person of the politician. One from among the citizens that has more responsibility for not distorting politics and, in that sense today more than ever, we are asked for a commitment to rehabilitate politics. Because when we want to blame someone we blame the politicians, and that blame is generalized to politics, and politics is one of the highest forms of charity, because it points to the common good.

The political vocation is a vocation—here I strain the word, only to indicate its nobility—an almost sacred vocation, because it means to help the growth of the common good.

There was talk of a transversal policy. It is urgent and rightly so. No more fragmentation and closed-in 'game reserves.' I would say that there is no transversality if there is no dialogue. If ideas do not come into confrontation searching for the common good, we become paralyzed. This is a good way to reorient politics in a creative direction.

Politics, I want to stress, is not only for managing crises. That may be true momentarily, to help emerge from a crisis. But it cannot be reduced to the management of crises. This would be like saying: "Well, everything has calmed down, now let's rest."

Creativity, fruitfulness. Let's etch that phrase "politics is not for managing crises" deep in our hearts. Sometimes we have to put out a fire, but the vocation of the politician is not to be a fireman. Politics is for creating, fertilizing.

In this state, uniting the political with the social, I want to remark on a problem that worries me and that may be a temptation in the face of the social crisis: that crisis management will lead the State to forgo its responsibility for social advancement and assistance. It is antihuman to privatize social advancement and social assistance. On this point the State must assume the role of facilitating, integrating, taking responsibility, auditing, and delegating, but it cannot decline the responsibility that is given to it by its own vocation: to take care of the common good of the people.

I said that this was a place for dialogue and human participation. And it is different when one meets through writings, articles, or from a distance or a bad confrontation, than when one meets in a relaxed atmosphere, knowing that we think differently, we have different points of view but we participate extensively, humanly, in the search for the common good.

The human dimension is key in the sociopolitical task, where the human person—every man and every woman—is the center of concern, the goal of action and also its subject. That is to say, we will create this human task if we integrate with others, not as professionals only, but as man and as woman—that is, put the meat on the grill.[1]

And the human, which is the value, is the opposite of the antivalue. The antivalue today, in my opinion, is human merchandise, that is, the commercialization of people. Man and woman become one more piece of merchandise in projects that come from outside, that take root in society and that somehow go against our human dignity. That is the antivalue. The human person as merchandise in the sociopolitical-economic system.

And regarding this value, the human, and its antivalue, human merchandise, I point to the two ends of life as a personal concern:

Children today are at risk, due to poor diet and bad or insufficient education, of not having the capacity to be fully integrated into society. It is possible we are creating a caste of *minus-habentes* (intellectually disabled). A child who does not have enough protein during the first two years of life will fall into the category of oligophrenia (mental and physical retardation). That is something we must avoid.

Today, childhood is being neglected and despised with impunity. We raised up our arms in horror when we read about the ship of slave boys

---

1. For Argentines, the expression "to put meat on the grill" means to follow through on a commitment.

recently in the newspapers.[2] That does not happen only there, it happens every time there isn't a childhood policy that saves the human person, the center of the person as a value. I mark that as a big concern.

And the other end of life: *older adults, the elderly.* With these two poles of life you cannot experiment, you should not experiment. Life must grow in children so that they can make a rich, big, and full contribution to society. And in the elderly must grow the wisdom they have accumulated throughout life.

That's what I wanted to tell you. Thank you again for participating.

➤➤ ◄◄

A Light That Is the Hope of the People of God

Homily, Christmas Mass during the Night—December 24, 2001, Year A

"The people who walked in darkness / have seen a great light" (Is 9:2). Isaiah's prophecy promises, amid the darkness, a great light. A light that is the hope of the people of God. A light that gives faith its foundation, its fidelity to God. That light is born in Bethlehem, it is gathered by Mary's maternal hands, by Joseph's affection, by the shepherds' haste. And they took responsibility for the hope of an entire people. Mary took responsibility in her solitude and her surprise when the angel said: "Nothing is impossible with God" (Lk 1:37), and she believed and took responsibility for the hope. Joseph took responsibility for that hope, when noticing the signs of motherhood and having decided to leave her in secret he listened to the angel's voice and accepted her, even though his heart didn't understand. On that sad night, when all the doors were closed, both took responsibility. They believed that the child was the hope and they took responsibility in that very adverse situation. They took charge when they went to the temple and recognized in these two elders the wisdom of all the people. Joseph and Mary took responsibility of that hope, when faced with the order: "Get up, take the child and his mother and flee to Egypt . . . for Herod is about to search for

---

2. The reference is to reports highlighting the slave trade from Africa to Europe by way of Libya.

the child, to destroy him" (Mt 2:13). Joseph and Mary took responsibility for that hope during those three days of anguish when the Child stayed in the Temple. And she—after so many years—returned to take responsibility for that hope in the dark midday of Calvary.

Today we are asked, facing this Child who is the light that illumines the darkness—the promised hope—to take responsibility as the two of them did. That we may take responsibility for that hope believing that nothing is impossible with God. Let us take responsibility in the midst of desolation and for tearing down the doors that are closed. Let us turn our efforts and our activity into building. Let us take responsibility for our elderly, who are the hope of a people because they are its wisdom. Let us take responsibility for our children, who are crushed and deprived of their faith by this civilization of consensus and devaluation. To take responsibility for hope is to walk with Jesus in the darkest moments of the cross, in moments when things are not explained and we do not know how they will proceed. Today the Argentines do not explain many things to us; neither do we know how they will proceed. Today it would be good if when looking at the child, Mary, and Joseph we would feel a voice: "Get up, take the Child and his mother, walk on the path of hope." Let us take responsibility for hope. That's what I want to ask tonight. It's that simple. Jesus is hope: Let us take responsibility for this hope. Let's do it working, praying, worshiping God, striving, not resting, looking for someone who had the doors shut, to open others for him or her; finding our elderly who suffer so much today and ask for their wisdom; taking care of the children.

Today, in the midst of this Argentine darkness, a light dawns, who is neither Tom, Dick, nor Harry but Jesus Christ. The only one that gives hope that does not disappoint. Let us take responsibility for Jesus Christ, for this hope and all its consequences as Mary and Joseph did. And today I would like to pray with my people the prayer that one of the great poets of our country prayed one sad Christmas night, asking the Lord to grant us the grace to take responsibility:

> Lord, who never denied me anything,
> I ask nothing for myself; I ask only
> For every aching brother,
> For every poor person in my beloved land.
> I ask you for their bread and their daily wages,
> For their pain as defeated birds,
> For their laughter, their song and their whistle,
> Today when the house fell silent.

With words, I ask you on my knees,
A crumb of your wonders,
A crust of love for their hands,
A hope, only an open door;
Today that the table was deserted
And they cry in the night, my brothers.
May it be so.

2002

You Are Anointed to Preach, to Heal, to Liberate

Homily, Chrism Mass—March 28, 2002, Year A

We are filled with hope by the image of an anointed Jesus consecrated to anoint his people, beginning with the neediest. This image also marks for us the road to follow at this moment of deep crisis in the life of our nation. The Father anoints his Son to be a man 'for' others. He anoints and sends him to announce the good news, to heal, to liberate. . . . Just as there is nothing in the Son that does not come from the Father, there is nothing in him that is not 'for' us. Jesus is anointed to anoint. And we, his priests, are also anointed to anoint.

In this image, something special draws our attention: Jesus reads Isaiah, sits down, and proclaims with devotion and simple majesty: "Today this scripture passage is fulfilled in your hearing" (Lk 4:21). Although the Lord had already been teaching in the synagogues (cf. v. 15) and his fame had spread throughout the region, it is evident that he is just beginning his mission. So, how is it possible to talk about fulfillment? This way of speaking shocked his countrymen, and they challenged him: What we have heard you did in Capernaum, do it here in your land, too (cf. v. 23). It's like saying to him: You, the anointed one, should try new miracles. This request for more signs will be a constant theme of those who refused to believe in Jesus.

It also gets our attention that the Lord speaks of fulfillment when he has just begun his mission. And does not that inner phrase resonate with us sometimes? Why don't you do, here and now, those miracles that we have heard you did then? This phrase makes us different from the ways of the Anointed One—in Jesus the promises are fulfilled every day . . . and when we do not see or can not see, the Gospel phrase should be: "I do believe, help my unbelief!"

The same thing that happens with the renewal each day in the Eucharist with simple bread also happens with the health and liberation that the Lord gives us. We can say that all the actions of the Anointed One, his announcements, his healings, the vision that he communicates to us, and the freedom he gives us, are characterized by simplicity. They are ordinary gestures and actions. They suffice for today, and—although their anointing was "once and forever"—they need constant renewal, constant updating, constant rootedness in the simplicity of every moment of our history.

This is how Jesus acts. For Jesus to heal a sick person from a particular illness meant also to anoint him to become, together with his anointed pain, a witness to the love of God associated with the saving Passion of the Lord. For Jesus, to give sight to the blind is not only so that they can see their own interests for themselves without the help of others; rather, it is to anoint the eyes so that faith will spring up and the practice of charity will be strengthened thanks to the joy that comes from "seeing what is not seen," from seeing with hope. Jesus liberates the oppressed not in the sense that by relieving them of any burdens they can run a race alone through life. Rather, to free ourselves from all slavery is to anoint, so that the anointed burden becomes the saving burden of the cross; and that, freed from all oppression, we can carry our cross with courage in order to follow the Lord by helping others to carry their own.

What I mean is that, because of its overabundance, anointing falls on the innermost being of the person, and not so much on the 'things' that it affects. The depth and efficacy of the anointing of the Lord are not measured by the number of miracles he can perform, or by how far he gets in his mission, or by the severity of his suffering. . . . The depth, which reaches the core of his bones, and the efficacy that makes all of him be salvation for those who approach him, lie in his intimate union and total identification with the Father who sent him. It is the anointing with which Jesus lives his union with the Father that precisely makes all his actions a fulfillment. The anointing is what transforms his time into *kairos*, into a time of permanent grace.

The mission is fulfilled "today" because the Lord not only gives bread but he himself also becomes bread. That liberation that he gives to the oppressed is fulfilled "today" because the Lord not only forgives, 'cleaning the stains' in other people's garments, but he himself 'becomes sin,' gets dirty, stays with the sores . . . and places himself in the hands of the Father who accepts him. That good news is fulfilled "today" because the Lord not only announces that he is going to do certain things, but he himself is the criterion that enables us to see through the light shed by each of his words.

We too, dear brothers in the priesthood, are anointed to anoint. Anointed, that is to say, united to the marrow of our bones with Jesus and with the Father. Like Baptism, the priestly anointing works from the inside to the outside. Contrary to what it seems, the priesthood is not a grace that comes from the outside and never stops entering the depth of our sinful hearts. We are priests in the most intimate, holy, and mysterious parts of our hearts, there where we are children by Baptism and dwelling places for the Trinity. Our moral effort is to anoint, with the deepest anointing, our external and daily actions, so that our whole life becomes, through our collaboration, what we already are by grace.

Anointed to anoint, that is, to incorporate every person into this union with the Father and the Son in the same Spirit. May the priestly anointing turn us into Bread while we anoint the daily bread in the consecration in each Eucharist and share it in solidarity with our brothers. May the priestly anointing turn us into men full of tenderness, while we anoint with balm the sick person's pain. May the priestly anointing liberate us from our sins while we anoint our brothers' sins with the Spirit of forgiveness, and help them carry their cross. May the priestly anointing turn us into the light of the world as we devotedly preach the Gospel following the Lord's command, and teach to observe everything that he told us. May the priestly anointing anoint our time and the use we make of it so that it becomes a "time of grace" for our brothers, while we follow—in the ecclesial rhythm of the Breviary— the ordinary course of the life the Lord gives us.

In the climate of lack of credibility in which we live, and in which every public person has to render accounts every day, may we not have the same experience as the compatriots of the Lord. May we not seek or claim any more trust than that which comes from the Anointing of Christ. As John says: "As for you, the anointing that you received from him remains in you, so that you do not need anyone to teach you. But his anointing teaches you about everything and is true and not false; just as it taught you, remain in him" (1 Jn 2:27). Only what is lived and done with anointing is worthy of trust. May Mary, who was the first to fully experience the presence of the Anointed within her, fill us with the joy of her hopeful vision and with her ecclesial tenderness open up for us the area in which—through our hands— the anointing of God may pass on to his faithful people.

＋＞ ＜＋

This Event Changes for Us the Meaning of History

Easter Vigil—March 30, 2002, Year A

The Gospel tells us about the women on the road to the tomb. They knew that Jesus was dead, and they walked in the certainty of this fact.

The unexpected occurs; the stone has been removed; an angel tells them, "Do not be afraid . . . he has been raised" (Mt 28:5–6). The fact transforms itself into an event; an event that changes for them the meaning of life, that changes for us the meaning of history. He tells them, "Go to Galilee and there you will see him." They return, and on the way they meet Jesus, and he also gives them the same command: Do not fear, tell my brothers to go to Galilee, and there they will see me.

It seems that everything has changed direction. Instead of going to the tomb, they have to retrace their steps, return to the Galilee where they first encountered Jesus, the Galilee where they first admired him and felt the awe that made them exclaim, "We have found the Messiah" (Jn 1:41). Time erodes. The memory of that first encounter had been lost. In the passage of time we always run the risk of losing our memory but he points the way: Return to the memory of the first encounter, return to the memory of the first love.

The event of the Resurrection of Jesus Christ invites all of us to retrace our steps toward the first call, the first encounter; to contemplate it, now with the hope that gives the certainty of victory, the certainty of prevailing. Returning to that first meeting, reliving what it was, but with the conviction that this journey was not in vain. It was a way of the cross, but also of victory.

And tonight, I cannot stop thinking about our people who today, in sadness, are facing a sealed stone that speaks of death, corruption, defeat. On this night, we are also reminded that everything is not yet finished; that there is hope; that death, corruption, and defeat promise nothing. And tonight we are told of hope, of promise, and we are invited to what? To retrace our steps, to reconnect with the road that forged us as a nation.

Today we ask that each one of us, in light of the event of Jesus Christ, look at our history, that we re-encounter it. Today we are asked to seek forgiveness. We are asked to make reparations, we are asked to work in the hope that the resurrection of Christ may become real in each of our lives, in our entire homeland. To retrace our steps!

And when I speak of the road, of the road traveled, I cannot fail to mention those who have walked the longest on the road of life: my dear elders, the wisdom of our people. To them I say: Do not fear. We know you are suffering much. We know that selfishness, ambition, theft, and corruption have taken away your rights and have brought you to the limits of your strength. But we also know that you can help us to retrace our steps as a nation, to recover what you sowed. To you we say in a special way: Christ has risen. There is our hope. Take us by the hand and help us to return to the Galilee of our first love.

On this night, when a fact is transformed into an event, let us see the power of the resurrection of Jesus Christ that is capable of changing things from within, of changing our hearts, changing our homeland. There is our hope. Let us not put it into promises, most of which, in the long run, become idols. How many things have we heard that they promised us! . . . How many things! . . . Let us not be fooled. The Lord is not there, in those promises.

He is risen. Retrace your steps. Go to the Galilee of the first love. As a people let us retrace our steps joining hands with our elders, who are our wisdom, and there we will find our first love again and will be able to be reborn as a nation. In a special way, I ask her who never lost faith, who never forgot her first love, who did not need to retrace her steps because her road was always alive in her heart. May Mary protect us as we retrace our steps to what gave us our foundation. May it be so.

→► ◄←

One's Word and Friendship

Message to the Educational Community—March 31, 2002

In life there are moments (few, but essential) when it is necessary to make decisions that are critical, total, and foundational. Critical, because they lie exactly on the line that separates commitment from hesitation, hope from disaster, life from death. Total, because they do not relate to an aspect, an optional 'matter' or 'challenge,' or a specific area of reality, but define a life in its entirety and for a long time. More than that, they shape the innermost identity of each individual. They not only take place in time but also give shape to our temporality and existence. It is in this sense that I use the third adjective: foundational. They create the basis for a way of life, a manner of being, of seeing and presenting ourselves to the world and to others, a certain position toward future possibilities.

Today I want to share with you the perception that we are precisely at one of these decisive moments. Not individually, but as a nation. It is a conviction shared by many, including the Holy Father, as he explained to us on our latest episcopal visit to Rome. Argentina is now at the brink of a critical, global, fundamental decision, to be taken by each one of its inhabitants: the decision to continue being a country, to learn from the painful experience of these years and start out on a new road, or to sink into dire poverty, chaos, loss of values, and decomposition as a society.

A Renewed and Audacious Hope

The purpose of this meditation is not to reinforce the feeling of threat, but on the contrary to encourage hope. I would like to expand on the reflections I shared with you a couple of years ago, but now from the specific and decisive experience of these recent months. Hope is the virtue of the arduous yet possible; it invites us, yes, to never stop trying, not in a purely willful manner, but by finding the best way to keep up our effort and use it for something real and specific. It's a virtue that sometimes pushes us to come forward, shout, and shake off our tendencies toward inaction, resignation, and failure. Yet, at other times, it invites us to keep quiet and suffer, nourishing our interior with the desires, ideals, and resources that will enable us—when the opportune moment, *the kairos*, arrives—to create more humane, more just, more fraternal realities. Hope not only relies on the resources of human beings but also tries to act in harmony with the work of God, who gathers up our efforts and includes them in his plan for salvation.

Our reflection on hope in the year 2002 has a fundamental difference from the one we shared with you in 2000, in that it comes at the very peak of the crisis, its most acute moment. But at the same time, I think I am not mistaken in observing that this peak is exactly the right moment, the point at which our history assumes a special gravity and the actions of women and men take on new significance. If gestures of solidarity and selfless love have always been a form of prophecy, a powerful signal of the possibility of another story, today their prophetic power is infinitely greater. They indicate the stepping-stones across the swamp, a direction to follow precisely at the point of being lost. Conversely, falsehood and theft (the main ingredients of corruption) are evils that destroy the community. Just the practice of corruption can definitively demolish this fragile construction that we, as a people, are trying to build.

If we give our assent to the word of the Gospel, we know that even apparent failure can be a path to salvation. This is what marks the difference between a drama and a tragedy. Whereas, in the latter, ineluctable fate drags human enterprise toward unmitigated disaster and any attempt to challenge it merely aggravates the irreversible end, by contrast in a drama of life and death, good and evil, victory and defeat are present as possible alternatives: Nothing could be further from stupid optimism, but also from tragic pessimism, because when we find ourselves at this perhaps distressing crossroads we can also try to recognize the hidden signs of God's presence, if nothing more, as an opportunity, as an invitation to change and action . . . and also as a promise. These words can take on a dramatic aspect, but never a tragic one. Take note: This is not theatrical posturing, but the conviction that we are in the moment of grace, in the spotlight of our responsibility as members of the community, which is to say, purely and simply, as human beings.

The City of God in Secular History

So, what now can Christian faith tell us about this critical moment, besides placing us on the steep and narrow path of freedom, without predetermined outcomes when it comes to the success or failure of our human endeavors? Allow me to make a sort of journey in time, to stand, almost sixteen hundred years back, beside the window through which a man watched as a world ended, without any certainty that something better would come afterward. I'm talking about Saint Augustine, who was Bishop of Hippo in North Africa during the last years of the Roman Empire.

Everything that Saint Augustine had known (and not only him, but his father, his grandfather, and many preceding generations) was disintegrating. The so-called barbarian peoples were exerting pressure on the edges of the empire, and Rome itself had been sacked. As a man formed by Greco-Roman culture, he was bound to feel perplexed and anguished in the face of the imminent fall of known civilization. As a Christian, he found himself in the difficult position of continuing to place his hopes in the Kingdom of God (which for too long, even then, had been identified with the Christianized empire) without closing his eyes to what was already an inevitable reality, historically speaking. And as a bishop, he felt bound by his duty to help his flock (and Christianity as a whole) not only to process the catastrophe without loss of faith but also to emerge from the ordeal with a better understanding of the mystery of salvation and increased trust in the Lord.

During that epoch, Augustine, a man who had known incredulity and materialism, found the key that could give shape to his hope in a profound theology of history, developed in his book *The City of God*. In it, going broadly beyond the 'official theology' of the empire, the saint presents us with a defining hermeneutical principle of his thought: the concept of 'two loves' and 'two cities.' In synthesis, his argument is that there are two 'loves': *self love*, predominantly individualistic, which uses others for its own ends, considers commonalities only in relation to its own uses, and rebels against God, and *holy love*, which is eminently social, aligns itself with the common good, and follows the Lord's commands. The 'two cities' are organized around these two 'loves' or ends: the 'earthly' city and the city 'of God.' The pagans inhabit one of them, the 'saints' the other.

But the interesting feature of Augustinian thought is that these cities are not historically verifiable, in the sense that they can be identified with one or another secular reality. The City of God is clearly not the visible Church: Many inhabitants of the celestial city are in pagan Rome, and many members of the earthly city are in the Christian Church. The 'cities' are eschatological bodies; only at the Final Judgment will they become clearly visible, like the chaff and the wheat after harvesting. Until then, here in history, they are inextricably intertwined. The 'secular' is the historical existence of the two cities. While they are mutually exclusive in eschatological terms, during worldly times—the *saeculum*—they cannot be properly distinguished and separated. The dividing line is . . . the personal and collective freedom of human beings.

Why am I mulling over these ancient thoughts of a fifth-century bishop? Because they teach us a way to see reality. Human history is the ambiguous field on which multiple projects are played out, none of them humanly immaculate. But we can consider that the 'profane love' and 'holy love' of which Saint Augustine spoke flows through all of them. All Manichaeism or dualism apart, it is legitimate to try to distinguish by seeing, on the one hand, historical events that are 'signs of the times,' the seeds of the Kingdom, and on the other the actions that—detached from the eschatological finality— only further frustrate man's highest destiny. That is, by perceiving reality through a theological and spiritual appraisal, from the point of view of the gifts of grace and temptations to sin that free will presents.

With these evangelical criteria in mind, I venture to share with you these reflections on the present reality of our country and, above all, the values at stake in that reality. Values or 'loves': that which attracts and moves our desires and energies, directing us toward grace or sin, making us members of one or other city, creating the innermost structure of our historical secular reality and—therefore—the specific path to salvation that God has placed beneath our feet. I shall try to extricate from recent events some fundamental directions that it seems necessary to pinpoint, in order to be part of a community quest for discernment and conversion, as proposed to us by John Paul II.

What Next, after the *Cacerolazos* Protests?

It may be obvious, but we are all aware that on that (first) night of the pot-banging protest,[1] something changed in our society. Not in the leadership, at least not primarily, but in the people. Within families, in the consciousness of every citizen who decided to abandon negativity or private grudges, mere ruminations of bitterness, to recognize their neighbor, their compatriot, united in weariness and rage if nothing else. In a few moments, the street stopped being a zone of passage, a place of otherness, to become a shared space from which to start out in search of other shared things that had been snatched away from us. Contrary to all technological mythology, public space again became the whole square, not just the stage. The same communications media, always omnipresent and at times almost creators of 'reality,' found themselves overwhelmed and had to focus on one or two nerve centers, while the people took over everything with their singing and pot-banging, on foot, on bicycles, in cars.

After that came the events we all know about and also the excesses and the various interpretations and readings of the protests. I don't intend to go into them. I wish only to refer to that moment of collective participation, seen as an indication of intent to reclaim 'common' ground, as a starting point for a reading of our deep-rooted reality.

---

1. The *cacerolazos*, or pot-banging, street protests started in Chile in the 1970s and spread to Argentina in the 1990s to vent rage for the inflationary prices of food, as well as corruption and injustice. They have continued to appear periodically in demonstrations against injustice and shortages of food, gas, and other necessities.

I suggest to you an 'indirect' path that traverses the very history of our national being, which, I hope, may be of help: to examine the verses of *Martín Fierro*, in search of a few key elements that can help us discover something of *'our own'* so that we can take up our history again with a feeling of continuity and dignity. I am conscious of the risks implicit in the reading I am urging you to share. We sometimes imagine values and traditions, even culture itself, to be a sort of ancient and unalterable jewel, something that remains in a space and time apart, unpolluted by the comings and goings of actual history. Allow me to express the opinion that such a mentality only leads to museums and, ultimately, to sectarianism. We Christians have suffered too much from sterile debates between traditionalists and progressives to allow ourselves to fall into attitudes like that again.

To me, what seems more fertile here is to recognize in *Martín Fierro* a *narrative*, a sort of 'staging' of the drama of constructing a collective and inclusive sentiment, a narrative that, transcending its genre, its author, and its time, can be inspiring to us 130 years later. Of course, there will be many who don't identify with an outlawed gaucho, fugitive from justice (and in fact, important figures in our cultural history have questioned the elevation of such a character to the category of national epic hero). Conversely, there will be no lack of people forced to recognize (in secret) that they prefer the Judge or Old Vizcacha, at least in terms of how they understand what is or is not worthwhile in life . . . and still others will certainly have felt like El Moreno, whose brother was stabbed by Fierro.

There's room for all. And it's not a case of installing a new Manichaeism. In a work of this scope, no one is totally good or totally bad. And although José Hernández showed no lack of political or even pedagogical intent in his construction of *The Flight* and *The Return*, the truth is that the poem transcended its circumstances to say something that speaks to the essence of our coexistence. It is from this transcendence, from the 'resonances' that it is able to create in us, and not from a useless dialectic on anachronistic models, that the poem must be approached.

Martín Fierro, the 'National' Poem

I. The Quest for National Identity in a Globalized World

It is a strange thing. Just on seeing the title of the book, even before opening it, I already find suggestive sources of reflection on the core elements of our identity as a nation: *The Gaucho Martín Fierro* (this was the title of the first book published, later known as *The Flight*). What does the *gaucho* have to do with us? If we were living in the countryside, working with animals, or at least in rural towns, in greater contact with the soil, it would be easier to understand. . . . In our big cities—obviously in Buenos Aires—many people will remember wooden carousel ponies or the corrals in Mataderos as the closest they've ever been to an equestrian experience. And is there any need to recall that over 86 percent of Argentines live in big cities? For most of our youth and children, the world of *Martín Fierro* is much more foreign than the mystical-futuristic worlds of Japanese comics.

This, of course, is closely connected with the phenomenon of globalization. From Bangkok to Sao Paulo, from Buenos Aires to Los Angeles or Sydney, very many young people listen to the same music, children watch the same cartoons, and families get their clothing, food, and entertainment from the same chains. Production and trade move across ever more permeable national borders. Concepts, religions, and lifestyles are brought closer to us by the media and tourism.

However, this globalization is an ambiguous reality. Many factors seem to be leading us to remove the cultural barriers that obstructed recognition of the common dignity of human beings, accepting the diversity of conditions, races, sex, or culture. It has never been more possible than now for humanity to build a multifaceted, supportive world community. But on the other hand, widespread indifference to increasing social imbalances, the unilateral imposition of values and customs by certain cultures, the environmental crisis, and exclusion of millions of human beings from the benefits of development raise serious questions about this globalization. Creation of a supportive and fraternal human family in this context remains utopian.

True growth in human awareness cannot be based on anything other than the practice of dialogue and love. Dialogue and love lead, through recognition of the otherness of others, to acceptance of diversity. Only thus can the value of the community be founded, not by requiring the other to bend to my criteria and priorities, not by 'absorbing' the other, but by recognizing the value of what the other is and celebrating that diversity which enriches us all. Anything else is mere narcissism, mere imperialism, mere foolishness.

This must also be read in the opposite direction: How can I create a dialogue? How can I love? How can I build something shared if I let what would have been my contribution be diluted, get lost and disappear? Globalization as a unidirectional and uniformist imposition of values, practices, and goods goes hand in hand with integration understood as cultural, intellectual, and spiritual subordination and imitation. So then, there is no room for prophets of isolation, provincial hermits in a global world, nor brainwashed, copycat passengers in the caboose, admiring the fireworks of the world (of others) openmouthed and applauding on cue. When people join the global dialogue, they bring the values of their culture and have to defend these values against any form of excessive absorption or 'laboratory synthesis' that dilutes them in what is 'common' or 'global.' And—on contributing these values—they receive from other peoples, with the same respect and dignity, the cultures belonging to them. Nor is there room here for messy eclecticism, because in this case a people's values become uprooted from the fertile soil that created and maintains their being, to be thrown together in a sort of curiosity shop where 'anything goes; we'll meet down there in the furnace.'[2]

1. The Nation as Continuation of a Shared Story

Going back to *Martín Fierro*, we are able to profitably open our 'national poem' only if we realize that the story it tells is directly relevant to us in the here and now, not because we are gauchos or wear a poncho, but because the drama Hernández narrates for us is set in real history, whose passage has brought us to where we are. The men and women reflected in the time of the tale lived here in this land, and their decisions, productions, and ideals shaped the reality that we are part of today and that today affects us directly. It is precisely that 'productivity,' those 'effects,' that ability to be set in the real dynamic of history, that makes *Martín Fierro* a national poem, not guitars, Indian raids, and improvised folksongs.

Here an appeal to conscience is needed. We Argentines have a dangerous tendency to think that everything starts today, to forget that nothing pops out of a pumpkin or drops from the sky like a meteorite. We have a problem here: If we don't learn to recognize and take on board the errors and achievements of the past that gave rise to the good and bad of today, we'll be condemned to an eternal repetition of the same, which—in reality—is far from eternal, as the rope can only stretch so far. . . . But there's more. If we cut our relationship with the past, we'll do the same with the future. It is high time to look around us . . . and inside ourselves. Wasn't there a denial of the future, a total lack of responsibility toward future

---

2. In Spanish, "*dale que va . . . allá en el horno nos vamos a encontrar.*" This is a line from the 1930s tango "El Cambalache," mentioned also in a homily to catechists in 2000, as representative of a widespread mentality among the people.

generations, in the levity with which institutions, property, and even people in our country were treated? The truth is this: We are historical people. We live in time and space. Each generation needs the previous ones and has a duty to those that follow. And this, in great measure, is what it means to be a nation: to see ourselves as continuing the task of other men and women who already did their bit, and as builders of a common space, a house, for those who will come after. 'Global' citizens: Reading *Martín Fierro* can help us 'come down to earth' and mark the boundaries of that 'globality,' recognizing the avatars of those who built our nationhood, adopting or criticizing their ideals, and asking ourselves why they succeeded or failed, so that we can continue forward on our road as a people.

2. Existence as a People Requires, above All, an Ethical Attitude which Springs from Freedom

In the face of the crisis, it is again necessary to answer the crucial question: What is the foundation of what we call the 'social bond'? What exactly is it, that thing we say is seriously at risk of being lost? What is it that 'binds' me, that 'links' me to other people in a place, to the point of sharing a single destiny?

Allow me to put forward a reply: It is a matter of ethics. The crux of the relationship between the moral and the social is found precisely in this space (which is also so elusive) where man is man in society, a political animal, as Aristotle and the whole classical republican tradition would say. It is this social nature of man that is the basis for the possibility of a contract between free individuals, as proposed by the liberal democratic tradition (traditions that are often opposed to each other, as shown by so many confrontations in our history). So, to consider the crisis as a moral problem, we need to refer once again to the universal, human values that God has planted in man's heart and that gradually mature as a result of personal and community growth. When we bishops repeatedly say that the crisis is fundamentally a moral one, we are not brandishing a cheap moralization, a reduction of the political, social, and economic to an individual matter of conscience. That would be false moralizing. We are not carrying grist to our own mill (given that conscience and morality are one field in which the Church has particular competence), but trying to point to the collective opinions that have been expressed in attitudes, actions, and processes of a historical-political and social type. The free actions of human beings, apart from their weight in terms of individual responsibility, have far-reaching consequences; they generate structures that endure through time and create a climate in which specific values can either occupy a central position in public life or become marginalized from the prevailing culture. And this also falls inside the moral sphere. That's why we need to rediscover the particular way of living together and forming a community that we have created for ourselves over the course of our history.

From this perspective, let us look again at the poem. Like all folktales, *Martín Fierro* begins with a description of an 'original paradise.' It paints an idyllic scene, in which the gaucho lives at the calm pace of nature, surrounded by his loved ones, working happily and skillfully, amusing himself with his companions and integrated into a simple, human way of life. What does this point to? First of all, the author was not prompted by a form of nostalgia for a 'lost Eden of gaucho life.' The literary conceit of painting an ideal scene at the outset is nothing more than a first presentation of the ideal itself. The value to be embodied is not behind, at the origin, but ahead, part of the project. At the origin is the dignity of the Son of God, the vocation, the call to embody a project. The end is being placed at the beginning (which is also a deeply biblical and Christian idea). The direction we give to our community life will have to do with the type of society we wish to form: It is the "telostipo."[3] That is the key to the nature of a people. It doesn't mean ignoring the biological, psychological, and psychosocial elements that influence the field of our decisions. We cannot avoid carrying the weight (in the negative sense of limits, conditioning, impediments, but also in the positive one of taking with us, incorporating, adding, integrating) of our received inheritance, the conduct, preferences, and values that have formed over the course of time. But a Christian perspective (and this is one of Christianity's contributions to humanity as a whole) knows how to value both the 'given,' which is already in man and cannot be otherwise, and that which springs from his liberty, his openness to new things, concretely, from his spirit as a transcendent dimension, always in accordance with the essence of the given.

That said, social constraints and the shape they have acquired, as well as the findings and creations of the spirit in order to constantly expand the horizon of human endeavor, together with the natural law of our conscience, come into action and take effect specifically in time and space: in a specific community, sharing one land, proposing common objectives, constructing their particular way of being human, of cultivating multiple bonds, together,

---

3. Bergoglio's neologism, from the Greek *"telos,"* purpose or objective, and *"tipos,"* meaning model, mark, or example, the amalgamation of elements that shapes a people.

as a result of so many shared experiences, preferences, decisions, and events. This is how we build a shared ethics and the opening toward a destiny of plenitude that defines man as a spiritual being. This shared ethics, this 'moral dimension,' is what enables the multitude to develop together, without becoming each other's enemies. Let us think of a pilgrimage. Leaving from the same place and heading toward the same destination allows the procession to keep together, regardless of the different rhythm or pace of each group or individual.

Let us now synthesize this idea. What is it that makes many persons into one people? There is first of all a natural law and then a legacy. Second, there is a psychological factor: Man becomes man by sharing communication, relationship, and love with his fellows. In word and in love. Third, these biological and psychological factors are actually manifested, really come into play, in free behavior. In the desire to connect ourselves with others in a particular manner, to construct our life with our fellow humans in a range of shared practices and preferences (Saint Augustine defined a people as "a multitude of rational beings united by agreeing to share the things they love"). The 'natural' grows into 'cultural,' 'ethical'; the gregarious instinct acquires human form in the free decision to become an 'us.' A choice that, like any human action, later tends to become a habit (in the best sense of the word), to generate deeply rooted feelings and produce historic institutions, to the point where each one of us comes into the world in the bosom of an already existing community (the family, the 'homeland'), without this negating the responsible freedom of each person. And all this has its solid foundation in the values that God imprinted on our human nature, in the divine breath that infuses us from within and makes us the children of God. This natural law that was gifted to us and imprinted on us so that it is 'consolidated by years, enlarged by time, refined by age' (cf. Saint Vincent of Lérin, 1st Commonitorium, chap. 23). This natural law that—throughout history and life—will consolidate, develop, and grow, is what saves us from the so-called relativism of values agreed by consensus. Values cannot be agreed on by consensus; they simply are. In the placatory game of 'agreeing on values by consensus' there is always the risk, and foretold result, of 'leveling downward,' which means things are no longer built on solid ground and the violent process of deterioration starts. Someone said that our civilization, in addition to being a throwaway civilization, is a 'biodegradable' civilization.

To return to our poem: *Martín Fierro* is not, of course, the Bible. But it is a text in which, for various reasons, we Argentines have been able to recognize ourselves, a platform from which to tell us something about our history and dream about our future:

> *I have known this land when the working man lived in it*
> *And had his little cabin / and his children and his wife . . .*
> *It was a delight to see / the way he spent his days.*

This, then, is the initial situation from which the drama starts. *Martín Fierro* is, first and foremost, an inclusive poem. Later, everything comes apart because of a sort of twist of fate, embodied by the Judge, the Mayor, and the Colonel, among others. We suspect this conflict is not just a literary one. What lies behind the text?

Martín Fierro, an 'Inclusive' Poem

1. A Modern Country, but for Everyone

More than an abstract epic poem, *Martín Fierro* is a work of protest with a clear intention: to oppose the official policy and propose the gaucho's inclusion in the country under construction:

> *He's a poor orphan, and he's the one / who gets crushed by destiny*
> *Because no one makes it their business / to stand up for his kind.*
> *But the gauchos ought to have houses / and a school and a church and their rights.*

And *Martín Fierro* took on a life beyond the author's intentions, becoming the prototype of the individual persecuted by an unjust and exclusive system. The poem's verses gave life to a certain type of popular wisdom received from the surrounding medium, which means *Fierro* speaks not only of the need to obtain cheap labor but also of the essential dignity of a man in his own land, taking care of his destiny through work, love, celebration, and brotherhood.

From here on, we can begin to move forward in our reflection. We need to know where we can rest our hope, the point from which to rebuild the social bonds that have been so bruised by these times. The pot-banging protest was a self-defensive spark, spontaneous and popular (although forcing its repetition over time causes it to lose some of its original expression). We know banging pots was not enough; what we most need today is to find the wherewithal to fill them. We need to reclaim, in an organized and creative way, the leading role we should never have relinquished, which also means we cannot now bury our heads in the sand again, leaving the leaders to do and undo. There are two reasons why we can't do that: because we have already seen what happens when political and economic power detaches itself from the people, and because reconstruction is not a task for the few but for everyone, just as Argentina is not just the ruling class but each and every one of us who live in this corner of the planet.

So what is the answer? I find the historical context of *Martín Fierro* significant: a society in formation, a project that excludes an important part of the population, condemning it to orphanhood and disappearance, and a proposal for inclusion. Aren't we in a similar situation today? Haven't we suffered the consequences of a country model constructed around specific economic interests, which excludes the majority, generates poverty and marginalization, and tolerates all forms of corruption so long as the interests of highly concentrated power remain untouched? Haven't we been part of this perverse system, partly accepting its principles—providing they didn't touch our pockets—and closing our eyes to those who fell outside and under the steamroller of injustice, until the latter practically expelled all of us?

Today we need to come up with an economic and social program, yes, but fundamentally a political project in the broadest sense. What sort of society do we want? *Martín Fierro* directs our gaze toward our vocation as a people, as a nation. It invites us to give shape to our desire for a society where there is room for everyone: the trader from Buenos Aires, the coastal *gaucho*, the northern shepherd, the northeastern craftworker, aboriginals and immigrants, insofar as none of them wants to keep everything for himself, ejecting others from the territory.

2. But the Gauchos Ought to Have a School . . .

For decades, schools were an important means of social and national integration. The child of the gaucho, of the migrant from the interior that arrived in the city, and even of the foreigner disembarking in this land found in basic education the resources that could enable them to transcend their origin and seek a place in the shared construction of a project. Today, too, with an enriching plurality of educational proposals, we should renew the commitment: everything for education.

In recent years, hand in hand with an idea of a country that no longer bothered much about including everyone and was even incapable of imagining its future, the educational institution saw its prestige decline, its support and resources diminish, and its place at the heart of society fade away.

The much referred-to case of 'escuela shopping[4] doesn't just lead us to criti-
cize certain specific cases we have witnessed. It calls into question a whole
concept, according to which society is a market and nothing more. The
school thus occupies the same place as any other moneymaking enterprise.
And we should remember, time and again, that this was not the idea that
developed our educational system and contributed, with errors and achievements, to the formation of a national community.

We Christians have made an undeniable contribution in this respect, over
many centuries. It is not my intention here to enter into polemics and differences of opinion that generally consume a lot of energy. I simply wish to
draw everyone's attention, and particularly that of Catholic educators, to the
highly important task we have on our hands. The depreciated, undervalued,
and even widely attacked everyday work of all those who keep schools going,
in the face of all sorts of difficulties, on low wages and giving far more than
they receive, continues to be one of the best examples of *what* we need to
opt for, once again: personal commitment to the project of creating a country for all, a project that goes from the educational, religious, or social to
the political in the highest sense of the word "community-building."

This inclusive political project is a task not just for the ruling party, or
even the ruling class as a whole, but for every one of us. The 'new time' ger-
minates from the real, everyday life of every member of the nation, from each
decision in relation to others, from our own responsibilities, from things big
and small. And all the more so within families and in our everyday school
or work life.

> But God will make it possible / for these things to be put right
> Though it's important to remember, / to make a good job of it,
> That when a fire's for heating / it has to come from underneath.

But this deserves a fuller reflection.

Martín Fierro: Compendium of Ethical Civics

Hernández was undoubtedly well aware that 'real' gauchos, of flesh and
blood, were not going to behave like 'English gentlemen' in the new society
that was being forged. Coming from another, unfenced culture, used to

---

4. A corruption scandal that occurred in 1990, when the city council sold a school in
Buenos Aires to a developer to turn it into a shopping mall and push the children to the
second floor. In 2011 it reverted to use as a school.

decades of resistance and struggle, alien to a world that was being built along parameters very different from theirs, they, too, needed to make a considerable effort to integrate, once the doors were opened to them.

1. *The Resources of Popular Culture*

The second part of our national poem tried to be a sort of 'manual of civic virtues' for the gaucho, a 'key' to integration in the new national society:

> And you must all have faith / in what my tongue declares to you:
> so don't misunderstand me, / there's no stain of greed in this.
> There'll be no leaking roof on the cabin / that has this book in it.

Martín Fierro is full of elements that Hernández himself had imbibed from popular culture, elements that, together with the defense of some specific and immediate rights, won it the great following it quickly acquired. Not only that, but over time, generations and generations of Argentines reread *Fierro* . . . and rewrote it, overlaying its words with their many experiences of struggle, their expectations, searches, sufferings. *Martín Fierro* grew to represent a country that was determined, fraternal, justice-loving, unbreakable. That is why it still has something to say today. That is why those 'words of advice' on how to 'tame' the gaucho far transcended the meaning with which they were written and are still today a mirror of civic virtues that are not abstract, but deeply embedded in our history. It is these virtues and values that we are now going to look at.

2. Martín Fierro's *Advice*

I invite you to read this poem once again. Don't do so out of merely literary interest, but as a way of listening to the wisdom of our people, which has been encapsulated in this singular work. Beyond words, beyond history, you will see that what still pulses in us is a form of emotion, a desire to twist the arm of all forms of injustice and lies and carry on building a history of solidarity and brotherhood, in a common land where we can all grow as human beings. A community where freedom is not a pretext for failing justice, where the law does not bind only the poor, where everyone has a place. I hope you will feel as I do, that this is a book that talks not about the past but about the future we can build. I am not going to prolong this already very lengthy message by expanding on the many values that Hernández puts into the mouth of Fierro and other characters in the poem. I simply invite you to look at them in depth, through reflection and—why not?—through a dialogue in each one of our educational communities. Here I will present just a few of the ideas we can reclaim, among many others.

2.1. Prudence or 'Artfulness': Acting out of Truth and Goodness ... or Convenience

A man is born with the astuteness / that has to serve him as a guide.
Without it he'd go under / but in my experience,
in some people it turns to prudence / and in others, artfulness.
There are some men who have their heads / full up with the things they know:
wise men come in all sizes, / but I don't need much sense to say
that better than learning a lot of things / is learning things that are good.

A starting point: 'Prudence' or 'artfulness' as forms of organizing one's talents and acquired experience. Appropriate behavior, within the truth and good that are possible here and now, or a knowing manipulation of information, situations, and interactions, motivated by self-interest. A mere accumulation of science (usable for any purpose) or true wisdom, which includes 'knowing' in the dual sense of learning and experiencing. 'Everything is permissible for me, but not everything is beneficial,' as Saint Paul would say. Why? Because together with my own needs, desires, and preferences there are those of others. And what satisfies one at the expense of the other ends up destroying both.

2.2. The Hierarchy of Values and the Success-Oriented Ethic of the 'Winner'

It's a bad thing to be attacked / either by fear or greed:
So, don't upset yourselves / over perishable goods.
Don't offer your wealth to rich men / and never neglect the poor.

Far from inviting us to scorn material goods as such, the popular wisdom expressed in these words considers perishable goods as a means, a tool for personal realization at a higher level. That is why it instructs us not to give to the rich (self-interested and servile behavior that Old Vizcacha's 'artfulness' would recommend) and not be miserly toward the poor (who do need us and, as the Gospel says, have nothing with which to pay us). Human society cannot follow the law of the jungle, where each person tries to grab what they can, whatever the cost. And we already know, all too painfully, that there is no 'automatic' mechanism that can ensure equality and justice. Only an ethical choice translated into actual practices, with effective means, can prevent man from preying on other men. But this is the same as postulating an order of values that is more important than personal enrichment, and therefore a type of riches that are superior to material ones. And we are not talking about matters that require a particular religious belief to be understood; we are referring to principles like human dignity, solidarity, and love.

> You call me 'teacher' and 'master,' and rightly so, for indeed I am. I, therefore, the master and teacher, have washed your feet, you ought to wash one another's feet. I have given you a model to follow, so that as I have done for you, you should also do. (Jn 13:13–15)

A community that stops kneeling down to wealth, success, and fame and is capable, on the other hand, of washing the feet of the humble and needy would be more in harmony with this teaching than the ethics of 'winning' (at any price), which we have sadly learned in recent times.

2.3. Work and the Sort of Person We Want to Be

> The law is that we have to work / because we need to buy.
> Don't expose yourself to suff'ring / that a wretched condition brings.
> A lot of blood runs from the heart / of a man who's obliged to beg.

Is any commentary required? History has branded our people with a sense of the dignity attached to work and the worker. Is there anything more humiliating than being denied the ability to earn one's bread? Is there any worse way of decreeing the uselessness and inexistence of a human being? Can a society that accepts such iniquity, defending itself with abstract technical considerations, provide a path toward the realization of human beings?

But this recognition that we all proclaim never quite materializes. Not only because of the objective conditions generated by the present terrible unemployment (conditions, it must be clearly stated, that have their origin in a way of organizing coexistence that places profit above justice and the law), but also because of a picaresque mentality (also called native wit!) that has come to form part of our culture. 'Save your skin' and 'get away' . . . by whatever means is easiest and most direct. 'Money brings money' . . . 'nobody got rich by working' . . . beliefs that have nurtured a culture of corruption that undoubtedly has something to do with these shortcuts, which many have used to try to excuse themselves from the rule of earning their daily bread with the sweat of their brow.

2.4. The Urgency of Serving the Weakest

The stork, when it gets old, / loses its eyesight, and then
all its young children undertake / to care for it in its old age.
You can learn from the storks / with this example of tenderness.

In the ethics of the 'winners,' anything that is considered useless is thrown out. This is the 'throwaway' civilization. In the ethics of a real human community, in that country we would like and which we can build, every human being is of value, and the elderly have intrinsic value, for many reasons: because of the duty of filial respect already present in the biblical Ten Commandments; because of the undoubted right to rest in the bosom of his community, earned by he who has lived, suffered, and played his part; because of the contribution that only he can still make to his society, since, as Martín Fierro himself says, "it's from old men's mouths / that truths come forth." There's no need to wait until the social security system, currently destroyed by pillaging, is rebuilt. In the meantime, there are countless small gestures and actions of service to the elderly that are within our reach with a pinch of creativity and good will. And similarly, we mustn't forget to think again about the real ways in which we can do something for children, for sick people, and all those who are suffering for various reasons. The belief that there are 'structural' issues that relate to society as a whole and the State in particular does not excuse us in any way from making our personal contribution, however small it may be.

2.5. No More Theft, Bribery, and Turning a Blind Eye

The carrion bird with its hooked beak / has a taste for robbery,
but a man with powers of reason / will never steal a cent
because there's no shame in being poor / but there is in being a thief.

This, in our country, has perhaps been one of the most forgotten teachings. But looking beyond it, as well as not allowing or justifying theft and bribery, we would have to take more decisive and positive action. For example, we can ask ourselves not only what things that are not ours we must not take, but also what things we can contribute. How can we present the idea that there is also 'shame' in indifference, individualism, withdrawing (stealing) one's own contribution to society to remain purely within a mind-set of 'minding my own business'?

> But because he wished to justify himself, he said to Jesus, "And who is my neighbor?" Jesus replied, "A man fell victim to robbers as he went down from Jerusalem to Jericho. They stripped and beat him and went off leaving him half-dead. A priest happened to be going down that road, but when he saw him, he passed by on the opposite side. Likewise, a Levite came to the place, and when he saw him, he passed by on the opposite side. But a Samaritan traveler who came upon him was moved with compassion at the sight. He approached the victim, poured oil and wine over his wounds, and bandaged them. Then he lifted him up on his own animal, took him to an inn, and cared for him. The next day he took out two silver coins and gave them to the innkeeper with the instruction, 'Take care of him. If you spend more than what I have given you, I shall repay you on my way back.' Which of these three, in your opinion, was neighbor to the robbers' victim?" He answered, "The one who treated him with mercy." Jesus said to him, "Go and do likewise." (Lk 10:29–37)

2.6. Empty Words, True Words

> If singing is your profession / make sure to sing from the heart.
> Don't tune your instrument / just for love of your own voice,
> and make a habit of singing / about things of consequence.

Communication, hypercommunication, noncommunication. How many of our words are superfluous? How much gossip, how much slander, how many lies? How much superficiality, banality, and timewasting? A wonderful gift, the ability to communicate ideas and feelings, which we don't know how to value or make use of in all its richness. Could we not find a way to avoid all 'singing' that is only 'for the love of talking'? Could we possibly pay more attention to what we are speaking too much or too little about, particularly those of us whose task is to teach, speak, and communicate?

Conclusion: One's Word and Friendship

Finally, let us quote that verse in which we have seen so clearly reflected the instruction to love in times of difficulty for our country. That stanza that has become a motto, a program, a slogan, but that we need to remember over and over again:

> Brothers should stand by each other / because this is the first law.
> Keep a true bond between you / always, at every time,
> Because if you fight among yourselves / you'll be devoured by those outside.

This is a crucial time for our country. Crucial and foundational, and for that very reason, full of hope. Hope is as far removed from expediency as it is from faintheartedness. It demands the best of us in the task of rebuilding what we share, what makes us a people. The only aim of these reflections has been to kindle a desire: to put ourselves to work, inspired and illuminated by our own history. To not give up the dream of a land of brothers that has guided so many men and women on this soil.

What will future generations say about us? Will we be able to meet the challenges facing us? 'Why not?' is the answer. Without grandiloquence, without messianism, without impossible certainties, it is a matter of once more delving bravely into our ideals, the ones that have guided us throughout our history, and starting right away to set in motion other possibilities, other values, other behaviors.

Almost in synthesis, here is the last verse from *Martín Fierro* that I will quote, a verse that Hernández places in the mouth of the gaucho's elder son, as he reflects bitterly on jail:

> *Because I suppose—though I'm ignorant—that out of all the good things*
> *which were given to proud man / by the Divine Majesty,*
> *Your Word is the first of them / and friendship is the second.*

The word that communicates and bonds us, allowing us to share ideas and feelings, provided that we speak the truth. Always. Without exceptions. Friendship, including social friendship, with its 'long arm' of justice, is the greatest treasure, the asset that can never be sacrificed for any other. It needs to be nurtured above all others.

One's word and friendship. "And the Word became flesh and made his dwelling among us" (Jn 1:14). He didn't build a separate abode; he became our friend. "No one has greater love than this, to lay down one's life for one's friends. You are my friends if you do what I command you. I no longer call you slaves, because a slave does not know what his master is doing. I have called you friends, because I have told you everything I have heard from my Father" (Jn 15:13–15). If we begin immediately to value these two assets, the history of our country could be different.

We conclude putting these wishes in the hands of the Lord, with a prayer for the country that the Argentine bishops have offered to us:

> *Jesus Christ, Lord of history, we need you.*
> *We feel wounded and overwhelmed.*
> *We require your relief and strength.*
> *We want to be a nation,*

Whose identity is passion for the truth
And commitment for the common good.
Give us the courage of the freedom of the children of God,
to love everyone without excluding anyone,
with preference for the poor and forgiving those who offend us,
abhorring hatred and building peace.
Grant us the wisdom of dialogue
and the joy of hope that does not disappoint.
You gather us. Here we are, Lord, close to Mary,
that from Luján tells us:
Argentina! Sing and walk!
Jesus Christ, Lord of history, we need you.
Let Yourself Be Possessed by the Truth.

➤➤ ◀◀

Let Yourself Be Possessed by the Truth

Homily, Mass for Educators—April 10, 2002

The presence of so many young people at the beginning of the school year gives me hope. It was funny, and I liked the expression of the leader "stubborn hope." Where there is a child who starts a school year, there is "stubborn hope." Where there is a man or a woman who begins his or her work in school, as a teacher, administrator, or board member, there is "stubborn hope." Where there is hope, there is joy. There is no grimace.

That is the first feeling I have today. Hope. Hope in everyone who is here, hope in you, students. Hope that you are on the path of light, the path of the one who works according to the truth. The way of truth. And truth is always combative, but it is also fought against. It is combative because it is fought against. Truth is not a thing; truth is the adherence of my heart to that which has been revealed to me. That which is evident to me, that which gives meaning to my life. You boys and girls give hope because you want to walk in the light of truth. The apostles, as we heard in the first reading, were persecuted for the truth that for them was never negotiable. Lying is the daughter of darkness; but between truth and lies is that spectrum offered by the market of semi-truths, of half-truths. The 'neither,' the language of 'neither.' It is not the 'yes-yes, no-no' but the 'neither-neither.' Where one can be accommodated according to whatever one wants, according to what suits. And that is the language of darkness.

However, darkness is not always darkness. There is darkness that is disguised as light—you should know that, boys and girls. We have heard the story of when the Indians were sold colored glass, telling them that it was precious stones. My grandmother called them 'chafalonería' (trinkets). Today there are so many colored glass sellers, and they tell you: This is the truth, that is the truth, it is the easy one, yours, the one you like. But the way of truth is arduous, you'd better believe it. It cost the apostles persecution and jail . . . it is arduous.

This is what I want to tell you as you start classes with this feeling of stubborn hope. Where truth is, there is light, but do not confuse it with a flash. Where truth is, there is joy within, not a circus. It is very easy to build a circus to laugh a while, and afterward remains an afterthought, a distortion. Defend the truth, seek the truth, let yourself be possessed by the truth, that is the arduous road and that which will give meaning to life and that which will fill you with joy and happiness! Knowing that the truth is not negotiable, it is not an easy thing.

And you, older people, working in the way of truth, helping the younger ones to grow in the truth, we must also talk to them about it being hard. Because it is very hard, in the easy world, to believe in the truth.

When a civilization loses its north star, the compass goes mad and starts spinning. Mark any direction, anything goes. But in this crazy compass there are two signs that are key. Two signs of profound existential disorientation. In a civilization that relativizes truth, always—and this is constant—you experiment on the children and the elderly. And our civilization performs experiments on the children and the elderly.

Open your eyes; do not join that game. The north of truth, the north of light, not the 'flash' that dazzles and then is reduced to darkness. When you experience the two extremes of life, you experience the hope of a people. Because children are the hope of a people and the elderly are the hope of a people. The children because they are going to replace us, they are the ones who will receive the torch. And the elders, because they are the wisdom of the people, are the ones who have to give us what they have lived on their way through life. And today, in this twenty-first century, so self-sufficient, men experiment on children and the elderly.

The compass is crazy. Even here, in this city, not everywhere, but there is the temptation to experiment on children and the elderly. It brings to mind ugly images, images from the first half of the last century. Let's see. How long will an old man live with 120 pesos[1] in his pocket without medicine and without a doctor? They experiment with the wisdom of old age. Or with the young they experiment with this value . . . no, let's try that other one . . . let's try this way . . . let's try there. And conscience is deformed, and they are subtly made to enter that world of relativism that is darkness disguised as light. And that not only in the cultural field, but also in the social field. Since last July 16 there are 192 children on the street, in the Bajo Soldati, as a result of an "eviction" from a settlement. And this, under the gaze of those responsible for the common good. There is experimentation with youth in the social field. There is experimentation with youth in the cultural field. There is experimentation with youth in ethics and morality.

Here the phrase of our Buenos Aires prophet does not fit with "anything goes . . . everything is the same" because that's the way "we'll meet down there in the furnace."[2] Only one thing is certain: the truth gives light, the truth cannot be negotiated, the truth is an arduous road, and the children and the elders are not for experimenting on.

To you, those who work in this noble task of making our children grow in truth, thank you. Thank you. From the heart. I know it's not easy for you. I know that the option to escape from the situation is always at hand. I really thank you from the heart. I feel indebted for what you do.

And to you, students, do not be afraid of work. Do not go for the easy road. Seek the truth, because only the truth will set you free.

May the Lord and Our Mother grant us this grace.

→→ ←←

We Have Reasons to Hope

Homily, Solemn Te Deum *on Independence Day—May 25, 2002*

He came to Jericho and intended to pass through the town. Now a man there named Zacchaeus, who was a chief tax collector and also a wealthy man, was seeking to see who Jesus was; but he could not see him because of the crowd, for he

---

1. In August 2002, when Bergoglio wrote, the equivalent in US currency was $33.24.
2. Another reference to the tango "El Cambalache," mentioned earlier.

was short in stature. So he ran ahead and climbed a sycamore tree in order to see Jesus, who was about to pass that way. When he reached the place, Jesus looked up and said to him, "Zacchaeus, come down quickly, for today I must stay at your house." And he came down quickly and received him with joy.

When they all saw this, they began to grumble, saying, "He has gone to stay at the house of a sinner." But Zacchaeus stood there and said to the Lord, "Behold, half of my possessions, Lord, I shall give to the poor, and if I have extorted anything from anyone I shall repay it four times over." And Jesus said to him, "Today salvation has come to this house because this man too is a descendant of Abraham. For the Son of Man has come to seek and to save what was lost." (Lk 19:1–10)

Perhaps, as very seldom in our history, this badly wounded society awaits a new coming of the Lord. It awaits the healing and reconciling entrance of the One who is the Way, the Truth, and the Life. We have reasons to wait in hope. We do not forget that his passing through, and his salvific presence, have been a constant in our history. We discover the wonderful footprint of his creative work in the incomparable wealth of our natural environment. Divine generosity has also been reflected in the life testimony of self-giving and sacrifice by our fathers and heroes, as well as in the millions of humble and believing faces, our brothers, those anonymous protagonists of work and heroic struggles, incarnation of the silent epic of the Spirit that founds nations.

However, we live very far from the gratitude merited by so many gifts we have received. What prevents us from seeing this coming of the Lord? What makes it impossible to "Taste and see that the LORD is good" (Ps 34:9) in the face of so much prodigality on earth and in men? What in our Nation hinders the possibilities of taking advantage of the full encounter between the Lord, his gifts, and ourselves? Just as in the Jerusalem of that time, when Jesus was crossing the city and that man named Zacchaeus could not see him among so many people, something prevents us from seeing and feeling his presence. In the gospel scene, we are given the key in terms of height and lowness. Height, because Zacchaeus is won over by the desire to see Jesus and, being small in stature, he goes forward and climbs a sycamore tree. No talent or wealth can replace being of low moral stature, or, in any case, if the problem is not moral, there is no way out for a downcast gaze, without hope, resigned to its limits, lacking in creativity.

In this blessed land, our guilt seems to have cast our gazes down. A sad inner pact has been forged in the hearts of many of those intended to defend our interests, with shocking consequences: The guilt of their deceit is pressing with its wound and, instead of asking to be healed, they persist and take refuge in the accumulation of power, in the reinforcement of the threads of a web that prevents them from seeing the ever more painful reality. Thus, the suffering of others, and the destruction provoked by the games played by those addicted to power and riches, are to them only game pieces, numbers, statistics, and variables of a planning office. As such destruction grows, arguments are sought to justify and demand more sacrifices hiding in the repeated phrase 'there is no other way out,' a pretext that serves to dull their consciences. Such low spiritual and ethical levels would not survive without the reinforcement of those who suffer from another old disease of the heart: the inability to feel guilt. The ambitious climbers, who behind their international diplomas and technical language, so easily interchangeable, disguise their precarious knowledge and their almost nonexistent humanity.

Like Zacchaeus, we can become conscious of our difficulty in living at spiritual heights—feeling the weight of wasted time, of lost opportunities— and rise up in a rejection of that impotence of carrying out our destiny, locked in our own contradictions. Certainly, it is usual that, faced with impotence and limits, we lean toward the easy response of delegating to others to represent our interests. As if the common good were a foreign science, as if politics—in turn—were not a high and delicate way of exercising justice and charity. Shortsightedness to see the passing of God among us, to feel gratified by and worthy of so many gifts, and not to have scruples in asserting them without renouncing our historic vocation of noninvasive overtures to other sister nations.

Like us, Zacchaeus also suffered that shortsightedness. However, the miracle happens: The evangelical character rises above his mediocrity and finds and climbs the height he needed. It is from our own pain and limits that we learn to grow, and from our own evils where a deep question arises: Have we lived through enough pain to decide to break old schemes, renounce such deep-rooted foolish attitudes, and unleash our true potential? Are we not facing the historic opportunity to review old and rooted evils that we have never finished tackling, and work together to resolve them? Do we need more blood to flow into the river, so that our wounded and failed pride will recognize its defeat?

Zacchaeus did not opt for resignation in the face of his difficulties, he did not give up his opportunity because of his helplessness; he went ahead, looked for the height from which to see better, and allowed himself to be found by the Lord. Yes, let yourself be found by the Lord, let yourself be impacted by your own pain and that of others; let failure and poverty take away prejudices, ideologies, numbing fads, so that in that way, we can feel the call: "Zacchaeus, come down quickly." This is the second key to this Gospel passage: Zacchaeus responds to a Jesus who calls him to come down. Come down from his self-sufficiency, from the character invented by his wealth; come down from the trap set up by his personal unfortunate complexes. In effect, no spiritual height, no project with great hopes, can become real if it is not built and sustained from below: from the lowering of one's own interests, from the lowering to the patient and daily work that kills all arrogance.

Today as never before, when the danger of national dissolution is at our doorstep, we cannot allow ourselves to be dragged down by inertia, to be sterilized by our impotence or frightened by threats. Let's try to locate ourselves where we can better face God's gaze into our consciences, to become brothers face to face, recognizing our limits and our possibilities. Let us not return to the arrogance of the century-old division between the centralist interests, which live on monetary and financial speculation, as the port did before,[1] and the imperative need of stimulation and promotion of an interior now condemned to be a tourist curiosity. Nor should we be driven by the arrogance of partisan internalism,[2] the cruelest of national sports, in which, instead of enriching ourselves with the confrontation of differences, the golden rule now consists in implacably destroying even the best of our opponents' proposals and achievements. Let us not be cut off by intransigent calculation (in the name of nonexistent coherence). May we not continue wallowing in the sad spectacle of those who no longer know how to lie and contradict themselves to maintain their privileges, their rapaciousness, and their quotas from ill-gotten gains, while losing our historic opportunities and locking ourselves in a dead end. Like Zacchaeus, we must be encouraged to feel the call to come down: to come down to patient and constant work, without possessive pretensions, but with the urgency of solidarity.

We have lived out many fictions, believing to be in the first world; we were attracted by "the golden calf" of the consumerist and well-traveled stability

---

1. Bergoglio refers to the attempt to capture all the income received from the very large traffic of the port in Buenos Aires to serve only the needs of the residents of that province, excluding the inhabitants of other provinces.

2. Internalism is the epistemological view that everything necessary to provide justification for a belief is immediately available in a person's consciousness without having to resort to external factors.

of some, at the expense of the impoverishment of millions. When dark com-
plicities from inside and outside become alibis of irresponsible attitudes
that do not hesitate to take things to the limit without caring for the damage: suspicious businesses, laundering to evade obligations, sectorial and
partisan commitments and supporters that impede a sovereign action, op-
eratives of disinformation that confuse, destabilize, and push toward
chaos. When this happens, the illusory temptation to demand scapegoats
for the supposed emergence of a better, pure, and magical class is of no use. . . .
It would be like climbing to another illusion. We must sadly recognize that
between ourselves and our opponents, there are many Zacchaeuses, with
different titles and functions, who exchange roles in a scenario of almost
authoritarian greed, sometimes with legitimate disguises.

It is best to let the Zacchaeus within each one of us allow himself to be
gazed at by the Lord and accept the invitation to come down. This call of
the Gospel is a remembrance and a path of hope. He who seeks and allows
himself to be reached by the sublime gives place to a new joy, to a possibility of redemption. And Zacchaeus redeems himself, gladly accepts the invitation from the only one who can reconcile us, God himself. He consents
to sitting at everyone's table, at the table of social friendship. No one asked
that publican to be what he could not be, but simply to come down from
the tree. He is asked to obey the Law of being one more, of being a brother
and compatriot that obeys the law.

This must be achieved: to enforce the law and allow our system to work
so that the banquet to which we are summoned in the Gospel becomes the
place of *encounter* and coexistence, of work and celebration that we want,
and not a shared coffee in haste with the swallows[3] interests of the world;
those who arrive, take, and depart. The law is the insurmountable condition of justice, of solidarity, and of politics, and it takes care of us, when it
comes down from the tree, it does not fall into the temptation of violence,
chaos, or revenge. Let us assume the pain of so much blood spilled uselessly
in our history. Let's open our eyes in time; a silent war is being fought in
our streets, the worst war of all—a war of enemies who live together and
do not see each other, because their interests intersect and are managed
by sordid criminal organizations and God only knows what else, taking

---

3. "*Intereses/capitales golondrinas*" refers to foreign money coming into a country for a short
time, extracting what it could, and then leaving, flitting away as quickly as a swallow
(*golondrina*).

advantage of social neglect, the decadence of authority, the legal vacuum, and impunity.

It is not the time to be afraid and ashamed of ourselves, we have a bit of Zacchaeus, and we all have enormous talents and values. We look with nostalgia at the natural riches, the brilliance of so many scattered compatriots, the silent and incredible resistance of a humble people who defend their resources and refuse to give up their faith and their convictions, who fight against degradation. Now or never, let us seek the recementing of our social bond—as we so often claim with society as a whole—and, like this repentant and happy publican, let us unleash our greatness: the greatness of giving and giving of ourselves. The great demand is to renounce the need to be always right, to maintain privileges, to have an easy life and income . . . to remain foolish and stunted in spirit. As in the evangelical call, on numerous occasions we have allowed ourselves to be visited by God. There the great and sublime have risen from us. In all of society there is a desire already alive, unavoidable, to participate and control its own representation, like that day we remember today in which the commune was constituted in the country's Council.[4]

In addition to climbing to see Jesus and then coming down to follow his invitation, there is a third key in the Gospel text: giving, giving of oneself to repair the evil done. Zacchaeus is inspired to return what was wrongly acquired, and to share. Like the converted Zacchaeus, this town feels the desire to "give half" and "return a fourfold." People desire to rescue work and generous solidarity, the egalitarian struggle and the social conquest, creativity and celebration from the depths of their soul. We know well that the people might accept humiliations, but not the lie of being judged guilty for not recognizing the exclusion of twenty million hungry brothers with trampled dignity. If Zacchaeus, before allowing himself to be found by Jesus, had devised a way for his debtors to sink lower and lower, he could not then claim alleged ethical obligations or exemplary punishments. Once converted you must recognize your usurer scam and return what you stole. Let us contemplate the end of the story: a Zacchaeus adhering to the law, living without complexes or disguises with his brothers, living and sitting next to the Lord, letting the initiatives flow with confidence and perseverance, able to listen and dialogue, and above all yielding and sharing with the joy of being.

---

4. This refers to the first national government formed after independence from Spain in 1810 and the assembly formed by notable citizens, celebrated each May 25.

History tells us that many peoples have risen from their ruins and abandoned their wretchedness as Zacchaeus did. It is necessary to give place to the time and the organizational and creative constancy, to appeal less to sterile claims, to illusions and promises, and to dedicate ourselves to firm and persevering action. Through this path hope flourishes; that hope that does not disappoint because it is God's gift to the heart of our people. Today, more than ever, hope gathers us. It inspires us and gives us the strength to rise and let God find us, let us lower ourselves in humble service, and give by giving ourselves. At times we dream of a call; we wait for it to be magical and enchanting. The path is simpler: We should only return to the Gospel, let ourselves look like Zacchaeus, listen to the call to the common task, not disguise our limits but accept the joy of sharing rather than the restlessness of hoarding. And then we will hear, addressed to our homeland, the word of the Lord: "Today salvation has come to this house. . . . For the Son of Man has come to seek and to save what was lost" (Lk 19:10).

➤➤ ◄◄

Remember How Your God Has Directed All Your Journeying

Homily, Solemnity of Corpus Christi and Consecration of Buenos Aires to Our Lady of Luján—June 1, 2002, Year A

On the feast of Corpus Christi, we remember the entire Easter season, which is concentrated on the feast of the Body and Blood of the Lord. The body of the Lord is our resurrected body, carried up to the highest heaven. A great believer used to say, "Heaven is the sacred intimacy of Holy God." Then, in the feast of Corpus Christi, we celebrate the physical place where this sacred intimacy of our Holy God opens for us and is offered for us each day: the Eucharist.

In these difficult times of our country when base morality seems to flatten everything, it is good for us to raise our eyes to the Eucharist and remember what is the hope to which we have been called. We are invited to live in communion with Jesus: "Whoever eats my flesh and drinks my blood remains in me and I in him" (Jn 6:56). That was Jesus' command when he said at the Last Supper: "Do this in remembrance of me" (1 Cor 11:24).

With the words of Moses that we heard in the first reading, we remember. We look back remembering everything the Lord did with us. In this square that should be the symbolic space of the Nation's promised land, and that sometimes becomes a battlefield and a desert place, the words of Moses to the people resound in our ears with dramatic realism. "Remember how for forty years the LORD, your God, has directed all your journeying in the desert, so as to test you by affliction and find out whether or not it was your intention to keep his commandments" (Dt 8:2).

Moses interprets the history of his people, those forty years of apparent failure, from the perspective of the salvific gaze of the Lord. There are no lost decades in the eyes of God.

There in the desert, at the precise moment when the people cannot find anything, except their limits, the Lord gives them a special food: manna, prefigurement and anticipation of the Eucharist. That bread from heaven has its particular characteristics. It lasts only a day; you have to share it with others, because if there's extra, it's no good; everyone gathers only what he needs for his family. The manna teaches the people to live "from our daily bread."

In the Gospel, Jesus reveals to us that he is the manna, he is the "bread that came down from heaven" (Jn 6:51). He is the Bread that gives Life, everlasting life: "My flesh is true food" (v. 55). Many disciples left him that day, because these words were very hard to take. They wanted something more concrete, a better explanation of how we can live with what Jesus tells us, with what Jesus gives us. On the other hand, Peter and the apostles bet on the Lord: "to whom shall we go? You have the words of eternal life" (v. 68). We too, as a People, are in a similar situation: a desert situation, a situation that demands from us decisions on which our lives depend. Facing the living Bread, as a faithful People of God, let the Lord tell us: My people, remember the bread that our Heavenly Father feeds you with and the false loaves that excited you and led you to this situation.

Remember that the Bread of Heaven is living bread, which speaks to you of sowing and harvest, because it is the bread of a life that has to die in order to nurture. Remember that the Bread of Heaven is a bread for each day because your future is in the hands of the Good Father and not only in men's hands. Remember that the Bread of Heaven is bread of solidarity that is not good if hoarded but is to be shared and celebrated as a family. Remember that the Bread of Heaven is bread of eternal life and not perishable bread.

Remember that the Bread of Heaven is broken so that you may open your eyes of faith and not be unbelieving. Remember that the Bread of Heaven makes you a companion of Jesus and allows you to sit at the Father's table, from which none of your brothers are excluded. Remember that the Bread of Heaven makes you live in intimacy with your God and fraternally with your brothers. Remember that the Bread of Heaven, so that you could eat it, was broken on the Cross and shared generously for the salvation of all. Remember that the Bread of Heaven is multiplied when you take care to distribute it. Remember that the Bread of Heaven, it is blessed for you, broken by His scarred hands for love of you, and the very Risen Lord serves it to you. Remember! Remember! Never forget it!

This memory around bread opens us to the Spirit, strengthens us, gives us hope. May this unwavering hope of sitting one day at the table of the heavenly banquet free us from wanting to sit at the banquet of the self-satisfied and proud, those who do not leave even the crumbs to feed the poorest. May living in the sacred intimacy of the holy God free us from the internal fratricidal policies that tear our Homeland apart. Satisfied by the humble bread of every day, may we cure ourselves of financial ambition. May the daily work for the bread that gives eternal life awaken us from the vain dream of wealth and fame. May the taste of shared bread shake from us from the murmuring and complaining tone of the media. May the Eucharist celebrated with love defend us from all spiritual worldliness.

We ask the Virgin for the grace to remember. Our Lady is the model of the Christian and ecclesial soul who "kept all these things in her heart" (Lk 2:51). We ask her to remind us always of the bread that gives us life and the wine that brings happiness to our hearts. May she never stop telling us in her maternal voice: "Do whatever [Jesus] tells you" (Jn 2:5). May the words of her Son be recorded in our hearts: "Do this in memory of me."

Consecration of the City of Buenos Aires to Our Blessed Virgin Mary of Luján at the End of the Celebration of the Solemnity of Corpus Christi

Our dear Mother, Virgin of Luján, I consecrate this city of Buenos Aires to your immaculate maternal heart. I consecrate to you each of your children. You know us well, and we know that you love us very much. Today, after having adored Your Son Jesus Christ, our elder brother and our God, I ask you to look at each one of us. I pray to you for every family in this city.

I pray to you for our children and our elders; for our sick ones; for those who are alone; for those who are in jail; for those who are hungry and have no work. For those who have lost hope; for those without faith. I also ask you for those who govern us and those who teach us. Our mother, I ask you to care for all of us with tenderness and to pass on to us your strength. We are your children. We put ourselves under your protection. Do not leave us alone in this moment of so much pain and difficulties. We trust in your Mother's Heart and we consecrate all that we are and all that we have. And above all, Mother, show us Jesus, and teach us to do what he tells us. Amen.

→→ ←←

"The Lord, Your God, Shall You Worship and Him Alone Shall You Serve"

Letter to Catechists—August 2002

The Lord, your God, shall you worship and him alone shall you serve. (Mt 4:10)

"Perhaps, as very seldom in our history, this badly wounded society awaits a new coming of the Lord. It awaits the healing and reconciling entrance of the One who is the Way, the Truth, and the Life. We have reasons to wait in hope. We do not forget that his passing through, and his salvific presence, have been a constant in our history. We discover the wonderful footprint of his creative work in the incomparable wealth of our natural environment. Divine generosity has also been reflected in the life testimony of self-giving and sacrifice by our fathers and heroes, as well as in the millions of humble and believing faces, our brothers, those anonymous protagonists of work and heroic struggles, incarnation of the silent epic of the Spirit that founds nations.

However, we live very far from the gratitude merited by so many gifts we have received. What prevents us from seeing this coming of the Lord? What makes it impossible to 'Taste and see that the LORD is good' (Ps 34:9) in the face of so much prodigality on earth and in men? What in our Nation hinders the possibilities of taking advantage of the full encounter between the Lord, his gifts, and ourselves? Just as in the Jerusalem of that time, when Jesus was crossing the city and that man named Zacchaeus could not see him among so many people, something prevents us from seeing and feeling his presence."

The homily for the *Te Deum* of last May 25 began with these words. And I would like that homily to serve as an introduction to this letter that with grateful affection I send to you in the midst of your silent but important task of building the Church.

I am not exaggerating when I say that we are in a time of "spiritual myopia and moral baseness" seeking to impose as normal a "culture of the low," in which there seems to be no place for transcendence and hope.

But as you well know by being a catechist, and through the wisdom that comes from the weekly encounter with the people, there continues to throb in mankind a desire and need for God. Faced with the pride and invasive arrogance of the new Goliaths, which from certain media and no less official dispatches, reinstate prejudices and autistic ideologies, now more than ever the serene confidence of David is necessary, so that, from the plain, the inheritance can be defended. That is why I would like to insist as I wrote to you a year ago: "Today more than ever, behind so many demands made by our people, one can discover a search for the Absolute that, at times, takes the shape as a painful cry from an outraged humanity: 'We would like to see Jesus' (Jn 12:21). There are many faces making this request of us, through a silence more telling than a thousand words. We know them well. They are in our midst; they are part of that faithful people that God entrusts to us. Faces of children, of young people, of adults. . . . Some of them have the pure look of the 'beloved disciple,' others, the downward gaze of the prodigal son. There is no shortage of faces marked by pain and despair. But all of them hope, seek, want to see Jesus. And that is why they 'ask believers, not only to 'speak' of Christ, but in a certain sense to 'show' him to them. . . . Our witness, however, would be hopelessly inadequate if we ourselves had not first *contemplated his face*' (NMI 16).

Because of this, I am encouraged to propose that we pause this year to deepen the theme of *worship*.

Today more than ever it is necessary to "worship in spirit and truth" (Jn 4:24). It is an indispensable task of the catechist who wants to be rooted in God, who wants to not lose heart in the midst of so much commotion.

Today more than ever it is necessary to worship in order to make possible the fellowship demanded by these times of crisis. Only in the contemplation of the mystery of Love that overcomes distances and becomes closeness will we find the strength not to fall into the temptation of passing by, without stopping on the road.

Today more than ever it is necessary to teach those being catechized to worship, so that our catechesis be truly an initiation and not only teaching.

Today more than ever it is necessary to worship without being overwhelmed with words that sometimes hide the Mystery, but rather give ourselves to the quiet full of admiration that falls silent before the Word that becomes presence and closeness.

Today, more than ever, it is necessary to worship!

Because to worship is to prostrate oneself, to recognize from the place of humility the infinite greatness of God. Only true humility can recognize true greatness, and it can also recognize that smallness which pretends to be greatness. Perhaps one of the greatest perversions of our time is that it is proposed to us to worship the human, leaving aside the divine. "Only the Lord shall you worship" is the great challenge before so many proposals of nothingness and emptiness. Not to worship the contemporary idols—with their siren songs—is the great challenge of today; not to worship what is not to be worshiped is the great sign of these times. Idols that cause death do not deserve to be worshiped, only the God of life is "divine or worthy of worship" (cf. DP 491).

To worship is to look with confidence at the One who appears as reliable because he is the giver of life, instrument of peace, generator of *encounter* and solidarity.

To worship is to stand before all that is not deserving of worship, because worship makes us free and makes us people full of life.

To worship is not to empty oneself but to be filled; it is to recognize and commune with Love. No one worships someone whom he does not love, no one worships anyone who is not considered his love. We are loved! We are loved! "God is love." This certainty is what leads us to worship with all our heart the One who "first loved us" (1 Jn 4:19).

To worship is to discover his tenderness, to find comfort and rest in his presence, is to be able to experience what Psalm 23 expresses: "Even though I walk through the valley of the shadow of death, I will fear no evil, for you are with me. . . . Indeed, goodness and mercy will pursue me all the days of my life."

To worship is to be joyful witnesses of his victory; it is not to allow ourselves to be overcome by the great tribulation but instead to taste beforehand the feast of the encounter with the Lamb, the only one worthy of adoration, who will dry all our tears and in whom we celebrate the triumph of life and of love, death and helplessness (cf. Rev. 21–22).

To worship is to draw closer to unity, to discover that we are children of the same Father, members of one family, as Saint Francis discovered: to sing praises in unity to all creation and to all men. It is to retie the bonds that we have broken with our earth, with our brothers; it is to recognize him as Lord of all things, kind Father of the whole world.

To worship is to say "God," and to say "life." It is to meet face to face in our daily life with the God of life, to worship him with our life and our witness. It is to know that we have a faithful God who has stayed with us and who trusts us.

To worship is to say, AMEN!

In greeting you on this Day of the Catechist, I want to thank you again for all your dedication to the service of the faithful People. And I ask Mary Most Holy to keep that thirst for God alive in your heart so that you can, like the Samaritan woman of the Gospel, "worship in Spirit and truth" (Jn 4:24) and many "began to believe in [Jesus]" (v. 39).

Do not stop praying for me so I can be a good catechist. May Jesus bless you, and may the Blessed Virgin take care of you.

→→ ←←

Get in Line and Walk

Homily, Shrine of Saint Cajetan—August 7, 2002

Dear brothers, dear friends and faithful of Saint Cajetan,

I want to greet all of you with these words of Saint Paul that are the best we can wish each other as Christians: I hope that everyone, that all of us, "Have among yourselves the same attitude that is also yours in Christ Jesus" (Phil 2:5). All the attitudes of Jesus revolve around a single attitude, the most profound: "No one has greater love than this, to lay down one's life for one's friends" (Jn 15:13). "You are my friends" (v. 14), Jesus tells us. And I have no other desire than to give my life for each one of you. I hope you feel the same: that everyone feels it toward me and also toward their friends, their children, their elders, their family. I hope that as a people we receive this grace: to feel the desire to give our lives for our brothers with whom we live in our beloved nation of Argentina.

This year's theme says: "With Saint Cajetan we claim nurturing bread and dignified work." Claiming the bread that feeds is a way of wanting to give life: We claim the bread because to give life you need to have bread to share. Before giving his life on the Cross, Jesus wanted to gather together with his friends around the table, he wanted to take the bread in his hands to break and share it, to break and share himself. To claim work that dignifies is a way of wanting to give life. We demand work because it is the dignified way to spend ourselves creatively for others. You cannot give your life without sharing bread or working. But neither is it truly a life unless you give it away daily. That is why our people do not sit down to wait for everything from their demands, but instead their demands involve sharing each day the little bit of bread they have and inventing a thousand solidary ways of working for the community. At the same time that we demand justice, we come here to pray to the Lord of life and to ask him for bread and work, through the intercession of Saint Cajetan.

"Have in you the same attitude that is also in Christ Jesus" (Phil 2:5). It is good for us to remember how at the worst moment of his life, on the night of betrayal and abandonment, Jesus had the noblest attitude. They were taking everything away from him and he turned himself into Bread for his people. He transformed the plundering into gift. "No one takes [my life] from me, but I lay it down on my own" (Jn 10:18). This silent example of Jesus, who carries the cross and assumes sin, including of those who kill him, contains an invitation. And there are people who accept that invitation, there are entire nations who rise from their ruins and with silent dignity put their hands to work and transform a situation of abasement and violence into a time of gift.

People who give themselves to work and if their salary is not sufficient they barter their goods with joy. People who give themselves to solidarity, and if they don't get enough bread, they break it and share it as necessary. People who give themselves to prayer and put their hope in the God of life. People who are able to make this "queue" that is the line of Saint Cajetan: a line that peacefully cuts across some streets, not to obstruct the passage of anyone but to show that the only true door is open—the narrow door that opens a breach to the intimacy of the Holy God in whom we are all brothers—a "queue" that is a bridge because it extends hands to Jesus Christ the true Bridge, between men of good will and our Father in Heaven.

Our faithful People have been demonstrating this faith forever. To demand life-giving bread and work is not something circumstantial or only to be pursued during difficult times. That is why this march, this demonstration, this 'line' from which for so many years our people stop their daily work to demand, together with Saint Cajetan, together with the Virgin, the attention of the Lord and of the brothers, all the marches, all the demonstrations, all the lines that are made in our country have to become contagious. In order to spread this grace is why we ask the Father to have the same attitudes that Jesus had.

We want to rescue those deep values that we have received as a people and, in these difficult moments, give a testimony of hope, of solidarity, of peaceful and insistent demands, with hunger and thirst for justice. As I have been saying to you, year after year, in this same Mass: We want to rescue that hope that contains the humble gesture of getting in line and walking— of getting in line like the grains of the saint's ear of wheat—remember?— to walk without trampling on anyone, without shortcuts, without being disappointed. We want to rescue the value of inclusion that our beloved shrine has, whose open doors welcome everyone without excluding anyone and that must be the image of our homes and our institutions. We want to rescue that strength of our faithful people who know how to "offer their shoulders" and carry the cross helping others. We want to rescue that solidarity, that spirit of the Good Samaritan that is in our faithful people and that leads them to "not pass by" in the face of pain and injustice, the desire to approach all who suffer to give a hand as Jesus did. We want to rescue the grace of that "Beatitude of Jesus to those who mourn" because they hunger and thirst for justice and receive from their hands the comfort we need.

That is why all together we are going to cry out to the Lord, together with Saint Cajetan, praying the beautiful prayer that was written for the novena:

We need to see your face
Observe the words from your mouth
Speak to your ear
Allow your eyes to see us
And when kissing you, Christ, seeing in you the features of your mother,
Of your saints, of your suffering people.
We want to see your face
God our friend
Companion on our journey.

→ ←

Communicator, Who Is Your Neighbor?

Keynote Address, Third Congress of Media Personnel—October 10, 2002

When facing the reflection of the topic that was proposed to me, as a Christian, I cannot at the outset omit the Gospel. Not only because the question of who is your neighbor is inspired by the parable of the Good Samaritan, but—and fundamentally—because the Gospel of the Lord is precisely to communicate good news.

The Gospel as Good News

"Go into all the world and proclaim the gospel" (Mk 16:15). ". . . teaching them to observe all that I have commanded you" (Mt 28:20): the law of charity. The Gospel is good news that we have the mission to announce to everyone and to do it "from the rooftops." And if we delve further, we see that the most profoundly human criteria of the announcement, also for the new media, are those of the Gospel. For this reason, I approach the subject from this perspective. On the other hand, the challenge presented by social media, with its technologies, its global reach, its omnipresence, and its influence on society and culture, are an invitation to dialogue and to the "inculturation of the Gospel" in them, while at the same time opening up an "evangelization of the media."

The Power of Social Media and Communicators

Today the profession of communicators and the technology of social media allow us to reach far and deep into the human heart, where important decisions are made. This is due to the powerful potential of the image to penetrate, stir, move, motivate, and affect our behavior. The image moves us, motivates our choices and decisions. It internally organizes the structure of the sense and meaning of existence; the image is generating the operational forces that move us. Like the creative Word of God, communicators can create or re-create an image of reality with only one word. And today's technology globalizes and makes simultaneous this power of the word.

That is why the actions and influence of the social media in society and in culture are so fascinating and powerful. They can help grow or disorient.

They can re-create things, informing us about reality to help us in the discernment of our options and decisions, or on the contrary, they can create virtual simulations, illusions, fantasies, and fictions that also move us to make life choices. This explains in part why investments in the development of technology for social media and for the production of images are so large. Social media are today the main instruments in the creation of culture. Thanks to the media, communicators reach huge audiences. I like to categorize this power that the media have with the concept of neighborliness. Its strength lies in the ability to get close and influence the lives of people with the same language that is simultaneous and global. The category of neighborliness involves a bipolar tension: to get close/to move away and—at the same time, inwardly—also has a tension by the way it does things: getting close for good and getting close for ill. In the practice of the media there is a way to approach for the good and another way to approach for the bad.

The Parable of the Good Samaritan

Taking this into account, we enter fully into our subject with the question: "Communicator, who is your neighbor?" which places us within the scope of the parable of the Good Samaritan. The question we pose for ourselves is the same one that the scribe (the communicator) put to Jesus: "And who is my neighbor?" As if to say, the commandment to love is clear to all, the problem is in the concrete: Who is it that I must love? How is neighborliness made real in the use of social media? Each neighbor individually, the totality of people, groups? . . . Can an evangelical message be given simultaneously that is not only highly personalized but also "global"? How do you love yourself through social media?

The Image of the Beaten Man on the Side of the Road

Although the image of the man beaten by the thieves and thrown on the side of the road is an image that points to the gospel behavior—ethical and moral—it is legitimate to transpose what is said of good to the field of truth and beauty. Even more: Truth and beauty are inseparable when we communicate; inseparable by presence or also by absence, and—in the latter case—the good will not be good, the truth will not be true, beauty will not be beauty. Currently there is an invisible majority of excluded ones, who are on the side of the road, beaten and robbed, and the media passes by them.

They exhibit them, pass on messages, make them speak. . . . Here neighborliness comes into play, the way of approaching them. The way in which it is done will determine respect for human dignity.

To Approach Well, to Approach Badly
from an Aesthetic Point of View

As well as at the ethical level, approaching well is for helping and not hurting; and at the level of truth, to approach well is to transmit truthful information; at an aesthetic level, to approach well is to communicate the integrity of reality in a harmonious and clear way. To approach badly is instead to approach with a disintegrating aesthetic that shuts down certain aspects of the problem or manipulates them, creating disharmony that obscures reality, disfigures it, and debases it.

To Approach Badly with a Disintegrating Aesthetic

When images and information have as their sole objective to induce consumption or manipulate people in order to take advantage of them, we are face to face with an assault, a beating. It is the feeling that you have many times before the bombardment of seductive and hopeless images. To feel bombarded, invaded, shocked, impotent to do something positive . . . feelings that are equivalent to those you have during an assault, an act of violence, a kidnapping. And precisely behind a disintegrating aesthetic that instills the hopelessness of being able to discover the truth and of being able to do the common good, it is necessary to know how to discern and be able to unmask the existence of political and economic interests of certain sectors that do not point toward the common good.

This disintegrating aesthetic operates in us in the same way that the 'law' and the 'liturgy' operated in the hearts of those who passed by the wounded: the Levite and the priest. They did not see the reality of a wounded neighbor, but the pseudo-reality of an 'outsider,' of a 'stranger' whom it is convenient to pass by. In those days what drove them away were their 'ideas' of the law and of the ritual service. Even today there is a risk that certain media will install a law and a liturgy that, in order to seek and serve other interests, will make us also pass by our actual neighbor.

To Approach Well, Communicating the Beauty of Charity in Truth

To approach well implies communicating the beauty of charity in truth. When the truth is painful and the good is difficult to perform, the beauty is in that love that shares the pain with respect and in a dignified manner. Against all sensationalism, there is a worthy way to show pain that rescues the values and spiritual resources of a people and helps overcome evil by force of good, to work together in the will to excel, in solidarity, in that proximity that enlarges us, open to the truth and the good. On the contrary, "confrontation and disqualification as a system, even through the irresponsible use of the media, are opposed to pluralistic and mature coexistence" as we, the Argentine bishops, have said.

Communicating What Has Been Contemplated

The first announcers of the Good News of Jesus Christ proclaimed it in terms of contemplation and witness: "What we have heard, what we have seen with our eyes, what we looked upon and touched with our hands concerns the Word of life—for the life was made visible; we have seen it and testify to it and proclaim to you the eternal life" (1 Jn 1:1–3). Faced with the infinite number of images that populate the world, only the austere exercise of contemplating the Face of Christ allows us to realistically mirror our condition wounded by sin in the merciful eyes of Jesus, and to discover in the Face of the Lord the face of our brothers so that we become more neighborly. Only the austere exercise of contemplating the Face of Christ allows us to discover the same Face of the Lord in the other in order to make us neighbors. Jesus is the visible Face of the invisible God, and the excluded and marginalized of today are the visible face of Jesus. Contemplation is what allows us to solve the paradox of making invisible faces visible.

To approach for good also always implies giving witness. Against the apparent neutrality of the media, only the one who communicates by observing his own ethics and giving witness to the truth is reliable to approach reality well. The personal testimony of the communicator is the very basis of its reliability.

Communicating with a Sense of Transcendence

Social media currently populates the world with images that are not windows to the Other. To approach well is always to show that image open to the Other, to transcendence, to hope, as shown by the images of the Virgin and the cathedrals. To approach well is the opposite of the frivolous approach of some media that convey a caricature of man. It is to show and highlight his dignity, the greatness of his vocation, the beauty of love that shares pain, the sense of sacrifice, and the joy of achievement.

The media can, unfortunately, be a mirror of society in its worst aspects or in the frivolous and narcissistic. But they can also be an open window through which the beauty of God's wondrous love flows in the marvels of his works, in the acceptance of his Mercy and in solidarity and justice with others.

Communicating the Beauty of Love That Shares Joy and Pain

The images in the parable of the oil and wine with which the Good Samaritan communicates his love to the wounded are two very decisive images for a communicator. What needs to be communicated should be perfumed oil for pain and delicious wine for joy. The beauty of love is joyful without being frivolous. We think about the beauty of a Mother Teresa or a Don Zatti,[1] whose luminosity does not come from any makeup or any special effects but from that radiance of charity when it wears out while caring for the needy, anointing them with that perfumed oil of their tenderness. Only the Samaritan enjoys the beauty of charity and the commitment to love and be loved freely. An experience that begins by being moved from the depths, by the tenderness of the heart; by becoming sensitive to beauty and the beauty of God in man ("The glory of God is man fully alive"),[2] to the beauty and joy of peace and the communion of man with God in humble service to the anonymous wounded, the unknown . . . on the margins of the city, the Market, society . . . out on the open road. . . . It is a different beauty. It is the beauty of Love.

---

1. Don Artemide Zatti was a priest born in Italy whose family migrated to Argentina when he was a child. Pope John Paul II beatified him in 2002.
2. Saint Irenaeus, bishop of Lyons and one of the early church fathers, lived in the second century.

In the broken Jesus of the cross, who has no appearance or presence in the eyes of the world and TV cameras, the beauty of the wondrous love of God who gives his life for us shines forth. It is the beauty of charity, the beauty of the saints. When we think of someone like Mother Teresa of Calcutta, our heart is filled with a beauty that does not come from her physical features or her height, but from the beautiful radiance of the charity toward the poor and disinherited that accompanies her.

In the same way there is a distinct beauty in the worker who returns to his house dirty and disheveled, but with the joy of having won the bread for his children. There is an extraordinary beauty in the communion of the family gathered at table and in the bread generously shared, although the table be very poor. There is beauty in the disheveled and rather elderly wife, who remains caring for her sick husband beyond her strength and her own health. Although the spring of courtship in youth has passed, there is an extraordinary beauty in the fidelity of couples who love each other in the autumn of life, those elderly ones who walk hand in hand. There is beauty, beyond the appearance or aesthetic of fashion in each man and woman who lovingly live out their personal vocation in selfless service to the community, for the homeland; in generous work for the happiness of the family ... engaged in the anonymous and impartial hard work of restoring social friendship. . . . There is beauty in creation, in the infinite tenderness and mercy of God, in the offering of life in service for love. To discover, show, and highlight this beauty is to lay the foundations of a culture of solidarity and social friendship.

Communicating with a Sense of Time, with Memory and Hope

The Pope speaks of Christian culture as news worth remembering (World Communications Day 2000). Rebuilding social bonds and social friendship requires the communicator to rescue from the embers of the cultural and spiritual reserve of our people the beauty of communion, of national community; to rescue and communicate the memory and beauty of our founding fathers, of our heroes, and of our saints.

This cultural reserve is the space of culture, of the arts, a fertile space where the community contemplates and narrates its family history, where the sense of belonging is reaffirmed, based on embodied values and imprinted in the collective memory. These communal spaces of fruitful, quasi-sacred leisure are often occupied today by social media with pastimes that do not always engender true joy and gladness. Merely punctual communication, lacking in history, has no sense of time and, consequently, does not create hope. On the other hand, the communicator—by his own vocation—is a reliable and qualified witness of the beauty of the wondrous love that becomes kindred, that becomes capable of assuming and continuing a history.

Conclusion: A Double Challenge

On the one hand, the Christian communicator has the challenge of knowing, feeling, and tasting the beauty of God's wondrous Love, living in the dead and risen Jesus Christ, in his Presence and merciful action among us, through the exercise of Contemplation. . . . This personal encounter with Jesus Christ is the light that allows us to discern the beauty of values, in the presence of the empty image of technical cosmetics.

The experience of the beauty of God's wondrous love, through the personal and communal encounter with Jesus Christ, is the motor for Christian creativity to communicate the Good News.

On the other hand, the challenge of sharing this beauty of God's marvelous Love with such a specific vocation, when the communications and information revolution in full transformation places the Church on a decisive path as it is to cross these new cultural thresholds, which require new energies and imagination to proclaim the one gospel of Jesus Christ, demands of the Christian communicator extensive training and true professionalism in order to use the technology and the language of the media competently.

The Other Good Samaritan

Saint Maximilian Maria Kolbe, martyr of charity, prisoner 16670 of Auschwitz, proposed by John Paul II for the use he made of social media, as patron of journalists in all branches of social communications, knew how to approach the wounded of the concentration camp. And there, where the jailers and executioners were stripping and beating, he became neighbor, like Jesus himself, offering up his life in the service of love, in place of Franciszek Gajowniczek, who had been sentenced to death. . . . He, as a model of all communicators, makes us see that the most competent way to communicate the Gospel of Jesus Christ is the beauty of the testimony of commitment to the truth and the gift of life for love.

Lord, may we become neighbors like the Good Samaritan of the Gospel, who is none other than you, transfigured by the beauty of God's marvelous Love for us; let our innermost being be moved and our heart be tender in the presence of our brother; may we discover the beauty of the marvelous Love with which we are saved, so that we may joyfully communicate the beauty of the commitment to love our neighbor according to the example of Maximilian Kolbe.

2003

To Educate Is to Choose Life

Message to the Educational Community—April 9, 2003

Introduction

Exactly one year ago, I began my message to the educational communities by talking about a critical and decisive moment in the life of our people. Many things have happened since then: suffering, confusion, indignation, but also so many men and women offering their shoulders to help their neighbors, rather than sheltering behind indifference or other people's desire to 'save their skins.' As a result, we are convinced that there is no need to wait for any 'savior' or 'magic' spell that can show us the way forward or enable us to fulfill our 'true destiny.' There is no 'true destiny,' there is no magic. What we have is a people whose history is full of questions and doubts, with its institutions barely standing, its values dangling from question marks, its basic tools only sufficient for short-term survival, things too 'heavy' to be entrusted to a charismatic or a technician, things that can be turned in a more favorable direction only by a collective action of historic creation. I don't think I'm mistaken in guessing that your task as educators will have to spearhead this challenge. Collectively creating a better reality, with the limitations and possibilities of history, is an act of hope. Not one of certainties or mere inclinations, nor of destiny or fate. It requires beliefs and virtues. To bring all the resources into play, plus an imponderable extra 'something' that makes it dramatic.

This year's reflection also has to do with hope, but quite particularly to do with an essential component of its active dimension: creativity. Because if we are at a moment of historic and collective creation, our task as educators can no longer be confined to 'keep on doing the same as always' or even 'resisting' an extremely hostile reality. It is time to create, to start laying the bricks for a new building in the midst of history, in other words, located in a present that has a past and—we hope—a future, too.

Utopia and Historic Creation

For us, talking about 'creation' has an immediate connotation with belief. Faith in God the Creator tells us that the history of mankind is not a boundless vacuum: it has a beginning and it also has a direction. The God who created heaven and earth is the same God who made a Promise to his people, and his absolute power is the guarantee of the effectiveness of his love. Faith in creation is thus a pillar of hope. Human history, our history, the history of each one of us, our families, our communities, the concrete history that we build day by day in our schools, is never 'finished'; it never exhausts its possibilities, but can always open itself to new possibilities, to things that have been disregarded until now. To what has appeared impossible. Because this history is part of a creation that has its roots in the Power and Love of God.

Once again, it is important to clarify that it is not some sort of battle of wills between pessimism and optimism. We're talking about hope, and hope doesn't feel at home with either of those options. We're going to focus on creativity as a feature of active hope. In what sense can we human beings be creative, be creators? Not, of course, in the sense of 'creating something out of nothing,' like God. Our creative capacity is far humbler and limited, given that it is a gift from God that, first of all, we have to receive. When it comes to exercising our creativity, we need to learn to move within the tension between novelty and continuity. That is to say, we need to allow the new to come starting from what already exists. For human creativity, there is neither 'creation out of nothing' nor 'identical repetition of the same.' To act creatively is to take seriously on board what already exists, in all its density, and find the path from which something new can appear.

At this point, we can once again refer, as we did last year, to one of the most significant masters of faith: Saint Augustine. In his work *The City of God*, this Church Father reflected on the sense of history from the perspective of eschatological salvation through Christ. The imminent fall of the Roman Empire heralded a profound historic novelty: the end of an era and the uncertain beginning of another. And Augustine set himself the task of understanding God's designs in order to illuminate the Church entrusted to his ministry. We already explained the central elements of this work in last year's message. Ultimately, we referred back to human history as a place of discernment between offers of grace, which seek the true fulfillment of man, society, and history in eschatological redemption, and the temptations of sin, which seek to construct a destiny by opposing the divine dynamic of salvation.

But this Augustinian thinking has other dimensions that can guide us in searching for a historical creativity. To benefit from its teaching, we need first to ask ourselves about the meaning of utopia. Utopias are primarily the fruit of the imagination, which projects into the future a constellation of desires and aspirations. A utopia takes its strength from two elements: on the one hand, the disagreement, dissatisfaction, or uneasiness generated by present reality, and on the other hand, the unshakable conviction that another world is possible. This is the source of its mobilizing strength. Far from being just a comforting fantasy, an imaginary otherness, utopia is a form that hope takes in a specific historical context.

All utopian constructs are fueled by the belief that the world can be perfected and human beings have the resources to achieve a fuller life. But this belief goes hand in hand with a real quest for mediations through which to realize that ideal. Because although the term 'utopia' refers literally to something that exists 'nowhere,' something that does not exist in any locatable way, it does not follow that it is completely removed from historical reality. On the contrary, it is posited as a possible development that is at present only imagined. Let us take note of this: something that does not yet exist, something new, but toward which we must move, starting from what there is. This is why all utopias include both a description of an ideal society and an analysis of the mechanisms or strategies that could make it possible. We can call it a projection toward the future that tends to return to the present in search of its possible ways forward, in this order: first, the ideal, vividly sketched, followed by certain mediations that could hypothetically make it viable.

But more than that, in its 'there and back' from the present, it fundamentally depends on the negation of undesirable aspects of present reality. It springs from rejection (not visceral but intelligent) of a situation seen as bad, unjust, dehumanizing, alienating, and so on. In this sense, it should be pointed out that utopia proposes something new . . . but without ever freeing itself from what exists now. It outlines the expectation of novelty based on the current perception of what would be desirable if we could free ourselves of the factors that oppress us, the tendencies that prevent us from reaching a higher level. Thus, we are able to see from two different sides the indissoluble connection between the desired future and the endured present. Utopia is not pure fantasy; it also criticizes reality and looks for new paths.

This rejection of what actually exists in favor of another possible world, expressed as a leap into the future that must then find its means of becoming viable, has two serious limitations: first, a certain crazy quality, linked to its fantastic or imaginary nature, which, when the emphasis is placed on that dimension rather than on the pragmatic aspects of its construction, can make it a mere dream, an impossible desire. The current 'realistic' use of the term contains echoes of this. The second limitation is that its rejection of present reality and its desire to install something new can result in an even fiercer and more intractable form of authoritarianism than the one it tried to overcome. How many times, in the course of human history, have utopian ideals given rise to every form of injustice, intolerance, persecution, abuse, and dictatorships of various stripes?

So, then, it is precisely these two limitations of utopian thinking that have discredited it in current times, either because of a supposed realism that confines itself to 'the possible,' with the possible being understood as just the interplay of dominant forces, ruling out human capacity to create reality out of ethical aspirations, or because of weariness with promises of certain new worlds that, in the last century, have brought only more suffering to the world's peoples.

And here we can reread *The City of God*. Utopia, as we know it, is a typically modern construct (although its roots are found deep in the millenarian movements of the second half of the Middle Ages). But Saint Augustine, by formulating his idea of two cities (the city of God, governed by love, and the earthly city, ruled by egoism) inextricably juxtaposed in secular history, gives us some clues to locating the relationship between novelty and continuity, which is precisely the crux of utopian thought and the key to all historical creativity. The City of God is in effect, first and foremost, a critique of the outlook that sanctified political power and the status quo. All the empires of antiquity were grounded in this form of belief. Religion was an essential part of the whole symbolic and imaginary edifice that upheld society, based on a sanctified power structure. This was not only the case for 'pagans'; once Christianity was adopted as the religion of the Roman Empire, it gradually became an 'official theology' underpinning political reality, as if it were already the Kingdom of God consummated on earth.

It was exactly this type of theological reading of a historical reality that Saint Augustine opposed in his writing. By showing the seeds of corruption in imperial Rome, he was breaking apart any identification of the Kingdom of Christ with the earthly domain. And by presenting the City of God as a reality present in history, but in a way that was intertwined with the earthly City and only 'separable' at the final judgment, he allowed for the possibility of another possible history that could be lived and constructed on the basis of other values and other ideals. Whereas according to the 'official theology' history was the exclusive and excluding abode of the self-referenced Power, in *The City of God* it becomes a space for a Freedom that welcomes the gift of salvation and the divine plan of a transfigured humanity and world. A plan that will be consummated in eschatology, it is true, but which can already, here in history, start generating new realities, overthrowing false determinisms, repeatedly opening up the horizon of hope and creativity with an 'extra' sense, with a promise that constantly invites us to keep on going.

We can also claim the 'utopian' moment of his criticism of the sacralized model and link it to the realism with which the Bishop of Hippo considered his active belonging to the Church. Because another aspect of our saint is his committed and real struggle to build a strong, united Church, centered on the experience of faith to which he himself was a privileged witness, but also taking shape in a historical, earthly manner in a specific community. His firmly held position against the Donatists (a schism that upheld a church of the 'pure,' with no place for sinners) clearly displayed the realistic belief that waiting for a new heaven should not leave us unresponsive to the challenges of the present and focused on 'purity' or 'nonpollution with earthly concerns,' but that—on the contrary—it should give us guidance and energy of our own with which to 'pummel' the clay of everyday life, the ambiguous clay of human history, to mold a world more worthy of the children of God. Not heaven on earth: just a more human world, while awaiting God's eschatological action.

Historical creativity, then, from a Christian perspective, follows the parable of the wheat and the chaff. It is necessary to project utopias, and, at the same time, it is necessary to take responsibility for what is already here. There is no clean slate, no new beginning. Being creative does not mean discarding everything that makes up present reality, however limited, corrupt, and worn out it may appear to be. There is no future without a present or a past: Creativity also means memory and discernment, equanimity and justice, prudence and strength. If we are going to try to contribute something to our homeland from the angle of education, we cannot lose sight of both poles: utopian and realist, because both are an integral part of historical creativity. We must encourage ourselves toward the new, without throwing out what others (and even we ourselves) have built with effort.

A Creative Figure in Argentine History

Let us look at this in a slightly more specific way. Why not try, while we're talking about it, to take a lesson from history? Thinking about the founding years of our nation, I met with a figure whose significant role in the early life of Argentina has generally gone unrecognized. I'm talking about Manuel Belgrano.[1]

What can be said about him, other than his participation in the First Junta and the creation of the flag? He wasn't a 'successful' man, at least in the ways we have grown accustomed to using that word in these times of pragmatism and foolishness. His military campaigns lacked the shine and depth that won José de San Martín the title of 'Liberator.' He lacked the writing and propaganda skills of a Sarmiento. As a politician, he was relegated to the backbenches. Nor was his private life particularly noteworthy: his health left much to be desired; he was unable to wed the woman he loved, and he died in poverty at the age of fifty. Nevertheless, Sarmiento called him "one of the few people who needs not beg forgiveness from posterity and the harsh verdict of history. His obscure death still provides the guarantee that he was an upright citizen, an irreproachable patriot." There are very few 'successful' figures in our national history of whom the same could be said. In fact, Belgrano, apart from his unquestionable personal virtues and deeply rooted Christian faith, was a man who was able, at just the right moment, to find the dynamism, drive, and equilibrium that are the hallmarks of true creativity: the difficult but fruitful union of realistic continuity and magnanimous innovation. His influence at the dawn of our national identity was much greater than is generally held; and that is why he can stand up and show us, at this time of uncertainty but also of challenges, 'how to do it' when it comes to laying lasting foundations in a task of historical creation.

---

1. Manuel Belgrano (1770–1820), Argentine economist, politician, and general, is a hero of Argentine independence. Among the leaders of the May Revolution of 1810, he was the designer of the country's flag.

A Creative Revolutionary

Belgrano lived in an era of utopias. The son of an Italian father and Creole mother, he had devoted himself to legal studies at some of the best universities of the metropolis: Salamanca, Madrid, and Valladolid. In the upheaval of late eighteenth-century Europe, the young Belgrano had not only learned the discipline he had gone to study but had also become interested in the whirlwind of nascent ideas that were shaping the new era—in particular, political economy. Firmly convinced by the most progressive ideas of his time, he didn't hesitate to formulate his own internal project: to put all this at the service of a great cause in the country of his birth. Thus, in 1794, he was appointed first Perpetual Secretary of the Royal Consulate of Industry and Commerce of the Viceroyalty of the River Plate, a post similar to today's Minister of the Treasury. It was unusual for strongly centralist Bourbon Spain to appoint the son of a colonial native and a foreigner to such an important post. But in Buenos Aires there was a shortage of men with his educational background. The new Secretary soon came face to face with reality in the Americas, when he tried to fulfill his task of stimulating production and trade with a truly transformational spirit. He quickly realized that his shining ideals of progress and the rights of man clashed with the conservative mentalities of the colonial administration and wealthy classes of Buenos Aires, traders who were benefiting from the Spanish monopoly and bootlegging.

> I realized nothing would be done to benefit the provinces by men who put their private interests before those of the common people. Nevertheless, since the duties of my employment allowed me to speak and write about such useful matters, I took it upon myself to at least sow the seeds which could someday grow to fruition, either because they had been cultivated by a few persons spurred on by the same spirit, or because the very order of things had caused them to germinate.

He expressed that in his brief autobiography. What were these seeds? In the words of our statesman, "To set up schools is to sow seeds in people's souls." Belgrano's revolutionary spirit rapidly discovered that the new, that which could one day be able to change a static and fossilized reality, would come into being through education. Therefore, he used all possible means to further the creation of elementary and specialized schools. The annual *Memoirs* of the Consulate, the newspapers *Telégrafo Mercantil* and, later, *Correo de Comercio*, were some of the means by which he tried to "sow" those "seeds." His preaching insisted on the need for technical education, designing projects for schools of agriculture, commerce, architecture, mathematics, and drawing. Out of all these, only the nautical and drawing schools came into being. Long before anyone else, Belgrano understood that education and even training in modern disciplines and techniques were key elements for the development of his native land. If his projects failed to materialize, it was because—as he himself wrote years afterwards—"all of them ran up against either the Government of Buenos Aires or the Court or, among the traders themselves, individuals who made up that body who could recognize no reason, justice, utility or need beyond their own mercantile interest; anything that conflicted with it was vetoed, without hope of appeal." But this could not make him give up his cause; one way or another he managed to carry on spreading his ideas and putting them into practice, because apart from being an idealist, the creator of the flag was extremely determined and not easily defeated, despite his moderate and conciliatory nature.

Besides his work toward economic development, Belgrano maintained that *"an educated people can never be enslaved."* Human dignity occupied a central position in his mentality, which was also both Christian and enlightened. As a result, he also campaigned for the creation of schools in towns and in the countryside, where all children could be taught to read and write, along with basic arithmetic, the catechism, and a few useful skills with which to earn a living.

> *"Those miserable hovels where you see hordes of children, who reach the age of puberty without having been schooled in anything other than idleness, must be addressed to the last detail,"* he wrote in 1796. *"One of the main means which should be adopted toward this end is free schools, where these unfortunates may send their children without having to pay the least thing for their instruction, there they may be taught good conduct and instilled with the love of work, since in a country where idleness reigns, trade declines and is replaced by poverty."*

The same spirit can be seen in his insistence (in the *Regulations of the School of Geometry, Architecture, Perspective and Drawing*, written in his own hand) on equal rights for Spaniards, Creoles, and Indians and that four places should be reserved for orphans, "the most dispossessed in our land." Similarly, Belgrano gave fundamental importance to the education of girls, at a time when practical recognition of equal rights and conditions for men and women was still a long way off. Here we see a true creator in action, someone who, far from feeling satisfied with the position he had reached and using it to his advantage, devoted the best of his energies to trying to bring about a new, different, better society for all. Open to the most advanced ideas of his time and—at the same time—keenly aware that no-body must be left outside this new world that was taking shape. But more than that, he was not an idealist who brushed aside the practical difficul-ties of his projects. For each one, he tried to envisage the means of funding, the material and human resources that would make it possible. In this re-spect he did not hesitate to contribute elements needed to sustain a serious educational enterprise. Shortly after the 1810 Revolution, he donated 165 vol-umes to the Buenos Aires Public Library (now the National Library). It is also known that he designated the 40,000-peso[2] prize money awarded him for his victory at the Battle of Salta to the construction of four schools in Tarija, Salta, Tucuman, and Santiago del Estero. He himself wrote the *Reg-ulations* for these schools, in which he detailed how those resources were to be used for the upkeep of teachers, to purchase supplies and books for the children of poor parents, and so forth. One notable detail is his insistence that the teacher should be considered a 'Father of the Nation' and hold a seat on the local council. Another not so noteworthy detail is that those schools were never built.

"What You See Is Not All There Is"

Before it seems as if the Archbishop is trying to unnecessarily become a his-tory teacher, I would like to extract from what we have seen a few teachings about creativity. Although the two eras are profoundly different, there is much that is permanent and current in Belgrano's attitude of trying always to look further ahead, not keeping to what was known, the good or bad of the present moment. This 'utopian' attitude, in the best sense of the word, is undoubtedly one of the essential components of creativity. To paraphrase (and invert) a popular expression, we could say that the creativity that springs from hope asserts that "what you see . . . is not all there is".

In this way, the challenge of being creative demands that we be suspicious of any speech, thought, assertion, or proposal that presents itself as 'the only way possible.' There is always more than one. There is always another pos-sibility. Maybe a more difficult one, a more committed one, more resisted by those who are comfortably installed and for whom things are going very well. . . . We Argentines have already suffered that type of speech over the last decade, with all the weight and brilliance of academia and science, with the supreme wisdom of technicians and titleholders. Vain promises from

---

2. Equivalent to US $60,000 today.

the gurus of the hour, and we have already seen where they have led. Today everybody seems to know 'what should have been done instead of what was done.' And everybody seems to forget that 'what was done' was presented by the economic gurus and opinion-makers in the media as 'the only way possible.' Being creative, on the other hand, is to state that there is always an opening somewhere. And it is not just about some idiotic optimism that we're trying to copy from a statesman two hundred years ago. The statement that "what you see is not all there is" is drawn directly from faith in the Risen Christ, the definitive novelty that declares all other acts provisional and incomplete, a novelty that measures the distance between the here and now and the manifestation of the new heaven and new earth. A distance only bridged by hope and its active component: the creativity that denies all false consummation and opens up new horizons and alternatives.

What can we say, then, about the 'tombstones' we place on others—a student, a colleague—when we pigeonhole them, label, them and bury them under a signboard, a definition, a 'concept'? How often do we close off a person's or an educational institution's paths to renovation and growth by declaring in resignation 'that's how things are,' 'that's how it works,' or 'so-and-so is hopeless'? Out of all possible institutions, it is precisely schools inspired by Christian faith that should least give in to resignation and staying with 'what we already know.' Our schools are called to be real, living signs that "what you see is not all there is", that another world, another country, another society, another school, another family are possible. As institutions, they are called to be the testing ground for new ways of relating, new paths of brotherhood, a new respect for the uniqueness of each human being, a new openness and honesty, a working environment whose hallmarks are collaboration, justice, and regard for each person, where there is no place for manipulative relationships, competition, 'backbiting' schemes, authoritarianism, or self-interested favoritism. Any closed, definitive argument always covers up multiple deceits; it hides what must not be seen. It tries to gag the truth, which is always open to the authentically definitive, which is not of this world. We are thinking of a school that is open to new things, capable of being surprised and itself learn from everything and everyone. A school rooted in truth, which is always surprising. A school that is a seed, in the sense described by Belgrano and, above all, in the sense of the Gospel, of a new, transfigured world.

I'll make you a proposal: In a society where lies, concealment, and hypocrisy have eroded the basic trust that forms the social bond, what new thing can be more revolutionary than the truth? To speak truthfully, tell the truth, express our criteria, our values, our views. If we forbid ourselves right now from continuing with any form of lying or pretense we will also become, as an overabundant result, more responsible and even more charitable. Lies dilute everything; the truth displays clearly what is in the heart. A first proposal: Let us always tell the truth in and from our schools. I can assure you that the change will be striking. Something new will appear in the midst of our community.

"The Whole Man, and Every Man"

There is one truly evangelical criterion that is infallible for unmasking 'single-track thinking' that closes the door to hope, and even false utopias that distort hope. That criterion is universality. "The whole man and every man" was the principle of discernment proposed by Paul VI in relation to true development. The preferential option for the poor espoused by the Latin American Episcopate sought exactly this: to include all people, in every one of their dimensions, in the project of a better society. That's why Manuel Belgrano's insistence on education for all, particularly including the neediest to ensure full universality, sounds so 'familiar' to us. Can a society that discards a large or small number of its members really be desirable? Even from a selfish point of view, how can I be sure that I won't be the next one excluded?

Perhaps our society has learned something of this over the last year. "The poor have always been with us," but in recent decades the institutions that tried to ensure that everyone had at least the chance to live with dignity have collapsed one by one. Ever-increasing unemployment was the clearest sign. Over a long time, work and social security gradually disappeared and became devalued, and provincial economies were dismembered. Today we are horrified to see children dying of malnutrition. But a few years ago, those of us who belonged to the world of consumerism could never have dreamed (nor wanted to dream) that while some people were becoming first world citizens, others were simultaneously descending into a sort of senseless, hopeless netherworld with no work or future, labeled 'inviable' or merely the object of (always inadequate) assistance by an unfair and heartless system. Until the 'corralito'[3] happened and everything collapsed, and then a lot

---

3. Informal name given to economic measures at the end of 2001 that banned all bank withdrawals in order to stop a bank run. These government edicts were in force for one year.

of Argentines discovered that the infernal machine was coming for them too, for the ones who had 'steered clear of things.'

If we accept that 'it's all right for some but not for others,' the door remains open for all the aberrations that come later. And that is also a central point of the creativity we're searching for. The capacity to always look at what is happening with the side that wasn't included in the calculations. To 'take another look' and make sure that nobody has been left out or forgotten. For many reasons: First, because in Christian thinking, every person has their place and every person is essential. Second, because an exclusive society is, in reality, a society that can potentially turn against everyone. And third, because those who have been forgotten will not so easily accept their fate. If they can't get in through the door, they'll try to come in through the window. And the result: the beautiful, exclusive, amnesiac society will have to become more repressive, to prevent the Lazaruses it left outside from sneaking in to snatch something from the rich man's table.

So then, one essential mission of any Christian educator is to actively opt for inclusion, to work toward inclusion. Wasn't it one of the Church's earliest practices to take education to the most forgotten? Weren't many congregations and educational works created with this aim? Have we always consistently followed this vocation of service and inclusion? What winds blew us off this evangelical true course? Because the Church also dreams of offering free education to all those who wish to receive its service, especially the poorest. But where does that leave us? Obviously, things don't drop from the sky like manna, and in these times, it is not easy to sustain our institutions. Of course, the State also has its responsibility and function and should guarantee in different ways that free, quality education is available to all, respecting the right to choose, which the poor also have. But now I want to talk instead about a question of mentality. The mentality with which we operate our schools, the mentality we transmit, the mentality with which we make decisions and choices. Our schools should be ruled by a clearly defined criterion, that of mutually supportive brotherhood. And that should be their badge of distinction in each and every one of their dimensions and activities and also, let me say, of every Christian teacher. Their work can never be just 'business.' No work is that, but yours for a special reason. It is a service to people, to the little ones, people who place themselves in your hands so that you can help them become what they can be. "Fathers of the Nation" Belgrano called them, and he called for you to be given a seat on the local councils. If only all our educational institutions could reward their teachers as they deserve! Not just economically, but also with respect, participation, and recognition. At the economic level, reality imposes undeniable limits. But everyone: teachers, pastors, fathers and mothers, children, we can all be signs of a different world where each person is recognized, accepted, included, dignified, and not just for their usefulness but for their intrinsic value as a human being, as a child of God. Called on to be creative at this critical moment for our country, we have to ask ourselves what we can do as a Church, as a school, as teachers, to contribute to a truly inclusive and universal mentality and practice and to an education that offers possibilities not just to a few but to everyone within our reach, through the various means at our disposal.

A second proposal: Let us dare to fully engage with the Christian value of mutually supportive brotherhood. We cannot allow the individualistic and competitive mentality so deeply rooted in our civic culture to take over our schools as well. Let us rise to the challenge of teaching and even demanding detachment, generosity, and that the common good must prevail. Equality and respect for all: foreigners (from neighboring countries), the poor and homeless. From our schools, let us fight all forms of discrimination and injustice. Let us learn and teach to give even out of the scant resources of our institutions and families. And let this be clearly visible in every decision, every word, every project. In this way, we'll be putting up a clear sign (even a polemical and conflictive one, if necessary) of the different society we want to create.

"The Road to Hell Is Paved with Good Intentions"

A third criterion to guide our creativity, once again recognizing it in the actions of the creator of the national flag, who always tried to safeguard the resources and means with which to carry out his projects. Neither intentions nor words are good enough. It is necessary to get the work done, and effectively so. It's all very well to talk of solidarity of a different society, to theorize about schooling and the importance of an up-to-date, personalized education with its feet on the ground. There are tons of words about the information society, about knowledge as the primary capital of today's world, and so on. But the road to hell is paved with good intentions. Real creativity, as we have seen, doesn't neglect the ends, the values, the meaning. Neither does it neglect the specific aspects of project implementation. 'Technique' without 'ethics' is empty and dehumanizing, a blind person guiding other blind people, but if objectives are formulated without properly considering the means of reaching them, they will be condemned to remain mere fantasy.

Utopia has, as we said, not only that capacity to mobilize by locating itself 'ahead of' and 'outside' the limited reality that can be criticized, but also, for the same reasons, a 'crazy' side of 'alienation,' since it fails to develop mediations capable of turning its attractive visions into possible objectives.

This means that in order to creatively confront the present moment, we must develop our capabilities ever further, refine our tools, expand our knowledge. Rebuilding our decaying educational system, from whatever lowly or exalted position we find ourselves in, calls for training, responsibility, and professionalism. Nothing gets done without the necessary resources, and not just economic ones but also human talents. Creativity is no task for the mediocre. But not for 'Illuminati' or 'geniuses' either; although dreamers and prophets are always needed, their words fall into the void without builders who know their trade.

The school that takes the risk of meeting these challenges will have to engage in a process of dialogue and participation in order to solve new problems in new ways, knowing that nobody has all the knowledge or inspiration and each person's responsible and competent contribution is essential. Socioeconomic exclusion, the crisis of meaning and values, and the weakening of the social bond are realities that touch all of us, but that especially affect our children and adolescents. It is necessary to search for effective ways of accompanying and strengthening them to face the risks awaiting them. And it is not just AIDS and drugs, but also individualism, frustrating consumerism, lack of opportunities, the temptation to violence and desperation, loss of bonds and perspectives, a reduced capacity for love. Are we ready? Do we have the right professional teams? Do we go out to look for experiences, knowledge, and proposals, or do we tend to stay with what we know, whether or not it has worked? Are we prepared to set up networks, generously open at the diocesan level? If we start with a true Christian mysticism of openness to the future and concrete, universal solidarity and supplement it with a careful and generous administration of our human and institutional talents, not remaining satisfied with what we already have but trying to continually perfect our skills and capabilities, we will be able to respond to the current moment with a true creative attitude.

And now for the third proposal: Let us not hesitate to search for the best in our schools. Let's leave behind a certain mediocrity, that let's just fix it with baling wire approach that has been habitual in our communities for so long. Let's make sure that our teachers, our principals, our chaplains, our administrative staff are really serious and good at their jobs. It's important to have the right spirit, but so too is professionalism. Not in order to follow the myth of 'excellence' in the competitive and nonsupportive sense it some-times has, but to offer the best of ourselves to our community and our country, putting our talents to their fullest use.

Creativity and Tradition: Building from the Healthy Side

Creativity, which is nourished by utopia, has its roots in solidarity, and seeks the most effective means, can still be affected by a pathology that deforms it to the point of making it into one of the worst ills: the belief that every-thing starts with ourselves, a defect that, as we have already pointed out, rapidly deteriorates into authoritarianism.

Let's go back to 1810. A few months after the May Revolution, Belgrano was sent on a military mission to Paraguay. A year later, he was placed in command of the Northern Army, with the mission of combating major roy-alist strongholds in Upper Perú. He held this post, with victories and de-feats, until 1814, when San Martín replaced him. We are obviously not going to list here the military campaigns led by the lawyer turned army leader, but I would like to draw your attention to a detail that illustrates the great man's attitude and can give us a platform from which to develop our final reflec-tion on creativity. You probably know that Belgrano was a leader who was truly recognized and loved by his subordinates, but also that he was the butt of jokes and sarcastic comments among the troops: that he was prudish and weak of character. . . . It is true that, to those soldiers, a son of wealthy traders, educated in the best centers of Buenos Aires and Spain, always de-voted to books and intellectual tasks, must undoubtedly have had a distant air. But it is also true that a large portion of those criticisms had to do with his moderate approach and, above all, with his strict prohibition on keep-ing company with women, consuming alcohol, fighting, card games, and other aspects of troop discipline. Belgrano believed that the military cam-paigns carried out in the name of the Revolution had to be on a par with the ideals that moved it, ideals of human dignity, liberty, and fraternity, all of them also based on Christian virtues. For that reason, he demanded of his troops that they demonstrate real integrity and respect for the commu-nities they passed through.

He showed particular severity in relation to anything that could scan-dalize the religious beliefs of people in the interior. In an edict to the troops on entering Upper Perú he ordered: *"respect is to be shown for the uses, cus-toms and even the concerns of local people; anyone who mocks them by action, word, or deed will be shot."* In addition to his own religious beliefs, he believed the meaning of the Revolution was at stake and, in the last instance, that of the nation he wanted to build. In fact, in one of his letters to San Martín, when the latter was already in command of the Northern Army, Belgrano wrote:

> you must wage war (in Upper Perú) not only with arms but with opinion, always taking your strength from the natural, Christian and religious virtues, since the enemy has done this to us, calling us heretics, and only by this means has attracted primitive people to arms, declaring to them that we were attacking religion. . . . You should not allow yourself to be swayed by exotic opinions or men who are ignorant of the country in which they have set foot.

These prohibitions were not unconnected with the fact that previous military and civilian leaders had seriously shocked the inhabitants of these regions with their attitudes and anti-Catholic rhetoric typical of the enlightened thinking of the French Revolution. Belgrano, on the other hand, knew that nothing can be built on the indiscriminate destruction of what came before, but that the identity and value of the other must be recognized.

And this is where we complete our consideration of creativity as located along the line of tension between novelty and continuity. If being creative has to do with the ability to open up to what is new, that doesn't mean the element of continuity with what went before can be neglected. As we said earlier, only God creates out of nothing. And just as there is no way to cure a sick person unless we start from what is healthy in them, we similarly cannot create something new in history except from the materials history itself offers us. Belgrano recognized that the united and strong America of his dreams could be built only on respect and affirmation of the identities of its peoples. If creativity is not capable of taking on the living aspects of what is real and present, it rapidly becomes an authoritarian imposition, a brutal replacement of one 'truth' by another. Could this be one of the keys to why we find it so difficult to take a more positive approach? If we always, in order to build, tend to pull down and trample on what others made before, how can we build anything solid? How can we avoid sowing new forms of hatred that will later overturn whatever we have managed to do?

This is why, if we as educators want to truly sow the seeds of a fairer, freer, and more fraternal society, we need to learn to recognize the historical achievements of our founders, our artists, thinkers, politicians, educators, pastors. Maybe now we have come to realize that during the time of the fat cows we allowed ourselves to be dazzled by a few colored baubles, fashions intellectual and otherwise, and forgot a few certainties very painfully learned by previous generations: the value of social justice, hospitality, solidarity be-tween generations, work as something that dignifies the person, the family as the basis of society.

Our schools should be a space where our children and youth can directly touch the vitality of our history. Not just by dressing up as *mazamorra*[4] sell-ers for the May 25 celebrations, but also by learning to reflect on the achievements and errors that have made up our national history. But for this to happen we all, as educators, need to have previously undergone the same process, together. Beyond the various options and ways of thinking, it is nec-essary to learn to reach basic, shared agreements—not based on the lowest common denominator—on which to start building. That is the only way to assert a collective identity in which we can all recognize ourselves.

To create from what already exists also means being able to recognize differences, prior-existing knowledge, expectations, and even the limits of our children and their families. We know that education is not, by any means, a one-way process. But do we follow that? Are we really prepared to let our-selves, the teachers, be taught? Are we capable of taking on a relationship from which we may all emerge as different people? Do we believe in our pu-pils, in the families in our neighborhood, in our people? The ability to 'build from the healthy side' is, then, the fourth and last criterion for cre-ative action that I want to share with you today.

And I'll put a last proposal to you: Let us propose models of life to our students. Postmodern culture, which dilutes everything, has declared all concrete ethical proposals to be out of fashion. Putting forward valuable ex-amples of service, struggle for justice, commitment to the community, holi-ness, and heroism tends to be seen as a sort of useless or pernicious time tunnel. And when the land is laid waste, what is left except the instinct to survive? Paraphrasing a song that you surely know and have sung, "Who said everything's lost? So many have offered their hearts,"[5] let us present testimonies with the conviction that those offerings will not have been in vain. And when faced with the leveling steamroller of "everything's the same, nothing is better," we will have placed unmissable signs that something new is possible.

---

4. *Mazamorra* is a Creole dish made with corn, milk, and honey or sugar.

5. The song is "Yo vengo ofrecer mi corazón" by the Argentine singer Fito Páez: "Quién dijo que todo está perdido? / Yo vengo a ofrecer mi corazón. / Tanta sangre que se llevó el río, / yo vengo a ofrecer mi corazón" ("Who said that everything is lost? / I come to offer my heart. / So much blood went down the river, / I come to offer my heart").

Conclusion

Our reflection has given us four teachings on historical creativity that must be brought into play in these times, four principles of discernment.

—Always look beyond: "What you see is not all there is."
—Always keep in mind "the whole man and every man."
—Always look for the most appropriate and effective means: "The road to hell is paved with good intentions."
—"Build from the healthy side," reclaiming positive values and actions.

And as one way (but not the only one!) of putting the above into practice, four proposals:

—Always tell the truth.
—Engage ourselves in mutually supportive brotherhood.
—Always develop our abilities further.
—Propose testimonies and specific models of living.

As in Jesus' miracle, our loaves and fishes can multiply (Mt 14:17–20). As in the example given by the Lord to his disciples, our small offering has maximum value (Lk 21:1–4). As in the parable, our small seeds grow into trees and bear fruit (Mt 13:23, 31–32). All of it from the living source of the Eucharist, in which our bread and our wine are transfigured to give us eternal Life. A huge and difficult task is asked of us. Through faith in the Risen One we can meet it with creativity and hope, always putting ourselves in the place of the servants at that wedding, surprised collaborators in Jesus' first sign, who followed only the instruction given by a woman: "Do as he tells you" (Jn 2:5). Creativity and hope make life grow. This year, in which, synthesizing all of this, we wish to emphatically say: To educate is to choose Life, let us beseech our Mother in the words of John Paul II in *Evangelium vitae*:

O Mary,
bright dawn of the new world,
Mother of the living,
to you do we entrust the cause of life:
Look down, O Mother,
upon the vast numbers
of babies not allowed to be born,
of the poor whose lives are made difficult,
of men and women
who are victims of brutal violence,
of the elderly and the sick killed

by indifference or out of misguided mercy.
Grant that all who believe in your Son
may proclaim the Gospel of life
with honesty and love
to the people of our time.
Obtain for them the grace
to accept that Gospel
as a gift ever new,
the joy of celebrating it with gratitude
throughout their lives
and the courage to bear witness to it
resolutely, in order to build,
together with all people of good will,
the civilization of truth and love,
to the praise and glory of God,
the Creator and lover of life.
Amen. (105)

➤➤ ◀◀

And the Truth Shall Set You Free

Homily, Mass for Educators—April 9, 2003, Wednesday
in the Fifth Week of Lent, Year B

Today in the last week of Lent, Jesus talks to us in a bipolarity of freedom and slavery. It is every person's battle: to be free or to be a slave . . . and it goes to the heart of each of us . . . it goes to our own being, it challenges us: Are you free or a slave? Are you free with the spontaneity that gives you the coherence of being a person? Or are you a slave because of the conditioning you accept, because of the limits you let turn into sin or simply because of autonomy?

In light of this bipolarity of freedom/slavery, today we start a school year, and today before you, boys and girls of our schools, and before you educators, whom I prefer to call teachers. Being an educator is a role; teacher . . . being a teacher is a passion. Before you teachers, I'd also like to pose this question: free or slave? And the key that solves the antinomy, in Jesus' words, is in the *truth*: "*If you remain in my word, you will truly be my disciples, and you will know the truth, and the truth will set you free*" (Jn 8:31–32).

What frees men, what makes them really free—persons—what anoints them in their whole potentiality is truth, whole, sometimes hard, sometimes grudgingly accepted, sometimes crucifying, but truth. Just as it is. Many times, the temptation of our weakness makes us avoid the truth, color it, diminish it, and even negotiate it or leave it aside.

To be teachers means to take the hearts of boys and girls and to instill in them, with teachers' passion, the passion for that truth that cannot be traded, that cannot be reached by consensus, leveling down our life's values. We all know that this civilization has become a market that sells half-truths that are lies. To take a boy or a girl along the path of half-truths, along the path of deceit, means to prostitute their hearts, to sow corruption instead of freedom.

Our vocation as teachers leads us to passionately sow the truth that will make them free, that will make them not give in before the latest fashion, before marketing, before the easiest things, before the "have it your way."

Truth makes us free, and this is what Jesus proclaims today, what is untrue enslaves us. To you, boys and girls, I ask you not to be afraid of truth, pursue it, don't be afraid of making mistakes while pursuing it, you will find it. But watch out for those who sell you deception, those who entice you with lies. Be careful of colored glass; today we are offered colored glass while telling us they are the most precious truth. To you, teachers, I want you to be passionate. And to you, boys and girls, I wish you a school year in the truth, so that it will make you free. May it be so.

→> <←

The Hope That God Would Care for Our Fragility

Homily, Chrism Mass—April 17, 2003, Year B

Today's readings talk to us about hope: the hope that God would care for our fragility.

Isaiah expresses the hope of the people by wishing that the Messiah would come to care for the poor's fragility, discouraged by all the bad news, brokenhearted, more than physically, living as prisoners to the interests of the powerful. And Isaiah announces that when the Anointed One comes, he will transform the desolate people into a priestly people by comforting them with the good news, so that they will proclaim that good news to others. By healing the brokenhearted and liberating them from all bondage, they will become ministers of reconciliation and freedom. By replacing their mourning garments with the oil of gladness, they will be recognized by everyone as being of the lineage blessed by the Lord (cf. Is 61:1–3, 6, 8b–9).

Jesus, in the passage from Saint Luke (4:16–21), consolidates this hope in himself and makes it his own. He turns it into a current event. He is the continuous source of this priestly grace, always available to the ones who risk entrusting their own fragility into his hands, for the ones who believe that the Scriptures and all human longing are fulfilled in the "now" of Jesus. That is why, today, as priests, we want to place into the Lord's priestly hands, as a holy offering, our own fragility, our people's fragility, the whole of humanity's fragility—their discouragement, their wounds, their mourning—so that, offered by him, they are transformed into Eucharist, the food that strengthens our hope and turns our charity into actions of faith.

Every offering and every dialogue between God and mankind have in Jesus the Priest that joyful and simple character of a beautiful Eucharist that links, in the tenderness of the bread, worship with life.

What is the meaning for us, priests and priestly people, that Jesus is Priest forever, mediator between God and humanity? It means that humble and joyful tone of the one who does not desire glory for himself but that his glory is to be a mediator so that the good of the people will be for the glory of the Father. It means that we, who take part in that priesthood, must be happy to be the humblest and most lowly servant of this mediation, which takes place through Jesus. It means that the whole Church must be so humble and peaceful, so tender and united that, as an entirely priestly people, it may be a place of mediation between God and the people who still do not know this grace and strive for a variety of other mediations. That is why I invite you, dear brothers in the unique priesthood of Jesus our Lord, to ask for this grace together, for each one of us and for the whole Church: that we may understand the wealth of the hope to which we have been called to be mediators, with Jesus and in Jesus, between God and humanity. Mediators that offer their own fragility, together with that of the entire people of God. That we may humble ourselves in such a way that it would be easy for our God and for our brothers and sisters to communicate through us. May our Heavenly

Father feel, as his beloved Son feels, that through us he may reach, with his blessing and with his word, the littlest of his children. May the people feel, as Jesus and Our Lady feel, that through us they may offer up to the Lord, their day-to-day sacrifices, those knitted by their work and family lives, and that they may tell God that they love, need, worship, and praise him from the bottom of their hearts. I ask you to care for your priesthood by caring for this offering.

We know that unity is protected by caring for mediations. And hope is the preeminent mediator when it is attentive to the small details where that mysterious exchange of fragility and mercy occurs. When there are good mediators, those who care about the details, unity is not broken. Jesus cared about the details.

The 'small detail' of noticing the missing sheep.

The 'small detail' of the wine that was about to run out.

The 'small detail' of the widow who offered her two small coins.

The 'small detail' of the one who did not forgive a small debt after having been pardoned of a large debt.

The 'small detail' of having spare oil in the lamps just in case the bridegroom arrived late.

The 'small detail' of noticing how many loaves of bread they had.

The 'small detail' of having a little fire ready and a fish on the grill while waiting for the disciples in the middle of the night.

The 'small detail' of asking Peter, among those other important things happening, if he truly loved him as a friend.

The 'small detail' of not having wanted to heal his wounds.

These are the priestly ways that Jesus has to tend to the hope that brings us together in unity.

The hope that none will be missing. The hope that joy will not end and may be overabundant and new. The hope that God is very pleased to see our most hidden loving acts. The hope that pardon is contagious. The hope that taking care of that one little light makes the feast brighter. The hope that there may be enough bread for everyone. The hope that he will always be waiting at the other shore.

The hope that, after all, what matters most to God is that we are his friends.

The hope that so much grief would not be forgotten but that God will kiss everyone's wounds, one by one, when they enter into Heaven, and that they will be a sign of a humble and grateful glory.

We ask Our Lady, mother of priests, mother of the priestly people, that she may take care within us, her children, of our hope's fragility, reminding us of what has been announced through her: that nothing is impossible for God.

→> ‹‹-

Paralysis Sickens Our Soul

Homily, Easter Vigil—April 19, 2003, Year B

Mary Magdalene, Mary the mother of James, and Salome set out at dawn. Tonight, we have also set out—following the journey of the People of God along the paths of the chosen, of promise and of the covenant. The journey of these women is embedded in this long walk of centuries . . . and in ours too. Because to be chosen and to be carriers of the covenant means to always be on the march. The covenant that God makes with his people and with each one of us is made precisely so that we may walk toward a promise, toward an encounter. This walk is life.

As a contrast, the stone is there. Motionless and sealed due to the conspiracy of the corrupt—a genuine obstacle to the encounter. These women walked vacillating between hope and hindrance; they went to the tomb to fulfill a work of mercy, but the specter of the stone made them doubt. They were moved by love but paralyzed by doubt. Just like them, we also feel impelled to walk, the desire to do great works. Inside our hearts we have a promise and the certainty of God's fidelity, but the doubt is stone, the seals of corruption are shackles, and many times we yield to the temptation of becoming paralyzed, without hope.

Paralysis sickens our soul, snatches away our memory, and takes away our joy. It makes us forget that we have been chosen, that we are carriers of promises, that we are marked by a divine covenant. Paralysis deprives us of the surprise of the encounter; it prevents us from opening ourselves to the "good news." Today we need to hear the good news again: "He is not here; for he has been raised" (Mt 28:5). We need that encounter that shatters stones, breaks the seal, and opens up a new path for us, one of hope.

The world needs this encounter, this world that has become a cemetery. Our homeland needs it. It needs the announcement that raises our spirits, the hope that impels us to walk, works of mercy, as those of these women who went there to do the anointing. We need our fragility to be anointed by hope; and may that hope spur us on to proclaim the good news and to anoint, in solidarity, the fragility of our brothers and sisters.

The worst thing that may happen is that we opt to choose the stone and the corruption of the seal, discouragement, to stay motionless without feeling chosen, without promise, with no covenant. The worst thing that may happen is that our hearts remain closed to the amazement of the life-giving announcement that drives us to keep walking.

This is the night of the announcement. Let us shout it with all our life: Jesus Christ, our hope, has risen! Let us proclaim that he is stronger than the weight of the stone and the provisional security offered by the corruption of the seals. Tonight, Mary already enjoyed her Son's presence. To her care we entrust our wish to walk impelled by the awe of the encounter with the risen Jesus Christ.

⤞ ⤝

Do Not Let Anyone Remain "at the Edge of Life"

Homily, Solemn Te Deum *on Independence Day—May 25, 2003*

There was a scholar of the law who stood up to test him and said, "Teacher, what must I do to inherit eternal life?" Jesus said to him, "What is written in the law?" He said in reply, "You shall love the Lord, your God, with all your heart, with all your being, with all your strength, and with all your mind, and your neighbor as yourself." He replied to him, "You have answered correctly; do this and you will live." But because he wished to justify himself, he said to Jesus, "And who is my neighbor?" Jesus replied, "A man fell victim to robbers as he went down from Jerusalem to Jericho. They stripped and beat him and went off, leaving him half-dead. A priest happened to be going down that road, but when he saw him, he passed by on the opposite side. Likewise, a Levite came to the place, and when he saw him, he passed by on the opposite side. But a Samaritan traveler who came upon him was moved with compassion at the sight. He approached the victim, poured oil and wine over his wounds, and bandaged them. Then he lifted him up

on his own animal, took him to an inn, and cared for him. The next day he took out
two silver coins and gave them to the innkeeper with the instruction, 'Take care of
him. If you spend more than what I have given you, I shall repay you on my way
back.' Which of these three, in your opinion, was neighbor to the robbers' victim?"
He answered, "The one who treated him with mercy." Jesus said to him, "Go and
do likewise." (Lk 10:25–37)

The Easter season is a call to be reborn from above. At the same time, it is
a challenge to rethink deeply and give new meaning to our whole lives—as
individuals and as a Nation—from the perspective of the joy of the risen
Christ, to allow hope of living like a true community to sprout from within
the very fragility of our flesh. From this mystery of intimate and shared
joy, we feel the resurgence of the May sun that Argentines have always
wished to see as a reminder of a glimmer of resurrection. It is the hopeful
call of Jesus Christ to have a resurgence of our vocation as citizens to build
a new social bond. A new call, however, that is always written as the fundamental law of our being: that society be in the pursuit of the Common
Good and, with this goal in mind, rebuild again and again its political and
social order.

The parable of the Good Samaritan is an illuminating icon, capable of
highlighting the basic choice that we must make to rebuild this country
that is such a deep part of us. In the face of so much pain, so many wounds,
the only way out is to be like the Good Samaritan. All other options end
either on the side of the robbers or on the side of those who pass by, without commiserating with the wounded one on the road. And "the homeland
should not be for us"—as one of our poets said—"only a *pain* on our side."
The parable of the Good Samaritan shows us the initiatives that can rebuild a community when carried out by men and women who feel and act
as true partners (in the old sense of fellow citizens). Men and women who
make it as their own and accompany the fragility of others; who do not
allow a society of exclusion to be built, but who draw closer—become
neighbors—and raise and rehabilitate the fallen, so that the Good will be
held in Common. At the same time, the Parable warns us about certain
self-referential attitudes that do not take care of the inescapable demands
of human reality.

From the beginning of the life of the Church, and especially by the time
of the Cappadocian Fathers, the Good Samaritan was identified with Christ
himself. He is the one who becomes our neighbor, the one who raises the
human being from the margins of life, the one who puts him on his shoulders, takes charge of his pain and abandonment, and rehabilitates him. The

story of the Good Samaritan, let us say it clearly, does not seek a teaching of abstract ideals, nor is it limited to the functionality of an ethical-social moral. But it is the living Word of the God who lowers himself and draws near to touch our most ordinary fragility. That Word reveals to us an essential characteristic of man, so often forgotten: that we have been made for the fullness of being; therefore, we cannot live indifferent to pain, we cannot let anyone remain "at the edge of life," marginalized from their dignity. This should outrage us. This should make us descend from our serenity to be "upset" by human pain, that of our neighbor, of the one who lives next to us, of our partner in this community of Argentines. In giving of ourselves in that way we will find our existential vocation, we will become worthy of this land, which never had the vocation to marginalize anyone.

The story is presented to us with the linearity of a simple narrative, but it has all the dynamics of that internal struggle that occurs in the defining of our identity, in every existence "that enters the road" in order to make a homeland. This is what I mean: If we set out on the road, we will inevitably run into, the wounded man. Today, and increasingly so, that wounded one is in the majority. In humanity and in our country. The inclusion or exclusion of the wounded at the side of the road defines all economic, political, social, and religious projects. Every day we face the option of being Good Samaritans or indifferent travelers who pass by. And if we expand our gaze to include the totality of our history and the breadth and length of the homeland, we are all or have been like these characters: We all have something of the wounded, something of a robber, something of those who pass by and something of the Good Samaritan. It is remarkable how the differences of the characters in the story are totally transformed when confronted with the painful manifestation of the fallen, of the humiliated. There is no longer any distinction between the inhabitant of Judea and the inhabitant of Samaria, there is not priest nor merchant; there are simply two types of men: those who take responsibility for the pain and those who pass by, those who bow down and recognize themselves in the fallen, and those who avert their gaze and accelerate the pace. In effect, our multiple masks, our labels and disguises fall. It is the moment of truth: Will we bend down to touch our wounds? Will we bend down so others may be carried on our shoulders? This is the challenge of the present hour, and we must not fear it. In times of crisis, the choice becomes urgent. We could say that at this moment, everyone who is not a robber or anyone who does not pass by is either wounded or is putting a wounded one on their shoulders.

The story of the Good Samaritan is repeated: It becomes increasingly obvious that our social and political neglect is making this land a desolate path, in which internal disputes and plundering of opportunities leave us all marginalized, thrown to the side of the road. In his parable, the Lord does not propose alternative ways. What would have become of that wounded one or of his helper, if the anger or thirst for revenge had gained space in their hearts? Jesus Christ trusts in the best of the human spirit and with the parable encourages the spirit to adhere to the love of God, reintegrate the hurt, and build a society worthy of that name.

The parable begins with *the robbers*. The starting point chosen by the Lord is an assault already consummated. But it does not make us stop to regret the fact; it does not direct our gaze toward the robbers. We know them. We have seen in our country the advance of the dense shadows of neglect, of petty interests of power and division using violence; there is also the ambition of public positions sought as booty. The question before the robbers could be: Will we make our national life a story that remains in this part of the parable? Will we leave the wounded man to run to take shelter from violence or to pursue the thieves? Will the wounded always be the justification of our irreconcilable divisions, of our cruel indifferences, of our internal confrontations? The poetic prophecy of Martín Fierro should warn us: Our eternal and sterile hatreds and individualism open the doors to those who devour us from the outside.

The people of our nation demonstrate, again and again, the clear will to respond to their vocation to be Good Samaritans with each other; they have trusted again in our democratic system despite its weaknesses and shortcomings, and we see how solidarity efforts are redoubled to reweave a society that is fracturing. Our people respond with the silence of the Cross to dissolute proposals, and they support to the limit the uncontrolled violence of those who are prisoners of criminal chaos.

The parable makes us look, twice, at *those who pass by*. This dangerous indifference to pass by, innocent or not, the product of contempt or a sad distraction, makes the characters of the priest and the Levite a no less sad reflection of that divisive distance, which many are tempted to put in front of the reality and the will to be a Nation. There are many ways to pass by that are counterparts of each other: self-absorption, disregard for the others, indifference, and another—just looking beyond. Regarding this last way of passing by, in some it is clear that we live with an outward gaze of our reality, always yearning for the characteristics of other societies, not to integrate them into our cultural elements, but to replace them. As if an impostor country project tried to force its place by pushing the other country. In this sense we can read today historical experiences rejecting the effort to gain space and resources, to grow in identity, preferring the advantage of smuggling, purely financial speculation, and the spoliation of our natural resources and—even worse—of our people. Even intellectually, the inability to accept our own characteristics and processes persists, as in so many nations, insisting on the disregard of their own identity. It would be naive not to see anything other than ideologies or cosmopolitan refinements behind these trends; rather, power interests emerge that benefit from the permanent conflict in the bosom of our people.

A similar inclination is seen in those who, apparently for contrary ideas, indulge in the petty game of disqualifications, even violent confrontations, or the well-known sterility of many intellectuals for whom "nothing is salvageable if it is not as I think." What should be the normal exercise of debate or self-criticism, which knows how to safeguard common ideals and goals, seems to be manipulated here toward the permanent state of questioning and confrontation of the most fundamental principles. Is it an inability to yield to the benefit of a minimal common project or the unstoppable compulsion of those who only become allies to satisfy their ambition for power?

Tacitly, the highway robbers have achieved as allies those who pass by on the road looking the other way. This closes the circle between those who use and deceive our society to deplete it, and those who supposedly maintain purity in their critical function but live from this system and our resources to enjoy them outside or maintain the possibility of chaos to earn their own ground.

We should not feel a call to deceive, to the impunity of crime, to the use of community institutions for personal or corporate gain and other evils that we cannot banish; they have as their underside the constant disinformation and disqualification of everything, the constant sowing of suspicion that diffuses mistrust and perplexity. The deception of "everything is wrong" is answered with a "nobody can fix it." And, in this way, disenchantment and despair are nourished. To sink a people into dejection is the closing of a perfect perverse circle: the invisible dictatorship of true interests, those hidden interests that took over the resources and our ability to opine and think.

Each of us, based on our responsibilities, must *put our country on our shoulders* because the time is getting short. We noted the possibility of a dissolution on other occasions, on this same commemorative date for our homeland. However, many followed their path of ambition and superficiality, without looking at those who fell by the wayside; this continues to threaten us.

Last, let us look at *the wounded one*. We citizens feel like him, badly hurt and thrown by the side of the road. We also feel deserted by our disarmed and deprived institutions, starved of the skills and formation that love of country demands.

Every day we have to start a new stage, a new starting point. We do not have to wait for everything from those who govern us; this would be childish, but rather we have to take an active part in the rehabilitation and assistance of the wounded country. Today we are facing the great opportunity to manifest our religious, filial, and fraternal essence to feel the benefits of the gift of the homeland, with the gift of our people to be other Good Samaritans who bear on themselves the pain of failure, instead of accentuating hatreds and resentments. As the casual traveler of our story, we need only the free, pure, and simple desire to be a Nation, to be constant and tireless in the task of including, integrating, lifting the fallen. Although the violent ones self-marginalize themselves, those who only have ambition for themselves, the spreaders of confusion and lies. And let others keep thinking about politics for their games of power, let us put ourselves at the service of the best possible for all. Begin from below and one by one, fight for what is most concrete and local, to the last corner of the homeland, with the same care that the traveler of Samaria had for each wound of the victim. Do not trust the repeated speeches and the supposed reports about reality. Let us take charge of our corresponding reality without fear of pain or impotence, because the Risen One is found there. Where there was a stone and a sepulcher, life was waiting. Where there was a desolate land, our indigenous parents and then the others who populated our homeland gave rise to work and heroism, organization and social protection.

The difficulties that appear enormous are opportunities to grow, and not the excuse for the inert sadness that favors subjection. We renounce the pettiness and resentment of sterile inside factions, of endless confrontations. Let us stop hiding the pain of our losses, and let us take responsibility for our crimes, dissensions, and lies, because only a reconciliation that makes reparation will raise us up and make us lose our fear of ourselves. It is not about preaching an ethics of reparation, but about facing things from an ethical perspective that is always rooted in reality.

The Samaritan on the road departed without expecting recognition or gratitude. Giving service provided satisfaction before his God and his life, and therefore it was a duty. The people of this nation long to see this example in those who make their image public; it takes greatness of soul, because only greatness of soul awakens life and convenes.

We have no right to indifference and disinterest or to look the other way. We cannot "pass by" as those in the parable did. We have responsibility for the wounded that are the nation and its people. Today begins a new stage in our country marked very deeply by fragility: fragility of our poorest and most excluded brothers, fragility of our institutions, fragility of our social bonds ...

Let us care for the fragility of our wounded people! Each one with his wine, with his oil and his horse.

Let us care for the fragility of our homeland. Each one paying from his pocket what it takes for our land to be a true Inn for all, without excluding anyone.

Let us care for the fragility of each man, each woman, each child, and each old person, with that attitude of solidarity and attentiveness, the attitude of the Good Samaritan's neighborliness.

May our Mother, Most Holy Mary of Luján, who has stayed with us and accompanies us on the journey of our history as a sign of consolation and hope, listen to our prayer as sojourners, comfort us, and encourage us to follow the example of Christ, the one who carries our fragility on his shoulders.

↠ ↢

Duc in altum, the Social Thought of John Paul II

Lecture on the Social Thought of John Paul II on the Dignity of Work—June 7, 2003

Duc in altum

Duc in altum! "Put out into deep water!" (Lk 5:4), without hesitation, into the depths. This exhortation of Jesus to Peter, which John Paul II himself endorses and transmits to us with renewed apostolic zeal, encourages us to enter today into his vast social thought. John Paul II is the pope who has written the most on the "social question"; his three encyclicals, innumerable speeches and homilies, and the constant allusion to the social dimension in all his documents surprise us not only for their vastness but also for the *breadth of horizons*, the *courage* and *depth* with which the Pope takes up all the social doctrine of the Church and re-presents it in a renewed and forceful way.

Going "into the depth" of his thought is akin to the incursions that the Lord made with his disciples, teaching them in the middle of the rich and mysterious reality of Lake Gennesaret,[1] symbol of the world and of history. Within the constricted format of *Laboren excercens* or *Sollicitudo rei socialis* all the social doctrine of the Church pulses in a universal and concrete model illuminated by the gospel. And in the sea air you can smell the promise of an abundant catch.

From the beginning of his pontificate, the 'Worker Pope' invites us to enter where the social life of man unfolds with the strength of oars and of nets being recast—the world of work and solidarity.

Duc in altum: With Broad Horizons

Committing oneself to the social question is to enter fully into the global question.

I start with a few words of John Paul II in *Novo millenio ineunte* (2001):

> Well known are the efforts made by the Church's teaching authority, especially in the twentieth century, to interpret social realities in the light of the Gospel and to offer in a timely and systematic way its contribution to the social question, which has now assumed a global dimension. (NMI 52)

For the Pope, "the ethical and social aspect of the question" must be presented "as an essential element of Christian witness" (ibid.). John Paul has the courage to reject as a "temptation" a "privatized and individualistic spirituality" (ibid.). His proposal is a spirituality of communion, a spirituality that considers the social dimension of man. The other, individualistic and hidden, has nothing to say of the implications of the Incarnation and, in the last analysis, of Christianity's eschatological tension" (ibid.). It is true that the hope of heaven makes us aware of "the relative character of history, but it in no way implies that we withdraw from 'building' history" (ibid.). The teaching of the Second Vatican Council is very current in this respect: "The

---

1. Also known as the Sea of Galilee or Lake Tiberias.

Christian message does not inhibit men and women from building up the world or make them disinterested in the welfare of their fellow human beings; on the contrary, it obliges them more fully to do these very things (GS 34)" (ibid.).

Duc in altum, in the voice of the Pope, is an exhortation that consoles and strengthens us to row into the new millennium and, with the light of the Gospel, illuminate the "social question" that has become a global issue.

Duc in altum is an invitation to commit ourselves to the task of building the world and pushes us to care for the common good of our fellow man as a duty that springs from the Gospel itself.

The Main Milestones for Social Doctrine in the Twentieth Century

The Pope himself has been the main protagonist of the Magisterium's effort to interpret social reality in the light of the Gospel.

John Paul II, in *Tertio millennio adveniente* (1994), reminds us of the main milestones of previous pontiffs' social thought, and of his own:

> *In the course of this century the Popes, following in the footsteps of Leo XIII, systematically developed the themes of Catholic Social Teachings, expounding the characteristics of a just system in the area of relations between labor and capital. We may recall the Encyclical* Quadragesimo anno *of Pius XI, the numerous interventions of Pius XII, the Encyclicals* Mater et magistra *and* Pacem in terris *of John XXIII, the Encyclical* Populorum progressio *and the Apostolic Letter* Octogesima adveniens *of Paul VI. I too have frequently dealt with this subject: I specifically devoted the Encyclical* Laborem exercens *to the importance of human labor, while in* Centesimus annus *I wished to reaffirm the relevance, one hundred years later, of the doctrine presented in* Rerum novarum. *In my Encyclical* Sollicitudo rei socialis *I had earlier offered a systematic reformulation of the Church's entire social doctrine against the background of the East-West confrontation and the danger of nuclear war. The two elements of the Church's social doctrine— the safeguarding of human dignity and rights in the sphere of a just relation between labor and capital and the promotion of peace—were closely joined in this text.* (TMA 22)

I. A Spirituality of Work

Keeping in mind the two elements of the Church's social doctrine that the Pope stresses—the safeguarding of human dignity and rights in the sphere of a just relation between labor and capital and the promotion of peace—we will be focused on the question of labor. And we will do it from the perspective of the "spirituality of work."

I will explain the reason for this option. In *Novo millennio ineunte,* that new spirituality of solidarity and communion, mentioned by the Pope, has a striking consolidation in what he describes as "a spirituality of work":

> One of the most notable events was the gathering of workers on 1 May, the day traditionally dedicated to the world of work. I asked them to live a spirituality of work in imitation of Saint Joseph and of Jesus himself. That Jubilee gathering also gave me the opportunity to voice a strong call to correct the economic and social imbalances present in the world of work and to make decisive efforts to ensure that the processes of economic globalization give due attention to solidarity and the respect owed to every human person. (NMI 10)

Explicitly, the Pope exhorts to join work to that spirituality of communion that he would like to be the paradigm for the Church in the new century. The characteristics of this spirituality are beautifully outlined:

> A spirituality of communion indicates above all the heart's contemplation of the mystery of the Trinity dwelling in us, and whose light we must also be able to see shining on the face of the brothers and sisters around us. (Ibid., 43)

Next, the Pope specifies three areas in which we need to "cultivate" communion in light of this presence of God in the face of every man. We would describe them like this:

Cultivating how to belong to a body:

> A spirituality of communion also means an **ability to think** of our brothers and sisters in faith within the profound unity of the Mystical Body, and therefore as "those who are a part of me." This makes us able to share their joys and sufferings, to sense their desires and attend to their needs, to offer them deep and genuine friendship. (Ibid.)

Cultivating a vision that values others holistically:

> A spirituality of communion implies also the **ability to see** what is positive in others, to welcome it and prize it as a gift from God: not only as a gift for the brother or sister who has received it directly, but also as a "gift for me." (NMI 43)

Cultivating how to give space to others and not to dominate their spaces:

> A spirituality of communion means, finally, to know how to "make room" for our brothers and sisters, bearing "each other's burdens" (cf. Gal 6:2) and resisting the

selfish temptations which constantly beset us and provoke competition, careerism, distrust and jealousy. (Ibid.)

We think that the spirituality of communion, with multiple resonances in each concrete area of ecclesial life, has a special flavor if we apply it to the spirituality of work that the Pope invited workers to cultivate. Let us note, by the way, that communion and work are the only two realities that in the document connote spirituality.

Duc in altum: With the Courage to Get Deep into the Topic

Work, Key to the Social Issue

Let us see why this is so.

Let us ask ourselves: What is John Paul II's conception of human work?

We all know that *Redemptor hominis*, his first encyclical (1979), was programmatic. The Pope thought that it was necessary to start from man, from that man whose profound and final meaning can only be found in Jesus Christ, the Redeemer of man. Two years later, in 1981, John Paul II published *Laborem excercens*. Another programmatic encyclical that John Paul II dedicated "to man" in the vast context of that reality that is work:

> *I wish to devote this document to human work and, even more, to man in the vast context of the reality of work. As I said in the Encyclical* Redemptor hominis, *published at the beginning of my service in the See of Saint Peter in Rome, man "is the primary and fundamental way for the Church," precisely because of the inscrutable mystery of Redemption in Christ; and so it is necessary to return constantly to this way and to follow it ever anew in the various aspects in which it shows us all the wealth and at the same time all the toil of human existence on earth.* (LE 1)

We highlight, first of all, this vision of the Pope who speaks of a spirituality that "begins and goes deep" in man's journey. A man, it is good to underline it, immersed in the mystery of Jesus Christ the Redeemer, not a man in his vertical dimension only, but a man contextualized in reality and in history from the point of view of work.

Where is the importance of work? Do not other values stand out more, such as solidarity and peace, which justice implies?

Let us hear what the Pope thinks of work in relation to the social issue:

> *While in the present document we return to this question once more—without*
> *however any intention of touching on all the topics that concern it—this is not*
> *merely in order to gather together and repeat what is already contained in the*
> *Church's teaching. It is rather in order to highlight—perhaps more than has*
> *been done before—the fact that human work is a key, probably the essential key,*
> *to the whole social question, if we try to see that question really from the point of*
> *view of man's good. And if the solution—or rather, the gradual solution of the*
> *social question, which keeps coming up and becomes ever more complex, must be*
> *sought in the direction of "making life more human," then the key, namely*
> *human work, acquires fundamental and decisive importance. (LE 3; cf. CCC*
> *2427)*

Just two years ago, on the occasion of the twentieth anniversary of *Laborem excercens*, John Paul II ratified this intuition of the beginning of his pontificate:

> *As long as man exists, there will be the free gesture of authentic participation in*
> *creation which is work. Work is one of the essential components in realizing the*
> *vocation of man who, in fulfilling himself, always discovers that he is called by*
> *God to "dominate the earth." Despite himself, he can never cease to be "a subject*
> *that decides about himself" (LE 6). To him God has entrusted this supreme*
> *and demanding freedom. From this viewpoint, today more than in the past, we*
> *can repeat that "human work is a key, probably the essential key, to the whole*
> *social question" (Ibid., 3).* (Message to the participants in the International
> Symposium on Labor on the twentieth anniversary of *Laborem excercens*,
> September 14, 2001)

The Pope makes this repetition from the perspective of the very essence of man, from which springs the mission to "dominate the earth," which implies the "free decision to be a collaborator of his Creator." Here underlies Romano Guardini's prophecy in his book *The End of the Modern World*, when he pointed out the fundamental motive of the paradigm shift that had been operating increasingly in our modern world. Guardini pointed out that the most encompassing and decisive feature of our current civilization was that power, increasingly, was becoming something anonymous. From that, as if from a root, arise all the dangers and injustices that we suffer today. And the antidote proposed by Guardini was none other than for each one to be responsible for power in solidarity. John Paul II's vision of human work is founded on this point: Work is *the place* where man freely decides to use power as a service and collaborate in the creative work of God for the good of his brothers.

II. The Man Who Works, Free, Creative, Participative, and in Solidarity

Work is the place where all the principles of the social doctrine of the Church and of society acquire real consolidation. John Paul II has always reaffirmed that the first firm point of the Social Teachings, from which all others derive, is that: *the social order has as its center man* . . . Man who works, we dare to add; man, who works, free, creative, participative, and in solidarity.

In this man who works, the other principles are focused and linked in a concrete way.

Through work the principle of the "right to common use" becomes concrete (LE 14).

Through work the legitimacy of private property, as an indispensable condition of personal and family autonomy, becomes real.

In valuing work—all jobs—as the source from which all the goods that allow the life of society to emerge, lies the concept of the duties and rights that the State must regulate and clarifies the State's own role as promoter and guardian of the common good.

III. Work: The Place Where All Social Transformations Gradually Take Place

This perspective, anchored in man who works, destroys all fatalistic and mechanistic conceptions when judging how and where large social transformations take place.

It would be a serious mistake to believe that the current transformations happen in a deterministic way. The decisive factor, in other words, the referee of this complex phase of change, is once again man, who must remain the true protagonist of his work. He can and must take charge in a creative and responsible way of the current transformations, so that they contribute to the growth of the person, of the family, of the society in which he lives and of the entire human family (cf. LE 10).

IV. Personalistic and Organic Vision of the Social Dimension of Work

Ten years after his first social encyclical, in *Centesimus annus* (1991), the Pope again placed man who works at the center of socioeconomic life:

> With the intention of shedding light on the conflict which had arisen between capital and labor, Pope Leo XIII affirmed the fundamental rights of workers. Indeed, the key to reading the Encyclical [Rerum novarum] is the dignity of the worker as such, and, for the same reason, the dignity of work, which is defined as follows: "to exert oneself for the sake of procuring what is necessary for the various purposes of life, and first of all for self-preservation." (CA 6)

The pontiff qualifies work as 'personal' since

> "the energy expended is bound up with the personality and is the exclusive property of him who acts, and, furthermore, was given to him for his advantage" (RN 130). Work thus belongs to the vocation of every person; indeed, man expresses and fulfills himself by working. At the same time, work has a "social" dimension through its intimate relationship not only to the family, but also to the common good, since "it may truly be said that it is only by the labor of workingmen that States grow rich" (RN 123). These are themes that I have taken up and developed in my Encyclical Laborem exercens (1, 2, 6). (CA 6)

Number 15 in *Laborem excersens* is key to an organic vision of the dignity of work from the perspective of the personalist argument.

V. The Relation between Work and Capital

In the necessary relationship that exists between work and capital, work has priority, since man "wishes the fruit of this work to be used by himself and others" (LE 15), and he also wants to be mutually responsible for and cocreator of the work he does. He desires "within the production process, provision be made for him to be able *to know* that in his work . . . he is working '*for himself*'" (ibid.):

> This awareness is extinguished within him in a system of excessive bureaucratic centralization, which makes the worker feel that he is just a cog in a huge machine moved from above, that he is for more reasons than one a mere production instrument rather than a true subject of work with an initiative of his own. The Church's teaching has always expressed the strong and deep conviction that man's work concerns not only the economy but also, and especially, personal values. (Ibid.)

VI. The Relation between Work and Private Property

From this perspective of personal values, John Paul II is at the core of the discussion between private ownership or socialization of the means of production and he says that the important thing, in either of the two systems that are adopted at the macrostructural level, is that man who works be aware that is working "for himself":

> The economic system itself and the production process benefit precisely when these personal values are fully respected. In the mind of Saint Thomas Aquinas, this is the principal reason in favor of private ownership of the means of production. While we accept that for certain well-founded reasons exceptions can be made to the principle of private ownership—in our own time we even see that the system of "socialized ownership" has been introduced—nevertheless the personalist argument still holds good both on the level of principles and on the practical level. If it is to be rational and fruitful, any socialization of the means of production must take this argument into consideration. Every effort must be made to ensure that in this kind of system also the human person can preserve his awareness of working "for himself." If this is not done, incalculable damage is inevitably done throughout the economic process, not only economic damage but first and foremost damage to man. (LE 15)

VII. A Just Wage

Within this vision of "working for himself," the question of salary is key:

> This consideration does not however have a purely descriptive purpose; it is not a brief treatise on economics or politics. It is a matter of highlighting the deontological and moral aspect. The key problem of social ethics in this case is that of just remuneration for work done. In the context of the present there is no more important way for securing a just relationship between the worker and the employer than that constituted by remuneration for work. Whether the work is done in a system of private ownership of the means of production or in a system where ownership has undergone a certain "socialization," the relationship between the employer (first and foremost the direct employer) and the worker is resolved on the basis of the wage, that is through just remuneration for work done. (LE 19)

At this point the Pope concentrates all of his vision on man who works. The living wage becomes the key point for verification of the justice or injustice of any socioeconomic system, since it is what makes the principle of "common use of goods" real:

> It should also be noted that the justice of a socioeconomic system and, in each case, its just functioning, deserve in the final analysis to be evaluated by the way in which man's work is properly remunerated in the system. Here we return once more to the first principle of the whole ethical and social order, namely, the principle of the common use of goods. In every system, regardless of the fundamental relationships

within it between capital and labor, wages, that is to say remuneration for work, are still a practical means whereby the vast majority of people can have access to those goods which are intended for common use: both the goods of nature and manufactured goods. Both kinds of goods become accessible to the worker through the wage which he receives as remuneration for his work. Hence, in every case, a just wage is the concrete means of verifying the justice of the whole socioeconomic system and, in any case, of checking that it is functioning justly. It is not the only means of checking, but it is a particularly important one and, in a sense, the key means. (LE 19)

Create Structures That Protect the Dignity of Work

Given that the real participation of all men in the universal destination of goods is at stake in decently remunerated work, the Pope urges institutions to "create structures that protect the dignity of work":

To deal with these problems, new forms of solidarity must be created, taking into account the interdependence that forges bonds among workers. If the changes in progress are profound, there must be a correspondingly intelligent effort and the will to protect the dignity of work, strengthening, at various levels, the interested institutions. Governments have a great deal of responsibility, but no less important is that of the organizations who defend the collective interests of workers and of those who provide work. All are called not only to foster these interests in an honest form and through dialogue, but also to rethink their own functions, their structure, their nature and their kinds of action. As I wrote in the Encyclical Centesimus annus, *these organizations can and must become places "where workers can express his/her own personality"* (CA 15). (Message of John Paul II to the International Symposium "Work as the Key to the Social Question," September 14, 2001)

This task of creating structures that protect the dignity of work entails a double requirement. For thinkers and researchers from different disciplines, the challenge is to "think with scientific rigor and wisdom" about the subject of work, so that they help to understand the change that is taking place in the world of work and to point out opportunities and risks. And for all Christians, the challenge lies in making "a preferential option" (CA 57) for the poorest, for those "excluded from work":

Today, furthermore, given the worldwide dimension which the social question has assumed, this love of preference for the poor, and the decisions which it inspires in us, cannot but embrace the immense multitudes of the hungry, the needy, the homeless, those without medical care and, above all, those without hope of a better

*future. It is impossible not to take account of the existence of these realities. To
ignore them would mean becoming like the "rich man" who pretended not to know
the beggar Lazarus lying at his gate (cf. Lk 16: 19–31). (SRS 42)*

Uniting, in one gaze, a spirituality of communion and a spirituality of work,
we can affirm that the common element of all spirituality of communion,
from the point of view of the subject, is the gaze of the heart. A loving gaze is
an integrating gaze. Faced with the concept that reduces work to mere
employment, which ultimately produces goods that only serve some, the
spiritual view considers work as an expression of all dimensions of man:
from the most basic, which makes the "realization of the person," to the
highest, which considers it a "service" of love.

From the objective point of view, that warm gaze, which is addressed simultaneously 'to the mystery of the Trinity and to the mystery of each human
face,' makes us value the binding nature of work, leads us to see every man
as "someone who belongs to me" and enhances each one's own effort as a
"gift for all." A human society is woven around these values without exclusions of any kind. At the same time, the work opens up for itself those "spaces
of participation" of which the Pope speaks, and turns them into spaces of
real, concrete, dignified participation.

Duc in altum: Toward the Theological Depth of the Dignity of Work

VIII. *The Preeminent Dignity of the Work of Jesus Christ*

Work fosters the dignity of man, linking his personal dimension and his
social dimension. Not only this, but it has an overarching dignity whose ultimate reason lies in Jesus Christ. This is what the Pope says in *Christifi-
delis laici:*

> *By work an individual ordinarily provides for self and family, is joined in fellowship
> to others, and renders them service; and is enabled to exercise genuine charity and
> be a partner in the work of bringing divine creation to perfection. Moreover, we
> know that through work offered to God an individual is associated with the
> redemptive work of Jesus Christ, whose labor with his hands at Nazareth greatly
> ennobled the dignity of work. (CL 43 from GS 67)*

If we properly value what it means that the Lord redeemed us with all
his life—his actions, words and gestures, joys and sufferings—then his
long years of silent and daily work in the small world of Nazareth should be
pondered by our spirits in all their magnitude. If they are hidden silently in

the Gospel, it is precisely because of this: the value of a spirituality of work is in itself silent, humble, contained. "The preeminent dignity of work" is how the Pope describes the work of Jesus, done with his own hands.

The dignity of work is rooted in the Trinity itself: "My Father is at work until now, so I am at work," says the Lord (Jn 5:17). It is precisely an image of work emphasized by the Pope that we may keep in our hearts in order to face the problems that darken the horizon of our time:

> We need but think of the urgent need to work for peace, to base relationships
> between peoples on solid premises of justice and solidarity, and to defend human
> life from conception to its natural end. And what should we say of the thousand
> inconsistencies of a "globalized" world where the weakest, the most powerless and
> the poorest appear to have so little hope! It is in this world that Christian hope must
> shine forth! (EDE 20)

In this world, the Pope states, "is where Christian hope must shine." And what is, then, the universal and concrete image that he presents to us as the clearest and most effective of Christian hope? It is the image of Jesus, Teacher of communion and service. The Pope says:

> Significantly, in their account of the Last Supper, the Synoptics recount the
> institution of the Eucharist, while the Gospel of John relates, as a way of bringing
> out its profound meaning, the account of the "washing of the feet," in which Jesus
> appears as the teacher of communion and of service (cf. Jn 13:1–20). (Ibid.)

The Lord wished to remain with us in the Eucharist, making his presence in this meal and his sacrifice (in the humble washing of the feet, slaves' work) the promise of a humanity renewed by his love.

In celebration of this 'work,' in which the Church imitates the Redeemer by 'doing the Eucharist,' we have a summary of all the eschatological tension of Christianity: the commitment to transform the world and all its existence so that it may become eucharistic:

> Proclaiming the death of the Lord "until he comes" (1 Cor 11:26) entails that all who
> take part in the Eucharist be committed to changing their lives and making them in
> a certain way completely "Eucharistic." It is this fruit of a transfigured existence
> and a commitment to transforming the world in accordance with the Gospel which
> splendidly illustrates the eschatological tension inherent in the celebration of the
> Eucharist and in the Christian life as a whole. (Ibid.)

I want to conclude these reflections by expressing our gratitude to the Holy Father from all of us for this rich doctrine about the social question that he has presented to us: within broad horizons, with the courage to go deep into the subject, and pointing out the theological depth of the dignity of work. Thank you very much, Holy Father.

-»- -«-

He Broke the Bread and Gave It to Them

Homily, Solemnity of Corpus Christi—June 21, 2003, Year B

The account of the Last Supper is always very moving. And even more so when we listen to it during the solemn feast of Corpus Christi. Gathered in this Plaza de Mayo, in front of our cathedral, summoned from all the parishes, as a family, as a people of God, the words of Jesus, the actions of the Lord, deeply touch our hearts: "While they were eating, [Jesus] took bread, said the blessing, broke it, gave it to [his disciples] and said, 'Take it; this is my body'" (Mt 26:26).

The Lord has just entrusted himself to his own, to open their hearts, saying that one is going to betray him. One who dips the bread in his own dish. But instead of continuing to talk about betrayal, Jesus focuses on the Covenant he wants to make with us. I would like us to pause for a moment at this image of Jesus giving the bread that he has just blessed and is breaking into little pieces. It is an image of fragility, a loving and shared fragility.

On Holy Thursday, the priests asked for the grace to "take care for the fragility of our people," making a holy offering of our own fragility. On May 25 we asked for everyone, as a Nation, the grace to "put our country on our shoulders" following in the footsteps of Jesus the Good Samaritan, who carries our frailties on his shoulders. Today the gospel gives us a deeper image: that of fragility not as a wound, not as weakness that the strongest person has to carry, but the fragility necessary for life to be: of the loving fragility of the Eucharist.

'Fragile' is 'what easily shatters.' And the evangelical image that we contemplate is that of the Lord who 'becomes little pieces' . . . of bread and gives himself. In the broken, fragile bread hides the secret of life, of the life of each person, each family, and the entire country.

How curious! We see fragmentation as the greatest danger for our social life and also for our inner life. On the other hand, in Jesus, this fragmentation under the form of tender bread is his most vital, most unifying
act: To give himself whole he has to be broken! In the Eucharist, fragility is
strength. Strength of love that becomes weak to be received. Strength of love
that is broken to feed and give life. Strength of love that is fragmented to be
shared in solidarity. Jesus breaking the bread with his hands! Jesus giving
himself in the Eucharist!

In this loving fragility of the Lord there is good news, a message of hope
for us. The generous and total dedication that Jesus wished to make to save
us was protected in the Eucharist against all the attempts of manipulation
on the part of men: from Judas, the high priests and elders, from the Roman
powers and also from all the distortions that would be tried throughout
history. At the dinner, with the washing of feet and with the Eucharist, the
message of the Covenant became clear: Jesus does not want to be anything
other than Bread of Life for men. For those who did not live this Covenant,
the scenes of the passion could suggest that the blood of the Lord was
wasted, that his body, hanging on the cross, was ruined, like a useless
waste. On the other hand, for those who commune with him, this Jesus,
pierced and bleeding, is more whole and alive than ever. There is already
hope of resurrection at the Last Supper.

Jesus' action of breaking the bread—fragile and tender—became the sign
to recognize the risen one: "He took bread . . . broke it . . . and they recognized him" (cf. Lk 24:30–31). For us too, this is the sign to believe in the risen
Jesus. "This is the sacrament of our faith," we say after the consecration and
we show the fragility of the bread, Body of Christ, divided and separated
from the Blood of the Lord that is contained in the chalice. This is the sign
for us to believe that the Lord gave himself for us. And by incorporating it
with faith, it gives us life, unites us in intimacy with him and with the Father,
unifies us interiorly, makes us one body with others in the Church. By contemplating the Eucharist, we believe. That is the strength of the fragility of
bread, the sacrament of our faith, until the Lord returns.

We turn to look now at the fragility of our people. With Jesus, our fragility acquires a new meaning. Fragility, it is true, causes various temptations: the temptation to live at the mercy of changing moods, the temptation
to delude ourselves with any promise of solutions that improve things just
a little, the temptation to remain isolated and fragmented each in our own
weakness. It is true—we cannot deny it—that fragility incites violent people

to rob the weakest. But it is also true, and more profound, that the fragility of our people is a fruit of their meekness, their desire for peace, that perseverance—which sometimes seems naïve—to renew hopes again and again. It is an evangelized fragility, in which there is much of the meekness and confidence of that Jesus who was announced to us here in our homeland from more than five hundred years ago and who has shared in our history. That is why, with Jesus, we want to be a people who take bread with their hands, who bless, break, and share it. We ask the Lord who becomes broken to give himself whole to each one, that he reconstitute us as a people, as Church and as society. Against the fragmentation that comes from selfishness, we ask for the grace of the loving fragility that comes from surrender. Against the fragmentation that makes us fearful and aggressive, we ask for the grace of being like the bread that is broken so that it will be sufficient. And not only for it to be enough, but for the joy of sharing it and exchanging it. Against the fragmentation of being isolated and immersed in one's own interests, we ask for the grace of being whole, each one in his post, fighting for all, for the common good. Against the fragmentation that springs from skepticism and distrust, we ask the Lord for the grace of faith and hope, which leads us to spend ourselves and wear ourselves out trusting in him and in our brothers.

May our Mother and Lady, the Blessed Virgin, who lived with the fragility of Jesus, who cared for it in the Child, and sustained it by bringing her Son down from the Cross, teach us the secret to look with faith at all human fragility and to care for it with charity, because it is the spring for authentic hope, through the real presence of Jesus in the Eucharist.

⇢ ⇠

Let Us Not Be Disheartened—We'll Find the Way to Start Over Again

Homily, Shrine of Saint Cajetan—August 7, 2003

Today's gospel shows us a very small event, something that lasted just two seconds, so fast, and so secret, that nobody heard of it. The only one who realized it was Jesus. He appreciated it, and he mentioned it to his disciples (cf. Mk 12:41–44). And thus, it became a big act, a teaching for everyone. Among all the people giving alms, Jesus paid attention to a humble woman who had lost her husband and was taking care of her family by herself. This lady put her two small coins that she had for her food that day in the Temple's alms box. Two small coins that made no noise as big silver coins do, but their tinkling resounded as a prayer in Jesus' heart.

Some people don't understand these gratuitous acts. They look at those of us who come to the Shrine of Saint Cajetan, and they don't understand and say: If they are jobless, why do they waste time standing in line to go inside? They come to ask for bread, and instead of buying it with the few coins they have, they make an offering, they give alms! If you don't look at people's hearts, as Jesus does, some things are not understood or are interpreted wrongly. Only Jesus understood the love and faith of this lady when putting her offering in the alms box for the poor. She trusted and risked everything to place all her hope in God's hands. She thought, if I am in a bad situation, I will help someone else who is worse off, and with this action I will ask the Lord to remember me and to bless my children. And the Lord, who is paying attention to these small details of those who love much, saw her, and her act was recorded in the living Word of the Gospel as the model for those small acts that fill us with hope. From time to time, we read news like this one in newspapers: The other day, a very poor mother returned an amount of money she found in her shopping cart. They are actions that last only one day in the papers, but in Jesus' heart the acts of those hands giving with hope, of those hands giving something back with sincerity, are recorded for ever.

This year's theme is: "Let us not be disheartened; taken by Saint Cajetan's hand, we'll find the way to start over again." Notice that he tells us not to be disheartened, to have hope, and to place everything in Saint Cajetan's hands. If you want to know if someone is hopeful or is disheartened, you have to look at their hands.

Today we'll look at hands. Saint Cajetan's hands that hold Baby Jesus and the ear of wheat. And we also look at our hands, one clutching two small coins for the alms collections, and the other with which we caress the image, placing there our family's fragility, our own fragility, our petitions and our gratitude, all our hopes wet with tears. . . . How many things there are in these hands that care for fragility, that break bread, that receive grace and that give what they have! In these hands lies the secret of starting all over again, of restarting the journey without being disheartened, filled with a hope that does not disappoint.

Hand in hand with Baby Jesus, we want to grasp our family's hands. Especially in these days when the family is attacked so much, wanting to destroy it in so many different ways. In that way, the hand of the Baby, tight and warm, turns our fragility into strength. Led by Saint Cajetan's hand, we want to take every Argentine's hand, especially of those who have lost their hope, so as to receive, together, the gift of bread and the gift of work. God, our Father, gives these gifts to those who want to include everyone. And if he offers them to everyone, without exclusion, nobody can deny them to us. They are an inalienable right. The bread and work that we receive together and that we share form our dignity, as persons and as a Nation. To recover them for everyone could take a little or a lot of struggle. Sometimes they have to be demanded, sometimes requested, and always shared . . . but knowing that they are not alms, but justice.

With the hand with which we receive grace, we want to acknowledge that every Gift and all justice comes first from God's hands before any man, before the heavy or weak hands of any government, before the "invisible hand" of any economic system.

And by giving our two small coins with the other hand, we want to testify that we are free and sovereign because we are the owners of giving, that from our own poverty and fragility, first we give and then we ask for.

Give us your hand, Baby Jesus! As our children do, who trust in us. We want to recover the courage to look forward and give everything for them. They are the hope of our people, and we don't want to let them down.

Give us your hand, Saint Cajetan! That hand holding the ear of wheat, and may the hope of daily bread and work lift up our fallen arms. We want to be a people who work as our elders did, and may this memory erase any delusion of earning our bread without the sweat of our brow.

Give us your hand, Heavenly Father! May we feel the Father's Providence, by receiving the Saint's grace. You know well what we need, our family, the Argentine family, trusts in you. We want to be a people that feels cared for in its own fragility. Lord, may no one say that you abandon us. For the honor of your name!

Give us your hand, our Blessed Mother! We have placed our hope in your hands. You are the one who tells us: "Do whatever he [Jesus] tells you" (Jn 2:5). In your maternal language, may this tender and demanding recommendation strengthen our hands, may they become agile and industrious for work, and may they be filled with the arduous joy of charity. You are the strong lady of our homeland, who every day places those two small coins in the alms box of every family, so that no one goes without bread.

Give us your hand, Lord, through your saints! . . . And led by Saint Cajetan's hand, let's not be disheartened! May we find the way to start over again.

→→ ←←

The Treasure of Our Clay

Message to Catechists—August 21, 2003

But we hold this treasure in earthen vessels, that the surpassing power may be of God and not from us. (2 Cor 4:7)

Throughout this year, we are trying, as an Archdiocesan Church, to take care of the "fragility of our people," even making it the theme and style of the archdiocesan mission.

Along these lines, I would also like the theme of "fragility" to be present in this letter that I write to you every year for the Feast of Saint Pius X, patron saint of catechists.

In 2002 I invited you to reflect on the mission of the catechist as worshiper, as one who knows to be before a mystery great and wonderful so that it overflows into prayer and praise. Today, I am encouraged to stress this aspect to you. Faced with a fragmented world, with the temptation of new fratricidal fissures in our country, with the painful experience of our own fragility, it becomes necessary and urgent, I would even dare to say, essential, to deepen our prayer and worship. This will help us unify our hearts and give us *'innards of mercy'* to be people of *encounter* and communion, who assume as their own vocation the responsibility for their brother's wounds. Do not deprive the Church of your ministry of prayer, which allows you to oxygenate your daily fatigue by bearing witness to a God so close, so Other: Father, Brother, and Spirit; Bread, Companion on our Journey, and giver of Life.

A year ago, I wrote to you: "Today more than ever it is necessary to worship in order to make possible the fellowship demanded by these times of crisis. Only in the contemplation of the mystery of Love that overcomes distances and becomes closeness, will we find the strength not to fall into the temptation of passing by without stopping on the road."

Precisely the text of the Good Samaritan (cf. Lk 10:25–37) sheds light on the *Te Deum* on May 25 this year. In it I made the invitation "to rethink and give new meaning to all our lives—as a people and as a Nation—from the joy of the risen Christ allowing hope, within the very fragility of our flesh, to live like a true community."

Announcing the *kerygma*, giving life new meaning, forming community, are tasks that the Church entrusts to catechists in a particular way. A big task that surpasses us and even at times overwhelms us. Somehow, we feel reflected in the young Gideon who before being sent to fight against the Midianites feels helpless and perplexed before the apparent superiority of the invading enemy (cf. Jgs 6:11–24). We too, faced with this new pseudo-cultural invasion that presents us with the new pagan faces of the "Baals" of yesteryear, we experience the disproportion of the forces and the smallness of the envoy. But it is precisely from the experience of one's own fragility that the strength from on high is evident, the presence of the One who is our guarantor and our peace.

Therefore, I am encouraged this year to invite you—with the same contemplative gaze that enables you to discover the closeness of the Lord of History—to recognize in your fragility the hidden treasure that confuses the proud and overthrows the powerful. Today the Lord invites us to embrace our fragility as the source of a great evangelizing treasure. To recognize that we are clay, vessels, and path, is also to worship the true God.

Because only those who recognize themselves as vulnerable are capable of solidary action. To be moved by ("move-with"), to have compassion (*"suffer-with"*) for one who is fallen by the wayside, are attitudes of one who knows how to recognize in the other his own image, a mixture of earth and treasure, and therefore does not reject it. On the contrary, he loves it, he approaches it, and, without looking for it, he discovers that the wounds he heals for his brother are a balm for his own wounds. Compassion becomes communion, a bridge that brings closeness and tightens bonds. Neither the robbers nor those who pass by the fallen one are aware of either their treasure or their clay. That is why the former do not value the life of the other and dare to leave him almost dead. If they do not value their own lives, how can they recognize a treasure in that of others? Those who pass by in turn, valuing their lives but partially, dare to look only at one part, that which they believe is valuable: They know they are chosen and loved by God (strikingly, in the parable, the two passersby are religious characters of Jesus' time: a Levite and a priest) but they do not dare to recognize the clay, the fragile mud. That is why they are afraid of the fallen one and do not know how to recognize him. How can they recognize the mud of others if they do not accept their own?

If something should characterize catechetical pedagogy, if catechists should be experts in one thing, it is in their capacity for welcoming, for taking responsibility for others, for seeing that no one is left by the side of the road. Therefore, given the seriousness and the extent of the crisis, faced with the challenge as an Archdiocesan Church to commit ourselves to *"take care of the fragility of our people,"* I invite you to renew your vocation as catechists and put all your creativity into knowing 'how to be' close to those who suffer, making a 'pedagogy of presence' a reality, in which listening and nearness are not only a style but the content of catechesis.

And in this beautiful artisan vocation of being 'chrism and caress for the suffering one,' do not be afraid to take care of the fragility of your brother out of your own fragility: your pain, your fatigue, your brokenness; God transforms them into wealth, ointment, sacrament. Remember what we meditated on together on Corpus Christi: There is a fragility, the Eucharistic one, that hides the secret of sharing. There is a brokenness that allows, in the tender gesture of giving oneself, to feed, to unify, to give meaning to life. On this feast of Saint Pius X, may you present to the Lord in prayer your weariness and fatigue, and that of the people whom the Lord has placed in your path. And let the Lord embrace your fragility, your clay, to transform it into an evangelizing force and a source of strength. This is how the Apostle Paul experienced it:

> We are afflicted in every way, but not constrained; perplexed, but not driven to despair; persecuted, but not abandoned; struck down, but not destroyed; always carrying about in the body the dying of Jesus, so that the life of Jesus may also be manifested in our body. (2 Cor 4:8–10)

It is in fragility where we are called to be catechists. The vocation would not be full if it excluded our mud, our falls, our failures, our daily struggles. It is there where the life of Jesus manifests itself and becomes a saving announcement. Thanks to it we discover the pains of our brother as our own. And from there, the voice of the prophet becomes Good News for all:

> Strengthen hands that are feeble,
> make firm knees that are weak,
> Say to the fearful of heart:
> Be strong, do not fear!
> Here is your God! . . .
> he comes to save you!

Then the eyes of the blind shall see,
and the ears of the deaf be opened;
Then the lame shall leap like a stag,
and the mute tongue sing for joy.

...

They meet with joy and gladness,
sorrow and mourning flee away. (Is 35:3–6a, 10b)

May Mary grant us the ability to value the treasure of our mud, to be able to sing with her the *Magnificat* of our smallness together with the greatness of God.

Do not stop praying for me that I may also live this experience of limits and of grace. May Jesus bless you and the Blessed Virgin guide you. With all my affection.

➤➤ ◀◀

"The People Who Walked in Darkness Have Seen a Great Light"

Homily, Christmas Mass during the Night—December 24, 2003, Year C

The prophetic announcement marks the beginning: "The people who walked in darkness / have seen a great light" (Is 9:1), a new direction for one's entire life, a direction for all of history that keeps us secure "as we await the blessed hope, the appearance of the glory of our great God and savior Jesus Christ" (Ti 2:13). Darkness and light, a path and hope, glimpse and manifestation. It is the prophecy of the chosen, of the promise and of the covenant. It is the path from the darkness of that sunset in the earthly paradise until that night in which the outbreak of "the glory of the Lord shone around them [the shepherds]" (Lk 2:9).

We too, pilgrims among the chosen, of the promise and of the covenant, come before the altar of God with the grief of so much darkness and the hope of finding the light; we approach the altar where the glory is hidden in a manger, and is shown to those with a humble heart who listen in awe to the heavenly hymn: "Glory to God in the highest / and on earth peace to those on whom his favor rests" (v. 14), and who believe with the faith of those who do not cheapen their consciences that "a savior has been born . . . you will find an infant wrapped in swaddling clothes and lying in a manger" (v. 12). Tonight, if we open our hearts, we too will have the possibility of contemplating the miracle of light amid our darkness, the miracle of God's strength amid fragility, the miracle of extreme greatness amid smallness.

We walk from faith to faith, in the pursuit of fullness and the meaning of our lives. And this path is true when we do not allow it to be trapped by the alienating noises of fleeting or lying propositions. We are part of the people of God who, day by day, want to take a step from darkness to light. We all want to find that light, that hidden glory, and we are willing because the same God who created us sowed that desire in our hearts. However, our hearts sometimes become hardened, whimsical, or, even worse, swollen with increasing arrogance. So, this desire to see the glory of the light is smothered and we risk living a meaningless life, of eroding in the darkness. Thus, we repeat the fact that God cannot find a place, as on that night in which Mary "laid him in a manger, because there was no room for them in the inn" (v. 7).

This is the tragedy of the soul becoming impatient while waiting; it entertains itself with false promises of light made by the Devil, whom Jesus calls "the father of lies" (Jn 8:44), 'the prince of darkness.' Then we begin losing hope in the promise, in the fidelity of the covenant with a God who does not lie "for he cannot deny himself" (2 Tm 2:13). We lose the deep sentiment of feeling chosen by the Father's tenderness. Doors are closed, and today, as always, in the world, in our city, in our hearts many doors are closed to Jesus. It is easier to be entertained by the lights of a Christmas tree than by sinking into contemplation of the manger's glory. And this anti-path, that is, the path of closing doors ranges from indifference to the killing of innocent people. There is not much difference between those who closed the doors to Joseph and Mary because they were poor foreigners, and Herod who "kills the little ones because fear killed his heart."[1] There is no middle ground: Light or darkness, arrogance or humility, truth or lie, we either open the door to Jesus who comes to save us or we close ourselves before the self-sufficiency and the pride of do-it-yourself salvation.

On this holy night, I ask you to gaze at the manger. There "the people who walked in darkness / have seen a great light" (Is 9:1), but it was seen by

---

1. Saint Quodvultdeus, *Sermoni sul Simbolo*, 2.

the people who were humble and open to the Gift of God. It wasn't seen by the self-reliant, the proud, those who enact their own laws, those who close doors. Let us gaze at the manger, and let us pray for ourselves, for our suffering people. Let us gaze at the manger, and let us tell our Mother, "Mary, show us Jesus."

2004

Throw the Nets in Deeper Waters

Homily, Ash Wednesday—February 25, 2004, Year C

Dear brothers and sisters,

During 2003 I asked you to dedicate the Archdiocesan Mission to care for the fragility of our people, taking responsibility for it from the very fragility of Jesus, God incarnate, who being strong became weak, being rich became poor, being great became small (cf. *Roman Missal*). In response, concrete actions have been carried out in some communities: more prayer, outreach, works of solidarity. . . . In others, little has been done yet. But we can certainly say that this deep pastoral concern is establishing itself in the Archdiocese.

The desire to care for the fragility of our people is a magnanimous longing that can be nurtured only in generous and solidary, simple and attentive hearts. Persevering in this purpose will be the fruit of the grace of the Holy Spirit that impels us to be close to all want and pain and sustains us in being constant.

We live in serious and disheartening situations that often lead to discouragement. We have reflected about them in each community in an effort to have them touch our hearts. To those who have not followed the plan prepared by the Archdiocesan Pastoral Council, I ask you to please do so during this year in order to be in harmony with this openness of the soul in order to care for the fragility of our people. It will be good for us to go back to these fragilities from within: e.g., those that touch the life of faith (how many kids do not know how to pray! how many young people are without horizons!), family life (lack of dialogue, abandoned old people . . .), social living (unemployment, hunger, injustice).

Faced with pain and disappointment, we Christians are called to hope. Not as a search for fantasy, but with the confidence of the disciple and apostle that "hope does not disappoint, because the love of God has been poured out into our hearts through the holy Spirit that has been given to us" (Rm 5:5). This hope is the anchor that is already moored in heaven and to which we cling in order to continue walking. Jesus himself comes to meet us and repeats to us, with serenity and firmness: "Do not be afraid" (Mk 6:50); "I am with you always, until the end of the age" (Mt 28:20); "Go, therefore, and make disciples" (v. 19). Going out to announce, being close to those who suffer from fragility, being fragile oneself, is possible only by trusting in that promise of the Risen Lord: "I am with you always" (v. 20). And because we are not superheroes or courageous fighters who blindly brag about their own strength, we act with the audacity of the disciples of Jesus, members of their family. The audacity of the brothers of the Lord.

This year I ask you to work with that audacity, with intense apostolic fervor. By taking responsibility for fragility—ours and our people's—we want to walk with audacity, that attitude that the Holy Spirit breathed into the Apostles and led them to proclaim Jesus Christ. Audacity, courage, speaking with freedom, apostolic fervor . . . all these are included in the word *parrhesia*, a word which for Saint Paul means 'the freedom and courage of a being, open in itself, because it is available for God and for the neighbor.' Paul VI mentioned among the obstacles to evangelization precisely the lack of *parrhesia*: "the lack of fervor. . . . It is the more serious because it comes from within. It is manifested in fatigue, disenchantment, compromise, lack of interest and above all lack of joy and hope" (EN 80). John Paul II speaks of ardor, apostolic zeal, courage, missionary drive (RM 30, 67, 91). And we remember the disciples of Emmaus in their encounter with the Risen Lord: "*Were not our hearts burning [within us] while he spoke to us on the way*" (Lk 24:32). Conviction in the work of the Spirit and zeal that springs from the encounter with the living Christ. Conviction and zeal that are necessary in us, the disciples, both to care for our fragilities and to announce the Risen Christ.

We often feel tired and fatigued. We are tempted by the spirit of sloth, of laziness. We also look at everything there is to do, and how small we are. As the apostles say to the Lord: "What good are these for so many?" (Jn 6:9). Who are we to take care of so much fragility? And therein lies precisely our strength: in the humble trust of those who love and know themselves to be loved and cared for by the Father, in the humble trust of those who know they are freely chosen and sent. The experience of Saint Paul was to carry a treasure in earthen vessels (2 Cor 4:7), and he transmits it to all of us. It is to look after oneself and others. He is not afraid to look at the earthen vessel precisely because the treasure inside is based on Jesus Christ, and from him comes the courage, the audacity, the apostolic zeal.

How many times we feel tempted to stay in the comfort of the shore! But the Lord calls us to sail out to sea and throw the nets in deeper waters (Lk 5:4). He calls us to announce him with audacity and apostolic zeal, to spend our lives in his service. Clinging to him, we encourage ourselves to follow him closely, each of us putting our charisms at the service of the community in the archdiocesan church. We will do it using diverse pastoral instruments harmonized by our Pastoral Plan that ends a new stage at the close of this year, with the activities proposed for the triennium 2002–2004. In the Episcopal Council we have seen the convenience of holding a Diocesan Assembly in 2005, which will allow us to grow in the sense of ecclesial belonging and participate in the reelaboration of our Pastoral Plan, taking into account the orientations of *Navega Mar Adentro*[1] [Go into Deeper Waters]. I have asked the Archdiocesan Pastoral Council to develop a path of preparation for that Assembly.

I would like to conclude by exhorting you once again to apostolic fervor with the words of Paul VI:

> Let us preserve the delightful and comforting joy of evangelizing, even when it is in tears that we must sow. May it mean for us—as it did for John the Baptist, for Peter and Paul, for the other apostles and for a multitude of splendid evangelizers all through the Church's history—an interior enthusiasm that nobody and nothing can quench. May it be the great joy of our consecrated lives. And may the world of our time, which is searching sometimes with anguish, sometimes with hope, be enabled to receive the Good News not from evangelizers who are dejected, discouraged, impatient or anxious, but from ministers of the Gospel whose lives glow with fervor, who have first received the joy of Christ, and who are willing to risk their lives so that the kingdom may be proclaimed and the Church established in the midst of the world. (EN 80)

I ask the Lord that we all may feel impelled by his love (2 Cor 5:14) and may be able to say with Saint Paul, "Woe to me if I do not preach [the gospel]"! (1 Cor 9:16). May the Mother of the Lord, who experienced the peculiar fatigue of the heart (RMA 17), accompany us and sustain us in our

---

1. Pastoral Guidelines for the New Evangelization, first prepared by the Argentina Episcopal Conference in 1990 as a response to John Paul II's call for a new evangelization. The guidelines were updated on May 31, 2003.

daily fatigue and obtain for us the grace of audacious evangelizing and apostolic zeal.

Please, pray for me. With fraternal affection.

→> <+-

The Reality of the Unborn Child

Homily, Day of the Unborn Child—March 25, 2004,
Feast of the Annunciation

Mary's 'Yes' opens the door to the long journey of the Son of God among us. Today begins this journey of the Lord, who "went about doing good" (Acts 10:38), cured our wounds with his wounds, proclaimed our triumph with his Resurrection. Jesus walks among his people ever since he was in his Mother's womb; he wants to follow all our steps, even the journey of the unborn child. He became equal to us in everything but sin. This event radically changes human existence. The Lord assumes our life and elevates it to the supernatural order. The presence of the Word of God made flesh transforms—without denying—everything that is human, elevates it, and places it in the dimension of the Kingdom of God. Thus, the unborn Jesus also enlightens the life of the person in his mother's womb. From our faith—through the mystery of the Incarnation of the Word—the human, what is in the order of the natural law, acquires the new supernatural dimension that, without denying nature, perfects it and leads it to its fullness.

With this event, a new perspective opens up for considering the origin and development of our life. In this particular case, Christ in Mary's womb is the hermeneutical key to understand and interpret the journey, life. And also the rights of the unborn child, to understand more clearly what the natural law already tells us on this subject.

Jesus comes as a child. He starts like every child and becomes a part of family life. The mother's tenderness toward the son who is coming, the father's hope (adoptive father in this case) who has bet on the future of the promise, the patient growing little by little every day until the moment of birth, all of this that occurs in the gestation of children, with Jesus acquires a new meaning that enlightens the understanding of the mystery of man and marks our existence with values that thrive in attitudes: tenderness, hope, patience. Without these three attitudes—tenderness, hope, patience—it is not possible to respect life or the growth of the unborn child. Tenderness makes us committed; hope thrusts us toward the future; patience accompanies our wait in the weary passing of days. And the three attitudes are like links of a chain for that life that grows day by day.

When these attitudes are not there, then the child becomes an 'object,' estranged from his father and mother, and many times 'something' bothersome, an intruder in the life of the adults, who aspire to live peacefully, withdrawn into themselves in paralyzing selfishness. From his Mother's womb, Jesus accepts running all the risks of selfishness. Once born, but still a child, he was subjected to the persecution of Herod who "killed children in the flesh because he was being killed by his heart's fear." Today, children and unborn children are also threatened by the selfishness of those who suffer from the shadow of despair in their hearts, the despair that sows fear and leads to murder. Today, our individualistic culture also refuses to be fruitful, takes refuge in a permissiveness that sinks ever lower, even if the price of that barrenness is innocent blood. Today we are also influenced by a theism that degrades everything related to the human, that theism "spray" that expects to replace the great Truth that "the Word is made flesh." Today's cultural proposal to withdraw into oneself in a selfishly individualistic dimension is built at the expense of the rights of persons, of children. These are the characteristics of a modern Herod.

The Incarnation of the Word, the unborn Baby Jesus in Mary's womb, once again summons us to have courage. We do not want to diminish ourselves in the superficial culture that destroys us and—because it kills little by little—always ends up being a culture of death. We want to reclaim the presence of Christ in his Mother's womb, a presence that reestablishes the reality of the unborn child. Our Yes to life is cemented here, a Yes motivated by the Life that wanted to share in our journey. In Christ the centrality of man as the masterpiece of creation reaches its fullness. By participating in this fullness, we understand more deeply the mystery of man from the moment of his conception and the natural ethical order that regulates this life.

On this day of the Incarnation of the Word, I want to ask our Mother, the Virgin Mary, to place us next to Jesus. May she grow in our hearts attitudes of tenderness, hope, and patience in order to protect all human life, especially the most fragile, the most marginalized, the most vulnerable.

→- -←

Where Did We Take the Fragility of Our People?

Homily, Chrism Mass—April 8, 2004, Year C

Dear brothers in the priesthood,

Last year's pastoral concern "to care for the fragility of our people" leads us to pray and to ask the Lord with the simplicity of servants: Where did we take the fragility that we looked for and are not taking care of? What is the grace that we should pray for in order to care for the most vulnerable, your favorite ones?

Let us bring to the heart today the Lord's gaze on so many occasions when, moved, he stopped to contemplate the fragility of his people. The compassion of Jesus was not something that absorbed him; it was not a paralyzing compassion, as often happens to us, but quite the opposite: It was a compassion that moved him to come out of himself with force, with audacity, to announce, to send on mission, to send to heal, as the gospel passage that we just read says (Lk 4:16–30).

There we contemplate the Lord assuming the mission of evangelizing with *parrhesia*. Let's look at the verbs that the Lord takes from Isaiah: "to announce" (*euangelizein*) and "preach" (*keruzein*), two actions that he performs driven by the Spirit that anoints him for the mission. Let's notice, for example, what he says about the "oppressed"; it is not simply freeing captives! The gospel says that the Lord comes "to send them (*aposteilai*) on a mission freed from their bondage." From among those who were once captives, the Lord chooses his envoys. Our Lord Jesus Christ bursts into our history—marked by vulnerability—with an unstoppable dynamism, full of strength and courage. That is the *kerygma*, the nucleus of our preaching: the emphatic proclamation of that irruption in our history of Jesus Christ incarnate, dead and risen.

In Jesus' diagnosis of the situation of the world there is nothing plaintive, nothing paralyzing. . . . On the contrary, it is an invitation to fervent action. And the greatest audacity consists precisely in the fact that it is an inclusive action, insofar as it associates the poorest, the oppressed, the blind . . . with the little ones of the Father. Associating them by making them partakers of the good news, participants in their new vision of things, participants in the mission to include others, once liberated. We could say, in our current language, that the gaze of Jesus is not at all a "welfare" vision of fragility. The Lord does not come to heal the blind so they can see the media spectacle of this world, but to see the wonders that God does in the midst of his people. The Lord does not come to free the oppressed because of their faults and those of unjust structures, or so that they feel good, but to send them on mission. The Lord does not announce a year of grace so that each one, healed of evil, will take a sabbatical year, but so that, with him in our midst, we can live our lives participating actively in everything that constitutes our dignity because we are children of the living God.

The Lord, when he looks at our frailty, invites us to take care of him not with fear but with audacity. "Take courage, I have conquered the world!" (Jn 16:33). "I am with you always, until the end of the age" (Mt 28:20). There-fore, consciousness of one's frailty, which Peter humbly confesses, does not cause the Lord to withdraw his invitation but moves him to send Peter on mission, to exhort him to sail offshore, to be encouraged to be a fisher of men (cf. Lk 5:8–10). The magnitude of the vulnerability of the faithful people, which fills the Lord with compassion, does not lead to a prudent calculation of our limited possibilities, as the apostles suggest, but urges them to trust without limits, to practice generosity and evangelical waste, as happened in the multiplication of the loaves. The sending forth by the risen Lord, who crowns the Gospel, is in keeping with the passage today, which is an inaugural moment: "Go, therefore, and make disciples of all nations, baptizing them . . . teaching them to observe all that I have commanded you" (Mt 28:19).

Apostolic audacity and courage are constitutive of the mission. The *parrhesia* is the seal of the Spirit, testimony of the authenticity of the *kerygma* and the evangelical proclamation. It is that attitude of "inner freedom" to openly say what has to be said, that healthy pride that leads us to "boast" of the Gospel we proclaim, that unwavering trust in the fidelity of the faithful Witness, which gives the witnesses of Christ the assurance that nothing "will be able to separate us from the love of God" (cf. Rm 8:38ff). If the pastors have this attitude, then the fragility of our people is well taken care of and directed. That is, then, the grace that we want to ask of the Lord so as to take good care of the fragility of our people: the grace of apostolic boldness, strong and fervent audacity in the Spirit.

We ask this, humbly and confidently, of Our Lady. Of her who has been called "the first evangelizer." Of her, the Eucharistic woman who gives us Christ and the one who exhorts us to "do whatever Jesus tells [us]" (Jn 2:5). She is the first to experience within herself the joy of going out to evange-lize and the first one to share in the unprecedented audacity of the Son and who contemplates and announces how God "has shown might with his arm, dispersed the arrogant of mind and heart. He has thrown down the rulers from their thrones but lifted up the lowly. The hungry he has filled with good things; the rich he has sent away empty" (Lk 1:51–53). From this audacity of Mary we are invited to participate as priests of the Holy Church. This area of evangelical joy—which is our strength—is where we must lead the fragility of our people that we went out to find. That is the good news: that the poor, the fragile and vulnerable, small as we are, have been regarded, like her, with kindness in our smallness, and we are part of a people to which the mercy of the God of our fathers has been shown from generation to generation.

⇥ ⇤

Remembering Returns the Women to Reality

Homily, Easter Vigil—April 10, 2004, Year C

The path of the people of God stops tonight in front of a tomb, an empty tomb. The body of Jesus, Son of the promise, was no longer there; only the sheets that wrapped him were visible. The journey of an entire people stops today as it once did before the rock in the desert (Ex 17:6) or on the seashore on the night of Passover, when the Israelites, "greatly frightened, . . . cried out to the LORD" (Ex 14:10) and furiously yelled at Moses: "Were there no burial places in Egypt that you brought us to die in the wilderness?" (v. 11). Tonight is not panic but the puzzlement (Lk 24:4) and terror (v. 5) of these women before the incomprehensible: The promised Son was not there. When they return and tell the Apostles everything (v. 10) "their story seemed like nonsense and they did not believe them" (v. 11). Puzzlement, terror, and seeming nonsense: feelings that are like a tomb, and where the centuries-long journey of an entire people stops. Puzzlement disorients, terror paralyzes, the appearance of being nonsensical suggests fantasies.

The women "bowed their faces to the ground" (v. 5). Puzzlement and terror prevent us from looking up to heaven; puzzlement and terror without a horizon distort hope. The women react with surprise at the accusation, "Why do you seek the living one among the dead?" (v. 5), but they are even more surprised with the prophetic word "Remember" (v. 6) . . . and the women "remembered his words" (v. 8) and it was then that what was going on outside was reflected in their hearts: The first rays of dawn dispel the darkness of doubt, fear, and bewilderment . . . and they run and tell what they have heard: "He is not here but has been raised" (v. 6).

Memory brings them back to reality. They recover the memory and the consciousness of being a chosen people; they remember the promises; they reaffirm themselves in the covenant, and they feel they have been chosen again. And so, a strong energy is born in the heart that is of the Holy Spirit to go and evangelize, to announce the great news. The whole history of salvation sets off once again. The miracle of that night at the Red Sea is repeated again. "And the LORD said to Moses: 'Why are you crying out to me? Tell the Israelites to go forward'" (Ex 14:15). And the people continued their journey with the running of the women who had remembered the promises of the Lord.

We have all at one time experienced, as persons and as a people, the feeling of finding ourselves stopped in our tracks, without knowing what steps to take. In those moments, it seems like the frontiers of life are closed, we doubt the promises, and a crass positivism arises as an interpretive key for the situation. In our consciousness, puzzlement and terror take control; reality is imposed on us as closed off, without hope, and we want to retrace our steps toward the same slavery that we had left, and we even reproach the Lord who set us on the path of freedom: "Did we not tell you this in Egypt, when we said, 'Leave us alone that we may serve the Egyptians? Far better for us to serve the Egyptians than to die in the wilderness'" (Ex 14:12). In these situations, as on the shores of the Red Sea or in front of the tomb, the answer arrives: "Do not fear" (v. 13), "Remember" (Lk 24:6).

Remember the promise but, above all, remember the story itself. Remember all the wonders the Lord has done throughout life. "Be on your guard and be very careful not to forget the things your own eyes have seen, nor let them slip from your heart" (Dt 4:9); when you are satisfied "be careful not to forget the LORD, who brought you out of the land of Egypt, that house of slavery" (Dt 6:12); "remember how for these forty years the LORD, your God, has directed all your journeying in the wilderness. . . . The clothing did not fall from you in tatters, nor did your feet swell these forty years" (Dt 8:2, 4); "Remember the days past" (Heb 10:32); "Remember Jesus Christ, raised from the dead" (2 Tm 2:8). The Word of God exhorts us in this way so that we continually reread our history of salvation in order to be able to keep going forward. The memory of the path traveled by the grace of God is strength and a foundation of hope to continue walking. Let us not allow the memory of our salvation to be atrophied by puzzlement and terror that may come over us in front of whatever tomb seeks to take over our hope. Let us always leave room for the Word of the Lord, like the women at the tomb: "Remember." In the moments of greatest darkness and paralysis, it is urgent to recover this Deuteronomic dimension of existence.

On this holy night I want to ask the Most Blessed Virgin to grant us the grace of the memory of all the wonders that the Lord has done in our lives, and that this memory shake us, impel us to continue walking in our Christian life, in the announcement that there is no need to search among the dead for the one who is alive, in the announcement that Jesus, the promised Son, is the Paschal Lamb and has risen. May She teach us to tell each other slowly and deliberately, with the certainty of someone who knows that she has been led throughout her whole life, what she surely repeated herself in that dawn while waiting for her Son: "I know that my vindicator lives" (Job 19:25).

→ ←

Education for Living

Letter to Educators—April 21, 2004

With audacity, between us all, an educational country.

Dear educators,

It's nothing new to say we're living through difficult times. You know it; you feel it every day in the classroom. You will often have felt yourself lacking in strength with which to respond to the burden of anxieties borne by families and the expectations placed on you. This year's message wants to start from that place and wants to invite you to rediscover the greatness of the vocation you have received. If we look at Jesus, the Wisdom of God incarnate, we can understand that difficulties become challenges; challenges call for hope and generate the joy of knowing they are the architects of something new. There is no doubt that all of that motivates us to keep on giving our best.

These things are what I would like to share with you today. As Christians, we have a specific contribution to make in our homeland and you, as educators, should be the protagonists of a change that cannot be delayed. It is for this change that I invite you and for which I place my trust in you and offer you my care as a shepherd.

During this last year, it has become popular to affirm that we Argentines have 'regained hope.' It remains to be seen whether it's that real hope which opens up a qualitatively different future (even though it may not have a clearly religious side to it), or whether we are prepared just to delude ourselves again, with all the risks that involves. Either way, we're going to take this 'change of mood' as the starting point for a few reflections. Sticking to what interests us here, which is the question of the values that sustain and justify our task as educators, I propose that we place ourselves in a scenario that may give rise to some interesting proposals: the scenario of rebuilding the community.

The panorama in our country over the last few years has made us recognize a 'fundamental' problem, a crisis of beliefs and values and, as with all moments of recognition, it confronts us with the challenge of finding a solution to it. That is where the idea of 'rebuilding' turns out to be much more than a metaphor. It is not a case of 'going backward,' as if nothing had happened or nothing had been learned. Nor is it about 'removing' something pernicious, a sort of tumor in our collective consciousness, supposing that 'before' this the organism was in 'perfect health.' If we talk about 'rebuilding' it's because we're aware of the impossibility of leapfrogging it and bypassing history. 'Rebuilding' means, in this case, to once again put aims, desires, and ideals first and to find new, more effective ways of guiding our actions toward those aims, desires, and ideals, linking efforts and creating realities (external and internal, institutions and habits) that make it possible to sustain a coherent and shared way forward.

Nobody can be unaware that education is one of the main pillars for this rebuilding of the sense of community, although it cannot be disassociated from other equally fundamental dimensions such as economics and politics. If the diagnosis is correct that locates the crisis not only in errors made by shortsighted macroeconomics (or with a distorted view of its place and function within a national community) but also at a political, cultural— and even more deeply so—moral level, the task will be long and consist more of 'sowing' than a series of quick fixes. That is why I do not think I am exaggerating when I say that any project that fails to give prominence to education will only be more of the same.

So now, as Christian educators faced with the challenge of making our contribution to rebuilding the national community, we need to effect a series of discernments as to what, at least in our opinion, should be prioritized.

The fruitfulness of our efforts doesn't just depend on subjective conditions, on the level of dedication, generosity, and commitment that we are able to achieve. It also depends on the 'objective' accuracy of our decisions and actions.

Understanding, interpretation, and discernment are essential moments of any form of responsible and consistent behavior, of any path in hope. As Christians, we have a starting point, a reference that is given to us as a light and guide. We're not walking blindly; we're not feeling our way ahead in our search for meaning, taking our bearings only by 'trial and error.' Christian discernment is Christian precisely because it takes Jesus Christ, the Wisdom of God, as its axis (cf. 1 Cor 1:24, 30). If it's a matter of trying to 'understand,' to 'make sense of,' to 'know' which direction to go in, we Christians have an inexhaustible fount, which is divine Wisdom made flesh, made man, made history. We must go back there, again and again, in search of illumination, inspiration, and strength.

1. Our Foundation: Christ, the Wisdom of God

(a). The Three Sides of Wisdom

What does it mean to speak of 'wisdom'? First, it clearly has something to do with knowledge. That is a first meaning of 'to know': to be familiar with, to understand. To be wise, to live with wisdom, involves many things, but the 'intellectual' aspect can never be omitted. As educators, a service to the wisdom of our people is—to a great extent—a service to cognitive growth. If we today take into account the experiential, emotional, bonding, attitudinal aspects . . . all those cannot exist at the expense of strong commitment to things intellectual. In that we should give some credit to the perhaps rather learned or encyclopedic matrix of 'foundational' Argentine education. Somebody who knows more, who has cultivated the capacity to acquire information, evaluate, and reflect and to incorporate new ideas and juxtapose them with existing ones to produce new meanings, not only possesses an invaluable tool with which to get ahead in the workplace and find 'success' in social life but also possesses extremely valuable elements for personal development, for growing in the sense of 'being' better.

It's not for nothing that the Church has always seen the importance, in education, of intellectual activity as well as strictly religious education. Knowledge not only 'doesn't take up space,' as our grandmothers used to say, but 'opens up space,' 'makes more room' for human development.

Here, still at the start of our meditation, we already have a specific point to review and discuss in our educational communities. We quite rightly put the emphasis on community life, on expanding our capacity to welcome and discipline, on creating human connections and environments of joy and love that can enable our children and youth to grow and be fruitful. And we do well to do so. Very often those basic contributions are denied them by a society that is increasingly harsh, success-oriented, competitive, individualistic. But all that cannot be done at the expense of the essential task of feeding and forming the intellect. Today the word 'excellence' is fashionable, sometimes with an ambiguous meaning, which we will return to later; but let's rescue from this fashion the imperative to work seriously to transmit and create all forms of knowledge. To paraphrase that trendy term, let's look for an 'intelligent' education.

But wisdom doesn't stop at knowledge. 'To know' also means 'to taste,' to savor. We 'know' knowledge . . . and we 'know' flavors also. What does this dimension contribute to what we've been saying so far? The 'affective' and 'aesthetic' aspects: We know and love what we know. Thus, educating is much more than offering knowledge: It becomes helping our children and youth to value and contemplate that knowledge, to give it flesh. It means working not only on the intelligence but also on the will. We opt for personal freedom as the ultimate synthesis of the human way of being in the world, but not an indeterminate (nonexistent!) freedom but one nourished by experiences of safety, joy, love given and received.

I'm not talking about whether children 'like' going to school. The quest for wisdom as a 'flavor' does not boil down to a question of motivation, even if it includes it. It's a matter of them 'feeling' the joy of the word, of giving and receiving, listening and sharing, understanding the world around them and the bonds uniting them, feeling the wonder of the mystery of creation and its maximum expression: humankind. Let's go back to these points. For now, let's make a note that our educational task has to awaken the feeling that the world and society are our home. Education 'for living': the essential path to being human and to recognizing ourselves as children of God.

I would still like to draw attention to a third 'side,' a third dimension of wisdom. A wise person is not only one who knows things, contemplates and loves them, but also one who manages to take part in them by choosing a path and the many concrete and even everyday options that faithfulness requires. That, then, is a 'practical' side, in which the previous two are resolved. This dimension coincides with the ancient meaning of 'Wisdom' contained in the Bible: the capacity to find one's bearings in life, so that prudent and skillful conduct can grow to fruition in a full and happy life. To 'know' what is 'worthwhile' and what is not, an ethical knowledge that, far from constraining and inhibiting human possibilities, unfolds and develops them to the maximum. A moral knowledge, as opposed to both 'immoral' and 'demoralized.' Also knowing 'how to do it': knowledge that is 'practical' not just in terms of the ends but with resources on hand to ensure that we don't stop at good intentions. This third dimension of wisdom is the one that King Solomon asked to be granted so that he could rule his people (cf. Wis 9:1–11).

We want a school of wisdom . . . as a sort of existential, ethical, and social laboratory, where children and young people can test which things allow them to develop fully and build up the necessary skills to carry out their projects in life. A place where 'wise' teachers—people whose day-to-day lives and demeanor represent a 'desirable' life model—can provide elements and resources that can spare those setting out on life's road some of the suffering of starting 'from scratch' and directly experiencing the pain of mistaken or destructive choices.

To encourage wisdom, which involves knowledge, appreciation, and practice, is an ideal worthy of presiding over any educational endeavor. Anyone who can bring something like this to their community will have made an incalculable contribution to collective happiness. And, as we were saying, we as Christians have in Jesus Christ a principle and an abundance of wisdom that we have no right to retain within our confessional spaces. This is precisely the kind of evangelization the Lord requests from us: to share a wisdom that was destined from the beginning to all men and women throughout all time. Let's renew with audacity the zeal of the proclamation, of the proposal that we know rewards the deepest searches, silenced by the maelstrom, let us do so every day and try to reach everyone.

(b). Building on Rock

This is our belief, as Christians. But we still have to engage in a long process of discernment in order to understand the radical change for which we are the vessels. After all, historical defeats and even the most unbelievable horrors and abominations that we have endured as a people have sometimes been led by our own brothers, who professed our same faith and shared our celebrations. Proclaiming the name of Jesus Christ does not exonerate us from error or evil. Jesus himself said: it is not enough to say 'Lord! Lord!' if the will of my Father is not done (Mt 7:21–23). It's not just a case of 'bad intentions' or 'wolves in sheep's clothing.' It's very easy to say, 'after all, really, deep down, they didn't really come from us': That's how we hold on to the certainties we give lip service to, throwing out any elements that would make us question ourselves about the depth and solidity of our beliefs and practices.

Let's continue listening to the Lord's words, which we have just recalled. In the following verses, Jesus continues his teaching with the parable of the man who built his house on rock. "The rain fell, the floods came, and the winds blew and buffeted the house. But it did not collapse; it had been set solidly on rock" (v. 25). The images of 'rain', 'floods', and 'winds' can give this construction a certain air of passivity: It simply 'withstands.' To 'withstand' by maintaining one's faith, one's convictions, in the midst of the world's adversities. But the immediate connection between the parable and Jesus' preceding words ("Not everyone who says to me, 'Lord, Lord' . . .") puts us in a completely different place; it means more. It is a case of doing "the will of my Father in heaven" (v. 21), or doing what Jesus, the teacher, tells us (Lk 6:46). It's a case of 'withstanding life's blows' and, even more, 'getting down to work' in a task that is closely linked to the Kingdom which is manifest through Jesus.

So, what does it mean to 'build on rock' in order to put into practice God's will? I think the idea of wisdom allows us to start making progress in our search. If the task, the specific task we have at hand, the educational task in the context of rebuilding community, requires a firm subjective commitment and a serious and lucid objective discernment, it then needs to be overseen by an intellectual, affective, practical Wisdom that fully brings into play at those three levels the model provided by Jesus. To confess that Christ is the Lord, to be his apostles in proclaiming the Gospel and in bringing his Kingdom into being, necessarily means to build on the rock of Wisdom made flesh in the dwelling of our identity as Christians and educators and of our educational work.

At this point, which we will have all undoubtedly reached on answering our vocation, certain misunderstandings can arise which introduce real temptations.

The first is for us to remain with a merely 'pious' understanding of the Wisdom made flesh in Jesus of Nazareth. To see it as just a subjective, 'interior' experience, leaving aside the 'objective' dimension, real observation of the world, the heart's movement in the light of that understanding, the solid determination that includes the creation of effective mediations through which to come closer to the ideal. It is the permanent temptation of the 'pseudo-mystical' tendencies of Christian existence.

This perspective, while certainly one aspect of the Christian Mystery (and of all religious mysticism), ends up being reduced to a sort of spiritual elitism, an ecstatic experience of the 'chosen' that breaks the link with real, tangible history. The enlightened elites deprive us, through their internal dynamism, of the sense of belonging to a people, in this case the people of God, which is now the Church. The enlightened 'elites' close off any perspective that can encourage us to keep moving ahead, diverting our action inwards, into immanentism without hope. At the core of this spirit elitism, which disempowers all wisdom, is a negation of the fundamental truth of our faith: the Word that came in the flesh (1 Jn 4:2)

In the New Testament, we have a specific example of this reductive emphasis: the first Christian community of Corinth, which motivated an emphatic letter from Saint Paul. These Christians of Greek origin had developed a concept of faith that was 'charismatic' but that separated experiences 'in the Spirit' (the gift of tongues, ecstasy . . .) from their corresponding moral and social commitments. Saint Paul had to reprimand them for this form of 'spiritual Christianity,' which lost connection with daily life at the tangible level. The concept was one more suited to the development of what we would today call New Age religion than to that of real faith in Jesus of Nazareth and his Good News. In times of orphanhood and loss of meaning such as we are experiencing today, this unilaterally mystical approach can undoubtedly provide a consoling and beneficial experience. But the truth is that after a while the mystery of the human condition of sinfulness undoes any pretensions of 'elevation above the mundane' that this deficient spiritualism involves, forcing it to reveal its hidden facet of lies and self-delusion.

How will a similar approach to Christian Wisdom affect our work in the classroom? Among other things, through a magical understanding of faith and in some cases the sacraments. It is not my intention here to analyze the sacramental life of our educational communities. I shall mention a few situations that arise, out of various possible ones: routine and absence.

Sometimes we absolutize the signs of meeting with God to the point of neglecting what those signs should mean; we simply invalidate them, making them lose substance and become mechanical. Similarly, we have sometimes relied too much on exalting the emotional during catechetical sharing,

youth retreats, in good times enjoyed on family day. . . . Moments of gratuitousness, yes, of celebration and joy, but at times so inconsistent. . . . Praise
and joy in the Lord are not 'instruments' or 'means' toward anything; they
express the splendor of a truly evangelical life, the resting place on a road
that has been traveled, the anticipation of happiness to come.

Finally, another way we may resemble Saint Paul's Corinthians: in the
cult of spontaneity . . . translated as improvisation. Justified criticism of bu-
reaucracy, of formality in and of itself, of adherence to procedure and regulations, of more importance being given to the 'spirit' than the 'letter,' can
all lead to mediocrity and inertia, even mere cult of personality, and ultimately to abandoning the mission entrusted to us, causing it to sink into
a sad parody of living and creative community, which, like all lies, has
short legs.

At the other extreme, Christian Wisdom becomes a predominantly 'objective' fact, a 'flag' that, like the image of the historical Christ who did not
remain in the tomb but was raised up as the Lord, identifies a new social
and cultural order that can be observed, a series of certainties identified with
some specific historical event. According to this reductive view, the 'objectivity' of Christ's Resurrection would give rise to the 'objectivity' of his triumph in history, similar to an identification between the Kingdom of God
and that of this world, which has happened over and over again in the history of the Church and already at the dawn of Christianity merited a significant page of criticism in the Gospel according to Saint John, in the
dialogue between Jesus and Pilate (Jn 18:33–37). Indeed, why would Jesus
decline to call on his angels to defend his Kingdom? Because that Kingdom
'was not of this world'; it wasn't another political, social, or cultural option
fatally linked to the passing nature of everything that is born, grows, and
dies within time.

And if 'mystical' Christianity gave rise to a sort of elitism or 'celebration
of narcissism,' its opposite, the 'historical' extreme, opens the doors to an
'authoritarianism of the spirit' that, just like the former, inevitably ends up
touching the 'flesh' of human beings. Because the historical condition as a
conflict of subjectivities, as an ambiguous area where things are never absolutely white or black (see the parable of the wheat and the chaff) always up-
sets 'perfect' and 'definitive' arrangements and forces them to show their
innate capacity for evil. Finally, the will to dominate that human beings carry
within them emerges, in this case camouflaged by contemplation of Christ's
victory over death.

This too can affect (and seriously distort) our service in the task of education. It is clear (although plenty of people would say the opposite, even today) that a model based on rigid historical identities, without room for dissent or even for diverse and plural choices and outlooks, can no longer be admitted, at least in our Western societies. The place of subjectivity in modern culture, acknowledging deviations and disagreements, is a human achievement; and evangelical inspiration has played a part in this development of the idea of the human person as the subject of inalienable freedom. At a religious level, too, human dignity demands a type of proposal and adherence to beliefs that have little to do with the imposition of an immanent and incontestable edict that shackles or diminishes the personal quest for God, compromising the ample capacity for such adventure that human beings have been given.

Our schools should never aspire to build a hegemonic army of Christians who will know all the answers; they should instead be places where all questions are welcomed, where, by the light of the Gospel, the search for personal fulfillment is actually encouraged, instead of being blocked with verbal walls, walls that are quite weak and will irreparably collapse soon afterward. It's a major challenge; it calls for depth, it calls for attention to life, it calls for healing and freedom from idols . . . and let's be clear here: Both the 'mystical' and the 'historical-political' approaches are a form of triumphalism, a real caricature of Christ's true victory over sin and death.

(c). Dimensions of Christian Wisdom

How, then, can we progress toward a positive understanding of Christian Wisdom? We know it's not possible here to take more than a quick glance, which is necessarily brief and limited. Nobody can aspire to exhaust the infinite riches of the Word made flesh with a simple string of human words. Instead, we invite you to search, pray, and delve deeply into the Scriptures and the many expressions of the Church's living tradition and teaching, to try to discover the accents and contours inherent in a faith that comes alive for today's world. I want to urge you to look more intently and vigilantly at the signs of the times, to a new strengthening of community reflection and prayer, to recreate that dialogue of salvation which at various points in history bore fruits of holiness and gave rise to unimagined instances of evangelism and renewal. This tells us to make time for common things, for seriously and enthusiastically opening ourselves up to building alongside others, putting our hearts into it.

In this respect, let me share with you, as a Shepherd, some ideas that it may be useful to bear in mind. Just a few ways in which the person and word of Jesus give shape to the ideal of wisdom outlined above.

First of all, Christian Wisdom as truth. Jesus defines himself that way (Jn 14:6). We must advance toward an idea of truth that is ever more inclusive, less restrictive; at least, if we are thinking about God's truth and not some human truth, however solid it may appear. God's truth is unending, it is an ocean of which we can barely see the shore. It is something we are starting to discover these days: not to enslave ourselves to an almost paranoid defense of 'our truth' (if I 'have' it, he doesn't 'have' it; if he 'can have it,' then it means that I don't 'have' it). The truth is a gift that is too big for us, and that is precisely why it makes us bigger, amplifies us, raises us up. And it makes us servants of such a gift. There's no relativism to it, just that the truth forces us to follow a continuous path toward a deeper understanding of it.

The Gospel of Jesus offers us truth: about God, about a God who is Father, a God who comes to meet his people, a free and liberating God who chooses, calls, and sends. Let us reread the parables and comparisons of the Kingdom: They talk about God. God goes out onto the roads because he prepared a festivity and wants everyone to enjoy it; God is hidden in small and growing things, although we don't know how to see him. God is infinitely generous; he waits until the last moment and goes in search of those who are lost. He overpays the workers who come late in the day but does not withhold his love from those who came early or from the brother of the prodigal son: On the contrary, he keeps them next to him and invites them to transcend themselves and become like him.

God . . . what can we say that will not be surpassed by the infinity of who he is! When we go back to drink from the well of the Gospel, we instantly realize how pathetic the 'images' of God manufactured by humans have been, often in our own image, throughout history. But there's more. We're talking about a God who didn't stay ensconced in his divinity. Everything we can say about him has had and has a 'human way' of existing: that of Jesus of Nazareth. That infinitely merciful and saving Father is not an unreachable figure: He carried out his work in the actions and words of the Teacher.

So Christian Wisdom is also truth about man. About the God-man and about the man called to live the divine condition. This is a message that is always new and always current. Even in times of technological globalization, when everything human seems reduced to bytes and it appears to have been decided that many outside the 'kingdom' now being set up are to be left out, there's a word of wisdom that repeatedly reminds us, to our ears and to the elements, from pulpits and Areopagi, and also from the Golgothas and the many hells on this earth, about the unshakable fidelity of a God who chose to become man so that men could be like God. And this precisely by following the opposite path than the one suggested by the Serpent in the Garden of Eden.

I ask myself whether those of us today entrusted with the mission of teaching are able to ponder all the beauty and explosiveness of this truth about God and man that we have received. Over a century ago (this year marks 110 years since his death), a Christian lived out his vocation as a teacher, journalist, and politician following these convictions, fully assuming his condition as a believer and man of his time, without dualism or timidity. I'm talking about José Manuel Estrada,[1] and I think it is important to go back to him, not only in light of the specific struggles through which he expressed his fidelity to the Church and his love for his country, but also starting from the very fact that he understood Christian truth as having a vast potential to elevate humanity and he refused to settle for anything less. For him, it was not a case of withstanding wind and rain, but of making the most of his abilities in the service of building a new society.

Fully a man of his time, he shared its questioning of the meaning of human life and accurately pinpointed the place where that feeling becomes both a query and an invitation to search, for all men of goodwill:

> The sciences of observation, whether in the material order such as chemistry, or moral order like philosophy, serve to classify facts, define phenomena, even to formulate their primary and secondary laws; but they are powerless to discover the higher bond which links them, within their metaphysical conditions of production, to a universal harmony, subject to a sublime law. . . . If man's ignorance were to consist only of his inability to appreciate phenomena and conditions, naturalism would suffice to gradually dissipate it. But one thing that will never disappear, neither from the mind of a Christian, nor from that of a logical atheist, nor from the spirit of one who raises himself a fraction above the level at which, by excess of primitive gradation, sheer bruteness and barbarism are almost indissolubly confused, even after exhausting all the curiosities of the visible and hidden world and the circumstantial querying of all experimental facts; it is this other curiosity: 'what am I?' or this other one: 'where do I come from?' or, finally, this harrowing

---

1. José Manuel Estrada (1842–97) was an Argentine writer and politician. A representative in the legislature, he was named director of Argentina's National University and Education Minister.

problem central to the gentleness of faith and the thorny anguish of incredulity or
doubt: 'where am I going?'

But Christian Wisdom, as Estrada also testifies, does not stop at words.
The dimension of Truth goes hand in hand with the Life and the Way. The
'three sides' of Wisdom are evangelically resolved in Jesus and in those who
followed his footsteps. The Truth about God and man is the beginning of
another way of valuing the world, our neighbor, life itself, our personal mission; it's the beginning of another Love. And, inevitably, it is the beginning
of ethical approaches and historical options that give shape to a tangible incarnation of Wisdom in our times.

I invite you to continue forward with me, reflecting on some of the ways
in which Christian Wisdom can mold our teaching vocation, translating the
revealed Truth into fundamental values and concrete actions.

2. Teachers with the Teacher

First, let us remember the starting point for our meditation: As Christians
committed to the task of education, we have a major responsibility today
and at the same time an opportunity to put our contribution to work. That
is why it is essential to 'get it right' when deciding what aims to prioritize,
based on wisdom matured by the experience of encountering the Lord. For
this, it won't hurt to once more ask ourselves the fundamental question:
Why are we educating? Why do the Church and the Christian communities invest time, goods, and effort in a task that is not directly 'religious'? Why
do we have schools and not hairdressing salons, veterinary clinics, or travel
agents? Is it for business reasons? There will be some who think so, but the
state of many of our schools refutes this claim. Is it to exert influence on
society, an influence we hope will somehow benefit us? It's possible that some
schools offer this 'product' to their 'clients': contacts, environment, 'excellence.' But that is not the reason why the ethical and evangelical calling inspires us to offer this service. The only motivation we have to do something
in the field of education is hope for a new humanity, for another possible
world. It's the hope that springs from Christian Wisdom, which reveals to
us through the Risen Christ the divine fullness we are called to.

Using the language and theology of his time, Estrada clearly proposed
this purpose of the educational task from the Christian perspective:

Do you see the people of this century busy with a tireless desire for perfection? We
also love progress and perfection, but a perfection suited to man in the totality of his

destiny and moral nature. Science is excellent, and I applaud and love it, because it
is the law of man to dominate nature; but it is also our law to aspire to supersensory
and immortal ends, and the purification of the soul and its union with God calls for
the adoption of means as supernatural as these ends. The condition and ultimate
goal of all progress is to restore the supernatural in man through the virtue of
Christ. Napoleon guessed it: to educate is to create.

If our schools are not the space where another humanity is being created, where another wisdom takes root, where another society is formed, where there is room for hope and transcendence, we are delaying a unique contribution at this time in history. If our schools do not give precedence to the word and love, over and above mechanisms of dominion and rivalry, we cannot speak of Christian schooling. If 'excellence' is not understood there as the excellence of charity, which surpasses all other 'virtues' (and skills), the Resurrection is far from our homes.

All this is not just poetry. In fact, many of the current 'values' of our society lose sight of this inclusive and transcendent Truth, which constitutes the sum of man and community. School can be just a transmitter of these 'values' or the cradle of new ones; but that calls for a community that believes and hopes, a community that loves, a community that is really gathered together in the name of the Risen One. Before planning and curricula, before the specific forms taken by rules and regulations, we need to know what it is we want to generate. I also know that to do this, the whole teaching community needs to be involved, in strong communion with a single feeling, becoming passionately involved in Jesus' project and all pulling in the same direction.

Many institutions encourage the creation of wolves rather than brothers; they educate for competition and success at others' expense, with just a few weak 'ethical' standards, upheld by destitute committees that try to alleviate the corrosive destructiveness of certain practices that 'must' be employed. In many classrooms, the strong and quick are rewarded and the weak and slow are scorned. In many, encouragement is given to being 'number one' in results, not in compassion. So then, our specifically Christian contribution is an education that testifies to and creates another way of being human. But that will not be possible if we simply confine ourselves to 'withstanding' 'rain,' 'flood,' and 'wind,' if we do not go further than mere criticism and smugly rejoice in being 'outside' the criteria that we decry. Another possible humanity . . . demands positive action; otherwise it will always be an 'other' that is merely invoked, while 'this' still exists and becomes ever more entrenched.

I believe that a more active stance inevitably requires us to overcome a few antinomies that have a more paralyzing than clarifying effect on us. Some types of inflexible antagonism end up exagerating the lights and shadows that promote those tendencies we consider to be the most negative. A real, determined, and responsible commitment invites us to step up in our discernment and overcome some clichés that have very deep roots in our communities. To do so, I put to you three interlinked challenges: to carefully ensure that our task bears fruit without neglecting the results; to give precedence to the criterion of gratuitousness without losing efficiency; and to create a space where excellence does not involve a loss of solidarity.

(a). 'Fruits' and 'Results'

Our task has one goal: to spark something in the pupils entrusted to us; to incite change, an increase in wisdom. We hope that children and young people will leave our classrooms having experienced a transformation, with more knowledge, new feelings, and also ideals within their reach. For the educator who aspires to be a teacher of wisdom, it is not enough to 'fulfill your obligations' neatly and carefully. Our outlook must go beyond necessary competence and professional integrity, to focus on what motivates the students who are the raison d'être of your vocation.

That transformation which we desire and hope for, on which we expend all our abilities, has multiple facets that need to work together in order to signify something better. In a way that is perhaps schematic, but useful for understanding each other, we can place ourselves in two dimensions, respectively called 'producing results' and 'bearing fruit.'

What do these two objectives involve? 'Bearing fruit' is a metaphor we take from agriculture, it's the way in which new things come into the world of living beings. We can also use the image of 'engendering': giving life to a new being. Whether vegetable or animal, the idea points to an internal process in the subjects. The fruit is formed from the same identity as the living being; it feeds from those energies that have already become part of its being; it enriches itself with the multiple internal identifications and is something unique, surprising, original. Nature does not produce two fruits that are exactly alike. In the same way, a person who 'bears fruit' is someone who has matured his or her creativity in a process of freedom, gestating something new from a truth that has been received, accepted, and assimilated.

How does this connect with our specific work? A teacher who knowingly tries to ensure that his work 'bears fruit' will never limit himself to hoping for something predetermined, being satisfied if the subject adapts to a mold considered desirable. He will not discard what is different and what calls into question any of his usual practices. He will not deceive himself with overadapted and unquestioning compliance on the part of his students. He knows that a question from his student is worth a thousand answers and will encourage searching while remaining alert to the risks it entails. When faced with questioning and rebellion, he will not try to bend wills and impose ideas but will encourage responsibility through intelligent criticism, with an open and flexible disposition that doesn't hesitate to learn by teaching and teach by learning. And when he encounters failures or mistakes, instead of denying them or triumphantly or bitterly emphasizing them, he will patiently resume the process from the point at which it became blocked or diverted, encouraging patient learning and also learning himself.

On the other hand, the metaphor of 'producing results' belongs to the sphere of industry, of serial and calculable efficiency. A result can be foreseen, planned, and measured. It involves control of each step taken, a set of perfectly determined actions that will have a foreseeable effect.

A society that tends to convert man into a puppet of production and consumption always opts for results. It needs control. It cannot make room for the new without seriously compromising its ends and increasing the level of already-existing conflict. It prefers the other to be completely foreseeable so as to achieve maximum profit with minimum cost.

But wisdom involves a maturation not only of content and values but also of skills. Any true transformation with a view to this other possible world we aspire to also requires know-how, an instrumental capability that needs to be incorporated according to an understanding of its logic. Our pupils have a right, above all, to their own autonomy and uniqueness, but also a right to develop proven, socially recognized skills in order to make concrete their desires and contributions in the real world. The teacher grounded in Christian Wisdom does not scorn the necessary effectiveness he must achieve, with all the effort that he supposes for himself and his students. He knows that moving from 'good intentions' to action means following the arduous path of technique, discipline, economy of effort, inclusion of others' experiences, and he is capable of persevering with his students along this path despite the fact that both they and he would sometimes prefer to take a short cut or stop at a resting place.

The root of the problem is that we Christians have often disassociated the 'fruits' from the 'results.' In this way, we neglect our training, we lower standards, when it would be better for the students if we could find a way to motivate and sustain the effort; we content ourselves with creating a good atmosphere and strong bonds, instead of using that structure as the foundation for a dynamic of creativity and productivity. Or, on the other hand, we take refuge in stereotypical behavior, correctly formulated beliefs, expressions that reflect the norm . . . all of it based on a freedom that is more 'tamed' than reinforced, thinking that with that we've 'educated!'

There's nothing worse than a Christian educational institution that bases its identity on uniformity and calculation, like that 'sausage-making machine' so crudely caricaturized a few years ago in the film *The Wall*. Our aim is not only to form 'individuals useful to society' but also to educate people who can transform it! This will not be achieved by sacrificing the maturation of skills, the consolidation of knowledge, the diversification of tastes, because, in the end, neglect of these 'results' will not create 'new men and women' but limp puppets of the consumer society.

It's a question of reconciling both extremes by combining them: 'educating for fruit,' making all possible tools available so the fruit can grow at all times in an effective way, thereby 'producing results.' Let us propose open, inspiring models and ideals based on the objectivity of truth, without imprinting the format we ourselves have found to express this dynamic, while at the same time developing the mediations needed so that children can mobilize their choices. Let us prefer free and responsible students, able to question themselves, decide for themselves, make right or wrong choices and keep on going, not mere replicas of our own achievements . . . or our errors. And precisely for this reason, let us be able to help them gain the confidence and security that spring from experiencing one's own creativity, one's own ability to successfully carry through to their conclusion one's own choices.

This involves a serious belief in all forms of dialogue, in the power of words. Words that are not idealized: words that can encourage and urge on, open doors and set limits, invite and forgive. All of which calls for some very difficult virtues: humility to know how to hold one's opinions in perspective, patience to know how to wait until the other is ready, and magnanimity to persevere and not tire of trying to give one's best.

(b). Gratuitousness with Efficiency

Quite rightly, we Christians try to give precedence in our schools to the criterion of gratuitousness. First, because of its intrinsic value: It is the quintessential sign of God's love and of love among human beings according to Christ's unconditional example. And second, because we know and suffer the consequences of extending economic criteria to all forms of human activity.

If by efficiency we understand obtaining maximum results from minimum output of energy and resources, then obviously an education for fruitfulness, value, and freedom will tend to reconsider all those relationships. There's no doubt the energy invested in our children and youth will be enormous, and the results will not always be what was hoped for. Furthermore, fruitfulness ultimately depends on each individual, which does not excuse us from assessing our task.

When left to itself, the criterion of efficiency will lead us to invest more where there is a better guarantee of success. Which is exactly what the prevailing success-oriented and elitist model does. Why spend money on those who will never get off the ground, asks the investor whose priority is to get a return. What's the sense in investing more and more so that the 'slowest' or most 'conflictive' can find their way forward? So that the 'less gifted' (and now there are moves to also factor in genetics to determine who 'can't') can 'squander' community assets, since they're never going to make the grade anyway?

But this logic of bad pedagogical humanism falls apart when we look at the core of our faith: The Son of God became man and died on the cross to save mankind. What is the ratio between the 'investment' made by God and the object of that expense? We could say without irreverence that there's nobody more 'inefficient' than God. To sacrifice his Son for humanity—a humanity that remains sinful and ungrateful to this day. There can be no doubt: The logic of the Story of Salvation is a logic of gratuitousness. It cannot be measured by 'should' or 'has,' nor even by the 'merits' we give value to.

Because we read in the Gospel that the mustard seed, such a tiny seed, grows into a huge bush and we understand the disproportion between action and effect, so we know that the gift is not ours to own and we try to administer it carefully and efficiently. We must be efficient in our mission because it is the Lord's work, and not primarily our own. The Word that is sown becomes fruitful in its own way, according to the soil on which it falls. But that is no reason for the sower to do his work clumsily and carelessly. The counterpart to divine giving is man's worship and gratitude; worship and gratitude, which carry a total respect for the wisdom shared, for the precious gift of the Word and of words.

Let us not be mistaken: Efficiency as a value in its own right, as the main criterion, is completely untenable. Today, when companies place emphasis on efficiency, it is clearly being used as a means to maximize profit. Well then, we too must be efficient in ensuring that 'profit' can be made for free. Efficiency at the service of a truly cost-free educational task. I am not talking here about tuition and contributions (if only we could find the formula so that the poorest of the poor may exercise their citizen right to choose our schools because they are also free!), but about an underlying attitude that permeates it. Neither the meaning nor the effectiveness of our task comes mainly from the resources used and their calculation; but that is precisely why we should put our best into it. Jesus also took that dimension into account; it was not for nothing that he told the parable of the talents.

This seriously commits us, as Christian teachers, to freely and carefully give what we have freely and carefully received, and it must similarly form part of the content of what we transmit. The teachers who wish to make Christian Wisdom the cornerstone of their lives and the meaning and content of their work will focus their attention on the atmosphere in the classroom and in the institution as a whole, on the attitudes they adopt and encourage, on the style of daily exchanges, and they will try to imprint on everything an atmosphere of gratuitousness, care, and generosity. Never an atmosphere of calculated, measured, and self-interested interactions, even if sometimes they feel tempted to be less generous in giving freely; nor an atmosphere of carelessness and scorn toward the property, time, sensitivity, and effort of each and every interlocutor in his task: pupils, colleagues, collaborators, families. Even though the deeply unsupportive culture in which we live pushes them daily to shrug their shoulders and say, 'What do I care?' they will feel a deep responsibility not to squander what belongs to all: knowledge, the school and all who take part in it, and the vocation of teaching.

And with this we come to our third and last challenge.

(c). The Excellence of Solidarity

The criterion that breaks with the logic of competitive individualism is ultimately that of solidarity. Here is where the contribution of Christian educators can become more critical and relevant, because, speeches aside, the 'ethics' of competition (which is nothing more than an instrumentation of reason to justify force) is the currency of the day in our society.

To educate for solidarity doesn't just mean teaching how to be 'good' and 'generous,' how to collect funds, take part in works of public welfare, support foundations and NGOs. A new mentality has to be created, which thinks in terms of community, of prioritizing the lives of each and every person rather than the appropriation of goods by just a few. A mentality born out of that ancient teaching of the Social Doctrine of the Church on the social function of property or the universal destination of goods as a primary right that precedes private property, to the point where the latter is subservient to it. This mentality must become the substance and thought of our institutions; it must cease to be a dead letter and come to life in real actions that piece together another culture and society. We must urgently fight to rescue real people, the sons and daughters of God, beyond any pretension to indiscriminately exploit the earth's resources.

Solidarity, then, is not just an 'emotional' or individual attitude but also a way of understanding and experiencing human society and actions. This should be reflected in ideas, practices, attitudes, structures, and institutions; it entails an overall appraisal of the various dimensions of existence; it leads to a commitment to embodying it in real relationships between people and groups; it demands not only 'private' or 'public' activity to alleviate the effects of social imbalances but also a search for ways to prevent those imbalances from arising, ways that will not be easy, let alone celebrated by those who have opted for and benefited from a model of egotistical accumulation.

This essential solidarity becomes a sort of 'trademark,' a 'seal of authenticity' of the Christian approach, of that way of life and that way of carrying out the task of education. We don't need any ideology critical of Christianity in order to put forward our new idea. Either we are capable of forming men and women with this new mentality, or we will have failed in our mission. This will also mean reviewing the criteria that have guided our activity until now. We need to ask ourselves:

Where is it, among us, that solidarity expressed as culture? We cannot deny that multiple signs of generosity exist among our people, but why don't they translate into a fairer and more fraternal society? Where, then, is the mark of the Risen One in the country we have built?

Maybe it's another case of disassociation of the ends from the means. But this statement merits closer examination. I already mentioned that today there is much talk about 'excellence,' sometimes from an unsupportive and elitist perspective. Those who 'can' demand 'excellence' because 'they pay for it.' This, unfortunately, is an argument that is heard too often to be ignored. The problem is that no one ever seriously questions what happens to those who 'can't,' let alone what causes the fact that some 'can' while others 'can't.' Like so many other things that derive from a long chain of human actions and decisions, that situation is seen as a given, something as natural as the rain or the wind.

So, now what would happen if we were to turn the question on its head and set ourselves the goal of achieving an excellence of solidarity? The dictionary of the Spanish Royal Academy defines 'excellence' as a 'superior quality or goodness that makes something worthy of special appreciation and consideration.' Going further back, we know that in ancient Greece excellence was a concept very close to virtue: perfection in an area valued by society. Not just 'appreciation,' but whatever deserves it: the superior ability that manifests itself in quality of action. Thus, to speak of an 'excellence of solidarity' would mean, at a first level, to present solidarity as a desirable asset, to elevate the value of this attitude and practice. Above all, it means doing our duties well and acting in accordance with the mission entrusted to every teacher, which begins—as Jesus himself showed by washing the feet of his disciples—with a profound personal, affective, and effective conversion, which translates into testimony: "If I, therefore, the master and teacher, have washed your feet, you ought to wash one another's feet. I have given you a model to follow, so that as I have done for you, you should also do" (Jn 13:14–15).

Second, it means perfecting that solidarity. There are times when we are asked to do more, to go beyond what we have been working on and offering at the behest or demand of the same pressing reality. We could talk of a 'superficial' solidarity and a 'fertile' solidarity. We know the first one: mere declarations, shows of generosity, periodic aid that sometimes hypocritically hide the true source of the problems. Or, in short, mere sentimentality, lack of vision, superficiality, and naiveté. Excellence of solidarity, on the other hand, means a complete way of thinking and living, as we said earlier; and more than that: effective concern to turn our supportive practices into actions that can really bring about change.

Here we can see a possible reason for what appears to be an impotence of solidarity. It's not enough to be 'good' and 'generous': It is necessary to be intelligent, capable, effective. As Christians we have placed so much emphasis on the rectitude and honesty of our love, on conversion of the heart, that we have sometimes paid less attention to objective success in our fraternal charity. As if the only important thing were the intention . . . and the necessary actions are neglected. This is not good enough; it is not enough for our neediest brothers, the victims of injustice and exclusion, who are not helped in their need by 'the inside of our heart.' Nor is it enough for us: A useless solidarity only serves to slightly palliate feelings of culpability. We need lofty aims . . . and adequate resources.

So, we can see, finally, that there is no reason to oppose solidarity and excellence, if we understand them in this way. Teachers who are knowledgeably rooted in the model offered by Jesus of Nazareth will be able to discern in their own hearts the motives for their commitment and self-giving and will find in their vocation, in their personal capacities, and in an active concern for formation and personal and community reflection, the means of creating change in their pupils, seeking after an inclusive and fraternal society. And they will do it with tangible initiatives ranging from the type of relationship he maintains and encourages with each of his students, to his participation in the educational community in a wider sense; from his spirit of companionship and solidarity at work, to the strength of his ethical and spiritual choices, always seeking to discover, from a perspective that combines intelligence with love, the best in each one of his pupils in order to encourage in them the 'excellence' of virtue, personal vocation, through which each of them will be called to live and plant the seeds of the Kingdom.

In this way, we come to the end of our reflection. Thinking about what we can and should contribute today to our country, we placed at the core of our consideration the dimension of Wisdom as revealed by the Gospel of Jesus. An ideal worthy of presiding over the best of educational endeavors!

Christian Wisdom, Truth, Life, and Way have illuminated us when it comes to discerning a few ethical guidelines and historical options for our teaching work.

Not contenting ourselves with words but building on rock will mean taking the meaning of our mission seriously: If our schools cannot germinate a new way of being human, another culture and another society, we are wasting our time. To progress in that task, I challenge you to overcome a few antinomies that stunt our growth.

First, to set ourselves the task of causing a transformation in our children and youth that will yield fruits of freedom, self-determination, and creativity and—at the same time—become evident as results in the form of truly useful skills and knowledge. Our objective is not to build islands of peace in a disintegrated society but to educate people with the capacity to transform that society. So, 'fruits' and 'results.'

And for that, we opt unwaveringly for the logic of the Gospel: the logic of gratuitousness, of the unconditional gift, but also trying to administer our resources with the greatest responsibility and seriousness. Only thus will we be able to distinguish what is free from what is indifferent and careless. Gratuitousness with efficiency.

Finally, going beyond the destructive ethic of 'dog-eat-dog' competition to carry forward a practice of solidarity that effectively identifies the roots of selfishness, not confining ourselves to mere speeches and complaints but placing the best of our abilities at the service of this ideal. Lofty aims and adequate resources: an excellence of solidarity.

Teachers with the Teacher: witnesses of a new wisdom, new and eternal, because the Kingdom that God has set in motion in our history calls on us to always hope for more, beyond all the searching and effort we can dream of. In this new universal reality, we can sow the seeds of a better humanity, a sign of what is to come.

Our vocation is nothing less than that. Are we forgetting our fragility? On the contrary, it inspires us to let ourselves be carried away, trusting as children, by the strength of the one who sustains and encourages us, the one who renews all things—the Holy Spirit. The Spirit through which Jesus is present in every Eucharist that is celebrated, as a sign of the Father's unending love, reuniting us and sending us out with the audacity to join forces in forging an educational country.

➤➤ ◄◄

Enter the Light Because the Truth Is There

*Homily, Education Mass—April 21, 2004, Wednesday,
Second Week of Easter, Year C (Transcript)*

The Gospel that we have just heard uses a phrase that can help us today to enter into the message for the day: "And this is the verdict, / that the light came into the world, / but people preferred darkness to light, / because their works were evil" (Jn 3:19).

The verdict of a person facing life, the verdict of a person facing himself, the verdict of a person facing God, is given in this fundamental option: Either I am not afraid of the light and I show myself as I am and assume all the consequences, or I hide in the darkness to cover the truth in the shadows of ambiguities or in those thousand and one unconscious, subconscious, or conscious defenses that we contrive.

When we enter the light, we appear as we are, and sometimes that hurts us, pains us a lot. But it is a fruitful pain, it is a pain that gives life, it is a pain that makes us grow. Darkness begins with the opposite sign, as good anesthesia; it does not hurt but leads you to disorientation, to self-deception; ultimately it doesn't have a way out.

Focusing education on this antinomy, light and darkness, is liberating because it puts us on the path of truth; truth tolerates light, darkness hides it, lies hide it, deceit hides a double life, hides everything that cannot stand up in front of the light.

I would like to ask all of you who work in education to notice a little if our path of educational leadership is not afraid of the light, and if we find that there is fear, then take courage and go forward but do not let ourselves be imprisoned by that fear that takes us into darkness.

And what is the way to enter the light cone, the truth cone? Words are not sufficient; there is no recipe. One can say do this, this, this, and this. Precepts are always incomplete because they deprive people of discovering step by step . . . discovering and having the admiration, the awe of discovery in the way of truth. Precepts can help a little like walkers help toddlers, but the way toward truth and growth goes for the light . . . for freedom. The way, then, more than words, more than ideas is actions, and actions are very simple, we just heard it in the letter to the Colossians: "put on kindness" (Col 3:12–15), that is, do not bite each other's ears . . . kindness. Put on heartfelt compassion. Compassion is not to have pity, it is to suffer with. Hearts open to suffer with the problems of others. To look around us and incorporate into our lives and daily walks, the problems of others.

And I insist again: Practice kindness, humility, gentleness, and patience. And, as if this were not enough, he says of patience: "bearing with one another and forgiving one another, if one has a grievance against another" (Col 3:12–15). Bearing with and forgiving one another, being humble and patient, being understanding are actions, works of neighborliness, works of charity, acts of love.

Are they love? No, they are not love. Love is much more, but these are acts born of love; therefore, the way to truth is not going to be shown so much by arguments and ideas as by attitudes toward life because these attitudes toward life, in some way, chip away at those starched hardnesses, those inhuman stances that in the last analysis distance us from an attitude of neighborliness, of reaching out to the one who needs us most.

The path of truth is that of light, it is only born from a heart that wants to love. *It's just that I do not know how to love, Father.* Nobody knows how to love; we learn every day. Take heart, how? With these little acts: kindness, heartfelt compassion, humility, gentleness, patience, and bearing with and enduring each other every day.

In the educational task this phrase weighs a lot, bearing with and supporting one another to walk together and grow; this is what I ask from you for this year's program.

Enter the light cone because the truth is there; but for this, to enter the light cone you need these attitudes, they will take us by the hand: attitudes of neighborliness. May the Lord grant this grace to everyone.

→> ←←

Wisdom Is the Bread That Opens Our Eyes

Homily, Solemn Te Deum *on Independence Day—May 25, 2004*

He came to Nazareth, where he had grown up, and went according to his custom into the synagogue on the sabbath day. He stood up to read and was handed a scroll of the prophet Isaiah. He unrolled the scroll and found the passage where it was written:

"The Spirit of the Lord is upon me, because he has anointed me to bring glad tidings to the poor. He has sent me to proclaim liberty to captives and recovery of sight to the blind, to let the oppressed go free, and to proclaim a year acceptable to the Lord."

Rolling up the scroll, he handed it back to the attendant and sat down, and the eyes of all in the synagogue looked intently at him. He said to them, "Today this scripture passage is fulfilled in your hearing."

And all spoke highly of him and were amazed at the gracious words that came from his mouth. They also asked, "Isn't this the son of Joseph?" He said to them, "Surely you will quote me this proverb, 'Physician, cure yourself,' and say, 'Do here in your native place the things that we heard were done in Capernaum.'" And he said, "Amen, I say to you, no prophet is accepted in his own native place. Indeed, I tell you, there were many widows in Israel in the days of Elijah when the sky was closed for three and a half years and a severe famine spread over the entire land. It was to none of these that Elijah was sent, but only to a widow in Zarephath in the land of Sidon. Again, there were many lepers in Israel during the time of Elisha the prophet; yet not one of them was cleansed, but only Naaman the Syrian." When the people in the synagogue heard this, they were all filled with fury. They rose up, drove him out of the town, and led him to the brow of the hill on which their town had been built, to hurl him down headlong. But he passed through the midst of them and went away.

Jesus then went down to Capernaum, a town of Galilee. He taught them on the sabbath, and they were astonished at his teaching because he spoke with authority. (Lk 4:16–32)

1. In these final days of the Easter season, on the eve of the coming of the Holy Spirit, we gather to return to the sources of the Argentines' May.[1] We return to the historical core of our beginnings, not to engage in formal nostalgia but to look for a footprint of hope. We remember the road we traveled to open spaces for the future. As our faith teaches us, from the memory of fullness it is possible to glimpse new paths. Starting with God's presence in our founding and his overwhelming saving grace in our history, it is possible to begin again, to be inspired, to strengthen oneself, to project oneself. The eve of Pentecost, the time of the Spirit, gathers the beleaguered believers of today, no less than the shaken and fragile apostles of that time, to begin again. The fragility of the boat should not cause fears or preventive actions; the immensity of the sea of life and history is softened by the wind, that breath of God that drives and leads us from the first day. Some true, mysterious, and unwavering confidence brought us Argentines to congregate, so many times throughout our history, in this Plaza de Mayo, as in that year of 1810, looking for the wind that will lead us on the right path.

2. The faithful who heard Jesus in his native Nazareth were also hopeful. There was respect and admiration for the authority that emanated from his person, and his words seemed to stir renewed air in the soul of the people. The proposal of that young Rabbi was something long awaited: "*Good News for the poor,*" a new way of 'seeing' life and the freedom longed for. That good news of Jesus is inclusive. To those whom he liberates and heals, he urges to liberate and heal others. Speaking with his people, Jesus himself feels confirmation that the prophetic words are fulfilled at the same moment he pro-

---

1. Bergoglio refers here to Argentina's Independence Day, May 25, celebrated each year with a solemn *Te Deum*.

nounces them. Enlightened and anointed, he speaks while moved by the Spirit. The Gospel story shows us clearly: There was the Spirit, a new time of God, a wind that is safe. And the people felt the same: There was applause and gestures of admiration.

However, the end of the story leaves us perplexed. Someone whispered slyly: "Isn't this the son of Joseph, the carpenter?" And then the mood of those present changed: They pushed him out and took him to a ravine with the intention of throwing him or stoning him. But *"Jesus passed between them and went on his way."* He went to Capernaum, a town in Galilee, to preach again in the open air, among the simple folk of the faithful town. He does not even behave like a rebel ready to present his chest to the stones.

3. Jesus, faithful to the prophetic style that accompanied his passage among men, makes symbolic gestures: What does leaving Nazareth, his 'homeland,' mean? I think I see here a strong protest against those who feel so included that they exclude others. They believe themselves to be so clairvoyant that they have become blind, so self-sufficient in the administration of the law that they have become wicked.

That is why Jesus withdraws and chooses the small path, going through the midst of his people, "the dark path" (of which Fray Luis de León spoke), which is precisely the path of the poor; that of the poor from any privation that means the spoiling of the soul and, at the same time, trust and dedication to others and to God. In effect, the one who suffers the dispossession of his goods, his health, irreparable losses, the security of the ego and—in that poverty—allows himself to be led by the experience of the wise, of the luminous, of the free, supportive, and disinterested love of others, he knows something or a lot about the Good News.

Argentines have suffered all these types of poverty; some live them and witness them for years and decades. Well, today as in that time, Jesus continues to slip away among the smallest and poorest of our people.

But, why does he leave those exasperated ones alone with their stones and their desire to throw over the cliff everything that does not agree with their ideas? What prevents them from traveling the path of listening to the Good News? Maybe the tacit confrontation, in their lives, between wisdom and illustration. What is wise is living life where prudence, the ability to understand, and the sense of belonging are clear. What occurred, on the other hand, may run the risk of being steeped in ideologies—not ideas—in prejudices, partisanship. The impatience of the enlightened elites does not understand the laborious and daily walk of a people, nor does it understand the message of the wise. And at that time there were also enlightened elites who isolated their consciences from the march of their people, who negotiated their sense of belonging and their faith. There also existed the leftist atheists and the nonbelieving rightists, unmoved in their marginal securities alien to all popular feeling. Something of that emotional closure, of those unfulfilled expectations, Jesus felt as true blindness of the soul. Such an attitude seems to evoke the histrionic, immediatist claims, those reactions and extreme superficial postures in which we tend to fall.

4. Not infrequently, the world looks with amazement at a country like ours, full of possibilities, lost in emergent postures and crisis and does not deepen on its social, cultural, and spiritual cracks, does not try to understand the causes, and disregards the future. Faced with this reality we should perhaps ask for light about the second prophetic promise: He has come to give sight to the blind, and to consider the fact of our blindness.

Let's admit it. We need the Lord to enlighten us because so many times we seem blind, and we live with ephemeral flashes that blur and dull our sight. It is like a whim of those who do not want to know anything of the clarity that springs from silent thought and take stock of our successes and mistakes. We do not seek the gentle light that springs from the truth; we do not bet on the strenuous wait that takes care of the oil and keeps the lamp lit.

The vain fruit of blindness is false illusion. We all hope for a prophetic and messianic force to free us, but when the path of true freedom begins with the acceptance of our little things and our painful truths, we cover our eyes and fill our hands with intolerant stones. We are ready for intolerance. We are stuck in our speeches and counterdiscourses, ready to accuse others rather than to review one's own stances. Blind fear is vindicating and often leads us to despise what is different, not to seeing the complementary; to ridicule and censor the one who thinks differently, which is a new way of exerting pressure and achieving power. Not recognizing the virtues and greatness of others, for example, and reducing them to the vulgar is a common strategy of cultural mediocrity of our times. Do not stand out! Do not challenge us . . . to see if we still have to get out of our numbness, from our comfortable peace of the cemeteries! *To think that he is the son of Joseph! they said . . .* anticipating in words what would happen in reality; and Jesus already received the first stone of our vulgarity.

Defamation and gossip, transgression with much propaganda, the denial of limits, the degradation or elimination of institutions, are part of a long list of plots with which mediocrity is concealed and protected, ready to blindly push off the cliff everything that threatens it. It is the era of 'weak thinking.' And if a wise word arises, that is, if someone who embodies the challenge of sublimity even at the cost of not being able to fulfill many of our desires, then our mediocrity does not stop until we throw him off. Heroes, great men, artists, scientists, or simply anyone who thinks beyond the thoughtless, prevalent discourse. We do not discover them until too late. We despise the "son of the carpenter." . . . But there is no shame for putting on the lamp stand the fatuous light of any perversion, portrayed day and night by images and abundant information; an enchantment with voyeurism where everything is allowed, where the marketer's enjoyment of the morbid seems to trap the senses and plunge them into nothingness. Forbidden to think and create. Courage, heroism, and holiness are forbidden. For these blind people, the suggestive and the subtle, the harmony of the beautiful, are not well seen, because they imply the modest and humble work of talent.

5. The vitality and creativity of a people, and of every human being, only occur and can be contemplated after a long journey accompanied by limitations, attempts and failures, crisis and reconstruction. . . . And the greatest sin of all the cultists of blindness is the identity vacuum that they produce, that terrible dissatisfaction that they project to us, not allowing us to feel comfortable in our own homeland. The deep identity is stripped away and an artificial, cardboard, made-up one is proposed. It is the contrast between what identifies a people and that other imported identity, built for the use and convenience of private sectors. Jesus, leaving the blind, chooses the humble path that leads him to the faithful people, the ones who stand in simple admiration before the teaching that returns sight to the blind who wish to see.

6. What do we see when we are allowed to open our eyes? We see God sneaking among his people, walking with them.

We see a Jesus with his feet on the ground, cultivating hearts as a good sower (and to cultivate is the root word of culture), developing the true food of the spirit, that which builds communion among the inhabitants of the nation. It is about that spiritual food, that bread, that when broken, allows us to see; that which is savored in the company of those who suffer daily, without seeking profit or income; that embraces all, even those who do not recognize it.

He who, with his mercy, takes responsibility for miseries and evils, without adulation or demagogic justification, without conceding to fashions and customs.

It is wisdom: the bread that opens our eyes and prevents us from the blindness of mediocrity, urging a life that tends toward the best and not the ethics of minimalism or the exquisite ethicism of the lab, and at the same time is the Wisdom that deeply understands and forgives everything.

It is the bread that makes us feel the support given by the sapiential constancy of walking through and touching concrete human pain, without ideological mediations or evasive interpretations made for public opinion.

And because it is given as Bread, it is Wisdom that with its testimony and its word knows that the soul of a people grows when the Spirit works in its deepest, most sensitive and most creative dimensions. That is his tireless educational challenge, far from pure encyclopedic or technocratic information, even further from subordination to power schemes. Because its true power is that of God's infinite and trusting love, not tied to races, cultures, or systems, which gives them their meaning and ultimate significance: to help to be and to delight in the joy of being, which demands giving and resists being locked in its own petty horizons.

7. Blindness of the soul prevents us from being free. In today's Gospel passage, many of those who longed for freedom, by raising their intolerant stones, showed the same cruelty as the invading empire. They wanted to get rid of the enemy outside without accepting the enemy inside. And we know that copying the hatred and violence of the tyrant and the murderer is the best way to be their heir. Therefore, when Jesus proposes, in line with Isaiah, liberation from captivity and oppression, we can ask ourselves: from what captivity and from what oppression? And answer: first, that of ourselves. That of our disorientation and immaturity, in order to claim the freedom from external oppression. If the chains were iron, if the presence of external armies were evident, so would the need for freedom be. But when captivity comes from our bleeding wounds and internal struggles, from compulsive ambition, from the compromises of power that absorb the institutions, then we are already captives of ourselves. A captivity that is expressed, among other things, in the dynamics of exclusion. Not only the exclusion implemented through unjust structures, but also the one we empower, that other form of exclusion through attitudes: indifference, intolerance, exacerbated individualism, sectarianism. We exclude others from their identity and remain captives of the mask; we exclude from identity, and we break up their sense of belonging ... because to have "identity" means to "belong." Only from belonging to a people can we understand the deep message of its history, the features of its identity. Any other maneuver

from outside is nothing more than a link in the chain; in any case there is a change of masters, but the status is the same.

8. The proposal is to free ourselves from our mediocrity, that mediocrity that is the best narcotic to enslave people. There is no need for oppressive armies. To paraphrase our national poem, we can say that a divided and disoriented people is already dominated.

A confused and mediocre media culture keeps us in the perplexity of chaos and anomie, in permanent internal confrontation and with the "current events" distracted by spectacular news so as not to see our incompetence in facing our daily problems. It is the world of false models and scripts. The subtlest oppression is then the oppression of lies and concealment . . . and yes, based on a lot of information, information that is opaque and, therefore, ambiguous.

Interestingly, we have more information than ever before, and, nevertheless, we do not know what is happening. Chopped, deformed, reinterpreted, the overabundant global information engulfs the soul in data and images, but without depth of knowledge. It confuses realism with manipulative, invasive morbidity, for which no one is prepared but that in its paralyzing perplexity produces propaganda revenues. It leaves disembodied and hopeless images.

9. But thanks be to God, our people also know the humble path of the daily grind, the same one of so many years of hidden life. Betting on the good and persevering without being sure of the result. They know the painful and peaceful but at the same time rebellious silence, of many years of misunderstandings, false promises, plundering violence, and injustices. However, they face their daily tasks, with much social exhaustion and webs of marginalization. Year after year, they renew their trusting expectations, making pilgrimages to so many places where God and his Mother await them for a comforting, strengthening dialogue.

These people do not believe in lying and mediocre plots. They have hopes but do not have illusions about magic solutions elaborated in dark arrangements and the pressures of power. They are not confused by speeches; they are getting tired of the narcosis of vertigo, consumerism, exhibitionism, and strident advertisements. To their collective conscience—the one that springs from the deep soul of our people—these things are only stonings. Our people know, they have a soul, and because we can speak of the soul of a people, we can speak of a hermeneutics, of a way of seeing reality, a conscience. I see in our Argentine people a strong awareness of their dignity. It is an historic awareness that has been molded by significant milestones. Our people know that the only way out is the silent but steady and firm road. The one with clear, foreseeable projects that demand continuity and commitment from all the participants in society and with all Argentines. Our people want to live and fulfill the call of Christ who walks among us, encouraging our hearts, one by one, reawakening the resources of our cultural memory. Our people know and love because they love the Father's Creation and the community, as our indigenous people did and do; because they plunge into and commit themselves to their ideals, as the Spaniards who populated our soil bequeathed to us; because they are humble, pious, and festive like our Creoles; because they are industrious and tireless, like our greatest immigrants.

10. We saw the Lord proclaiming his message in the midst of his people. We observe how the enlightened elites do not tolerate the patient daily path of the humble and simple and, driven by their exquisite hysteria, seek to push them off the cliff and to stone them. We point out the values of a people with God in their humble path. We traversed our historical path as a people and observed our contradictions. We feel the need to be cured of our blindness and freed from captivity and oppression. The sapiential appeal that we can make today, inspired by the Gospel, is from all appearances very clear: Any profound transformation that aims for serenity of spirit, toward co-existence and toward greater dignity and harmony in our homeland, can be achieved only from our roots; appealing to the consciences that seek and commiserate, that enjoy others and commit to them, that accept the pacifying order of the just law and the memory of the collective achievements that form our common being. Appealing to the consciences that do not get lost in the blindness of secondary contradictions, but focus on the great challenges, and commit their priority resources to make this their educational project, for all generations and without limits.

The Word, like history, leaves us a code where we can see ourselves as in a mirror. But, in addition, there are also mirages. Today, as always, Argentines must decide. Not doing it is already a decision, but a tragic one. We either choose the mirage of adherence to the mediocrity that blinds and enslaves us, or we look at ourselves in the mirror of our history, assuming also all its obscurities and antivalues, and adhering wholeheartedly to the greatness of those who gave everything for the homeland, without seeing the results, of those who walked and still walk the humble path of our people, following in the footsteps of that Jesus who passes among the proud, leaving them bewildered in their own contradictions and seeking the road that exalts the humble, a road leading to the cross on which our people are crucified, but which is a path of certain hope of resurrection; hope that no power or ideology has yet been able to strip from them.

→► ◄←

"He Spoke to Them about the Kingdom of God"

Homily, Solemnity of Corpus Christi—June 12, 2004, Year C

In this passage of the Gospel, a word resounds with special insistence, full of nuances for us: "the crowd." It begins by saying that the Lord "spoke to the crowds about the kingdom of God" (Lk 9:11).

After having slipped away from those who wanted to stone him, the Lord went to speak to the simple people. Many times, the Gospel shows us Jesus in the midst of the people: "a large crowd of people followed him" (Lk 23:27), and the Lord spoke to them at length, healed them, welcomed them, chose his apostles from among them, whom he sent in turn to go into that crowd.

I would like to stop today to contemplate with you that special relationship of Jesus with the crowd. People follow him and listen because they feel that he speaks differently, with the authority that he gives to the authentic and coherent being, not having double messages or double intentions. There is joy and rejoicing when they listen to the Master. People bless God when Jesus speaks because his discourse includes them all, personalizes them and makes them the people of God. Have you noticed that only the scribes and the Pharisees, whom Jesus calls hypocrites, always ask, "To whom are you speaking?" "Do you say it for us?" "By saying this you also offend us!" People do not ask that question; it is more for them, they wish, they want, that the Word be for them. They know that it is a word that does good; that the one who says, "this is for me," that word heals, improves, cleanses. . . . It's funny, while some dislike that the Lord speaks in parables, people imbibe his parables and transmit them from mouth to mouth; they receive everything—the content and style of Jesus. The crowd was thirsty for that new Word, thirsty for the Gospel, thirsting for the Word of God.

Following the Lord that afternoon, the crowd enters in the open field with him, without noticing either the time or the distance. The disciples express their concern: "Dismiss the crowd," and Jesus immediately retorts: "Give them some food yourselves" (Lk 9:12–13).

At that moment, at the time for eating, the crowd stops being anonymous and becomes, according to the disciples' calculation "about five thousand *men*" (v. 15). Jesus tells them: "make them sit in *groups* of up to fifty people." Actually, the Lord uses an expression as if he were saying "on tables" of fifty people ("*klisias*" is the "space where a group lies down to eat"). Tables of fifty guests, and the food is placed in the middle, and from which all are served.

This table is already an image of the Kingdom. Jesus uses it again in the parable of the vigilant servants who wait for their Lord to return from the wedding (cf. Lk 12:35–38). To those he finds watching, Jesus says that "he will gird himself, have them recline at table, and proceed to wait on them."

Here begins the inclusive force of the Eucharist, which turns the multitude into groups of communities, measured by their ability to share bread.

And there is still a third mention of the crowd. When it is thus organized, in such a familiar human setting, which transforms a group into a community of companions, then the Lord takes the five loaves and the two fish, and raising his eyes to heaven he blesses them, shares them, and gives them to the disciples to serve to the crowd.

That crowd is already a transformed, personalized, familiar crowd. That community is the area in which the blessing and the miracle take place. In that community, everything was enough for everyone, and there were leftovers: "They all ate and were satisfied. And when the leftover fragments were picked up, they filled twelve wicker baskets" (Lk 9:17).

Once again Jesus in the midst of us as a crowd urges us to organize ourselves in communities according to the availability of bread. Organize yourselves as they do in retirement centers, in the school cafeterias, in foster homes, in neighborhood parties, in work cooperatives, in Caritas, in parishes.

Let the possibility of sharing bread be the measure used.

Organize yourselves so that you do not need to count the children or the elderly, because they are already included where those who support the home, eat.

Sadly, current statistics speak separately of children and the elderly, because they also speak of unemployed individuals. The Lord's numbers are different: He points to community and solidarity, he sees "tables of fifty," groups of relatives and friends, like those who gather at parties, at religious celebrations . . . it is the starting point for the Lord to organize his Community, his Church. It must be our starting point to organize the parish, the neighborhood, and the homeland.

Only Jesus sees us this way. Only his living bread has the strength to give cohesiveness to the crowd. Only the strength of his death on the cross to become bread can turn crowds into communities. And we ask him:

Lord, give us this Bread always!

We want to be a community that shares the bread that you bless and distribute.

We want to be a community that is organized following your model, to allow you to serve us and transform us.

We do not want to eat our bread alone: neither that of faith nor that of work.

We do not want to "fire" the crowds that, when summoned, seek you and desire you, even without knowing it many times.

We do not want to accept the statistics that have already discarded so many of our brothers.

We each want to follow you and receive you and share you "at your table of fifty."

We want to be communities that live off the strength the Eucharist gives, to announce with our life more than with words, that truth of the Gospel that is transcendent because it speaks, beyond individualism, of a Kingdom that is already in our midst when we come together to share the bread in your name, Lord.

To our Mother, to Mary, who notices when there is no wine, that wine that is the joy and hope that summons "tables of fifty," that wine that is festive and gives meaning to all the rest of work and effort. We ask you, with your mother's heart, to make us feel and live in the community of the Living Bread and the New Wine that your Son gave us and that we adore and celebrate with fervor.

→► ◄←

"Get Up and Eat or the Journey Will Be
Too Much for You!"

Letter to Catechists—August 2004

"Get up and eat or the journey will be too much for you!" (1 Kgs 19:7)

Dear catechists,

As a Diocesan Church we walk a path that will have a strong moment of the Spirit: the next Assemblies of the People of God. I hope that this time of preparation implies starting on a path of community discernment through prayer.

As the Church in Argentina we make a pilgrimage to Corrientes where, in a few days, we will gather together as a faithful People around the Eucharist, to ask the Lord that the daily celebration will help us realize the dream, postponed so many times, of a truly reconciled and solidary Nation. We do it with the sad realization that there are people who do not have anything to eat in this land blessed with bread.

Finally, the Buenos Aires catechists initiate, with the catechists of the whole country, a pastoral journey that will culminate with the celebration of the National Meeting of Catechists (ENAC 2005) in the Shrine of Luján next year. This will be a propitious time to reflect on the identity and the person of the catechist, also remembering with gratitude the faces of the past that, as faithful witnesses, knew how to make their ministry fruitful.

Identity, memory, belonging to a people that knows itself as pilgrims on the way.

In this dynamic reality of the Church I want, as we near the feast of Saint Pius X, to send you my greetings and grateful affection for the Day of the Catechist. I want to share with you some reflections that lately have been in my prayer, in line with what I wrote to you on Ash Wednesday, when I invited you to take care of the fragility of our brothers with the audacity of the disciples of Jesus who trust in his Risen presence.

Our Church in Buenos Aires needs that *audacity* and *fervor*, works of the Holy Spirit, that lead us to announce and loudly proclaim Jesus Christ with our whole lives. It takes much boldness and courage to keep walking today amid so much perplexity.

We know that we may be tempted to allow ourselves to be trapped by the paralyzing fear that sometimes is masked by withdrawal and realistic calculations and, in other cases, by constant repetition. But it always hides the cowardly and conformist vocation of a minimalist culture accustomed only to the security of walking on the edges.

Apostolic audacity will involve search, creativity, sailing into the deep!

In this spirituality of the journey, the temptation to betray the call to march as a people is also great, renouncing the mandate to be on pilgrimage for the craze of running the marathon of success. In this way we mortgage our style, adhering ourselves to the culture of exclusion, where there is no place for the elderly, the annoying child, and there is no time to stop at the edge of the road. The temptation is great, especially because it is based on new modern dogmas such as efficiency and pragmatism. Therefore, it takes a lot of daring to go against the current, not to renounce the possible utopia that is precisely the inclusion that marks the style and pace of our step.

Walking as a people is always slower. In addition, all know that the road is long and difficult. As in that foundational experience of the people of God through the desert, fatigue and bewilderment will not be lacking.

It has happened to all of us at one time or another to find ourselves stalled and disoriented along the way, not knowing what steps to take. Reality is often imposed on us as closed off, without hope. We doubt, like the people of Israel, the promises and presence of the Lord of history, and we allow ourselves to be enveloped by the positivist mentality that tries to be the key for interpreting reality. We renounce our vocation to make history to join the nostalgic chorus of complaints and reproaches: "Did we not tell you this in Egypt, when we said, 'Leave us alone . . .'?! Far better for us to serve the Egyptians than to die in the wilderness" (Ex 14:12). Apostolic fervor will help us to remember, not to give up freedom, to walk as a people of the Covenant: "Be careful not to forget the LORD, who brought you out of the land of Egypt, that house of slavery" (Dt 6:12). As catechists in difficult times, you must ask God for the audacity and fervor that will enable you to help us remember! "Be very careful not to forget the things your own eyes have seen" (Dt 4:9). In the transmission and celebration of memory we will find as a people the necessary strength to avoid falling into fear that paralyzes and causes anguish.

This journey of the people of God recognizes seasons and rhythms, temptations and trials, events of grace in which it is necessary to renew the covenant.

Also, today, in our walk as the Church in Buenos Aires, we are living a very special moment that we dare to envision as a time of grace. We want to open ourselves to the Spirit to let him move us spiritually so that the next Diocesan Assemblies can be truly the "Time of God" where in the presence of the Lord we can deepen our identity and become aware of our mission. To be able to create a fraternal experience of communal discernment in fellowship where prayer and dialogue allow us to overcome disagreements and grow in community and missionary holiness.

Like all walking, it forces us to get going, keep moving, it unsettles us and puts us in a situation of spiritual struggles. We must pay special attention to what happens in the heart; be attentive to the movement of different spirits (the good, the bad, your own). And this for discerning and finding the Will of God.

It will not be surprising that in this path that we begin to travel there appears the subtle temptation of the 'alternativist' seduction, that expresses itself in never accepting a common road, to always present other possibilities as absolute. I do not refer to healthy and enriching pluralism or nuances at the time of community discernment; but the inability to walk with others, because deep in the heart the preference is to walk alone on elitist paths that, in many cases, lead to selfishly falling back on oneself. In contrast, the catechist, the true catechist, has wisdom that is forged through nearness to people and the richness of so many shared faces and stories that distance them from any updated version of 'enlightenment.'

It should not be surprising that the evil spirit also becomes present on the road, the one who rejects all newness. The one who clings to what has been acquired already and prefers the security of Egypt to the promises of the Lord. That evil spirit leads us to gloat over difficulties, to bet on failure from the beginning, to dismiss 'with realism' the crowds because we do not know how, we cannot and, deep down, do not want to include them. No one is exempt from this evil spirit.

Hence, the invitation to renew the fervor is an invitation to ask God for a grace for our Church in Buenos Aires: "*The grace of apostolic boldness, strong and fervent audacity in the Spirit.*"

We know that all this spiritual renewal cannot be the result of a movement of will or a simple change of mind. It is grace, interior renewal, profound transformation that is based on and supported by a Presence that, like that afternoon of the first day of new history, makes its way with us to transform our fears into zeal, our sadness into joy, our escape into an announcement.

All we need is to recognize him as at Emmaus. He continues to break the bread so that we also will be recognized at the breaking of our bread. And if we lack the audacity to take on the challenge of being the ones who provide the food, let us activate in our lives the mandate of God to the tired and overwhelmed prophet Elijah: "*Get up and eat or the journey will be too much for you!*" (1 Kgs 19:7).

In thanking you for all your journey as catechists, I ask the Lord of the Eucharist to renew your ardor and apostolic fervor so that you never get used to the faces of so many children who do not know Jesus, the faces of so many young people who wander through life without meaning, the faces of the crowds of excluded ones who, with their families and elderly people, struggle to be a community, whose daily passage through our city hurts and questions us.

More than ever, we need your close catechist gaze to contemplate, move, and stop as many times as necessary to give our walk the healing rhythm of neighborliness. And you can thus make the experience of true compassion, that of Jesus, that far from paralyzing, instead mobilizing, impelling you to leave with more force, with more audacity, to announce, to heal, to liberate (cf. Lk 4:18–19).

More than ever, we need your delicate catechist's heart that allows you to contribute, from your experience of accompaniment, the wisdom of life and the processes where prudence, the ability to understand, the art of waiting, the sense of belonging, to care in this way—among all—for the sheep that are entrusted to us, from the enlightened wolves that try to scatter the flock.

More than ever, we need your person and your catechetical ministry so that with your creative works, we can, like David, play music and bring joy to our people's tired walking! (cf. 2 Sm 6:14–15).

I ask you, please, to pray for me to be a good catechist. May Jesus bless you and the Blessed Virgin guide you.

→‣ ‹←

The Lord Gives Us a Bread
That Puts Us Back on the Road

Homily, Shrine of Saint Cajetan—August 7, 2004

Today, the Word of God speaks to us of paths. The path of disenchantment and the path of hope. Elijah, pursued by King Ahab and Queen Jezebel, takes the path of flight and hopes for death: "Enough, Lord! Take my life, for I am no better than my ancestors" (1 Kgs 19:4). The disciples from Emmaus, saddened by Jesus' death, leave the community united in its affliction waiting for the Lord and return home: "we were hoping . . ." they tell the Stranger who accompanies them along the way, but "it is now the third day since this took place" (cf. Lk 24:13–35), as if to say 'nothing more is going to happen here. Let's go.'

But the Lord appears on these paths of disenchantment and comforts the downhearted. The angel says to Elijah: "Get up and eat, or the journey will be too much for you!" (1 Kgs 19:7). Jesus approaches the disciples from Emmaus and consoles them as he keeps them company along the way. Jesus' 'challenges' are filled with a love and understanding that make them react: "Were not our hearts burning within us while he spoke to us on the way and opened the Scriptures to us?" (Lk 24:32)

But the key to strengthening these disheartened people is in the bread. The Lord feeds them with the bread of sojourners. That bread that is viaticum, bread for the journey, the bread that restores strength and hope. Bread that restores them, with new strength, for their mission and community. Elijah rose up, he ate and drank, and with the strength provided by that food he walked forty days and nights to God's mountain, where the Lord appeared to him as a soft breeze. When the disciples from Emmaus gave hospitality to their traveling companion without knowing he was Jesus, they recognized him when he broke bread for them and, having eaten it, "they set out at once and returned to Jerusalem where they found gathered together the eleven and those with them" (v. 33).

The Lord also wants to give us, who are coming to Saint Cajetan, this same bread, from the hands of the Saint, which provides strength for working and for the community. As always, we come with hope, but sometimes that hope wants to turn away from the path of men, it wants the true peace that is found only in God. "Enough, LORD! Take my life, for I am no better than my ancestors" (1 Kgs 19:4). That phrase strikes a chord in our hearts. Sometimes we feel that all we have left is our God and there is nothing more we can do on this earth. There is too much injustice, poverty and violence. . . . And yet the Lord gives us a bread that puts us back on the road with renewed strength and sends us back to our work, our family, our homeland: You still have a long way to go. There is so much to do! And with the Lord as our food we fear nothing. There is no discouragement or obstacle that this bread cannot transform into life and the will to keep on struggling and walking.

Elijah ate only this bread, in the solitude of the prophet. The young disciples from Emmaus ate it together, as friends who start out together on the road back to hope. We eat it together, as Church, as people of God. And the strength of this bread increases with our unity and fellowship.

There is a bread for celebration, a bread that is the product and reward of work, the joy of eating together. But bread is also bread that is eaten on the way to work, that gives us the strength to do difficult tasks. That is the bread we're looking for today: the bread that gives us strength. The bread that provides energy. The bread that makes us feel like working and persevering. The bread that is shared along the way with our companions. That bit of bread we eat as we're working, and that helps us make it through the day. This is the bread we want to leave to our young people, because they are our hope; the bread of work that restores dignity and pulls us through.

This bread that gives us a beautiful image of the Eucharist, the one that travels with us, meaning bread for the road. It's like the bread roll carried in our bag as a token of family love; it's the warmth of home that reaches all the way to our workplace, if we have one, or the places where we look for work. It's a bread that encourages us to fight for our family, as if it were saying, 'Let's go!' That 'let's go!' reminds me of the title of the Pope's latest book: *Rise, Let Us Be on Our Way*. And I want to say to our youngest in particular: 'We go trusting in Christ. It is he who will keep us company on our way to the destination only he knows.' Because he is the bread; he became the Eucharist to walk beside us.

Rise and eat! Eat this bread, which gives us the strength to work for our families. Rise and eat! Eat this bread, which restores our dignity and restores our will to keep on struggling and fulfill our mission. Rise and eat! Eat this bread, which we share with our fellow travelers and which makes us feel like brothers, like people of one country, people of God.

We ask the Virgin, our Mother, who sees when we lack this bread, who always places in the hands of our women a roll for the journey in their children's schoolbags and the husband's pocket, to show us how to search in our hearts with true hope, certain that we will always find this bread for the journey, this bread which is Jesus.

May Saint Cajetan the patron saint of bread and work grant us, and especially those men and women who are heads of households, that while we look for the work that allows us to bring home bread we may also receive that other small, simple, and sufficient bread that allows us to get up every day and walk, full of energy and hope, along the Lord's path. That is how we can leave our young people that same precious gift our parents left to us: the bread that always gave them strength to work.

→→ ←←

"Be Reconciled with God"

Homily, Tenth National Eucharistic Congress—September 2, 2004

"Be Reconciled with God"

In this quite beautiful climate at the Eucharistic Congress, already in our second day, the parable of the Prodigal Son wants to talk straight to our hearts.

So, let's open our hearts wide.

May every person open their heart, looking at the Virgin, feeling Jesus' presence in the Eucharist who, silently, has been accompanying humanity for two thousand years.

Let's open our family's heart, each one his or her own, feeling their parents' and siblings' heartbeat, their spouse's and the youth's, the children's and grandparents.'

Let's open our hearts as the faithful People of God who travel in Argentina under the mantle of the Virgin, of Our Lady of Itatí . . . [1]

Let's open our hearts and let's be reconciled with our Father, God.

Let's say with the prodigal son, who in a moment of grace realized that the deepest cause of his situation of misery was to have separated his heart from his Father's: "I shall get up and go to my father!" (Lk 15:18).

Each one should say so in his or her own heart. And they should also say it in that realm where their own heart is a shared heart, responsible for the hearts of everyone, in solidarity with the hearts of their own people. From

---

1. The Virgin of Itatí is a devotion very dear to Argentines after a statue of the Blessed Virgin brought by two Spanish missionaries to the village of Itatí disappeared in 1615 following a looting. It was later found in the nearby Paraná River. A shrine was erected to celebrate the miraculous discovery and, shortly after, a miracle happened, and it repeated itself many times: The face of the Virgin was surrounded by a radiant light, as was first witnessed by Fray Gamarra, who was officiating that day.

there, each one may say, prodigal people: Get up and return to your Father! It's time you stop longing to eat the pods of the swine. No one gives them to you. Thanks be to God. It's better this way. Because it's time you long for *children's bread* again.

You are impoverished; you have squandered some of your inheritance and some has been stolen. It's true. But you keep what is most valuable: the embers of your dignity always intact and the little flame of your hope, which lights again every day. You keep that spiritual reserve that you have inherited.

See that your Father never stops going to wait for you on the terrace at every sunset . . . to see if you come back.

Set off on the path to go back, your eyes fixed on those of your Father, who widens the horizon so that you give as much as you can.

By seeking after false gods, you turned this blessed land into a foreign one. And today it seems that your horizon has become smaller, that your hope has shrunk.

But that's not true. If you look up, if you remember, if you return and convert with all your heart, the same soil on which you trod will become your Father's House again.

That Father's House where the values of the humble house of Joseph and Mary in Nazareth are practiced.

The Father's House that is an inn where the wounds of victims of robbers are cured.

The Father's House where the Son's wedding banquet is celebrated, and everyone is invited, without excluding anyone, except for those who do not wish to attend.

The Father's House which, as Jesus assures us, has many rooms and where he himself serves us, as he did at the Last Supper.

And it makes you feel like a people and a family!

Also, let the Father tell us, as he told the angry son: *Enter the feast with your brother!* Every heart must hear this invitation, by which the Father wants to convince his older son that forgiving his brother is the path to life.

Each one of us also has something of that older son within. Let the Father tell us:

It is time you stop hearing the bitter complaining inherent in a heart which does not value what it has, of a heart that compares itself in the wrong way.

It's time you dare to share the children's bread with your brother.

Stop longing for your own young goat and listen to these words from your Father: "My son, everything I have is yours" (Lk 15:31).

Be reconciled with God, with yourself, and with your brother!

But from the bottom of your heart.

The Eucharist is the bread of reconciliation that goes to the bottom of each of our hearts. And it reconciles and nourishes that inner place where the person is the true self and more than themselves, because it is God's dwelling place, where each heart is the heart of the entire family and of all the people.

With just a few of these hearts, which allow themselves to be fully reconciled, reconciliation will spread to all the people.

Hearts like that of Saint Roque González de Santa Cruz, S.J.,[2] who founded these lands and their cities on the culture of work and on the forgiveness of his own enemies. A broken heart that the Lord covered with incorruptibility!

Prodigal and rebellious people; people who suffered at the hands of robbers; people with strong spiritual resources: Be reconciled with God!

Our Lady of Itatí, we entrust to you this reconciliation that transforms the hearts of each person and of all peoples. Her most beautiful miracles have been a recurring presence and a transfiguration that attracts with its glory. As Fray Luis de Gamarra said in 1624: "There was an extraordinary change on her face; she was more beautiful than ever before."

Those transfigurations of our Lady, which emerge from her pure and loving heart, are a sign of predilection for our people. And they are also an announcement: Transfigured Mary of Itatí transfigures us. She tells us the Word of God: "So whoever is in Christ is a new creation: the old things have passed away; behold, new things have come. And all this is from God, who has reconciled us to himself through Christ and given us the ministry of reconciliation" (2 Cor 5:17–18).

By looking at her, we understand: "If sin is distance and discord, reconciliation is approach and reunion, an overcoming of enmity and a return to communion. God reconciles us in Christ. He is the beginning and the end of filial reconciliation, by which repented men come back in trust to the Father's loving arms."[3]

---

2. Roque González de Santa Cruz (1576–1628) was a martyred Jesuit priest. Born in what is now Paraguay, he founded many missions there and in Argentina. He was canonized by Pope John Paul II in 1988.

3. X National Eucharistic Congress, Working Document.

She invites you, people of the homeland: Be reconciled with God!

With her, we pray to Jesus, and beg him, with the words of this prayer: "May his Eucharist fill the hearts of the Argentine people and inspire their projects and hopes."[4]

→▸ ◂←

Let's Be Quiet in Our Hearts and Be Accountable for Our Brothers and Sisters

Remarks, Selichot Service in Preparation for Rosh Hashana at the Synagogue on 2049 Vidal Street—September 11, 2004

Today we have come before the Lord. We can imagine the scene as at the beginning of the book of Job (1:6). There the Lord asks questions, and these move the heart, unveil intentions. We are before him, willing to listen. Let's allow his questions to move us within, to make us transparent. Let's not be afraid of Truth if we recognize or proclaim it before him because "Merciful and gracious is the LORD, slow to anger, / abounding in mercy. / He will not always accuse, / and nurses no lasting anger" (Ps 103:8–9).

And as in that sunset in the beginning, today he asks each one of us about ourselves: Adam, "Where are you?" (Gn 3:9). He questions our direction. Do we know where we are in relation to him, in relation to what he wants from us? Or have we eaten from the forbidden tree and are trying to hide ourselves? (cf. v. 11). The question makes us aware of our limits, our flaws, our nakedness. We only have two directions, to camouflage them or ac-knowledge them. Where am I in relation to God? Where am I in relation to myself? Today is the 'right time' to reposition ourselves. So many times, we get off the path! So many times, our compass goes crazy and we lose our sense of direction! Today we must answer truthfully, to look inside our hearts. Not to be afraid, but to tell the truth. Where am I? And not try blaming others: "The woman whom you put here with me—she gave me fruit from the tree, so I ate it" (v. 12). To reposition myself within and be-fore God. And to redirect my heart by converting myself to him.

---

4. Ibid., closing prayer.

Today he also asks us a second question: "Where is your brother?" (Gn 4:9). Before he asked about our relationship with ourselves and with him; and now with our neighbors. He did not want us to be isolated, but to constitute a people, a family. When we are disoriented from ourselves and from God, this disorientation also affects our relationship with our brothers and sisters; and we answer: "I do not know" (ibid.), or we go further and want to justify ourselves: "Am I my brother's keeper?" (ibid.). My brother: so many men and women whom I forgot because of my selfishness. The Lord asks us about the orphan and the widow, the foreigner and the slave. Let's be still in our hearts and be accountable for our brothers and sisters.

These two questions fulfill his mandate: "Hear, O Israel! The LORD is our God, the LORD alone! Therefore, you shall love the LORD, your God, with your whole heart, and with your whole being, and with your whole strength" (Dt 6:4–5) and "You shall love your neighbor as yourself. I am the LORD" (Lev 19:18); we are asked to fulfill that mandate that must become flesh in our lives and in our teachings for our children: "Take to heart these words which I command you today. Keep repeating them to your children. Recite them when you are at home and when you are away, when you lie down and when you get up" (Dt 6:6–7).

This is our memory. Let's not lose it. And, when listening to these two questions today, let's focus on recovering the memory too. In everyday life, our fascination with idols weakens our memory. Together with these two questions today, we are asked to recover our memory: "Be on your guard and be very careful not to forget the things your own eyes have seen, nor let them slip from your heart" (Dt 4:9). Let's recover the memory of our personal history and of our history as a people: "I led you for forty years in the wilderness. Your clothes did not fall from you in tatters nor your sandals from your feet" (Dt 29:4). When we lose the memory of the path we traveled, we also avoid the two previous questions. We don't know what to answer to the questions "Adam, where are you?" and "Where is your brother?" simply because we have forgotten from whence we come, because we have lost the compass of our belonging to a people. And when you lose your compass, you fall into idolatry. Today we should ask ourselves this by remembering the Lord's mandate: "You shall not go after other gods, any of the gods of the surrounding peoples" (Dt 6:14). Idolatry seeps into our lives in thousands of ways, we're offered idols at every step, but we ourselves are the most dangerous idol when we want to take God's place. That subtle selfishness turns us into the only reference point of all being.

To recover memory with a child's piety and, while we examine ourselves about the two questions asked by the Lord to us, to babble our history with a heart that wants to be converted to the Lord: "My father was a refugee Aramaean who went down to Egypt with a small household and lived there as a resident alien. But there he became a nation great, strong and numerous. When the Egyptians maltreated and oppressed us, imposing harsh servitude upon us, we cried to the LORD, the God of our ancestors, and the LORD heard our cry and saw our affliction, our toil and our oppression. Then the LORD brought us out of Egypt with a strong hand and outstretched arm, with terrifying power, with signs and wonders, and brought us to this place, and gave us this land, a land flowing with milk and honey" (Dt 26:5–9). This is the memory that today leads us to conversion.

And our memory points also to the Lord's memory: He waits for us, he remembers us with the hope that we return to the first days: "I remember the devotion of your youth, how you loved me as a bride, following me in the wilderness, in a land unsown" (Jer 2:2). We remember feeling remembered; we want to love by feeling loved first. He waits for us; he is first to love us as the almond tree is the first to flower.[1] To be converted in this way, contemplating so much love, becomes a feast and, amid repentance and a resolution of conversion, let's fraternally repeat: "Today is holy to the LORD your God. . . . Do not lament, do not weep! Do not be saddened this day, for rejoicing in the LORD is your strength!" (Neh 8:9–11).

⤏ ⤛

It Is Possible to Be Holy

Closing Presentation at the Congress on Veritatis splendor—
September 25, 2004

More than ten years after the publication of the Encyclical *Veritatis splendor*, the John Paul II Chair has begun its activities with a Congress that leaves an enormous wealth in our local churches that we must continue unpacking and spreading.

---

1. A reference to the almond tree in Israel, the first to flower in winter.

How can we carry out this work, how can we deepen and communicate the experiences and reflections we have shared during these days?

I would like to answer this question from a triple and complementary perspective: one, which I consider to be the fundamental one; another, which is the indispensable instrument; the third, which is one of its most precious and expected fruits.

The first perspective offers us the centrality of grace in the moral life as conceived in the light of Revelation.

The second is the perspective of evangelization as an indispensable reality, not only because there is a "command" from the Lord, but above all because he has communicated a new life to us, and that life leads to and demands communication.

The third is the perspective of the relationship between the Gospel of grace and the cultural and political life of human beings.

I. The Centrality of Grace in Christian Moral Life

"For God all things are possible" (Mt 19:26). The conclusion of Jesus' dialogue with the rich young man is doubly disappointing: The young man goes away saddened because he had many possessions and the disciples, moved and perplexed, ask themselves in front of Jesus: "Who then can be saved?" (v. 25).

"For God all things are possible," Jesus responds with clarity and firmness, announcing and communicating to us the *Gospel of grace*. It is not possible for men to live the holy law of God while following Christ without grace, that is, without the new life of the Spirit, without being led by the Spirit (cf. Rm 8:14).

The moral life of men of all times is called to be "led by the spirit" (ibid.). "To imitate and live out the love of Christ is not possible for man by his own strength alone. He becomes *capable of this love only by virtue of a gift received*" (VS 22), and "Christ's gift is his Spirit, whose first 'fruit' (cf. Gal 5:22) is charity: 'God's love has been poured into our hearts through the Holy Spirit which has been given to us' (Rm 5:5)" (VS 22).

Saint Augustine cogently asked himself: "Love brings about the keeping of his commandments; but does the keeping of his commandments bring about love? Who can doubt that it is love which precedes? For he has no true ground for keeping the commandments who is destitute of love."[1]

---

1. Lectures on the Gospel according to John, Tractate LXXXII, Chapter 15:8–10, 3.

This brings us to a fundamental conclusion that the Pope makes explicit: "Love and life according to the Gospel cannot be thought of first and foremost as a kind of precept, because what they demand is beyond man's abilities. They are possible only as the result of a gift of God who heals, restores and transforms the human heart by his grace" (VS 23).

Proposing Christian morality from the perspective of the *precept*, from a *commandment*, may explain in part why contemporary man, especially among our peoples of Christian tradition, fell into a serious temptation: Faced with the impossibility of observing the holy law of God, man wants to decide himself what is good or bad (cf. VS 102).

We must remind the frail man of today, even more, we must announce and joyfully bear witness to him, that "temptations can be overcome, sins can be avoided, because together with the commandments the Lord gives us the possibility of keeping them" (ibid.), and that, "Keeping God's law in particular situations can be difficult, extremely difficult, but it is never impossible" (ibid.).

Presenting and witnessing Christian morality from the centrality of grace, is to present it and give witness to it in light of hope. Has not today's man traded hope for optimism? Do we not feel around us the anguished cry of so many who are disappointed, hopeless?

Only with the help of grace, the gift of the Spirit, and the collaboration of our freedom is it possible for all people today to live their existence in this world in the light of hope.

Hope that it is possible to be honest, it is possible to live in truth, in justice, and in love. In a word: *it is possible to be holy*. It is possible to build a new civilization centered on love and life. It is possible to trust in the mercy of the Father who opens the doors of his eternal dwelling place in the hope of a life that will never end. Everything is possible because of the gift of grace from Jesus who died and rose.

II. Evangelization, Witness, and Announcement of New Life

Only the one who lives by the Spirit in loving obedience to the Father witnesses in his daily actions the new life of grace and feels the need for that life to be communicated to all men, feels the need of the joyful proclamation of the Gospel of grace. "Woe to me if I do not preach it" (1 Cor 9:16), exclaims the apostle after his personal encounter with the risen Christ who calls him to faith and conversion.

"Evangelization is the most powerful and stirring challenge which the Church has been called to face from her very beginning" (VS 106). Today, particularly, we are living the moment of a "formidable challenge to undertake a *new evangelization*" (ibid.). This exciting challenge is made more urgent by the reality of "dechristianization, which weighs heavily upon entire peoples and communities once rich in faith and Christian life, involves not only the loss of faith or in any event its becoming irrelevant for everyday life, but also, and of necessity, *a decline or obscuring of the moral sense*. This comes about both because of a loss of awareness of the originality of Gospel morality and because of an eclipse of fundamental principles and ethical values themselves" (ibid.).

Our peoples are living the irruption of a *non-Christian or dechristianized cultural form*. The subjectivist, utilitarian, and relativist tendencies, not only as pragmatic positions but also as theoretically consolidated conceptions, shape our world and seriously challenge us.

In addition, the great migratory movements of our world and the reality of religious diversity, particularly coming from the East, pose for evangelization the delicate challenge of the encounter between different cultures and interreligious dialogue.

Thus, "*Evangelization*—and therefore the new 'evangelization'—*also involves the proclamation and presentation of morality*" (VS 107). Jesus not only called to faith but also to conversion (cf. Mk 1:15).

For the *moral presentation* to be an *indispensable component* of evangelization, the living witness of holy men and women is necessary. This witness is the clearest sign of the *holiness of the Church that comes from Jesus Christ*.

The Church, in her wise moral pedagogy, has always invited her children to find in her holy men and women, above all in Mary and Joseph, "the model, the strength and the joy needed to live a life in accordance with God's commandments and the Beatitudes of the Gospel" (VS 107).

In the context of the new evangelization, which also involves Jesus' moral design, "appropriate allowance is made both for God's *mercy towards the sinner who converts and for the understanding of human weakness*" (VS 104).

But this understanding can never mean a compromise and a falsification of the measure of good and evil to which God calls us in his holy law, to adapt it to the existential circumstances of people and human groups. "It is quite human for the sinner to acknowledge his weakness and to ask mercy for his failings; what is unacceptable is the attitude of one who makes his own weakness the criterion of the truth about the good, so that he can feel self-justified, without even the need to have recourse to God and his mercy" (ibid.).

The reflection that theology must elaborate on the moral life—as well as the formation and action of the various pastoral agents, in particular, priests and catechists—finds its genuine place in the context of the new evangelization.

The Church needs moral theologians who deepen the moral proposal of Jesus, make it understandable to contemporary man, and thus render their irreplaceable service to the new evangelization.

The dedication of many in the cultivation and teaching of moral theology constitutes a true charism of the Spirit and an ecclesial ministry. Moral theologians are called to live their charism and ministry in *"a profound and vital connection with the Church"* (VS 109).

This connection with the Church implies, on the one hand, service to the People of God so that they may be helped, not impeded, to apply the faith more directly and deeply to their lives. On the other hand, the moral theologian is called to develop his mission by keeping a link with the charism and the ministry of the Magisterium of the Pope and the Bishops.

The charism of the moral Magisterium, far from impeding the development of moral theology, gives the theologian indispensable moral certainty to progress in the knowledge of moral truth and formulate it more adequately. In this sense, a link of close *charismatic communion* must be established between moral theology and moral teaching, with the awareness that *dissent* from the moral Magisterium "is contrary to ecclesial communion" (VS 113). The faithful have the right to receive the moral doctrine of the Church in all its integrity.

In addition, the moral theologian must necessarily use the results of the sciences of man and nature, aware that they only give an "empirical and statistical normalcy." Therefore, "the human sciences, despite the great value of the information which they provide, cannot be considered decisive indications of moral norms" (VS 112).

The other pastoral agents who actively participate in evangelization, particularly priests and catechists, must exercise their ministry with true ecclesial responsibility and conscience, knowing that their recipients expect from them "the truth that sets them free."

III. The Gospel of Grace and Cultural, Social, and Political Life

A final aspect that I would like to emphasize about the teachings contained in *Veritatis splendor* is the relationship that exists between the Gospel of grace and the cultural, social, and political life of men. We can say that the Pope's encyclical has laid the definitive foundations of a personalist Christian morality, which does not enclose the person in individualism, but rather inserts it into the necessarily communal dimension of existence. Every moral question is simultaneously personal and social.

This clearly appears in the Pope's categorical defense that "the absolutely essential demands of man's personal dignity must be considered the way and the condition for the very existence of freedom" (VS 96).

This defense of personal dignity is addressed to *each man* and to *all men*, "not only for individuals but also for the community, for society as such" (ibid.).

The absolutely inalienable prerogatives of the personal dignity of each man and of all men constitute "the unshakable foundation and solid guarantee of a just and peaceful human coexistence, and hence of genuine democracy, which can come into being and develop only on the basis of the equality of all its members, who possess common rights and duties. *When it is a matter of the moral norms prohibiting intrinsic evil, there are no privileges or exceptions for anyone.* It makes no difference whether one is the master of the world or the 'poorest of the poor' on the face of the earth. Before the demands of morality, we are all absolutely equal" (ibid.).

In the end, only a morality that acknowledges certain norms as valid, always and for everyone, with no exception, can guarantee the ethical foundation of social coexistence, both on the national and international levels (cf. VS 97).

In the face of serious forms of social and economic injustice and political corruption affecting entire peoples and nations, there is a growing reaction of indignation on the part of very many people whose fundamental human rights have been trampled upon and held in contempt, as well as an ever more widespread and acute sense of the *need for a radical* personal and social *renewal* capable of ensuring justice, solidarity, honesty, and openness (cf. VS 98). "At the heart of the *issue of culture* we find the *moral* sense, which is in turn rooted and fulfilled in the *religious sense*" (ibid.).

Only based on the "truth that makes us free" is it possible to solve the serious problems of peoples and nations, particularly that of the most diverse forms of *totalitarianism*: "Totalitarianism arises out of a denial of truth in the objective sense. If there is no transcendent truth, in obedience to which man achieves his full identity, then there is no sure principle for guaranteeing just relations between people. Their self-interest as a class, group or nation would inevitably set them in opposition to one another. If one does not acknowledge transcendent truth, then the force of power takes over, and each person tends to make full use of the means at his disposal in order to impose his own interests or his own opinion, with no regard for the rights of others. . . . Thus, the root of modern totalitarianism is found in the denial of the transcendent dignity of the human person who, as the visible image of the invisible God, is therefore by his very nature the subject of rights which no one may violate—no individual, group, class, nation or State. Not even the majority of a social body may violate these rights, by going against the minority, by isolating, oppressing, or exploiting it, or by attempting to annihilate it" (CA 44, cited in VS 99).

For this reason, the Pope affirms in a lucid diagnosis of reality, today we face a challenge no less serious than that of the totalitarian ideologies of the twentieth century: "This is the risk of an alliance between democracy and ethical relativism, which would remove any sure moral reference point from political and social life, and on a deeper level make the acknowledgment of truth impossible. Indeed, 'if there is no ultimate truth to guide and direct political activity, then ideas and convictions can easily be manipulated for reasons of power. As history demonstrates, a democracy without values easily turns into open or thinly disguised totalitarianism'" (VS 101; citing CA 46).

In this broad perspective of the moral life posed by the Pope, we can say that the Encyclical *Veritatis splendor* is the Magna Carta of Freedom for the human person, for families, nations, and humanity. At the end of the second millennium and in the perspective of the new, it lays the foundations of an integral humanism that is called to be the soul of a new universal civilization: *the civilization of love and life.*

IV. Conclusion

At the end of the encyclical, the Pope turns to the *mercy* of the Father communicated in his Son Jesus Christ by the gift of the Spirit, in the figure of Mary, Mother of God and Mother of mercy.

Mary is the mother of mercy because Jesus, her Son, is sent by the Father as a revelation and communication of his Mercy, and she encourages us and guides us to follow him.

Mary is the mother of mercy because Jesus, on the Cross, entrusts to her his Church and all humanity.

Mary is the mother of mercy as a luminous sign and a clear example of moral life by living her own freedom by giving herself to the Father and welcoming the gift of the Father.

Mary is the mother of mercy because she invites every human being, in the celebration of the Marriage of her Son throughout history, to welcome "the Truth that sets us Free" by *always doing what he tells us* (cf. Jn 2:5).

Let us entrust to Mary, mother of mercy, the teachings of this Magna Carta of Freedom, *Veritatis splendor*, so that the *Splendor of Truth* may illumine our lives, that of our ecclesial communities and of all humanity.

Thank you very much.

→⊱ ⊰←

We Want to Be One People, We Want to Be Family

Homily, Thirtieth Youth Pilgrimage to Luján—October 3, 2004

"Mother help us. We want to be one people."

For thirty years now, as a believing people, we have shared this ritual of coming to our Mother's, house and we do it with our trust placed in her, who receives and protects us.

Thirty years ago, young people made a pilgrimage here, to pray for the Homeland. Today, we share that same desire: to be one people. And here we are together receiving the same care from the Mother.

We celebrate what it meant to have walked these kilometers, to have passed in silence before the Image, glancing at her. To tell her what we brought with us along the way. What many people asked us to tell her once we saw her. Concerns that are shared in her House, which is our house, the house of our family, the house of our people.

Since we were young, many of us were brought here to receive Baptism and to see her Image that stayed here to receive us. And this is how we got to know this House and it began to be familiar to us, and we got into the habit of coming to visit the Virgin, to be close to her, to have this encounter that gives us rest.

And so, our people have been growing with these simple and profound things. There are many stories of lives that have been rebuilt here. As a people, our roots are anchored in the longing for fraternity and the desire for family. Today, we come to tell the Mother that we want to be one people; that we do not want to fight with each other; to ask her to defend us from those who want to divide us. That we want to be a family, and for that, we do not need any vindictive ideology that claims that it will redeem us. Her motherly affection is enough for us, of her we ask, "Mother, we want to be one people."

We do not stop thanking her that the Image of her clean and Immaculate Conception has miraculously stayed on the banks of the Luján River, founding this City. That is why, as a pilgrim people, we continue to realize that we grow, because here there is someone who summons us and brings us together. Looking at this, her house and our house, we tell her: "Mother, we want to be one people."

We know that Mary, after the cross, held the body of Jesus. It is a sad and sacred moment, and while we remember it, it gives us hope because it is the great affection of our dear Mother. Here is the greatness of God. In times when everything seems to be lost, God shows his greatest love, which makes us strong. It is the love that we carry today in our hearts, it is the blessing that fills us and makes us carry many of our brothers that, after returning from this visit, surely, we will have to lift up. With this desire of helping each other, we tell her: "Mother, we want to be one people."

May nothing separate us from all this that we believe in so much. May no one come to deceive or divide us. These are the wonders of God, he wanted them this way. In the silence of the miracle of the carts,[1] a miracle without words was built, a miracle that the Virgin tells slowly to each one, to the hearts of her children, on these pilgrimages. We came to rest from our journey, a rest for the heart. Let's go back home renewed. Here we leave everything that we find difficult to bear alone every day. We carry in our hearts the joy of having been close to the one who wanted to stay and protect us. And with great faith let's say together: "Mother help us, we want to be one People."

→> <+-

---

1. According to tradition, oxcarts once were transporting two icons of the Virgin. They stopped at the edge of the Luján River, forty-two miles from Buenos Aires. Every attempt to move the animals was useless until one of the two images of the Madonna was removed and left where a church, now a basilica, was built.

The Existence of the Pastor Is Expressed in Dialogue

Homily, Funeral Mass for Cardinal Juan Carlos Aramburu,
Archbishop Emeritus of Buenos Aires—November 22, 2004

The death of our pastor reminds us of his entire journey as a priest: his hopes, his work, his discreet and laborious elderly years. The Lord called him precisely when he was about to go to carry out his ministry, the ministry he never stopped rendering: hearing confessions. Behind that intense life, of his activities and concerns, he had—as every pastor—a dialogue with the Lord. It is the dialogue between Jesus and his disciple. A dialogue that begins with a glance, a word: "Follow me," and continues to grow throughout a lifetime. The existence of the pastor is expressed in that dialogue, an existence that, in its deep intimacy, only the two of them know; and they walk together through this existence. The dialogue between the pastor and his Lord takes a lifetime and is always projected further on: toward the people of God whom he must serve, and toward eternity.

We recently heard, in the Gospel, how this dialogue has a bit of miracle, of silence . . . and a lot of love. The pastor knows that he is before his Lord and for that "none of the disciples dared to ask him, 'Who are you?' because they realized it was the Lord" (Jn 21:12). They had known him with that certainty that only the heart provides, when love purifies one's glance: "It is the Lord" (v. 7). And this is so because, beyond the miracle, the silence and the certainty, the dialogue between the pastor and his Lord is a dialogue of love, a dialogue of love between two pastors: "Do you love me?" "Tend my sheep" (v. 16). The pastor remains almost perplexed in his love: on the one hand looking at his Lord, who asks him to profess his love, and on the other hand committed to the brothers who are entrusted to him and whom he is asked to serve out of love.

This is how Jesus and the pastor that he chose looked into each other's eyes; this is how they talked in a dialogue of a total life commitment. Over the years this dialogue grows, ages, matures, until it fully identifies with the destiny of his Lord: They will "lead you where you do not want to go" (v. 18), yes, "where you do not want to go," as it happened to the Lord himself: "If you are willing, take this cup away from me; still, not my will but yours be done" (Lk 22:42).

"Follow me," "Do you love me?" "Tend my sheep," "Let yourself be led where I wish." . . . Such is the axis of the dialogue between the pastor and Jesus, until the fullness of his existence, the time of the serene, steady, resignedly happy, and bright confession: "I am already being poured out like a libation, and the time of my departure is at hand" (2 Tm 4:6–7).

Is it like this, brother Juan Carlos, bishop and disciple of the Lord, we want to ask him. And surely, remembering the long and fruitful path traveled while following Jesus, he will look at us with that mischief that characterized him; and, with that great equanimity he possessed, he will answer us: So it is: "I know him in whom I have believed" (2 Tm 1:12).

→— —←

Jesus Already Warned Us That These Things Would Happen, and He Told Us Not to Be Afraid

Letter to Consecrated Men, Women, and the Faithful—December 1, 2004

Dear children and brothers and sisters,

For some time now, there have occurred in the city some public expressions of mockery and insults against our Lord Jesus Christ and the Blessed Virgin Mary, as well as several expressions against the religious and moral values that we profess. I am addressing you today deeply pained by the blasphemy perpetrated in the Recoleta Cultural Center, on the occasion of a plastic arts exhibit. I also regret that this event is being held in a Cultural Center that is supported by funds from the taxes paid by Christian people and people of good will.

Jesus had already warned us that these things would happen, and, with much tenderness, he told us not to be afraid, that we are his little flock, that we should persevere in the struggle for the faith, and in charity, waiting for him, praying with the true confidence of children to the Father who loves us.

To address this blasphemy that shames our city, I ask you, all of us together, to make an act of reparation and a prayer for forgiveness. For this reason, next December 7, the eve of the Solemnity of the Immaculate Conception, I invite you to make it a day of fasting and prayer, a day of penance on which, as a Catholic community, we ask the Lord to forgive our sins and those of the city. May our Mother of Luján accompany us with her affection.

→- -←

Give Us a Sign

Homily, Christmas Mass during the Night—December 25, 2004,
Year A (Transcript)

When we see Jesus amid fatigue and work, amid conflicts with the educated elites of that time (the Pharisees and Sadducees), we see how they often asked him for a sign: "We wish to see a sign from you" (Mt 12:38). Jesus preached, and people followed him as no one else; he healed, he raised people from the dead . . . but they asked for a sign. The sign they saw was not enough. We can imagine that it was not enough because that educated elitism shut down their consciences; that is a valid explanation. But there was something else: Not even the person most unwilling to listen to God's voice is deprived of the instinct of knowing where he is and the direction where he should search. They sensed that raising the dead, healing the sick was not "the sign." That's why once Jesus told them, you will be given the sign of Jonah (that is, the resurrection), they asked for the transcendental and unmistakable sign where God is fully revealed; and by that they made no mistake, even those who were further away, not even Herod. They were frightened and urged on by the heart's religious instinct, which drives us to look for and distinguish where God is.

They asked for a sign. . . . On the other hand, that happened to the Saints, too. Saint John the Baptist, in jail, was suffering a lot, and he saw Jesus preach, but he felt puzzled; in the loneliness of his prison cell he started to doubt and sent Jesus a question: "Are you the one who is to come, or should we look for another?" (Mt 11:3). He asked for the sign, looked for the sign of God's revelation, that which had been proclaimed by the Prophets and that for which the people of Israel had been waiting for hundreds of years. They asked for the "great sign."

In the story of Jesus' birth, which we have just heard, when the angels announce to the shepherds that the Redeemer was born, they tell them:

"And this will be a sign for you: you will find an infant wrapped in swaddling clothes and lying in a manger" (Lk 2:12). This is the sign: the total self-emptying of God. The sign is that tonight, God fell in love with our smallness, and turned himself into tenderness; tenderness for all fragility, for all suffering, for all distress, for all searching, for all limits; the sign is God's tenderness, and the message sought by all who asked for signs from Jesus, the message sought by all who were disoriented, even Jesus' enemies and those who looked for him from the bottom of their hearts, was this one: they sought God's tenderness, God made tenderness, God caressing our misery, God in love with our smallness.

This is proclaimed to us today: God's tenderness. The world keeps going; men keep looking for God; but the sign continues to be this one. By contemplating the baby born in the manger, by contemplating the God who became a little boy in love with our smallness, tonight this question is appropriate: What about God's tenderness for you? Do you allow yourself to be caressed by that tenderness of a God that loves you, by a God made tenderness? Or are you unfriendly and don't allow God to look for you? No, I look for God, you might say. Your search for God is not the most important thing; what is most important is that you allow God to search for you in his tenderness, his caresses. This is the first question that this Baby asks us merely by his presence today: Do we let that tenderness love us? And furthermore: Do you also have the courage to make yourself tender for every difficult situation, for every human problem, for those close to you, or do you prefer the bureaucratic, fast, cold, efficiency-based solution, not the evangelizing one? If so, are you afraid of the tenderness that God showed you? And this would be the second question of today: Do we bear, in our behaviors, that tenderness that should accompany us throughout our life, in times of happiness, of sadness, of the cross, of work, of conflict, of battle?

The response of a Christian cannot be anything but God's response to our smallness: tenderness, meekness. Remember that time when Jesus and his Apostles were not welcomed in a town of Samaria, John suggested to Jesus, "do you want us to call down fire from heaven?" (Lk 9:54); that is the same as saying "we go inside and damage everything." And Jesus "turned and rebuked them" (v. 55); he chastises them, today he would tell them that this is not being a Christian. Also remember that night when Jesus was arrested, and Peter unsheathed his sword, herald, defender of the emerging Church, unhappy advocate (a few hours later he betrayed him) and Jesus told him: "Put your sword back into its sheath. . . . Do you think that I cannot call upon my Father and he will not provide me at this moment with more than twelve legions of angels?" (Mt 26:52–53), but my path is different; it is tender-ness. Even in times of conflict, in times in which you are slapped in the face, when they slap one cheek offer the other and continue being tender. This is what Christmas Eve brings us. When we see that God falls in love with our smallness, becomes tenderness to caress us better, a God who is completely meek, who is close, who is our neighbor, we can only open our hearts and tell him: Lord, if you did it this way, help us, give us the grace of tenderness in life's painful situations, give us the grace of being close to our neighbor before every human need, give us the grace of being meek before every con-flict. Let's ask for it, this is a night for asking . . . and I dare to give you some homework: Tonight, or tomorrow, before Christmas day ends, take a moment of silence and ask yourself, What about God's tenderness with me? What about my tenderness with other people? What about my ten-derness in extreme situations? What about my meekness at work and in conflicts? And may Jesus answer you; he will do so.

May the Virgin grant you this grace.

→> <+

Index of Scriptural References

Index

abortion, John Paul II on, 14
accountability, 279–81; for Church's sins, 240–41
action(s), 258; and compassion, 232; Good Samaritan and, 201; and openness, 31
Ad gentes divinitus (Vatican II), 107
admiration, capacity for, 87
Advent, 29
aesthetics, aestheticism, 54; Good Samaritan and, 164; and wisdom, 239
AIDS, 80
alienation, 42, 79. *See also* orphanhood
alternativism, 272
ambition, 66
Anna, saint, 4, 95, 116
Annunciation, 230–31
anointing, xxix–xxx, 3–5, 27, 59–61, 121–23
anthropology, 21
antinomies, xli–xlii, 7, 14, 191, 249, 256, 258
Aperite portas Redemptori (John Paul II), 29
apocalyptic mentality, 50, 54
Aramburu, Juan Carlos, 290–91
Archdiocesan Catechetical Encounter (EAC), 41–43, 106
Archdiocesan Days for Social Ministry, 114–16
Archdiocesan Department for Parochial Schools, 25–26
Archdiocesan Pastoral Council, 227
Argentina, xiii–xiv, 270–72; Belgrano and, 178–88; and Cajetan, 159; and decision making, 125–45; and education, 28; and hope, 237; institutions in, 183; *Martín Fierro* and, 125–45; prayer for, 144–45; reputation of, 262; and unity, 288–89
Argentinian Independence Day (May 25), xxiii–xxvi, 5–11, 63–67, 98–104, 147–53, 196–202, 259–67; origins of, 152, 152n4
artisans: catechists as, 221; educators as, 92–93
Ash Wednesday, 227–30
attitude, 99; and action, 233; Belgrano and, 181, 187; of care, 92–93; and education, 184, 253; of Jesus, 69–70, 159–60
audacity, 56–57, 228–29, 236; and action, 232–33; catechists and, 270–73; of Mary, 233–34

Augé, Marc, 81n2
Augustine of Hippo, saint, 127–29, 135, 174–77, 282
authenticity, and service, 98–104
authoritarianism: spiritual, 243; utopianism and, 176
authority, and education, 22
availability, and openness, 31

Beatitudes, 111–13, 161
beauty: Good Samaritan and, 163; media and, 165–68
Belgrano, Manuel, xiii, 178–88; accomplishments of, 179–80; background of, 179, 178n1; character of, 178
belief, and creativity, 174
Bergoglio, Jorge Mario: elected pontiff, xxxvii; on homilies, xi–xii, xxi–xxii; influences on, xix–xx, xli
Bible, 53, 87–89; and Christian wisdom, 244–47; reading, recommendations for, xxi, 109–10
bio-technology, 48
blindness, of soul, 262–65
bread, xxvii, xxx; anointing and, 122; and Corpus Christi, 154, 214–16; loaves and fishes, 104–5, 268; manna, 12, 154; and May 25, 9; and work, Cajetan and, xxvii, 15–16, 112, 160, 216–19, 273–76
Buenos Aires, xxiv; beggars in, 31n1; blasphemy incidents in, 291–92; consecration to Our Lady of Luján, 155–56; economic issues in, 150, 150n1; visitor experience in, 77–78
business culture, 79

cacerolazos (pot-banging protests), xiv, 129–30, 129n1
Cajetan of Thiene, saint, xxvi–xxvii, 15–16, 69–71, 111–14, 159–61, 216–19, 273–76
capital: internationalization of, 19; work and, John Paul II on, 209
caring, 92–93; culture of, 93; Good Samaritan and, 202
Catechism of Catholic Church, 107, 110

299

(continued)

Library of Congress Cataloging-in-Publication Data

Names: Francis, Pope, 1936– author. | Spadaro, Antonio, editor. | Herrera,
    Marina, translator.
Title: In your eyes I see my words : homilies and speeches from Buenos
    Aires / Jorge Mario Bergoglio, Pope Francis ; edited by Antonio Spadaro ;
    translated by Marina A. Herrera ; introduction translated by Elena
    Buia Rutt and Andrew Rutt
Other titles: Sermons. Selections. English
Description: New York : Fordham University Press, 2019. | "This book was
    originally published in Italian as Jorge Mario Bergoglio, Papa
    Francesco, Nei tuoi occhi è la mia parola: Omelie e discorsi di Buenos
    Aires." | Includes bibliographical references and index. | Contents:
    Volume I: 1999 to 2004 | Summary: "Pope Francis was a first in many
    ways: the first pope from the Americas, the first Jesuit, the first
    Francis, the first child of immigrants from the old world, nurtured and
    transformed by the new world, and returned to lead the whole world. His
    eloquent homilies and speeches have inspired the faithful of Argentina
    for decades, largely through his gift of oratory, tracing back to his
    time as a bishop, archbishop, and cardinal in his home country. To be
    published in English for the first time in their entirety and with
    contextual annotations, In Your Eyes I See My Words, Volume 1, collects
    his homilies and speeches from 1999 to 2004. Volume II spans from
    2005–2008, and Volume III, from 2009–2013, concludes with his prophetic
    last homily before being elected to the papacy"—Provided by publisher.

Identifiers: LCCN 2019028502 | ISBN 9780823285600 (hardback) | ISBN
    9780823285617 (ebook)
Subjects: LCSH: Catholic Church—Sermons.
Classification: LCC BX1756.F677 S4713 2019 | DDC 252/.02—dc23
LC record available at https://lccn.loc.gov/2019028502